The Armed Forces of Asia

Series editors: **Professor Desmond Ball**, Strategic and Defence Studies Centre, Australian National University; **Air Marshal Ray Funnell** (Ret'd), Principal of the Australian College of Defence and Strategic Studies.

The Armed Forces of Asia series presents single-country studies of the nations in the arc from Pakistan in the west to the Russian Far East in the north. Each title provides a succinct survey encompassing each service of the armed forces including territorial and paramilitary formations. It assesses the role of the armed forces with regard to national defense and security policy, and their social, political and economic functions. It analyses their defensive and offensive capabilities and the ambitions of sectors within the armed forces establishments.

THE ARMED FORCES OF ASIA SERIES

The USA in the Asia–Pacific Region	Stanley B. Weeks & Charles A. Meconis

Forthcoming titles

Australia	David Horner
Burma	Andrew Selth
India	Vijai K. Nair & K.K. Hazari
Japan	Akio Watanabe & Naoko Sajima
Malaysia	Joon-Num Mak & Russ Swinnerton
North Korea	Joseph Bermudez Jr
Pakistan	Pervaiz Iqbal Cheema
Papua New Guinea	Ron May
Philippines	Carolina G. Hernandez & Gina Pattugalan
Russia in Asia	Greg Austin & Alexei D. Mouraviev
Singapore	Tim Huxley
South Korea	Taeho Kim
Taiwan	Andrew N.D. Yang
Thailand	Noel Adams
Vietnam	Carlyle Thayer

THE ARMED FORCES OF CHINA

YOU JI

I.B. Tauris *Publishers*
LONDON • NEW YORK

To all of my family

Published in 1999 by I.B.Tauris & Co Ltd
Victoria House, Bloomsbury Square, London WC1B 4DZ
175 Fifth Avenue, New York NY 10010

In the United States and Canada distributed by St. Martin's Press
175 Fifth Avenue, New York NY 10010

ISBN 1 86064 499 6 hardback
ISBN 1 86064 487 2 paperback

A full CIP record for this book is available from the British Library
A full CIP record for this book is available from the Library of
Congress

Library of Congress catalog card: available

Manufactured in Singapore

Foreword

It is fair to say that, since the end of the Cold War, China has emerged as the country of greatest concern in Asia in strategic and regional security terms.[1] It could become the world's largest economy by around 2030, but it is more likely to be the second largest. It has the fastest-growing defence budget in Asia, amounting to a two-fold increase in real terms since 1988. In the mid-1990s, it had the most active nuclear weapons development program in the world.

China's capabilities for operating in the Western Pacific are growing significantly. The Chinese navy has recently acquired or is in the process of acquiring two Luhu (or Type 052) destroyers, one modified Luda destroyer, one Luda III destroyer, two Sovremenny destroyers (from Russia), a new class (Jiangwei) of missile frigates, and new classes of resupply and amphibious assault ships for sustaining operations farther from shore and for longer periods. China's power projection capabilities in the South China Sea have been enhanced with the construction of an airbase and anchorages on Woody Island (Lin-tao) in the Paracel Islands, and the acquisition of an air-to-air refuelling capability for its naval air forces. China is also acquiring several types of modern aircraft from Russia, including 72 Su–27 Flanker strike/fighters, and MiG–31 Foxhound interceptor fighters. For the longer term, China's defence planners remain actively interested in the acquisition of some aircraft carrier capability.

These Chinese developments are generating strong apprehensions throughout East Asia. Some countries, such as Taiwan and South Korea, have felt a compelling need to counter some of the new Chinese capabilities with their own programs. In Southeast Asia, there is concern about the possibility that China might be able to assert supremacy over the South China Sea. More generally, the region is disturbed by the lack of transparency attending the Chinese policies and acquisitions—with respect to the strategic purposes of the new capabilities as well as the ultimate dimensions of the Chinese build-up.

This book by You Ji is itself a major contribution to the promotion of transparency. The most knowledgeable young specialist on Chinese defence matters, You Ji portrays the prevailing strategic objective: the development of a high-technology defence force designed for modern warfare in the information age. He describes in unprecedented detail and assesses comprehensively the current and projected Chinese defence capabilities.

China's domestic situation is so complex and uncertain that it would be unwise to draw premature conclusions about its emergence as an active and substantial international power. There are two broad possibilities for China's future: China could continue to reform both economically and politically, becoming more powerful but constrained by growing economic interdependence from being a strategic threat to the region; or, it could attempt to maintain its repressive political system, with some loss of economic dynamism but still with respectable increases in its national power, and a more aggressive foreign policy. 'At the moment,' according to You Ji, China 'is poised to move decisively in either direction.'

For other countries in the Asia–Pacific region (including the United States of America), the wisest approach would be to maintain some form of balance of power system (in which China would be accepted as a legitimate and fully functioning party), while at the same time engaging China in multilateral dialogues, confidence-building arrangements, preventive diplomacy and other forms of security cooperation. This is a very delicate and difficult exercise, which requires great care and sensitivity as well as informed analysis, for which reading this book is indispensable.

Desmond Ball
Strategic and Defence Studies Centre
Australian National University, Canberra

Contents

Tables, figures and maps

TABLES

FIGURES AND MAPS

Preface

In 1993 I first raised the argument at a conference at the Australian National University (ANU) that China's national defence strategy had been transferred from Deng Xiaoping's 'people's war under modern conditions' to the post-Deng 'regional limited war under high-tech conditions'. Few China specialists accepted my view. It was understandable because at the time it was still the Deng era. However, a number of researchers at the PLA National Defence University and the PLA Academy of Military Science supported me. This gave me additional confidence to continue my research project on China's armed forces in the information age. Therefore, my first acknowledgement must go to these officers, although their names have to remain anonymous.

In the next few years I visited China frequently to obtain more information for the book. During these fieldwork trips I received enormous help from many friends who are working or used to work in the Chinese defence establishments. From my conversations with them I learned a lot about the PLA's efforts to modernise itself for a possible war in the new millennium. Although I cannot list their names here, their help will always remain in my memory.

In preparing the book I benefited from a number of visiting fellowships which helped me carry out research and writing. In 1993 I received an Australian Defence Department fellowship and worked for three months in the Strategic and Defence Studies Centre at ANU. This period of research laid down the foundation for the subsequent writing. In 1994 I furthered my research on the PLA in the Contemporary China Centre at ANU and the Australian Defence Studies Centre, the Australian Defence Force Academy. Each of these centres provided me with visiting fellowships and office facilities. Without their assistance it would have been difficult for me to continue my study. Here I would like to express my special thanks to Dr Jonathan Unger of the Contemporary China Centre, and Dr Anthony Bergin and Dr Bob Hall of the Australian Defence Studies Centre for their great encouragement and assistance. The Australian Defence Studies Centre published part of the contents of this book in its monograph series.

My heart-felt gratitude goes to Professor Desmond Ball, who recommended me to participate in the *Armed Forces of Asia* series. Moreover, Professor Ball has been a constant source of guidance and help for almost a decade. I also owe a big debt to Dr Denny Roy, who put in a lot of his precious time and energy in preparing the manuscript for publication. It has been greatly appreciated.

During the last stage of writing, my employer—the University of New South Wales—provided a research grant for me to finish the project. The grant allowed to make a fieldwork trip to China and enabled me to obtain precious information on the latest development of the Chinese armed forces. This has updated the coverage of the PLA to the middle of 1998, making it the leading-edge study of the PLA in the world. The Humanities Research Program of UNSW also provided funding to assist the work of indexing, making maps and proofreading. The author is grateful for the help of professors Roger Bell and Cornal Condren.

Finally, I'd like to thank my family members and my friends for their support. Particularly I want to thank You Xu and Lin Yan, who have helped to collect a great deal of useful research material.

It is my sincere hope that this book may contribute to our understanding of the PLA, which will play an increasingly larger role both in China's domestic politics and international security-making. Of course, due to my limited analytical capacity, there may be many errors and misjudgements. The responsibility is always mine.

Glossary of acronyms

A–5	single-engined ground attack aircraft
AA	anti-aircraft
ACV	air carrier vehicles
AEW	anti-electronic warfare
APEC	Asia Pacific Economic Cooperation
ARF	ASEAN regional forum
ASEAN	Association of Southeast Asian Nations
ASW	anti-submarine warfare
AWACS	airborne early warning and control systems
CC	Central Committee
CCP	Chinese Communist Party
CEP	circular error probability
CEW	counter-electronic warfare
CIS	Commonwealth of Independent States
CMC	Central Military Commission
CODAG	combined diesel and gas (propulsion system)
COSTIND	Commission of Science, Technology and Industry for National Defence
CSCE	Council for Security Cooperation in Europe
CTBT	Comprehensive Test Ban Treaty
C³I	command, control, communication and intelligence
CZ	*Changzheng* series missile carriers
DF	direction finding
ELINT	electronic intelligence
ESF	PLA Navy East Sea Fleet
EW	electronic warfare
EWC	electronic warfare countermeasures
FF	fast frigate

GEA	ground effect aircraft
GED	PLA General Equipment Department
GLD	PLA General Logistical Department
GPS	global positioning system
GSD	PLA General Staff Department
HF	high frequency
Hong–6	medium-range bomber (Tu–16)
IDF	indigenous developed fighters
IISS	International Institute for Strategic Studies
IRBM	intermediate range ballistic missile
IRST	infra-red search and track
IT	information technology
IW	information warfare
J–7III	single-engined fighter
J–8II	twin-engined fighter with limited ground attack capability
KMT	Kuomintang
LSM	landing ship medium
LST	landing ship tank
MAAFC	PLA Military Area Air Force Command
MAC	PLA Military Area Command
ME	military expenditure
MFN	most favoured nation
MIRV	multiple independently retargetable re-entry vehicle
NAF	PLA Navy Air Force
NDU	National Defence University
NIEs	newly industrialised economies
NPT	Non-proliferation Treaty
NSF	PLA Navy North Sea Fleet
O&M	operation and maintenance
ONI	US Office of Naval Intelligence
OSO	(CIA) Office of SIGINT Operations
PAP	People's Armed Police
PLA	People's Liberation Army
PLAAF	PLA Air Force
PLAAMS	PLA Academy of Military Science
PLAN	PLA Navy
PMC	Post-Ministerial Conference
PRC	People's Republic of China
R&D	research and development
RMA	Revolution in Military Affairs
SAM	surface-to-air missile

SATCOM	satellite communications
SININT	signal intelligence
SLBM	submarine-launched ballistic missile
SLOC	sealane of communications
SMF	PLA Strategic Missile Force
SSBN	nuclear-armed submarine
SSF	PLA Navy South Sea Fleet
SSN	nuclear attack submarine
STOVL	short take-off and vertical landing
Su–27	twin-engined multi-role aircraft
Yun–8	medium-range transport aircraft

Introduction

Thinking strategically about China is a key question in our current efforts to construct a stable post–Cold War world order. China is rising but its future is still uncertain. This is a challenge both to western powers and China's neighbours.[1] And this challenge is multi-dimensional: political, economic and military. The answer to this challenge has also to be multi-dimensional and a sensible one as well. Otherwise, it just contradicts our efforts to bring about a peaceful environment in the region. In essence, thinking about China strategically means looking at China not as it is but over a fairly long period of time.

If we employ a trend-analysis to examine China's armed forces, we are witnessing a strong military in the making. The Chinese People's Liberation Army (PLA) is undergoing a fundamental change under a new national defence strategy which guides the PLA to meet the challenge of a changed security environment following the demise of the bipolar system. Moreover, the strategy has been the PLA's response to the Revolution in Military Affairs (RMA) brought about by the astonishing development in information technology since the 1980s. At the same time, however, the Chinese armed forces have to overcome a long and painful transition both in military thinking and hardware acquisition. Even if the PLA is fully prepared to embrace the best ideas in the RMA and transform it accordingly as quickly as possible, it will still take one or two decades of strenuous work. Even by then, whether it has caught up with the current western technology will remain an open question. Much depends on whether China's economic growth is sustained for a fairly long period and the international situation remains peaceful.

THE CHALLENGE OF STUDYING THE PLA

The Chinese military constitutes an interesting object to study: conceptually, it is more and more receptive to new ideas and forward leaning in force modernisation; technologically, however, it remains backward. Nevertheless, it confronts real security challenges, or, put in a more blunt way, real prospects of actions. Indeed, what makes the study of the PLA interesting is our puzzle of how it overcomes the gap between its fairly advanced new thinking and the technological predicament in translating the new thinking into practice. To students of the Chinese military, this is more of a challenge than a puzzle. Now we have to study it from a new angle. As compared with the recent past when the PLA's modernisation was driven by an obsolete military strategy (the doctrine of people's war under modern conditions), we have to presume that this time the PLA has set its guidelines right, which may greatly shorten its catching-up process. Additionally, the guidelines have been set right not only in the military field. More profound is the fact that China's economic system has been geared towards the market economy. As proved by the experience of other major western powers, the thirst for market profits generates great energy for industrialisation which may eventually boost the country's scientific and technological development. China's opening up to the world also provides it with much needed overseas markets, technology and capital for its economic take-off, which will in turn drive the military modernisation in the fast lane.

This is the fascinating part of our study of the Chinese military: advanced in thinking, backward in equipment; driven by powerful ambitions but challenged by genuine security threats. Often such a military force appears to be stimulated into action fairly easily, so as to disguise its reality of being ill prepared. This we saw from the Taiwan episode in March 1996. As Taiwan's political elites from both the ruling party and the opposition party push for the independence course, a sea battle across the Taiwan Strait is now assessed by the PLA as a likely scenario of an armed conflict it has to get ready for. According to a senior security expert in the Beijing Institute of Contemporary International Relations— which, as the top think-tank under the Ministry for State Security, regularly presents policy proposals to the Politburo's Leadership Group for Foreign Affairs—the initial trend of non-military-confrontation among major powers in the first years of the post–Cold War era has turned in the direction of potential confrontation since 1995. China's security environment will gradually worsen and by the third decade of the new century a war (most likely across the Taiwan Strait) may become inevitable.[2]

Somehow, the PLA seems to believe that threat of action may be the best form of war prevention at its current stage of development. When it becomes a true military heavyweight in the new century, there would be little need for such reckless action. Then it might face reduced prospects of being provoked.[3] In the longer term, however, the increasingly outward reach of the PLA, as seen mostly by its navy's enlargement of defence depth in the high seas, may increase encounters with the superpower. Indeed the show of force by two US aircraft carrier battle groups close to the Taiwan Strait in March 1996 made the PLA high command feel insecure and convinced it with whom it would eventually have to deal with.[4] If such incidents occur repeatedly, this would offer the PLA a convenient reason to demand more budgetary allocations for hardware upgrading. For instance, the new Sino–Russian arms deal in early 1997, which included sales of two of the best Russian destroyers, has been interpreted as China's direct response to US intervention in Taiwan affairs.[5] As China's armed forces set out to acquire an international status in the next century, the question 'Does a strong Chinese military matter?' will be discussed more seriously by countries in Asia and the Pacific. Yet in order to answer the question of how it matters, we need to apply objective analysis, which constitutes the focus of this book.

This study is a concentrated effort to assess China's armed forces, its current state of affairs and, more importantly, its developmental trend in the next few decades. It does not cover every aspect of the PLA. For instance, it tries to deal with the history of the PLA as lightly as possible. It does not touch upon the PLA's history between 1927 when it was established and 1949 when the People's Republic of China was founded after 28 years of armed struggle. For the sake of linkage, it mentions a few major events in the lead-up to the adoption of Deng Xiaoping's post-Mao defence strategy of people's war under modern conditions in 1981, which was formally approved by the Chinese Communist Party's Central Military Commission in 1985. One of the reasons for this biased treatment of history is that many books have been written on the PLA's growing path. The focus of this book is on its present and future. Neither does the book touch upon the issue of civil–military relations. This by no means belittles the key political role played by the PLA in Chinese politics. The author feels that should be the subject of a different book; this one concentrates on the PLA purely from a defence point of view.

THE TREND ANALYSIS

From this angle we shall see that the PLA's quest for high-tech military power is intended to re-orient China's preparation for war through creating greater depth in defence. This will inevitably set a more forward posture by creating forward defence frontiers. It may also make the PLA appear to be more offensive-capable. While it is wrong to equate a forward military posture to an expansionist military policy, there is no doubt that the consequences of the PLA being an offensive power will produce long-term implications for the balance of power in post–Cold War world politics and, particularly, for the regional security environment. In a way China's efforts to catch up with advanced military powers may generate spillover effects of a regional arms build-up, although each of the participants in this build-up may not be entirely motivated by the PLA's modernisation program.

Related to the creation of a forward posture is force redeployment that the PLA is currently conducting in response to China's changed security concerns. Put in simple terms, as the Russians are no longer regarded as posing any immediate threat, the PRC's defence gravity is being shifted from the three norths, namely, north, north-east and north-west China, to south and east China, where preparedness has been uplifted to cater for potential regional armed conflicts. This strategic move has been reflected by the PLA's efforts at reinstituting war zones in south and east China. In this process new command and control establishments are put in place and battlefield construction (*zhanchang jianshe*) has been stepped up in strategic war directions. To meet the challenge of new campaign modes brought about by the information age, all the services will be required to learn and participate in united warfare. Training has thus been geared to joint operations. The whole of the logistical supply networks are undergoing reform to become more effective in supporting fast response actions.

Another new development in the Chinese armed force is what the PLA defined as two fundamental changes: change from a quantitative military to a qualitative military; and change from a military that is manpower-intensive to one that is knowledge-intensive. The first task for the change is force restructuring, which entails two key parallel missions in the PLA's modernisation:

setting priority in the development of services and prescribing an overall size for the PLA in the era of the RMA. For the former preferential treatment has been given to the specialised services, the air force, navy and the Strategic Missile Force (SMF), since the mid-1980s. The adoption of a high-tech oriented defence strategy has only highlighted the urgency for the selective upgrading of the key services. At the same time the ground force will be continuously reduced in number. As a result, the dominance of the army in PLA politics will gradually weaken, although it will still possess disproportionate influence in the whole of China's armed forces.

In the PLA's new priority sequence of services development, the air force has been on the top of the list of selective modernisation in the last six years. This can be seen clearly from the huge amount of foreign exchange spent on the purchase of advanced aircraft and air defence systems, by far the largest outlays. The navy has occupied an important place in this priority list, too, thanks to the fact that if there is any future armed action involving China, the navy will bear the first brunt, be it in the South China Sea or across the Taiwan Strait. Simultaneously, China's strategic missile force—the Second Artillery by its official name—continues to enjoy favourable treatment. The reason is not hard to understand. Nuclear deterrence is still regarded as the foundation upon which China's entire national security is based. Moreover, in the last decade or so, the PLA's strategic missile force has formulated a priority program of developing conventional missiles, a program that parallels the nuclear one. While the PLA believes that nuclear missiles are indispensable in dealing with the superpower, they are increasingly unusable in the post–Cold War era. Conventional missiles, however, may exert enormous deterrence in limited high-tech conflicts concerning, for instance, territorial disputes. This missile diplomacy will gain more and more currency in the years ahead. In a way we are witnessing China's strategic missile force breaking away from its decades-long mentality of 'how to hide' and may have acquired an urge of 'how to fight'.

The adoption of the new strategy also settled a protracted debate among senior PLA officers over how large the PLA should be. In the early 1990s the PLA high command was nervous about the domestic situation following the Tiananmen incident and about international uncertainties as a result of the collapse of the USSR. It proposed to maintain the large size of the PLA as it was in the 1980s. In 1997 Jiang Zemin announced at the Party's 15th National Congress that the PLA would reduce its number by 500 000 men. Further cuts will be made in the years to come when the situation is considered as warranting it. By the end of the 1990s the size of the PLA will be the smallest in half a century, indicating a major turn in the direction of its development—namely from development based on quantity to quality. Finally the PLA has embarked on the direction of development that other advanced military powers have pursued in the recent past.

The PLA's modernisation efforts are ambitious and comprehensive. However, the Chinese military leaders have not underestimated the present backwardness of the PLA. They agree to the consensus by most western analysts that the PLA is one or two generations behind the current military technology of the major western powers. By the Chinese' own account the PLA is in a dangerous transitional process. Many obsolete weapons need to be decommissioned but replacements are hard to come by. This 'vacuum' worries PLA generals who do see real security threats around them. This serves as the background for large increases of military budget since 1989, and it is very fortunate for the PLA that Russia suddenly opened its arsenal for China to shop. With a 'quick fix' from foreign purchases, the PLA may gain some confidence in fighting a middle-level high-tech conflict, the confidence it would not have had otherwise.

What is more important for this 'quick fix' is the breathing time for the PLA to tackle the weak linkages in its war preparation with concentrated financial resources. This resulted in a middle-course modernisation program. On the human side a small number of elite troops (rapid response units) have been established and equipped with the best weapons the PLA can obtain. On the hardware side a pocket of excellence has been achieved thanks to fairly sufficient funding concentrated in certain areas and acquisition of foreign arms. The PLA has full recognition that its search for high-tech power is based on the long term. Having obtained a limited amount of high-tech weaponry and thus a limited level of deterrence for regional conflict, the PLA is not in a great hurry to catch up with the best armed forces in the world. In the final analysis the Chinese military leaders have wagered its eventual power on the country's economic and technological take-off, unless the world situation changes dramatically.

METHODOLOGY

This book is an attempt to evaluate strategically these major ingredients of China's armed forces. This is difficult because the

PLA is a closed book to all analysts within China and outside it. Before Deng Xiaoping opened China to the world, the PLA was just a riddle. Some information leaked out but there was no way of confirming it until it became old news. Even today students of the PLA are confronted with the problem of secrecy surrounding its command and control structure, weapons programs and financial situation. Perhaps the majority of PLA officers and men do not have any real grasp of how it operates except for a small number of senior generals in *Sanzuomen* where the General Office of the CMC is located and in the West Hill where the First, Second and Third Departments of the General Staff Department handle the top secret affairs.

However, we now at least have better access to PLA publications. Dr Pillsbury's collection of the PLA's research on RMA opens a window on the minds of important PLA researchers.[6] Well received outside China, his book is one vivid example showing how eagerly senior PLA staff wanted to communicate with their colleagues in the west, in a language we are familiar with. In recent years more and more PLA journals and books have become available in market places in China, some of which are even for *junnei* (within the armed forces) distribution. This has provided a valuable opportunity for us to obtain first-hand research material on the PLA, and thus achieve a better understanding of it.

Like Pillsbury I have found that reading PLA publications is very helpful. Although they are not policy statements, during the long period of research I do find that many of the ideas carried in these research articles become policies later on. After all, many of the authors are key policy advisers to the top military leadership and they like to publish, as publications have become a standard criterion for promotion both in research institutions and in active service. A number of promising top generals such as Liu Jingsong, former commander of Shengyang Military Area Command (now president of the PLA Academy of Military Science), Xin Shizhong, president of the PLA National Defence University, and Liu Zhenwu, commander-in-chief of the PLA's Hong Kong Garrison, all publish frequently in the journals I read and collect. I have been mostly impressed by the openness and insight of PLA authors. It is said that Jiang Zemin, chairman of the Central Military Commission of the Chinese Communist Party and commander-in-chief of the Chinese armed forces, spots talented young officers through reading their published articles in key PLA journals. To some extent PLA publications reduce the level of speculation with which we study the PLA, although they cannot resolve many questions we still have. Since 1990 I have collected a large number of PLA publications, on which this book is based.

Their articles and books reflect a specific culture and mentality. The authors are at once full of confidence in winning the next war and have strong worries over the PLA's current level of modernisation. Sometimes their criticism on certain national policies is so sharp that I speculate that there exists a level of freedom of ideas within the PLA such as I never thought before—it is certainly against my own experience of being born and brought up in the PLA. For instance, their ideas on national security and threat perception are visibly different from what we hear from the personnel of the Ministry of Foreign Affairs. Nevertheless, they are not unacquainted with the views and concepts held by western military researchers. Some of them have achieved very sophisticated knowledge of foreign armed forces, from their overall national defence strategy, operational principles of individual services, collaborative efforts with allied forces, to the missions of one particular army. From these writings we see the clear influence of western military science and ideology. In fact this book is written with unprecedented use of PLA publications. As such, the book is very much a study of the PLA from the PLA's perspective.

I have also conducted many interviews with PLA officers during the two years of writing this book. Through these interviews I gathered both valuable information about the military modernisation in China and the personal opinions of the officers on many issues facing this huge country. I later decided to exercise strict restrictions in citing oral sources. Partly this is because there are no independent channels to certify how authentic the information is. In fact, published sources have already provided more credible material to support my argument. More importantly, this book is not meant to be intelligence analysis. When I did use the account of interviews, that was because I felt the points made sense and were logical. Of course I may be wrong. Given the secrecy of the subject, as I mentioned earlier, I am sure this book contains many errors and therefore hope readers will demonstrate a high level of tolerance when they do not agree with me.

Chapter 1 reviews the evolution of China's military strategy. Comparisons are made to the three strategies under which the PLA has been guided in the last three decades but the emphasis is on the difference between the Dengist strategy and the post-Deng strategy. It also focuses on how the PLA has learnt modern warfare through studying the recent armed conflicts in the world, particularly the Gulf War in 1991. Chapter 2 is a study of the PLA's

recent reforms, as embodied in its force restructuring and redeployment. It shows how the Chinese armed forces are positioning
themselves for a war in the new century. Chapter 3 selectively
analyses the main features of the PLA's new strategy, including its
new R&D priorities, principles for budgetary allocations, weapons
programs, the timetable for China's space program and so on.
Chapter 4 deals with the new development in China's strategic
missile force. It concludes that the Chinese nuclear force is com-
pleting a transition from 'hide' to 'fight'. Chapter 5 is on the PLA's
efforts to modernise its air force, transforming it from a basically
defensive force to one that is more offensively oriented. Chapter 6
examines the maritime strategy of the PLA Navy and its progress
towards achieving the status of a bluewater power in the next
century. Chapter 7 explores the implications of the Chinese military modernisation on world politics in general and the regional
security landscape in particular, as seen by both major western
powers and China's immediate neighbours.

1

Embracing Revolution in Military Affairs

The PLA is in the midst of a fundamental change under a new military strategy termed as 'high-tech national defence strategy' (*gaojishu guofang zhanlie*), a new phrase now commonly used by Chinese generals.[1] This new strategy was the outcome of a lengthy debate among PLA commanders in the 1980s in response to the recognition that high technology was revolutionising military science. The collapse of the USSR, precarious Sino–West relations, and the Gulf War also stimulated the PLA to reposition itself in the post–Cold War era of multipolarity. Towards the end of 1992, the supreme command of the Chinese armed forces, the Party's CMC, finally reached a consensus on the guiding principle for China's military modernisation in the 1990s and beyond. This principle has been best summarised by Admiral Liu Huaqing's call 'to fight a modern war under high-tech conditions'. General Zhang Zhen, ranked second in the PLA's high command during most of the 1990s, specified the strategy by calling on the PLA to achieve 'five breakthroughs' in its military thinking, tactics, training, R&D and force structure.[2]

A study of any country's military strategy reveals the nature of its armed forces—whether its force structure and deployment posture are defensive or offensive. It can also tell us what potential threats the country has identified and what measures its military has adopted to respond. Different strategies also entail different emphases in training and weapons acquisition. These are crucial areas where research can be conducted to review the evolution of China's military strategy in the post-Deng era, shedding light on the PLA's ambitions and developmental trends in the years to come.

1

THE EVOLVING NATIONAL DEFENCE STRATEGY

The history of the PLA since 1949 has included a number of events that have heavily influenced China's national defence strategy. In the 1960s and 1970s coping with the threat of a Soviet land attack guided the formulation of China's military strategy. Based upon Mao Zedong's people's war doctrine, the PLA strategy in the 1960s and 1970s stressed numerical strength, which was thought to compensate for inferior weaponry. For a nation that was still struggling with a subsistence economy and short of advanced military facilities, Mao's idea of mobilising the civilian population for a protracted war was at the time the only feasible means of deterring a powerful adversary. That the Soviet Union failed to do to China what it did to Hungary, Czechoslovakia and Afghanistan showed its appreciation of the prospective prohibitive cost in invading a country of China's size and huge hostile population. 'People's war' has been an effective deterrent precisely because it makes virtues of these factors and exploits China's few advantages.[3]

FROM POPULOUS DEFENCE TO ACTIVE DEFENCE

The people's war strategy underwent a number of changes in the 1970s and 1980s, as it was modified by 'modern conditions'. However, the main thrust of the strategy remained largely intact at all three levels: technical, tactical and operational. Technically, the deployment of large quantities of low-tech hardware was a necessity, partly because sophisticated weapons were either unavailable or too costly. Indeed, the country's general low level of technological development at the time required a protracted period of R&D for any modern weaponry. Tactically, this led to an emphasis on human engagement with enemies at close range and with superior numbers of infantry soldiers. Although increased attention was given to the idea of combined campaigns, the PLA's mainstay military concepts reflected the man–rifle era, sadly reminiscent of the heroic scene of Polish cavalry charging against German tanks. As a result, at the operational level, the PLA still stuck firmly to its traditional combat guidelines: waging campaigns through the manoeuvre of large masses of soldiers in offence and deploying fixed positional warfare in defence.

For instance, the prospects of a large-scale Soviet land invasion in the late 1960s dictated, at the technical level, that the Chinese develop as many anti-tank and anti-aircraft artillery (AA) weapons as possible. This oriented the PLA towards a defensive posture at the tactical level. At the operational level, where Chinese forces were inadequate to hold back an invasion through line defence in the border areas, plans for quick retreat had to be drawn up to avoid a frontal confrontation with large columns of tanks. This meant that the enemy would be allowed to reach into the heartland where, by trading space for time, the PLA could regroup its main forces for counter-offensive campaigns in selected strategic directions, leaving other areas for guerrilla warfare. So China's military strategy in the Mao era really reflected China's technical and tactical weakness in coping with superior opponents. Nevertheless, for over two decades the doctrinal defects in this costly strategy persisted, leaving the PLA mired in the era of 'cold weaponry', while elsewhere in the world the high-tech revolution carried modern warfare into the information age.

Mao's death in 1976 created an opportunity for the PLA to break away from the Maoist mentality. By the end of the 1970s the PLA had accumulated a considerable amount of heavy military hardware. More importantly, it had achieved a limited second-strike nuclear capability. These factors gave the PLA high command a measure of confidence in proposing plans to prevent potential invaders from marching into China's interior. Some senior PLA generals began to advocate a basic revision of Mao's people's war strategy.[4] Their views were adopted by Deng Xiaoping, who in the early 1980s put forward a new version of China's national defence strategy: 'people's war' under 'modern conditions'.[5] The essence of the term 'modern conditions' was a change in emphasis from a focus on populous defence to that on a relatively well trained and equipped professional military. More concretely, the PLA believed that it should withstand a Soviet land attack through reinforced positional warfare, particularly in the key strategic regions such as those around major cities in north and north-east China. This new defence guideline was later formally coined as the 'active defence doctrine' (jiji fangyu). General Yang Dezhi, former chief of the General Staff Department, elaborated the doctrine in the following terms: 'instead of allowing the enemy to move fairly freely into the country, the PLA should firmly stick to positional defence in order to weaken the enemy's massive invasion and then wage counter-offensive campaigns with concentrated and combined forces'.[6] Politically, the revision revealed a Party and military consensus that allowing the enemy into China's heartland would cause serious damage to the Party's legitimacy. Economically, it was recognised that by the time the enemy was 'lured' into the heartland, much of the country's vital industries and transportation nodes would have been destroyed.[7]

DENG XIAOPING'S MILITARY REFORMS IN THE 1980s

In a meeting with Party leaders on 2 March 1983, Deng proposed that the PLA's war strategy be altered from preparation for an early all-out war with the USSR to one of 'steady development' in a changed international environment of lasting *détente*. The proposal assumed that the Soviets were mainly focusing on the European theatre and preoccupied with the threat posed to it by a hardline US foreign policy. Thus the PLA enjoyed a historic opportunity of development and reform: barring an imminent attack, the PLA was no longer forced to keep a giant army, and produce and deploy expensive but ineffective low-tech equipment for the worst-case scenario. China could now focus on developing economy, science and technology, which would provide the PLA with a more solid base for modernisation.[8] Deng's new line of thinking focused more on upgrading military hardware to suit modern conditions than retaining those elements prescribed by the people's war doctrine. He particularly called for large-scale force reduction and singled out the R&D of advanced weapons to be the priority for the PLA. In doing so he created a path for the PLA to professionalise, with far-reaching consequences.[9]

In December 1985, the CMC formally adopted Deng's proposal and renamed the PLA's war doctrine 'active defence strategy in the new era'.[10] In this context 'active' means holding the invaders outside the country's key areas, beyond the borders if necessary. It also indicates a determination to launch large-scale counter-offensives after blunting the enemy's initial attack. 'Defence' means *bentu fangyu*, or territory defence, a premise stemming from the principle of non-expansion.

In the wake of its transformation from quantitative to qualitative development, the PLA launched a number of far-reaching military reforms in the 1980s. First, a force reduction and restructuring was initiated in 1985–86, formally discarding a long PLA tradition that identified strength with large numbers of infantry soldiers. To this end, the PLA demobilised one million officers and men, reduced the number of its regional commands from eleven to seven, disowned construction and railway units, transferred the command of the militia to local civilian government, and merged its 36 armies into 25 combined group armies (including the 15th Airborne Corps).

Second, Deng's strategy gave prominence to the professional training of the officers and men. In 1982, Deng instructed the PLA to reform its national education system. By mid-decade a new three-tiered system of defence tertiary institutions was established.[11] On the very top are the PLA National Defence University and the PLA Academy of Military Science, which offer advanced courses for commanders at the army level or above. At the second level there are about a dozen command academies run by the headquarters of each service. They assume the task of training divisional and regimental commanders. At the third level, about 100 institutions recruit cadets both from within the armed forces and from among high school graduates, turning them into leaders of PLA basic units and technical staff. The CMC further prescribed that by the year 2000 most PLA officers would have to acquire tertiary qualifications.[12] It was hoped that as the quality of officers' education and technological hardware gradually improved, so would the level of professionalism of the PLA. This would be reflected in the elevation of its corporate spirit, commitment of the officer corps to acquiring the newest knowledge of military science, a sense of discipline in the rank and file, and flexibility in the face of unexpected strategic developments. In the words of a senior PLA officer, the goal is to build the PLA into a 'military of intelligence'.[13]

Third, Deng's idea of military modernisation decisively influenced the PLA's protracted debate over whether the people's war doctrine was out of date. Deng tried to reconcile the arguments for and against the doctrine. To some extent, Maoist military thinking was still enshrined in the PLA. Most of the top generals in the 1980s had been imbued with this strategy throughout their long professional careers. Moreover, the history of contemporary warfare had proved the usefulness of the strategy, first in Vietnam and then in Afghanistan. The idea of 'bleeding the invaders' in a protracted war remained attractive to China's defence planners, who knew clearly that for both political and social reasons the western powers had little capacity to sustain large numbers of human losses. Deng's revision of Mao's strategy addressed two dimensions of China's military strategy: according to a very influential general, Song Shilun, the PLA would build up an active defence to prevent the invaders from entering China's territories, both land and maritime. When this failed, a people's war would be waged within the territory to wear down powerful enemies.[14]

Indeed, General Song's understanding still serves as the foundation for China's active defence today.

In sum, the PLA's modernisation efforts yielded mixed results in the 1980s. On the one hand, while addressing doctrinal defects, the groundwork had been laid for force restructuring and improved military thinking and general training. The 'war game' tactics of different services had been updated to suit contemporary warfare. Yet the PLA's modernisation advanced slowly. Theoretically, the doctrine of active defence, mainly designed to defeat a Soviet land attack through positional warfare, seemed to be out of step with the evolution of international affairs, as the Cold War confrontation gradually drew to an end. As a result, this strategy could not provide practical guidance for the PLA to assess its security concerns, which were centred principally on territorial disputes in the second half of the 1980s. When limited conflicts in regional flashpoints were regarded by the PLA as its most likely war fighting scenarios, mass mobilisation and large-scale military operations seemed to be out of touch with reality. In the 1990s, when conflict scenarios are dominated by high-tech weaponry, the term 'people's war under modern conditions' has become even more self-contradictory, conflating two very different strategies of relying on population power (people's war) on the one hand or firepower (modern conditions) on the other. Deng's strategy fomented confusion regarding the basic direction of the PLA's development.[15]

THE EMERGING POST-DENG NATIONAL DEFENCE STRATEGY

Deng's strategy did not explain to the PLA how to fight in the new era. A transitional pause in the formulation of strategic guidelines resulted due to uncertainties both in domestic politics and the international situation at the turn of the 1980s and 1990s. Fortunately for the PLA two historical events occurred soon enough to make the pause short. First the succession arrangement in political and military leadership was worked out during the period 1989–1992, although it took a few more years for the leadership to consolidate. The Gulf War erupted in 1991, which for the Chinese high command shed light on the future direction of military modernisation. Nevertheless, the quick adoption of a new strategy was significant in a number of ways. Politically, it showed the strength and far-sightedness of the post-Deng CMC established in the CCP's 14th National Congress in October 1992.[16]

Members of the CMC in 1998 are: Jiang Zemin, chair; Zhang Wannian, executive deputy chair; Chi Haotian, deputy chair and minister for national defence; Fu Quanyou, member and chief of general staff; Yu Yongpo, member and director of the General Political Department; Wang Ke, member and director of the General Logistical Department; Cao Gangchuan, director of the General Equipment Department; and Wang Ruilin, member and deputy director of the General Political Department.

The strength and far-sightedness of the post-Deng CMC leadership can be seen from the following three angles, each in sharp contrast to the PLA's well-known inertia of the past: the new CMC was able to revise Deng's strategy while Deng was still alive; the new CMC was able to respond to the new technological revolution in a quick and down-to-earth manner, sometimes against serious ideological taboos; and the new CMC was able to use the new strategy as a banner to unify the faction-ridden PLA. In a way this was a repetition of what Liu Huaqing did to the navy in the early 1980s when he successfully united the admirals with his bluewater strategy. Indeed, the new consensus on the PLA's future direction of development has provided concrete criteria for personnel appointments, indoctrination of soldiers, and identification of potential opponents. It has served as a new rallying point to boost the PLA's corporate spirit and interest, thus contributing to an unprecedented level of unity among the top echelon of military commanders.[17]

The PLA has finally recognised that fighting wars in the high-tech era requires hardware superiority, sound tactics and a suitable force structure. Jiang Zemin remarked during his inspection tour of the PLA National University of Science and Technology in early 1991 that any future war would be a war of high-tech, a war of multi-dimensions, a war of electronics, and a war of missiles. The PLA had to be ready for such a reality.[18] Under the new guidelines, for instance, the PLA has speeded up its efforts to build a qualitative military by initiating another round of force reductions. The army is supposed to be trimmed by 500 000 men (more on this in the next chapter). At the same time, the specialised services continue to enjoy greater priority for modernisation. Enormous efforts have been made to strengthen the second-strike nuclear deterrence capability, create offensive air power and develop a bluewater navy.[19] Textbooks in the military institutions have been completely rewritten in the last few years so as to highlight the changing nature of future warfare. In 1993 a comprehensive reform was carried out in the area of military training. Soldiers are now drilled not only to learn high-tech wars but to learn how to fight specific high-tech enemies. Furthermore, China's new defence strategy has reoriented R&D and weapons programs towards research focused on military space facilities, fixed-energy weapons, laser equipment and electronic technology. Logically, this demands a continuing and sizeable increase in the military budget, as high-tech-driven military modernisation is bound to be expensive.

What is the relationship between Deng Xiaoping's doctrine of fighting a people's war under modern conditions and the post-Deng strategy of fighting a future war under high-tech conditions? The latter has clearly evolved from the former. Both envisage active defence to hold an enemy's invasion at bay. This sharply contrasts with Mao's strategy of luring the enemy into the heartland. Both prefer advanced military hardware to manpower and have set out to build a high-quality standing army. Both emphasise combined military operations (the post-Deng strategy places even more stress on united military operations, and the decisive role of the specialised services, for example the nuclear force, air force and navy).[20]

Yet they differ in several important respects. First, the post-Deng strategy calls for the linking of active defence and forward defence, which may mean power projection beyond the country's land borders. This is a radical departure from Deng's active defence, which was confined basically to territorial defence in a form of positional warfare around major cities. Deng's defence is 'active' only compared to Mao's passive people's war. Forward defence is the key to the new strategy, as it recognises that in a high-tech war the enemy can strike from a great distance. This has forced the PLA to project its strategic depth, which, according to PLA war planners, should not be restricted within Chinese borders. For instance, air defence should be stretched even beyond the enemy's first line airbase.[21] Moreover, one form of this forward defence is forward deployment in areas subject to overlapping territorial disputes. As an expression of sovereignty claims, this entails the permanent stationing of PLA units in, and regular military exercises around, these areas. In some extreme cases, this even entails a demonstration of war brinkmanship to protect China's vital national interests, such as its sovereignty and territorial integrity.

Second, the high-tech defence strategy is largely an offensive-oriented strategy reflecting the PLA's shifting emphasis towards the 'active' versus the 'defensive' side of war preparation. In a way this is a reverse of Deng's doctrine. According to some PLA strategists, China's post–Cold War military guideline should be changed from

Deng's *yifang weizhu fangfan jiehe*, or 'defence as overall posture, offence as the supplement', to *linghuo fanying gong fang jiehe*, or 'adroit response based on a combination of offensive and defensive capabilities'.[22] Active defence is now understood as capturing the nature of high-tech warfare: the evolving high-tech hardware is highly biased toward a fast offensive strike because technological innovation has increasingly blurred the boundaries between offensive and defensive weaponry. Thus it is the offensive side that can seize the first initiative of the war and has the best chance of success.[23] The offensive posture is especially crucial for a weak military in a high-tech war.

In practice the post–Cold War uncertainties have required the PLA to enhance rapid response capabilities to cope with new sets of events, expected or unexpected. Under some circumstances active defence can mean pre-emptive offensive campaigns to neutralise an imminent threat.[24] PLA strategists argue that a country's need to protect its territorial integrity dictates a forward posture. Take Taiwan as an example. Here the Chinese are politically and diplomatically reactive to the efforts of the independence movement. Militarily, however, the PLA has to develop a capability powerful enough to deter any such attempt by the Taiwan authorities. If this fails, it has to launch an offensive operation. Inevitably the PLA has to formulate its detailed invasion plans based on available offensive weaponry. More importantly, this propensity to employ military forces is closely linked to the concept of military deterrence at various levels of possible armed conflict. A strategy of deterrence against foreign invasion differs from that of safeguarding national sovereignty. Generally, a defensive-oriented military strategy cannot make the latter credible. This is especially true when the political forces for separatism have the support of a high-tech military.[25]

Third, China's post-Deng strategy is forward-leaning in both political and military terms. Politically, the high-tech focus aims at defence against strategic concerns, namely the major military powers.[26] At the same time the strategy is flexible in principle, catering to different scenarios, from major high-tech wars to small-scale border rifts. This is the response of China's armed forces to the country's changing security environment in the post–Cold War era (more on this in a later section). Militarily, China's post-Deng defence strategy is not just a change in doctrinal concepts. It is forward-looking, as it is geared to preparation for warfare in the next century. Therefore, it prescribes concrete measures for weapons programs, force restructuring, campaign tactics, and national defence research priorities, which do not aim at equipping the PLA in the near future but at the new frontiers of high-tech break-throughs some decades from now. The PLA's enthusiasm for the 'Revolution in Military Affairs' (RMA) has surprised top experts in RMA in the United States.[27] Indeed, one of the major changes in China's armed forces in the post-Mao era has been a high level of far-sightedness in war preparations. Immediately after the offi-cial adoption of Deng's 'people's war under modern conditions' in 1985, the CMC launched a nationwide campaign to study how the PLA would fight in the turn of the century. In a keynote speech to the PLA's first all-services conference in 1986, General Zhang Zhen said he believed that if the PLA could not foresee the developmental trend of military science, it would be further left behind.[28] China's new defence strategy requires all the armed forces to study how to fight a war beyond the year 2020.

Establishing the proper direction of development may be more important than the immediate availability of military hardware for the future of the Chinese armed forces. An example of the far-reaching impact of China's post-Deng defence strategy is the major re-ordering of the PLA's theoretical and applicable research priori-ties. In the past, PLA researchers were inclined to study the PLA's war history. For instance, about half of the research projects in the PLA Academy of Military Science were engaged in continuous evaluations of the PLA's successful campaigns between 1927 and 1953. In 1993 Jiang Zemin instructed the PLA research bodies to shift their research focus from the past to the present. More concretely, he decided that over 60 per cent of research projects had to serve the PLA's current needs (for example, restructuring), practical war plans (for example, force redeployment), and likely operations in the future (for example, the way in which men and weapons are related).[29] Consequently, the PLA's research on major practical issues (*zhongda xianshi wenti*) and its theoretical explo-ration of the RMA have been combined together under the post-Deng military strategy.

Finally, the high-tech defence strategy has been viewed as a driving force for the development of science and technology for the whole nation. Indeed, the Chinese technocrats-turned-leaders have made it a state policy to enter the high-tech race with the industrialised countries.[30] They have not failed to notice that the US technological race with the USSR helped it to achieve a superior position in the post–Cold War world economic compe-tition. Defence-related high-tech has always led scientific and technological revolutions. The applications of military information technology can be wide-ranging and profitable. The PLA has been very supportive of the Party's concern about the country's economic security, now seen as built upon a scientific and technological competitive edge.[31] As the civilian and military leaders share the same policy objective in placing high-tech development as the top national priority, the PLA has vigorously followed the Party's call to convert much of its military-industrial complex to dual use (that is, producing goods for sale on the open market as well as military material).

THE LESSONS OF THE GULF WAR AND THE HIGH-TECH STRATEGY

One of the most decisive catalysts for China's post-Deng strategic change was the Gulf War, which Chinese strategists regarded as the inevitable pattern of high-tech armed conflict beyond this century.[32] During the Gulf War all military headquarters throughout the country received round-the-clock satellite coverage of the action and set up special research task forces to follow any signs of new progress in military tactics and technology.[33] In November and December 1991 the CMC convened a series of meetings to analyse the research findings. CMC chairman Jiang Zemin and then vice chairmen Yang Shangkun and Liu Huaqing were present at a number of report sessions. They asked a large number of questions concerning the weaponry and tactics employed by the Allied forces in the war. Some of the questions were particularly searching, such as how the PLA would cope with the Allies' specific weaponry (for instance, the F–117 Stealth aircraft), and its tactics if it were in Iraq's place. Many of these questions went unanswered, which seriously worried the Chinese top leadership.[34] Subsequently, the CMC called for a serious study of high-tech warfare throughout the whole of the armed forces.

Since the end of the Gulf War, there has been a sustained campaign to study the whole process of the Desert Shield and Desert Storm campaigns. The depth of research, the absence of ideological constraints and the wide range of participants from top brass to ordinary soldiers have been unprecedented in the PLA's history. Detailed war actions by both sides were video-taped by PLA research institutes or purchased by PLA overseas missions. Edited versions were used later as compulsory teaching material and references for the training of officers and men. For the first time since 1949 the daily coverage of the war by PLA newspapers and journals effectively exposed the three-million-strong armed forces to every kind of high-tech weapons and operational tactics used in the war. They were implicitly told that these were the likely situations which China's potential enemies might impose upon the PLA. All this has exerted a profound impact on the PLA, whose rank and file had hitherto been sheltered from knowing too many details about the sophisticated weapons of its potential adversaries. In a way this historical exposure reflected the confidence and resolve of the PLA's new leadership to catch up technologically with the west. The results of this study campaign are quite impressive: there has emerged a 'high-tech wave' among the rank and file members of the PLA. As one senior PLA officer put it, what would defeat the PLA in future wars was not its obsolete weapons but its obsolete ideas. Following are a few major lessons that the PLA has learned from the Gulf War.

Electronic warfare is decisive to the result of the entire war

The PLA has made enormous efforts to analyse why the Iraqi armed forces became paralysed immediately after Desert Storm was launched. The Chinese noticed that at the beginning of the war, together with other channels of intelligence, 34 specialised satellites were deployed in the space above the Gulf area. Capable of image resolution of half a metre, they easily detected every major movement and position of the Iraqi forces. On the ground 39 intelligence-gathering stations joined forces with various kinds of reconnaissance aircraft to form a multi-dimensional intelligence network that provided a large amount of reliable information for the Allied forces. The Gulf War has clearly shown that information, one of four basic elements of modern warfare, has risen to parallel the importance of the other three (people, weaponry, and battlefield circumstances).[35] Superiority in information control made it possible for the Allied forces to work out detailed plans of attack later. Indeed, a military victory in the high-tech era requires a great deal of intelligence gathering for precise target acquisition and identification.[36]

To the PLA it was the use of a computerised C^{3}I system that distinguished the Gulf War from any of the previous ones.[37] The first combat use of the Global Positioning System, as the PLA noticed, conveniently connected the Allied headquarters and field units and provided accurate three-dimensional flight and navigation guidance to the Allied air force and navy throughout the conflict. Computers of various sizes from 'super' to 'personal' quickly transmitted information, processed intelligence reports, arranged flying sorties, assigned targets, and coordinated the operations of different war theatres. For instance, the PLA conducted specific research on how the computer system of the US Air Force made possible the 'zero stock' in the Gulf theatre by flying in from home 95 per cent of the needed supplies.[38]

The PLA also eagerly studied the uses of electronic warfare in the Gulf War. One report noted that while the 42-day bombing of Iraq's C³I system by the Allied air force failed to eliminate the system's physical existence, the three-day electronic blockade at the beginning of Desert Shield achieved the desired result: to completely paralyse the Iraqi C³I system. This 'soft warfare', as the PLA termed it, such as attack on the enemy's C³I system through a computer virus, has become a strategic rather than tactical component of any future wars.[39] The PLA reported, for instance, that during the Gulf War the US employed special software chips to contaminate the French-made printers of Iraq's air defence computer system, and as the virus spread to the main computer system of the Iraqi armed forces, Iraq's C³I system was fatally disrupted.[40] This was an alarming learning process for the PLA, since a large number of its major computer systems were imported from western countries.

High-tech weaponry is the key to victory in future wars

The PLA saw the Gulf War as the testing ground for the most advanced military technology. Stealth technology, for instance, helped F–117As penetrate Iraq's air defence system independently of other supporting aircraft. This was in sharp contrast to the traditional method of a strike employing large bombing packages. Hence they were able to achieve a significant level of surprise even after war was declared. With only a small number of sorties, the F–117As destroyed a disproportionate 30 per cent of the first-day targets and about 50 per cent of all original targets with strategic importance. All this would not have been possible without precision guided munitions, which comprised only 5 per cent of all explosives dropped.

The PLA's study of the Patriot missile led to the conclusion that the age of a 'dog-of-war' type missile exchange has come. Technologically, this means that the outcome of future wars will be highly dependent on the development of sophisticated radar acquisition/guidance systems, high-speed but small-sized computers, and advanced electronic micro-chips. Militarily, this places the side without sophisticated anti-missile technology in an extremely difficult position. Without an effective anti-missile system, all military units would be exposed to the enemy's long-range missile attacks, which could be devastating. The outcome of such a war would have been half-decided before human engagement had even begun.[41]

The PLA also closely monitored the performance of technologies that helped the Allied forces to fight effectively at night, such as infra-red, laser, millimetre-wave radar, and heat imagery. While some PLA analysts ridiculed the Iraqi forces for passively hiding under the sand and relying on the darkness, they expressed grave worries that the PLA's traditional strong point, its ability to fight at night, might have evaporated given the highly developed night vision equipment available to its potential opponents. One research article commented that when infra-red and heat-imagery facilities of the US ground forces could—through magnifying the night light by 60 000 times and detecting a temperature difference of 0.056°C of objects—expose the enemy's tanks and personnel at four and one kilometres respectively, the prevailing mentality of the PLA— 'it is safe unless sighted by eyes'—had become more dangerous than ever before.[42]

The Gulf War has stimulated the PLA to study how and how far the development of high-techology has affected military strategies and tactics. The general application of laser, stealth, micro-electronic and infra-red technologies has translated the great potential of the scientific development into battlefield reality. The PLA concluded that high-tech multiplies the capabilities of conventional weapons systems, and hence changes the nature of combat. The wide use of computer simulation technology, for instance, has remarkably improved US campaign tactics. During the Gulf War, about 1000 computerised simulating models of combat were proposed to the Joint Chiefs of Staff, which selected 178 of them. These models provided to the commanders assessments of all likely options of attack and measures to deal with the worst-case scenarios. The PLA therefore cautioned its researchers against exaggerating some seeming loopholes in the US operations by judging these on the basis of their limited knowledge of high-tech wars and on the PLA's own traditional military thinking.[43]

Air power is crucial to success in modern warfare

The Gulf War marked the ascendancy of air forces in modern warfare. Western analysts watched the success of Allied air forces in the Gulf War and concluded that, with air superiority, almost anything was feasible and, without it, everything was difficult.[44] The PLA has generally accepted this assessment, representing a visible departure from its time-honoured emphasis on the decisiveness of the ground force. The political implication of this is the gradual erosion of the mentality that humans are superior to machines. As one senior PLA air force theorist commented:

> It is inevitable that a military has to evolve from drawing physical strength from numbers (*tineng*) to relying on technological hardware (*jineng*) to becoming eventually a military of intelligence (*zhineng*). The Gulf War has proved the ascendancy of the air force. It is a fact that the air force has played and will continue to play a decisive role in the high-tech limited wars. This dictates a qualitative change in the utility of different services.[45]

The PLA's new appreciation is fundamentally based on the study of the performance of the Allied air force in the Gulf War. Numerous articles have been published in PLA journals showing how the Allied air force provided a platform for transporting 80 per cent of troops to the theatre in a short span of time, for waging an electronic campaign that paralysed the Iraqi defence system, and for delivering the bulk of the bombs that destroyed Iraq's capability for effective resistance. Above all, the PLA agreed that it was air power that frustrated Saddam Hussein's desire to engage the Allied forces in protracted ground battles so as to extract heavy casualties. Air superiority is thus seen as instrumental in fulfilling the objective of modern warfare: not taking enemy territory, but destroying the enemy's defence capability through superior firepower. This has been a profound lesson for the PLA, with major implications for its war doctrine and preparation.[46] Chapter 5 will deal with this in more detail.

In short the PLA concluded that with the advanced technology, the Allied forces turned the Gulf War into a war of attrition. Air power had reached a new plateau where techniques of target acquisition, movement, invasion and resupply became so routinised that the application of operational tactics was reduced to a minimum. This now challenges the PLA to contemplate whether it could win its next war with any major high-tech powers.[47] Indeed, the central theme of the PLA's study of the Gulf War has been the question of what the PLA must do, in theoretical and practical terms, to win such a high-tech war.

SINIFYING THE REVOLUTION IN MILITARY AFFAIRS

The concept of the Revolution in Military Affairs (RMA) has been discussed in academic papers for some time but only recently was it brought to prominence by Desert Storm. It is a surprise that the Chinese are among the first enthusiastic learners and have benefited tremendously from the concept in setting up their development goals in the decades ahead—surprise in the sense that RMA is a western invention but embraced by a communist military so eagerly. This tells a lot about the PLA today as compared with its recent past. As pointed out by Michael Pillsbury, the PLA's elaboration of the RMA has shaken up western notions about the backwardness of Chinese strategic planning. Indeed, the very fact that RMA is studied in China is an indication of the PLA's advance; besides the Chinese, only American and Russian strategists have written on the subject.[48]

The advanced thinking on the future warfare is also reflected by the PLA's full understanding of the effects of RMA on the military establishments. As pointed out by an American professor at the Armed Forces Staff College, 'the Chinese defence analysts appear to be at the cutting edge of the implications of information war for traditional institutions such as the military'.[49] Major General Chen Youyuan, director of the Officers Training Bureau in the General Staff Department, praised the ideas related to RMA, saying: 'The revolution in information technology changed with each passing day the battleground structure, operation modes and concepts of time and space while dealing blows to the traditional "centralised" and "tier-by-tier" command structure.'[50]

In his influential article, published in *The Journal of the PLA National Defence University*, General Chen well summarises the key features of the RMA, as understood by the PLA. According to him, RMA is profoundly altering the world military in the following areas: RMA is changing the components of the armed forces, especially for the campaign formation between different services; is introducing new combat means; is generating much large combat space; is creating new modes of operations; and is inventing new methods of combat engagement. All this in turn propels the military establishments to make theoretical breakthroughs so as to accommodate these new developments in technology and combat operations. Thus the PLA together with other advanced military powers enter an exciting era of new military thinking, new military ideas and new military concepts.[51]

In PLA writings about RMA, future warfare has never been

studied so thoroughly. As mentioned earlier, the PLA was quick to learn immediately after the Gulf War that high-tech wars will not be fought along fixed defence lines. The line between battle-ground frontier and its depth will become very thin. Trench warfare will be rare to see. In recent years they have accumulated more knowledge in studying ideas of US and Russian RMA experts. Andrew Marshall, Stephen Blank, Martin Libiki, and others have been quoted frequently. As of May 1998 PLA thinkers have come up with a number of new ideas that they want to incorporate into their planning for the long-term modernisation of the Chinese armed forces. Among other things the following are their findings:

- Strike from long distance. New sophisticated terminal guid-ance systems and precision weapons have made possible beyond-vision attack. This will save human engagement and greatly reduce casualties. PLA researchers have noticed the US's new concepts of combat such as 'disengagement and indirect assault', and 'concentrated firepower but dispersed manpower'. They agree with the claims by US military experts that in the not too distant future tank battles, aircraft 'dog-fights' and exchange of fire by warships' big guns will become history.[52]

- Small-size campaign formation without compromising the strength and outcome. Crack force structure and simple-layer command are more suitable for information warfare, which is characterised more by combat between hardware than between men. At the same time digitalisation and precision ammuni-tion have multiplied the firepower of campaign units. There-fore, a small high-tech force can overpower an army ten times more numerous. Digitalisation in particular is a key indicator of a military of the future.

- Linkage between superiority in information and victory of an operation. Information technology has not only become an indispensable means for better command and communication, but it has also constituted an effective weapon to be used to kill the enemies directly. Combat between opposing militaries is first of all between their information capabilities. In a way superiority in information is superiority in combat operation.[53]

There is no doubt PLA theoreticians are copying the thinking of their US colleagues. At present most of them still belong to the school of high-tech warfare, which differs from the school of RMA in that the latter takes a more integrated view on the features of information warfare. It aggregates all the features of IW and analyses them in a forward-leaning manner. In contrast the majority of PLA commanders are in the school of high-tech warfare, as represented by Admiral Liu Huaqing, who emphasises only individual aspects of IW.

Although the number of true believers of RMA in the PLA remains small, they are wielding increasingly more influence, thanks to the personal support of the CMC chairman Jiang Zemin. A few years ago only a small number of PLA researchers were talking about RMA. Now it has become a vogue. It is safe to predict that the future development of the PLA will be guided quite visibly by the idea of RMA.

On the other hand, however, the Chinese are not only learning the idea. They are sinifying it according to their own tradition, current practice and future needs. RMA has pitfalls and deceptions. Gao Jinxi, deputy president of the PLA National Defence University (NDU), cautioned those bold advocates of the concept about the danger of copying foreign military ideas mechanically:

> Inserting some high-tech weapons into the PLA's traditional war doctrine would not be successful. More importantly, in creating new doctrine all the factors of the high-tech limited wars have to be studied. Especially it has to be tested in the comparison of available armament to the PLA and its potential opponents. The primary task of studying RMA is to find effective methods to win a high-tech war by using inferior hardware.[54]

In other words the PLA is injecting Chinese characteristics into RMA. By the definition of Professor Zhu Guangya, China's top defence scientist, RMA is the product of socio-economic and technological development. It is the organic and timely combination of advanced weapons systems, new military theoretical guidelines and effective force structure. This combination can generate qualitative change in the employment of military power.[55] The Chinese believe that the new military revolution is still in its formative years. Therefore, it is not too late to catch up with this crucial developmental trend. The key to success is to have a correct understanding of what RMA means, especially, of what it means to the Chinese military modernisation. With a proper understanding achieved, the PLA has to do a lot of careful research on how to apply it in its policy process regarding force restructuring, weapons R&D, equipment and preparation for actions.

In order to meet the challenge of IW the Chinese armed forces have formulated a number of principles of learning RMA. First, the PLA must further emancipate the minds of the officers and men and upgrade the war-fighting theories of the PLA. Major-General Li Youyuan argued that revolution in military technology will not automatically produce theoretical guidelines. Without new combat theory, technology cannot win the war by itself. However, new theory will not be invented without a fundamental change in the mentality of PLA senior officers. In fact RMA is seen as not only bringing pressure to bear on the PLA, but also opening up new opportunities: it provides the best stimulant for the PLA to shake off its historical burdens rooted in its old military strategies.

Second, the PLA must broaden its horizons and closely follow the major military powers regarding their new theories and practice. The PLA now believes that the recent limited high-tech wars have provided very good study cases for China to understand the logic, operation features and combat patterns of its potential adversaries. These should serve as a useful reference for the PLA to work out countermeasures. At the same time the PLA should use these cases as a guide to develop its own combat theories and principles.

Third, the PLA must study information warfare very carefully in order to learn its merits and, simultaneously, find its points of weakness. This is crucial for the PLA, which will for a long time have to rely on inferior weapons to fight powerful enemies.

Fourth, the PLA must employ advanced means to improve its research on RMA. Senior officers and ordinary soldiers alike are encouraged to learn military science and technology. Knowledge of social science and other disciplines should be applied in the research on RMA. It is very important, for instance, for the PLA to use computer simulation systems to reconstruct major high-tech operations of the major powers in their recent limited wars.

People may concede that the Chinese can copy American thoughts but whether they can also materialise RMA is not at all obvious.[56] However, one thing is certain. The PLA is very serious about RMA this time. One clear example is the establishment of a General Equipment Department immediately under the CMC (whose functions will be discussed in the next chapter). Another indicator has been the renewed discussion in recent months of abolishing the seven Military Area Commands. The PLA high command invited debate among top brass in the early 1980s about whether to replace all MACs with strategic direction field armies. For instance, the Shenyang MAC would be restructured into Northeast China Direction Field Army. The difference between the two was that the former was at once a level of administrative agency and operational command. This made the leadership structure unwieldy. Instructions from the CMC had to be relayed through several layers to reach the units they should go to quickly. In comparison the Northeast China Direction Field Army was merely a level of operational command. It was more directly connected to the CMC. Another advantage of the reform was to uproot the too-intimate political and economic ties between the PLA's regional command and the local civilian government. However, the debate did not bring any concrete results due to the resistance of military regions. Later on the CMC abolished the attempted reform simply by saying that the conditions were not ripe.[57]

Since 1997 a new round of discussion of the same theme has been carried out among PLA leading agencies. This time the 'conditions' may be 'ripe'. It has been proposed that the current seven MACs may be substituted by five strategic war zones. There are several merits in this reform. I have already mentioned the simplified command structure between the central military authority and the basic campaign units (group armies or divisions). Political need is even more pressing. However, the motivation is also rooted in the need to initiate a thorough overhaul of the PLA's command structure in order to suit it better in information warfare. For instance, the war zone concept will guide the integration of all services in united operations under a united command (more on this in Chapter 2). It will be very interesting to watch the outcome of this reform.

THE DOCTRINAL PRINCIPLES OF THE HIGH-TECH STRATEGY

It may be an exaggeration to claim that the PLA has shifted to a high-tech oriented military strategy just because of the Gulf War. Discussions on how to meet the challenge of the information age have been going on in the PLA since the mid-1980s. In 1987 a strategist in the PLA Academy of Military Science (PLAAMS) stated that a qualitative change in military science was in the making. This change was stimulated by the development of high-tech conventional armoury, such as laser and fixed-energy weapons systems, whose effect was increasingly approaching that of nuclear weaponry.[58] The learning experience of the Gulf War has only hastened the PLA's grasp of the nature of China's potential future wars. In a sense the PLA was fortunate to have been exposed to such international events and technological development at a time when its leadership was under minimal ideological constraint. This unprecedented level of political relaxation has helped PLA researchers to take a realistic approach to the study of military science. In close association with Admiral Liu Huaqing and General Zhang Zhen, who represent mainstream PLA policy opinions, war planners in the navy, the PLA Academy of Military Science and the PLA National Defence University have spearheaded the study of advanced western military ideas and convinced the PLA top brass that times have changed. These war planners are young, well read, visionary, and anxious to create a new PLA that is more professional than revolutionary. They favour China's modernisation but reject its wholesale westernisation. They entertain strong nationalist feelings but oppose closed-doorism. More interestingly, they see communism as irrelevant to China's self-strengthening but accept the Party as the vehicle for that national purpose. They seem to harbour a suppressed ambition, recognising their country's present state of military backwardness.[59]

A two-tiered national defence doctrine

China's two-tiered national defence doctrine simultaneously seeks to improve its capability to deter nuclear powers through its own nuclear capabilities, and to augment its conventional capability to tackle crises along China's peripheries. The second-tier war preparation received a great deal of attention in the late 1980s.[60] In the 1990s the PLA's post-Deng strategy has somewhat revised the second-tier emphasis. Recognising that a focus on small neighbouring states would not provide a basis for a comprehensive modernisation program for the military of a big country such as China, the PLA has again highlighted potential conflict with the major powers at the second tier, as mentioned earlier. In the revised hierarchy of importance, at the first tier, constantly upgrading nuclear weapons is viewed as crucial to coping with the potential threat posed to China by America's strategy of 'global deterrence' and its mentality of Containment Number Two.[61] As pointed out by one senior PLA analyst, 'We must have a clear vision of the future posture of nuclear powers. Any relaxation will put us in a sorry position'.[62] Even at the second tier any possible conflict involving China is perceived as high-tech warfare, as all the major regional military powers have acquired high-tech weapons in recent years. Under these circumstances the PLA's second-tier military readiness must be advanced through raising the level of firepower of conventional weapons, and especially through introducing more high-tech hardware to the PLA Navy (PLAN) and Air Force (PLAAF).[63]

The relationship between the two tiers is dialectical, which realistically reflects China's perception of imminent and potential threats in the era of Cold Peace. The US is considered to be more offensive and adventurous now that it has become the sole super-power.[64] Therefore the first tier has been given top-priority status in military modernisation. On the other hand, however, even under rising American pressure—as after the post-Tiananmen sanctions—the PLA still believes that such pressure will not be translated into any armed confrontation in the foreseeable future. Therefore, the PLA continues to pay due attention to limited regional wars, a major contingency of the second tier in China's defence strategy. During much of the late 1980s the PLA high command concluded that limited regional conflicts along and beyond the country's borders were unavoidable and constituted the more likely scenarios that the PLA would have to deal with.[65] This recognition enriched the PLA's military thinking and rectified a visible weakness in its preparation for war: an obsession with an all-out war which had prevented an in-depth study of limited wars both in theoretical planning and in the development of appropriate weaponry.[66] A limited regional war caused by territorial disputes would render irrelevant the traditional Maoist war strategies and tactics such as mass mobilisation and luring the enemy into the heartland for a protracted manpower-intensive engagement. Nor, during a limited regional war, would the positional defence against massive invading armies—the core of the Dengist active defence doctrine—help in achieving the PLA's objectives.

Lieutenant-General Mi Zhenyu, a top PLA strategist, summarised seven main features of a limited regional war. These features reflected the PLA's understanding of modern warfare:

1   Limited objectives which restrict the scale, means and the timing of the war.
2   Very often these objectives are more political-diplomatic oriented than military (for example, wiping out the enemy's manpower).
3   The conflict process is under greater central control, with a political settlement seen as the end result.
4   A complicated international background which makes the conflict more unpredictable and fast-evolving.
5   Although the war is limited, the preparation for it is intensive because the room for failure is very narrow.

6   Pre-emptive attack (surgical strike) is a major form of action.
7   Despite the short duration of conflicts, it is very costly, since a large quantity of high-tech weapons of mass destruction is employed.[67]

The PLA's post-Deng defence strategy has further broadened the concept of regional limited wars as defined by General Mi, bringing the major powers into the picture. This is a significant departure from the concept's previous narrow focus on China's immediate neighbours. The evolution of the two-tiered defence strategy now deals, at both tiers, with long-term potential threats, mainly from the major powers. At the second tier, a local limited war is understood as a war with the involvement of major powers. In an acute regional crisis China may clash directly with major powers. In such a case, China must be prepared to counter each of an escalating series of levels of coercion. At the beginning the PLA may have to deal with the challenge of a 'no-fly-zone' imposition, possibly over the Taiwan Straits. Chinese analysts see the 'no-fly-zone' as a frequently used post–Cold War demonstration of superior power over weaker states.[68] The next possible step up is a surgical attack against PLA facilities for political and diplomatic purposes by the superpower. Indeed one feature of such an action against China could be an air or missile punishment without a real invasion.[69] This possibility of a 'limited surgical attack' against China, the type the US waged against Libya, particularly concerns Chinese war planners because the PLA has little capability to counter such a lightning military action.[70]

In the short run, however, the flashpoints that exist along Chinese peripheries still occupy a central place in China's war preparation. In recent years a new situation has emerged that requires the PLA to contemplate a regional military power joining forces with a superpower to challenge China's vital national interests. One clear example is the US's silent support of Taiwan's separation from the mainland. This point will be discussed in more detail in later chapters.

In terms of military equipment, the conduct of future limited regional wars would require of the PLA greater firepower, more effective command and control systems, and better logistical supply networks. The PLA's new focus on limited regional wars in the 1980s stimulated it to develop more suitable weapons for regional flashpoints.[71] For instance, more special equipment was provided to the newly created mountain brigade at the Sino–Indian borders and to special jungle units along the Sino–Vietnam borders, while the navy gradually extended its power projection capabilities into the South China Sea.[72]

The new campaign tactics in a high-tech war

Since the emergence of the post-Deng defence strategy, the PLA's traditional war tactics have been thoroughly reviewed, which has strongly affected its campaign theories and training programs. PLA planners have learned from the Gulf War that a high-tech war entails a complete set of new military tactics. Iraq had some high-tech weapons but it had not developed appropriate tactics to use them to its best advantage.[73] During the Gulf War all Iraq could do was to maintain the tactics of line defence, waiting to be wiped out by the enemy's superior firepower. This was a profound lesson for the PLA, as its doctrine of active defence and associated campaign tactics heavily emphasised positional warfare, a legacy from its earlier war design against the probability of a Soviet land invasion. Lieutenant-General Hu Changfa, deputy president of the PLA National Defence University, made the following summary at an all-armed-forces conference on campaign theory in late 1996:

> The changes in the international strategic environment and the wide application of high-tech in the military realm have posed an enormous challenge to the PLA. Now we are facing new forms of warfare, new opponents in future wars, new campaign tactics and new patterns of engagement in campaigns. How to win the next war under high-tech conditions is the primary task of study in front of us.[74]

To tackle this task the PLA has first identified the new forms of its most likely forms of engagement in a high-tech campaign. According to General Hu, there are two basic forms. The first is mobile operations and the second is united operations.[75] Mobile operation dictates a fundamental revision of the PLA's operational doctrine centred on positional warfare and promotes a kind of non-line defence warfare. The PLA has realised that line defence belongs to the era of rifles, guns and tanks, while the non-line defence is the key feature of high-tech warfare, requiring long-range mobility and an effective attack at the enemy's defence depth. Inevitably the campaign operations have to be supported by satellite guidance and multi-dimensional strike capabilities.[76]

Therefore the essence of mobile operation is offensive-oriented operation (gongshi zuozhan), which will be the main form of the PLA campaign engagement with its opponents.[77] To PLA theoreticians, mobile operation is seen as a key component of a campaign in the information age. High-tech limited wars are characterised by non-fixed campaign battlefields, fast change in operation formats, and little distinction between the front line and the defence rear. Only through mobile operations will the PLA take the initiative of the war. Mobile operations are also required by China's strategic landscape. In future campaigns the PLA may be confronted with the mission of operating in multiple strategic directions and over a vast space of war zones. It has to move very rapidly in order to establish regional superiority in terms of manpower and hardware.

Closely related to mobile operation is united operation. Together they constitute the main features of a high-tech campaign. United operation is seen as reflecting the nature of the information age that the PLA has to embrace. For a long time combined operations remained the PLA's basic campaign typology. Most campaigns were designed to be centred around the ground force operations. 'Combined' referred to employment of different arms of services (junzhong) within the army: units of tank, artillery, anti-chemical warfare, engineering corps, telecommunications and others were brought together to execute a joint campaign. Specialised services such as the navy, the air force and the strategic missile force were, however, given only a minor role. This campaign form was in agreement with the level of China's overall military modernisation: the specialised services were left far behind in hardware development. Certainly the PLA's doctrinal defects were also to blame for the state of affairs. After all the Chinese armed forces grew from the ground force and were dominated by it.

Now the PLA high command believes that the time has come for the rectification of the flaws both in campaign theory and typology. Information warfare has raised the status of specialised services to parallel the ground force. In recent years the special services have made some progress in both theoretical guidance and hardware modernisation, making them more capable of supporting joint operations. More importantly, fighting with the new war opponents requires a more crucial participation of the specialised services. According to Lieutenant-General Hu, in China's future major strategic war direction, landing operations of some scale will be the PLA's primary task. Landing operations have to be united operations, which makes them the basic form of campaign under high-tech conditions.[78]

The following are two of the new principles regarding campaign tactics that the PLA has developed in its current study of high-tech warfare.

1   In the future united campaigns, strategic operations and tactical operations have become less distinguishable. A tactical campaign now assumes the same far-reaching political significance that is traditionally applied to strategic operations. A victory of a campaign operation is normally the fulfilment of a strategic design, as is its failure.

2   A traditional campaign involves massive manpower and large quantities of equipment and can last for some extended time. A high-tech campaign can, in contrast, be very short and directly involve only a small number of people. Moreover, such a campaign can be conducted in a limited space—an attack on a small target, for example.[79]

In projecting a future campaign operation, PLA strategists have simulated a battle against itself that is launched using electronic warfare, followed by a large-scale air attack and an integrated air and ground assault. Since 1991 numerous academic papers have been published exploring the countermeasures available to a military engaged in such a high-tech war with inferior equipment. Exercises and training have focused on how to increase survivability and mobility for such an armed force. These have already triggered a profound change in the mentality of senior army officers. An ongoing debate asks whether there is still a need to train soldiers as intensively as before with traditional combat techniques such as short-distance infantry fighting (grenade-throwing or bayonet charges), and how to realise the tactical value of massive attacks at night on an enemy equipped with sophisticated night vision weaponry. One researcher argues that these old strong points of the PLA may have become its liability in the information age:

> It would be a lot better if we set out now to upgrade our C^3I and weapons systems and establish our own defence theories under the conditions of high-tech wars rather than waste time and energy repeating those obsolete combat principles. Our training programs must aim at enhancing troops' capabilities to withhold the enemy's attack of high-tech weaponry.[80]

From these analyses we may see a major PLA effort to follow the world-wide trend of military development. And this effort is accompanied by the PLA's willingness to address its past theoretical defects in military thinking. This may represent major progress in China's grasp of the nature of a high-tech future campaign which is serving a two-tiered purpose of being both a strategic–political endeavour and a tactical operation.

2

Positioning the PLA for a 21st-century war

Since the early 1990s the PLA has accelerated the pace of its modernisation. One visible difference between this round of military reform and the previous ones lies in the PLA's efforts to remedy the doctrinal deficiencies which in the past stood in the way of a thorough transformation of China's armed forces. In the current round of military reform the new PLA leadership has tried hard to match its war-fighting doctrine with the reality of future high-tech warfare. This has generated a very dynamic evolutionary process, affecting almost all aspects of Chinese military development. This chapter selectively analyses some of the changes that are taking place in the PLA, namely its efforts to restructure and redeploy its services and units, which may serve as the best example to show the PLA is geared to fight a war in the new millennium.

FORCE RESTRUCTURING

Until recently, alterations in the structure of China's armed forces have been insignificant: the PLA ground force in 1997 still comprises over 75 per cent of all four services combined, only a minimal decrease compared to a few years ago. This has put the PLA in sharp contrast to the composition of other major military powers, whose ground forces make up only half of total military personnel, and therefore it has to further adjust its force structure to catch up with the world trend. In this process China should particularly learn from the evolution of the force structure of the western advanced military powers (see Table 2.1).[1]

A number of factors have obstructed the PLA's restructuring efforts in the past. First, the low level of China's economic devel-

Table 2.1 Manpower ratios of the services of major military forces (per cent)

Total	Army	Navy	Air force	Missile force
China	70	9.4	16	4.6
USA	34	40	26	
Russia*	47	17.6	14.7	13
UK	47	22	31	

Note: *Internal security troops not included.
Source: Hu Guangzheng 1997, p. 124.

opment meant that the government could not afford to provide the PLA with enough of the sophisticated weapons systems necessary for enhancing the specialised services (the air force, navy and Strategic Missile Force). Second, the PLA has been burdened by an obsolete notion that the country's national defence is fundamentally continental. More importantly, the PLA was created as a ground force. Specialised services appeared in its force structure only after the army had achieved absolute control over all of the armed forces. Both air force and navy headquarters were not established until after the PLA won the national civil war. Even today China's armed forces are still called the People's Liberation *Army*. As a result infantrymen have long dominated the top brass and they have the best chance of being promoted to the CMC. Domination by infantry officers has inhibited the restructuring of the PLA to suit modern warfare, which inevitably calls for an enhanced role for the specialised services.

Signs of change have begun to register since the mid-1990s and a long, dynamic trend has gradually taken shape thanks to both internal and external stimuli. Since the late 1980s rapid economic growth has led to unprecedented financial allocations for the modernisation of the military. With the military budget doubling every four or five years, the PLA is now able to undertake long-term development projects that are costly and technologically demanding.[2] The availability of advanced weapons systems in the world market widens the PLA's opportunities to restructure its force components through a new combination of manpower and equipment. And the unprecedented level of foreign currency reserves, standing at US$140 billion at the beginning of 1998, makes overseas purchases more feasible. The timely adoption of a high-tech national defence strategy by the post-Deng leadership marks a far-reaching departure from the old tradition and mind-set, and is in itself a significant milestone in the PLA's modernisation. Force restructuring is now viewed as an inevitable response to information warfare (IW). More than at any time in its history the PLA has realised that a scientific force structure can serve as an effective force multiplier.[3]

Without fundamentally changing the current manpower scale of China's armed forces, the latest round of PLA restructuring has been centred on two major questions: how to create an over-all force structure that can effectively coordinate all different services at the strategic level and in united strategic campaigns; and how to regroup units of different services that can completely fulfil the potential of PLA firepower at the tactical level. For the former, the PLA high command has given special attention to united warfare as the future form of combat and thus tried to incorporate all the four services into an organic whole. Under this guidance, the PLA is rectifying the current imbalance in its force structure, which highlights the predominance of the ground force. In planning its over-all force development, the PLA is studying how to enhance new specialised services such as space units and electronic warfare units, based on the model of the armed forces of major powers. At the tactical level combination (*hecheng*) is the key word for the restructuring. This combination emphasises scientific pooling of components of various services in a basic combat unit so as to increase the degree of coordination in campaign operations.[4] This principle is implemented at various levels in the ground force from group army to regiment.

Strengthening specialised services

Even before the Gulf War a consensus existed in the PLA high command that modern warfare would elevate the position of specialised services in the military. In a CMC conference in 1989, Yang Shangkun, then deputy chairman of the CMC, ordered that research on the PLA's force structure be stepped up and that the development of the navy and air force should be given priority.[5] Essentially China's quest for a suitable force ratio among the four services has been an integral part of its quest to become a high-tech military power, although for the time being the restructuring has merely entered a preparatory stage.

Two elements have been crucial in guiding the PLA's restructuring efforts: new military thinking and the gradual introduction of advanced hardware. As mentioned earlier, the PLA has increasingly embraced the idea that a high-tech war is by nature an offensive war. Since the specialised services are regarded as the main vehicles for offensive operations, they have gained a special status. Moreover, the PLA's projected defence in depth will eventually give the specialised services a leading role—only these can move into international air and maritime space. According to Lieutenant-General Xu Fangting, the PLA's future war actions will take the form of united campaigns in which the air force, navy and Strategic Missile Force play a decisive role.[6]

The PLAAF, for instance, is now regarded as crucial for a PLA version of the Air–Land War doctrine: its service is required for clearing up all road-blocks for the prosecution of a united operation. The PLA high command has identified air superiority as a crucial precondition for winning any future battles. Although top priority in air force development does not automatically mean enlargement in its size, the current number of personnel in the PLAAF will likely persist despite the fact that eliminating all outdated aircraft will reduce its current size by a large margin. For the future's sake the CMC is reluctant to let go many trained aviators. Even the obsolete aircraft, such as the J–6s, are seen as still useful in short-distance and low-altitude dog-fights. Given the fact that it is impossible for the PLAAF to obtain sufficient numbers of aircraft of the fourth generation, concentrated employment of J–6s could, for instance, lend temporary but valuable support in a cross-Taiwan-Strait air war, which would likely be fought at a relatively short distance and low altitude. Therefore the current manpower level of the PLAAF will stay steady in the next decade.

The story of the PLA Navy is similar. The profound change in its doctrine from in-shore defence to bluewater defence has placed greater emphasis on the strengthening of naval striking capabilities. This transition has also been given a powerful push by the changing national mentality: China is both a continental and a Pacific power.[7] Up to now a large-scale Chinese naval build-up has been inhibited by China's general low level of economic and technological development. However, the PLA's restructuring has taken a long-term approach to naval build-up. High on the country's military R&D agenda are projects for constructing a number of large and medium-sized warships capable of long-distance navigation.[8] More detailed analysis on this point will be found in the navy chapter.

While the air force and navy are to be enhanced, it has also been proposed that the anti-electronic warfare and anti-air attack units should be upgraded to the level of independent arms of service. In due time, space military systems as well will acquire an important place in the PLA's force structure. It is also suggested that the airborne units, which are seen as the best fast response troops, should be greatly enlarged and independently run by the CMC headquarters.[9]

The following is an example that vividly demonstrates how the PLA high command formulates its restructuring plans. The CMC's enlarged conference in 1987 discussed a comprehensive reorganisation plan for the PLA. In the plan, six departments of specialised arms of the GSD, namely Departments of the Artillery, Armoured Corps, Telecommunication Corps, Engineering Corps, Electronic Warfare and Ground Force Aviation would merge into one department, the newly established Department of Specialised Arms (*Bingzhongbu*) under the headquarters of the General Staff Department. The CMC approved the merger of five departments except for the Electronic Warfare Department, better known as the Fourth Department of the GSD. Instead the CMC directed that the Fourth Department should rather be enhanced with more technical personnel and financial input. Indeed, now that PLA strategists have reached a consensus that future warfare will be transformed from three-dimensional warfare (the land, air and sea) to five-dimensional warfare (adding outer space and electromagnetic space), China's military space unit and the electronic warfare force have the best chance to be converted into independent services in the 21st century. The retention of the Fourth Department reflects the PLA's recognition that force structure must be established according to the evolution of military science and technology, which has certainly dictated that in high-tech warfare victory depends more and more on those newly emerging services. Without new thinking in force structure, no matter how hard the PLA tries to increase its firepower, the PLA's traditional establishments (*bianzhi*) would greatly weaken the effect of the military high-tech it already possesses.[10] In comparison to the fast growth of the specialised services, the infantry will play a gradually decreasing role in future wars.[11]

Reduction of force scales

Different defence strategies catering to different threat perceptions have an important bearing on projected force levels. After 1974, when Mao Zedong entrusted Deng Xiaoping with the everyday affairs of the CMC, Deng initiated two major rounds of force reduction, each time as a result of a changed focus in the national defence strategy. In 1975 the CMC concluded that a massive Soviet invasion was more of a myth than reality. With Mao's support and Deng's guidance, the CMC implemented a three-year plan of force reduction, cutting the overall force level of the PLA from 6.1 million to 4.5 million, making it the largest reduction in the history of the PLA since the PRC was established in 1949. The army was reduced by 32 per cent, the Strategic Missile Force by 27.2 per cent, and the air force by 13.4 per cent. The staff of the headquarters from the CMC to the eleven Military Area Commands (MACs) were trimmed by 32.2 per cent. Only the navy increased its number of sailors. Within the ground force, field army infantrymen were cut back by 28.6 per cent; border troops by 18.3 per cent; local garrisons by 34.5 per cent; and artillery units by 10 per cent. The deepest reduction took place in the engineering corps and the railway corps, the former being cut by 62 per cent and the latter by 65 per cent.[12] This line of thinking also informed the PLA's reduction a decade later when the emphasis shifted to fighting a flexible limited regional war, which was thought to involve no large-scale military campaigns, but instead required a quick and effective response to actions along China's land borders.[13] As a result one million soldiers were demobilised in the mid-1980s.

Towards the end of the 1980s, new plans were drawn up to further trim the PLA, but these were delayed by the Tiananmen incident of 1989. According to General Zheng Wenhan, the PLA was charged with both internal and external tasks. Internally it needed to maintain a fairly high level of strength in order to deal with difficult political situations. Externally, the PLA had to confront increased western pressure, as embodied in the US-led political and military sanctions against China. Even though immediate threats from the north subsided with the end of the Cold War, in the longer run, the PLA believed that it had to maintain a large foundation (size) for fighting a possible all-out war, which warranted a properly large structure. In other words, since China is a major power with multiple potential threats, it has to be capable of engaging in a two-front war.[14]

Only when the post-Deng leaders felt a degree of confidence after stabilising the 1989 turbulence did they go ahead with the post-Deng round of force reduction in 1992. Generally speaking the reductions have been unfolding simultaneously on three different fronts, although the pace of implementation has varied greatly in each. The first task was to trim the PLA central command. Following Deng's instruction that a scale-down of the PLA must start from its headquarters, a major reform was taken within the General Staff Department in September 1992, which dismantled the commands of the five first-grade departments, as mentioned earlier.[15] This streamlining was formally announced by the PLA only a year later with the establishment of the department made known to the public.[16]

Similar cuts also took place in other headquarters of the ground force, such as in the General Political Department and the General Logistical Department (GLD). For instance, two first-grade departments in the GLD, namely the Department of Military Transportation and the Department of Military Equipment were merged with other departments with a deep cut of their personnel. This round of reform reduced the size of the PLA central command by 30 per cent.

According to one senior PLA researcher, the rationale for the merger was that the PLA central command had over 300 specialised agencies at the divisional level or above. If each of them issued only one instruction a year to the combat units at lower levels, it would still make the running of these units difficult because it meant that these units received about one instruction a day, instructions they have to implement, and be prepared for inspection. This is not to mention the fact that many of the instructions are overlapping and confusing.[17]

A new round of streamlining in the headquarters took place in early 1998 when the PLA introduced the most important restructuring in its high command. Since the mid-1940s the top leading structure of the PLA has been composed of three departments: the General Staff Department, the General Political Department and the General Logistical Department. In April 1998 a new General Equipment Department (GED) was created, parallelling the other three in bureaucratic ranking (see Figure 2.1).

The GED has taken over the functions of weapons R&D, testing, acquisition, allocation and related matters formerly assumed by the various top agencies in the PLA headquarters. For instance, it has incorporated the Department of Equipment in the GSD, administrative and operational missions of the Commission of Science, Technology and Industry for National Defence (COSTIND) under the State Council, including R&D projects and procurement agencies in the GLD and other services. The State Council's new COSTIND has become an all-civilian agency with much narrower responsibilities in China's weapons development. The two most important bureaus in the commission are the State Aerospace Administration, headed by Luan Enjie; and the State Nuclear Administration, headed by Zhang Huazhu. Its chief task is now to oversee the conversion of military production into civilian production in the country's industrial–defence complex.

Figure 2.1 The structure of the PLA high command

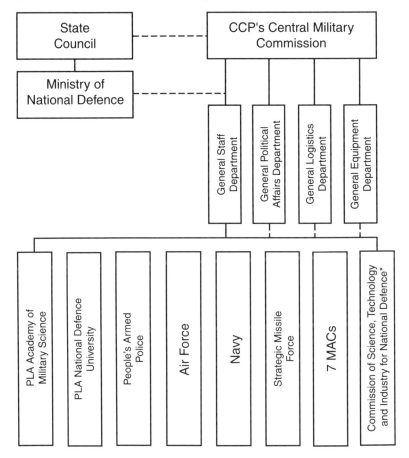

Note: * The Commission of Science, Technology and Industry for National Defence is not the new commission of similar name under the State Council. However, the one in the chart may have been merged with the General Equipment Department.

Coordination of military-related hardware production in the civilian sector is its secondary mission.

The significance of the creation of this GED can be seen from the following two angles. First, it constitutes an effective measure towards realising the high-tech defence strategy. Without a sufficient amount of sophisticated high-tech weaponry, the strategy will remain an empty shell. The new department reflects the determination of the CMC to concentrate all resources it can to advance weapons R&D and to quicken the process of equipping combat units with the best hardware. Second, the department is also a concrete step towards translating the theory of RMA into practical application. For instance, the GED will facilitate weapons R&D and acquisition in accordance with the requirements of united warfare. One precondition for this is to rectify the current state of affairs in weapons development by different services, which can be summarised as uncoordinated, with an effect of weakening the united campaign capabilities of the PLA. The GED will have power to oversee weapons programs of all services in order to make them serve the purpose of united warfare.

The second wave of reductions involved the transformation of a large number of non-combat personnel into civilian officers (*wenzhi renyuan*). For instance, medical officers in military hospitals not attached to combat units were deprived of their military rank. This principle was also applied to scientific research institutions. Many active duty officers assigned to work in enterprises run by their army units were required to give up their military rank as well. Moreover, the CMC reiterated the principle that PLA combat units should surrender their profit-seeking enterprises to the Production Management Bureau established at the CMC Headquarters, after which these enterprises would be demilitarised. This again affected a large number of officers and men. One important task in this round of force reduction was the amalgamation of tertiary military institutions. The merger of specialised central commands paved the way for the regrouping of military tertiary institutions, because each of the specialised arms of the services ran several institutions and teaching content was often duplicated. For instance, under the Armoured Corps Department of the GSD, there were different command institutes for training officers at division/regiment levels, at battalion/company levels, and for teaching technical staff. Now the upper level institutes formerly run by the individual specialised arm commands have merged into one directly under the control of the new Department of Specialsed Arms. Some lower level institutes were dismantled and their teaching programs relocated to some general army tertiary institutions. As a result, 21 defence-related educational colleges were decommissioned with the effect of cutting back large numbers of servicemen.

The third major effort of force reduction concerned the demobilisation of up to 500 000 officers and men by the year 2000. A major follow-up move of the PLA's one million men cut in the mid-1980s, this round of reduction will streamline the army by 19 per cent, the navy by 11.6 per cent and the air force by 11 per cent according to China's second *Defence White Paper*, published in July 1998. The whole endeavour is pursued simultaneously on three fronts. The first is the priority task, which is to further trim the PLA's central bureaucracies. In 1998 alone over 50 000 officers from the leading PLA agencies will be demobilised. More will have to go in the following years.[18] The second is aimed at reducing the numbers of the army to a substantial degree. This involves cutting two to three group armies and transferring a dozen or so regular army divisions into the People's Armed Police (PAP) or defence reserves. The purpose is two-fold: saving money and enhancing social stability at a difficult time of transition in China. At the same time, however, the basic structure of these divisions is preserved for a possible quick reorganisation in the event of a crisis. As maintenance for the PAP is much cheaper, this transfer allows the CMC to allocate more funding for the remaining army units, especially for those designated as 'fist divisions'.[19] Indeed, this unprecedented effort has marked a new stage for correcting the manning ratios of the four major services in the PLA.

The third function of the reduction of half a million men is to further adjust men–power structure in combat units according to weapons upgrading programs. Elimination of obsolete weaponry entails cuts in personnel. For instance, the replacement of old infantry guns and AA artillery with conventional tactical missiles has reduced the size of artillery brigades in group armies. When anti-tank missiles replaced anti-tank guns in the artillery units of group armies the number of gunners was cut by two-thirds.[20] In the meantime a large number of positions for political officers were removed. Among these were deputy posts for political directors and instructors at battalion level and below. At the same time restructuring also occurred in the navy and air force. The central theme was to raise the ratio of the units operating high-tech weaponry in the overall service structure and to gradually eliminate the equipment regarded as useless in a high-tech war.

Creating combined army units

Restructuring in the PLA ground force has been centred around the transformation of infantry armies into group armies that are capable of launching combined campaigns. A major component of the PLA's high-tech defence strategy is the new role envisaged for group armies in future wars characterised as highly mobile but limited in scope. In such warfare, theatre campaigns are seen as the most likely form of PLA actions, and group armies are the basic combat units at the strategic/tactical campaign levels.

Although the reform was launched as early as the beginning of 1980s, and all group armies have been in existence, except for a few elite units most of the group armies are only in organisational form without a qualitative change from their infantry nature. The reason for this is that the PLA cannot provide the sophisticated hardware to establish many specialised units required to make them a true group army, largely due to lack of financial resources and technology. For instance, many group armies have no established aviation wing in their structure. Neither have they the full-fledged electronic warfare composition designed for their force structure. Probably it will be well into the next century before the PLA ground force can become truly group armies.

Traditionally, the PLA ground force had a 'three–three' structure: an army contained three infantry divisions, which contained three regiments, which contained three battalions, which contained three companies. Under the assumption that a major war was forthcoming, the structure of all the armies in the ground force was about the same: centred on large-scale infantry divisions and equipped with similar hardware, regardless of their different missions and locations.[21] This simple structure could not easily accommodate the specialised arms of services which were under separate commands and were fairly detached from the commands of infantry armies and divisions. Given the fact that the PLA ground force is enormously inadequate at conducting united campaigns, the primary mission of army restructuring is to incorporate the specialised services in the army into the structure of group armies, which will then be restructured into different types of group armies: mechanised with heavy equipment, motorised for high mobility, and lightly-equipped for complicated landscapes. Each type will cater to different tactical missions. The third task is to introduce into group armies new specialised services such as tactical missile troops and electronic warfare units. Eventually, specialised arms personnel will make up the majority of officers and men in all group armies, and they will operate as an organic whole to engage in all types of united campaigns. The following are the principles under which the restructuring proceeds.

1   The restructuring should help make the army capable of offensive attack in depth.
2   The restructuring must be guided by the theory of combined operations, namely the Chinese version of the 'Air–Land War' theory of multi-dimensional warfare.

3   The restructuring must place due emphasis on electronic warfare at the tactical level.
4   The restructuring should prepare the combat units for both a high-tech conventional war and a tactical nuclear war.[22]

In summary the restructuring not only aims to reduce the group armies in size and to integrate them with other services, but also to render them more diverse and thus capable of carrying out a variety of missions.[23]

Eventually all group armies are required to be capable of independent frontal strike, deep penetration, and fast encirclement from all directions. These tough requirements force group armies to be capable of moving fast, obtaining reliable intelligence information, operating effective long-distance telecommunications networks, coordinating long-range artillery and missile support, and conducting air lift and assault. To be more concrete, the restructuring will create mixed group armies that follow the Russian model. Each PLA group army may have one or two tank divisions/brigades, two or three motorised infantry divisions/brigades and two artillery divisions/brigades (one for attack and one for air defence). Whether a division or brigade is established depends on what type of group army it is. A heavily-equipped mechanised group army normally contains divisions, while a motorised group army normally has infantry divisions but tank and artillery brigades.

One particular feature of the army's restructuring is the introduction of a combat aviation wing in group armies, which is worth some detailed analysis. For the PLA the establishment of ground force attack aviation units was an important step in bringing its ground force up to the general level of military modernisation in the world. Partly it was influenced by the learning experience from the Vietnam and Middle East wars in the 1970s, where attack and transport helicopters were extensively used to enhance the army's offensive depth, especially as tank-killers. The Department of Army Aviation in the GSD was formally established in 1985, and was charged with coordinating the creation and training of the army aviation units in the PLA. In January 1988 the first regiment of attack helicopters was established in the 38th Group Army, which was hailed as the PLA's first practical success in shifting its operating principles from horizontal combination to vertical combination.[24]

Subsequently serving as the model for all other group armies to follow, this regiment was composed of a few attack helicopter squadrons, a transportation squadron, a squadron of specialised helicopters (that is, those for reconnaissance and communications), and a number of fixed-wing aircraft such as the transportation aircraft. Before long the 39th Group Army was also enhanced with an aviation regiment. All five group armies that are earmarked as the national strategic reserve force are to be equipped with an aviation regiment as soon as they are in the financial position to do so. Then the regional fast response troops will receive the same treatment. Eventually, all other group armies, as well, will have aviation units in their structure. Now the major difficulty for a quick implementation of this plan seems to be financial, as aircraft are expensive. Moreover the PLA has only a limited range of choices for helicopter types. Yet at least one group army in each Military Area Command will have the aviation regiment before the end of the century. Some advanced tactical corps (two or more group armies combined, similar to US group armies in size) will also be strengthened by a transportation helicopter regiment.[25]

In addition to the aviation wing all group armies are designated to receive tactical missile regiment/battalions, telecommunication corps, engineering corps, electronic warfare (EW) units and anti-chemical warfare units. For example, since the mid-1980s the PLA has significantly enhanced its mobile battleground electronic intelligence (ELINT) capabilities. Soon after group armies were established the CMC instructed that EW units in the ground force should be strengthened by creating new EW establishments directly under the command and control of the headquarters of group armies and divisions. These EW units are equipped with truck-mobile ELINT, high frequency (HF) direction finding (DF) and jamming facilities. At the group army and divisional levels two truck-mobile ELINT/EW systems are detected by western intelligence sources: Model 970 and the BM/DJG–8715 systems. The former is a radar jamming system which includes an I/J band receiver for measuring the bearing, frequency and other parameters (such as antenna rotation speeds) of hostile radars, and which can be used in conjunction with a pulse analyser to measure parameters such as pulse widths, pulse repetition frequencies, and radar illustration. The latter system features a wide frequency coverage, automatic classification and identification of a variety of radar threats, monopulse auto-angular tracking with high DF accuracy, and a multi-threat jamming capability.[26]

The introduction of new specialised arms of services into group armies has effectively improved the combat structure of the ground force. By the mid-1990s the number of soldiers in these specialised arms of the services has now exceeded that of infantry soldiers for the first time in the PLA's history. And officers with higher education qualifications reached over 50 per cent.[27] Access to a satellite communication network and various military computers has been made available to ground force units and thus improved their rapid response time to a crisis. For instance, electronic mail and facsimile machines have become widely used in the army. The overall structural change in a group army allows it to incorporate more tanks and heavy artillery into its battle array, thus significantly lifting its firepower. At the basic combat levels, infantry regiments have become mechanised. In the first decade of the new century armoured personnel carriers will be the main battlefield transportation. Combat vehicles and self-propelled howitzers and guns will gradually replace a large number of other types of artillery.

FORCE REDEPLOYMENT

Closely related to the PLA's force restructuring has been its endeavour of force redeployment. While both respond to the changing perception of security threats, the latter effort has been more target-specific and is revealed in war game plans (*zhandou yuan*). These plans map out detailed prescriptions for PLA actions in future wars of different types and intensities. In the 1950s the plans were aimed mainly at frustrating a possible large-scale invasion by the remaining Nationalist armed forces in Taiwan with US military support. A number of huge defence projects were constructed in east and south-east China. Army units throughout the country were trained to deal with specific war scenarios. They manoeuvred repeatedly in the designated front areas, drilled for certain types of warfare customarily employed by the Taiwan and US armed forces, and conducted counter-offensive operations in predetermined directions. In the 1960s and 1970s war game plans were overwhelmingly geared toward the scenario of a massive surprise attack by the USSR. This required enormous preparations for protracted trench warfare in a number of defence lines along the Sino–Soviet and Sino–Mongolian borders. *Sanbei*, or the 'three norths' (north China, north-east China and north-west China) became the focus of those war game plans. Many large defensive projects were launched around Beijing, Shenyang, Langzhou and other political and economic centres.[28] The bulk of the Cold War period saw two major troop redeployments designated to meet the needs of the two strategic north–south shifts mentioned above. The first redeployment occurred in 1958 when the CMC relocated two armies to the Fuzhou Military Area Command and again in 1962, when another two-plus armies were moved into the area. In late 1969 and early 1970 the CMC transferred five armies from south China northward toward the Sino–Soviet border, which was the largest troop redeployment since the founding of the PRC in 1949.

Towards the end of the Cold War the PLA readjusted its war game plans several times according to the changes in the strategic environment.[29] For instance, the easing of tensions along the Sino–Vietnam and Sino–Russian borders has been matched by an increase in the intensity of potential crises across the Taiwan Straits. For a while the worsening Sino–US relationship forced the PLA to prepare itself better for confrontation with the American military. A new round of force redeployment is under way to meet the challenge of the changing security landscape in East Asia.[30] Generally speaking, the redeployment can be summarised as *beishou nangong*, or taking a strategically defensive posture in the north but preparing a potentially offensive posture in the south and east.[31] The new efforts have entailed the following missions: reinstituting war zones, strengthening fast response units, and reconstructing designated battlefields.

Reinstituting war zones

The definition of the concept
War zone (*zhanqu*), a term very frequently used by PLA officers in recent years, describes a strategic region embracing several provinces and is similar to the English notion of theatre of war. The provinces concerned tend to have close historical, economic and political ties. Traditionally China is divided into six strategic zones: north China, north-east China, north-west China, south-west China, east China, south China. Each of them contains the basic geopolitical and geo-economic ingredients for forming China's theatres of war. The reduction from eleven MACs to seven in 1985 (see Table 2.2) highlighed again the texture of these six strategic regions and reflected China's perception of security threats.[32] For instance, when Deng Xiaoping ordered the amalgamation, there were two MACs in south-west China: Kunming MAC and Chengdu MAC. One had to go, but the question of which one generated heated debate in 1983–84. Both Kunming, the capital of Yunnan Province, and Chengdu, the capital of Sichuan Province, are major regional cities and met the criteria for housing the PLA's regional command. Initially, the dominant opinion favored Kunming as the site, largely because the on-going Sino–Vietnam border

Table 2.2 The PLA's seven Military Area Commands

MAC	Areas included	Commander	Political commissar
Beijing MAC	Beijing, Tianjing, Hebei, Shanxi, Inner Mongolia	Li Laizhu	Du Tiehuan
Shenyang MAC	Jilin, Heilongjiang, Liaoning	Liang Guanglie	Jiang Futang
Jinan MAC	Henan, Shangdong	Qian Guoliang	Xu Caihou
Nanjing MAC	Zhejiang, Jiangsu, Jiangxi, Fujian, Shanghai, Anhui	Chen Binde	Fang Zuqi
Guangzhou MAC	Guangdong, Guangxi, Hong Kong (for CMC), Hainan, Hubei, Hunan	Tao Bojun	Shi Yuxiao
Chengdu MAC	Sichuan, Chongqing, Yunnan, Guizhou, Tibet	Liao Xilong	Zhang Zhijian
Lanzhou MAC	Shaanxi, Gansu, Qinghai, Xinjiang, Ningxia	Guo Boxiong	Wen Zongren

conflicts required the headquarters to be closer to the battlefields. At the last minute Deng vetoed the motion and decided on Chengdu. He believed that the Sino–Vietnam border rift was not highly strategically significant and that Chengdu was traditionally the centre of south-west China and more important in political and economic terms.[33]

A similar type of calculation can be applied to Jinan Military Area Command, which geographically belongs to the east China region and therefore stands outside the six strategic zones. Of the two provinces under Jinan MAC, Shangdong belongs to the east China strategic region and Henan to the central/south China strategic region. This fact has stimulated discussions since the late 1980s about whether to keep Jinan as an independent MAC. The basic reason for retaining the Jinan MAC is that it is supposedly strategically irreplaceable. Geographically, the Shangdong peninsula protects the oceanic approach to Beijing and the huge North China Plain. Militarily, Shangdong is close to the Korean peninsula, where tensions remain acute, and to Japan, which embodies many strategic uncertainties that require vigilance. Henan Province is the transportation hub linking north and south/east China.[34] The retention of the Jinan MAC is important for frustrating any landing attempts by possible invaders in that area. So each of the two provinces is home to high-profile PLA group armies which can be dispatched quickly to other strategic areas during crises.[35]

The link between a MAC and a war zone lies in the PLA's psychological and practical preparation for future wars. The MAC is more of a concept of military geography and administration, while war zone is more of a concept of military operations. The shift of emphasis from the former to the latter indicates an increase in readiness for action, although the armed forces have not actually been placed on alert status. Indeed, the concept is an important part of China's high-tech defence strategy: war zone campaigns (zhanqiu zhanyi) constitute the chief form of limited high-tech wars. In the future a limited war is most likely to be centred on one of China's war zones, and may be conducted in relative geographic separation from the other war zones. However, any such campaign will be of strategic significance because even a tactical battle is politically crucial for national security. As one senior PLA researcher has pointed out, war zone campaigns are targeted mainly at the major world military powers. Therefore the study of war zone campaigns should be directed toward fighting wars at all levels: high intensity as well as low intensity, with emphasis placed on the former.[36]

The promotion of war zones for MACs signals China's deepening perception of an impending conflict. The term war zone has appeared repeatedly throughout the PLA's history, but it tends to be emphasised only when Chinese commanders sense an external security threat. The term has now become a buzzword in PLA writings, and was especially popular during China's military exercise close to the Taiwan Strait in 1996. The choice of this more menacing term is not merely a play on words. It involves institutionalising three 'capabilities': sustainable economic support (building an economic foundation that can be called upon to support large-scale military actions at a short notice), mobilisation for war (a whole set of mechanisms that can maintain regular reserves and quickly enlist new conscripts in large numbers), and combat operability (the enhancement of battlefield reconstruction, about which more will be said later).[37]

War zone command

The reinstituting of the war zone concept in PLA vocabulary has heralded a far-reaching reform of the leadership structure in MACs. In preparation for future high-tech wars a war zone high command is to be created using one of several forms of command and control. For a tactical campaign of strategic significance, a CMC representative system may be established at the top command level in the war zone, a practice similar to that of the USSR during World War Two. The representative is directly responsible to the supreme command in Beijing, commands and coordinates all PLA units in the war zone, and can issue direct orders to the civilian government in the region. For a lesser operation, a joint 'geographic war direction' headquarters (*fangxiang zhihuibu*) is to be established, usually with the commander of the MAC as the commander-in-chief. He is to be assisted by the regional heads of all services. A team of advisers from the CMC may also be sent to the site for liaison with the supreme command.[38]

The purpose of creating such a leadership structure is to bring all regional military units and civilian supporting resources under more integrated command and control. Coordinating fairly independent large-scale united campaigns by all four services is a key aspect of the war zone concept. As a profound reform of the Chinese military system, this entails a long-term plan to establish joint command headquarters, redeploy the four services under a united system, and train the regional units for united warfare.[39] More concretely, the reform serves:

1   to bridge the gap in C³I currently existing between the four services in the MAC;
2   to remove the existing logistical barriers between the different services so as to facilitate a unified supply system (*sanjun lianqin*);
3   to lay down groundwork for joint exercises of all services, for the purpose of launching united campaigns in the future, as mentioned earlier; and
4   to place the regional units under tighter central control.

The last point is also politically important because the direct involvement of the central authorities in war zone command and control may help to inhibit the potential emergence of military regionalism, which may gather strength during the difficult social transformations now going on throughout China. Overall, the efforts to reform the MAC command and control mechanism are practical measures to raise the PLA's professionalism and combat efficiency.

The series of united live-ammunition exercises in the Nanjing War Zone in March 1996 served as an experiment to test some of the basic designs of the war zone command model. These games involved PLA units of four services from outside of the Nanjing MAC, and required a medium level of civilian mobilisation in a number of coastal localities. Some of the activities were even conducted outside the Nanjing MAC. For instance, missiles were fired in the Jilin Base by the Strategic Missile Force. Thus it was apparent that the Nanjing MAC, which is largely a regional ground force body, could not effectively carry out the organisation of these exercises by itself. Establishing joint headquarters became a necessity. When the headquarters were created, they were headed by General Zhang Wannian, former chief of the general staff and currently executive deputy chair of the CMC, who served as the representative of the supreme command in Beijing. The headquarters comprised top brass of all four services, commander-in-chief of the Nanjing MAC and the leading Party and government figures from the provinces affected by the exercises. This all-embracing but highly concentrated leadership ensured a smooth implementation of the war games and constituted a new model of command and control for future war zone operations by all seven military regions. Indeed, all top commanders from the other six MACs were present during the exercises.

Upgrading readiness

Parallel to reinstituting war zones are the PLA's efforts to upgrade combat readiness for possible armed conflicts. The main purpose of this upgrading is to develop various types of fast response units for dealing with unexpected events. At the same time, however, the regular combat units are not to be compromised too much even when the budgetary allocations favour the crack units. Two means of improving readiness are the creation of duty-specific military units and battlefield reconstruction.

Creating duty-specific units
Since the second half of the 1980s the PLA has moved to establish duty-specific units in all four services. In the ground force, for instance, four different combat formations came into existence as a result. At the top level are the national strategic reserve troops, composed of five heavily equipped mechanised group armies, which are traditionally the PLA's elite units. In the PLA terminology, they are also called the strategic force on duty (*zhanlie zhiban budui*), which highlights their primary function as reinforcement for any war zone at short notice. Among them the 38th and 39th Group Armies have basically completed the transformation in

terms of equipment, while the other three are still in the process of upgrading.[40] These group armies are all deployed in strategic locations (see Figure 2.2 for the deployment of the group armies).

For instance, the 38th Group Army seals off the last Yan mountain pass leading to Beijing from the north. The 27th Group Army assumes the same mission but defends another strategic juncture towards Beijing. The 39th Group Army is responsible for the defence of north-east China's heavy industrial base and for reinforcement of all other group armies in the Shenyang MAC.

More importantly, as the central strategic forces, the group armies involved are entrusted with key trans-regional combat missions. In any large-scale armed conflict involving China they will be the main thrust/reinforcement force directly controlled by the country's supreme command. Therefore, they have been granted all possible battlefield training. The 47th Group Army, although permanently deployed in Shanxi, has been on the move all over the vast western China. In the mid-1980s, for example, it, together with the 27th Group Army, was dispatched to the Sino–Vietnam borders to gain real combat experience. The 54th Group Army is deployed in Jinan MAC but it shoulders the mission of support for military actions in east China in the east and north China in the north.

As the PLA's focus of war preparation is shifting from the 'three norths' to east and south China, the group armies in the strategic force are constantly engaged in long-range manoeuvres in the southern military regions. Moreover, in order to raise their 'strategic readiness', they have designated new specific opponents in their exercises at the campaign level. One vivid example of such training efforts can be seen from a major 'clash' in north-east China between the 39th Group Army and one US army deployed in the Far East. Under the direct leadership of General Zhang Zhen, the PLA National Defence University formulated very detailed air–land battle protocols to guide different stages of action, including anti-air attack, anti-electronic warfare, anti-tank invasions and a counter-attack by a group army. The design and conduct of such sophisticated campaign exercises show the PLA has made significant progress in organising joint operations.[41]

The next layer of duty-specific units consists of special combat units established at the central and MAC levels. These units are special in the sense that they are commissioned with special tasks (for example, psychological warfare and intelligence/counter-intelligence warfare) and trained to fight in special circumstances (for example, infiltration of the enemy's rear lines). The CMC has

Figure 2.2 Chinese military regions, districts and headquarters of group armies

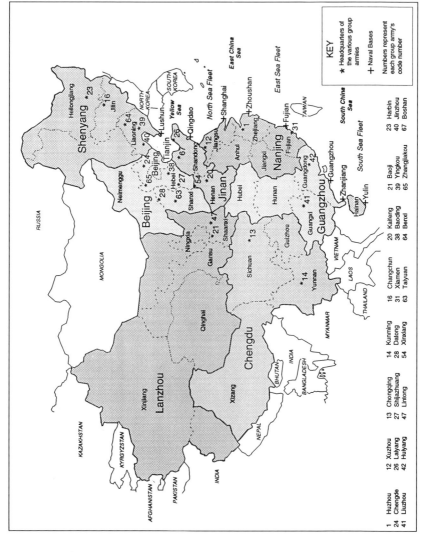

designated a few crack units as centrally-sponsored special units, although during peaceful times they are under normal command and control of their MACs. These units are formed at the divisional/brigade level, and possess the most advanced weapons systems available to the PLA, such as access to satellite information. As fast response units, they are not necessarily heavily equipped but highly mobile, and are capable of all types of operations, including airborne, in any kind of weather and at night. They are specifically trained to cope with 'hot-spot' contingencies. The air force's 5th Airborne Corps is the largest unit that may be put under the direct command of the CMC in the event of an emergency. The Marine No. 1 Brigade is another such unit that has received special treatment, including generous budget allocations. At the level of military regions special units are integrated into the group armies, but their command and control can be quickly transferred to the MAC in crisis situations. These special units, normally at brigade/regiment levels, are entrusted with the mission of dealing with the war zone's predetermined adversaries. They are equipped according to the war zone's geographic features and weather conditions, and pre-positioned around flash points within the war zone. For instance, special brigades for both tropical jungle warfare and freezing high plateau warfare have been formed in the Chengdu MAC in order to respond quickly to difficult situations along the Sino–Vietnam and Sino–Indian borders. In the Nanjing MAC, because of the long distance between the MAC headquarters and the front line in Fujian Province, a sub-area fast response command has been created with considerable decision-making power. At the same time a highly mobile crack unit which comprises the four services is made available for the Nanjing MAC to cope with emergency situations.[42]

The third level of duty-specific units consists of the majority of China's field army units: the group armies that normally assume specific missions of territorial defence in the MAC. This is the major reason why most of the group armies are stationed fairly permanently in the same MAC. They are repeatedly trained in the area so the soldiers become familiarised with the defence facilities, climate, landscape, and social environment in the region. It is important not to forget that each MAC may be as large as a medium-sized country, which means that these group armies are often exposed to rather diverse circumstances. It is not customary for the group armies to be transferred, however, because once in a new MAC it takes time for it to reach the same level of readiness it had in its original MAC. Plans for restructuring and redeployment often take this factor into consideration. One example is retention of the 31st Group Army, which has been deployed in Fujian Province since the 1950s. The 31st Group Army is not regarded as an elite unit and it could have been disbanded in the 1985 force reduction had it not been long established and well-positioned to deal with the Taiwan situation. Replacement of this Army with another one may at the time have caused a temporary drop in readiness in this crucial defence sector.[43] Nevertheless, the PLA's recent redeployment efforts have eroded the permanence of the group army. Following the example of the five national strategic reserve group armies, as mentioned earlier, since 1993, when the PLA's new training program took effect, all group armies have been conducting a certain number of trans-regional exercises in order to familiarise themselves with likely war scenarios in other war zones.[44] This step has been regarded as very important by the PLA high command, which calculates a high probability of having to reinforce local troops with other group armies in the priority areas, particularly those in south and east China. Readjusting the future missions of group armies without redeploying them is a cost-effective way for the PLA to respond to the fluid security situations confronting China in the post–Cold War era in Asia. For instance, one new training item for the elite group armies since the mid-1990s has been maritime warfare, involving long-distance navigation and landing exercises.

The fourth layer of duty-specific units is the lightly-equipped local garrison force. This is normally viewed within the PLA as a second-rate force. Traditionally, garrison forces comprise two major parts: independent divisions (*dulishi*) under the command of the PLA provincial military district (normally two to three in each district); and garrison divisions (*shoubeishi*) that assume the tasks of border security, protection of major military bases such as naval ports, and defence of some strategically important areas. In the 1985 round of troop reductions the PLA transformed the bulk of those independent divisions into the PAP, and they have now become the main force responsible for the PLA's internal duties: suppression of political protest and maintenance of local public security. For a brief period they were under dual civilian (the State Council and provincial government) and military (the CMC) leadership, with the former playing a more direct role. After the Tiananmen incident, the military command became more responsible for the PAP's everyday administration. Moreover, the CMC has assumed authority over the appointment of officers, although the State Council and provincial government are still consulted in the selection process. To cope with socio-political uncertainties in the 1990s, some of the PLA's elite units were transferred into the PAP, for example, one entire division from the 24th Group Army. In the current round of troop reductions more group army divisions may be transferred into the PAP. There is no doubt that the reinforcement of the PAP is also meant to address the worsening law and order problems in Chinese society at large. Indeed many of the transformed divisions will reinforce the PAP's fast response units, established in all major industrial provinces and municipalities after the turbulent events of 1989.[45]

Deployment readjustments are currently under way among the garrison divisions. The scaling down of the force level along the Sino–CIS borders may have led to the dismantling or transfer of a number of these divisions. At the same time, however, the non-defence-related responsibilities of the garrison divisions have increased. This is especially true in certain areas in the Xinjiang Uygur Autonomous Region, where extreme Muslim minority groups have stepped up separatist activities. In southern and eastern China, where the major standing army units are focusing on contingency tasks and training, the garrison divisions have become more involved in political and economic security missions in the areas covered by their units. They are engaged, for example, in off-shore anti-smuggling activities. In localities close to the 'flash points' (that is, the Taiwan Strait), some garrison divisions have even received specific training in order to serve as the second-line reinforcements for the group armies in the war zones. Increasingly they have become an indispensable link in the four-in-one national defence system: the field army (group armies), the local garrison units, the People's Armed Police and defence reserves (see Figure 2.3).

Battleground construction

Crucial to the effort to upgrade the PLA's readiness for action is battleground reconstruction, which requires the modernisation of military facilities in the war zones for specific contingencies. Defence-related projects have always constituted an important part of the PLA's preparation for war. During the decade of the Cultural Revolution (1966–76), in order to cope with the increased Soviet threat the CCP leadership undertook to build a Chinese-style Maginot defence trench line in the 'three norths'. About 330 defence networks at the divisional level were constructed. Among these networks one particular project was to build permanent 'artificial mountains' in the plain areas. These fortifications were designed to serve as barriers to Soviet tank invasions and as shields for the key

Figure 2.3 PLA ground force structure

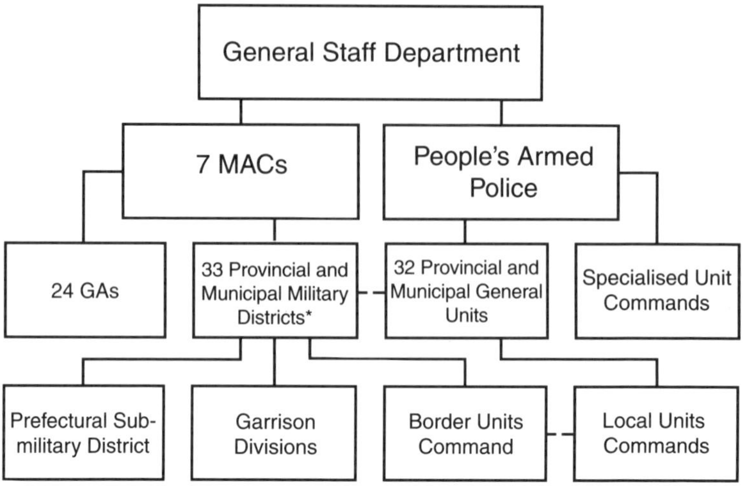

```
                    ┌─────────────────────────────────┐
                    │    General Staff Department      │
                    └─────────────────────────────────┘
              ┌──────────────┴──────────────┐
        ┌───────────┐               ┌──────────────┐
        │  7 MACs   │               │People's Armed│
        │           │               │    Police    │
        └───────────┘               └──────────────┘
   ┌─────────┬──────────────┬──────────────┬──────────────┐
┌───────┐ ┌──────────────┐ ┌──────────────┐ ┌──────────────┐
│24 GAs │ │33 Provincial │ │32 Provincial │ │Specialised   │
│       │ │and Municipal │─│and Municipal │ │Unit Commands │
│       │ │Military      │ │General Units │ │              │
│       │ │Districts*    │ │              │ │              │
└───────┘ └──────────────┘ └──────────────┘ └──────────────┘
   ┌──────────────┬──────────────┬──────────────┐
┌──────────────┐┌──────────┐┌──────────────┐┌──────────────┐
│Prefectural   ││Garrison  ││Border Units  ││Local Units   │
│Sub-military  ││Divisions ││Command       ││Commands      │
│District      ││          ││              ││              │
└──────────────┘└──────────┘└──────────────┘└──────────────┘
```

Note: *Including the PLA's Hong Kong Garrison command.

transportation hubs in the nearby capital cities. Each of them could contain a strengthened battalion and was capable of withstanding a direct hit by a 1000-pound bomb. In 1971 alone 310 000 PLA soldiers were engaged in building defence fortifications nation-wide, digging 120 000 metres of tunnels and constructing fortresses comprising 686 000 cubic metres in total.[46] With the recent shift in defence focus to east and south-east China, these huge projects are now considered an enormous waste of money and resources.

While steel and concrete were being wasted in the north as seen from today, for two decades defence facilities in east China suffered from a dire shortage of funding and material input. When the post-Deng high-tech military strategy addressed the new security threats in the east, the PLA found that enormous efforts were needed to meet the new requirements.

Since the 1990s battleground construction has been pursued simultaneously on two fronts. The first involves enhancement of combat facilities for all services. The second is to launch a large number of logistical supply projects to service the combat facilities in those strategic war directions. The central theme of battleground construction in recent years has been to fit the preparation for war into the gradual transfer of the country's centre of defence gravity from north to south.

As far as the first front construction is concerned, each service has worked out its list of most needed facilities in the pre-planned war direction. For example, the SMF considers that the inadequate number of missile launch bases in the vast areas of east China has posed a serious obstacle for combat readiness. Lack of launching sites and lack of crucial launching information for the sites currently under construction have caused difficulties for the quick and sufficient deployment of its strategic nuclear and conventional tactical missiles in response to a crisis situation. One important task in the PLA's force redeployment and battleground reconstruction in the 1990s has therefore been to increase the number of launching sites for the SMF in south and east China.

At the turn of the 1980s and 1990s a number of the best launching brigades were transferred from north China to east and south China. Some of them changed their equipment from short- and intermediate-range tactical missiles to the latest generation of China's intercontinental strategic missiles. In 1993 the No. 1 Strategic Missile Brigade, one of the transferred units, tested the first of China's latest version intercontinental missiles in south China, despite a long tradition of such launches in the north.[47] Moreover, battleground reconstruction for the SMF also entails other missions such as collecting geographical and meteorological information in those areas where the SMF's mobile units may launch missiles against the designated targets.

Other services have also stepped up their battleground construction efforts. For the PLA Air Force (PLAAF), for instance, the imbalanced distribution of airports in north and east China has to be rectified. As east China will become the most important war direction in the next decades, the PLAAF is confronted with an acute shortage of airports in the front line. And its second ring of airports is too far away from the possible air-battle areas. Therefore, the PLAAF has decided to improve the front-line airport arrangement (more on this in Chapter 5). Another immediate task for the PLAAF's battleground construction relates to the construction of basic facilities for its air defence systems, especially the early warning sites. At the moment the density of the air defence network is considered far too sparse. Therefore, increasing the number of air defence points has become an urgent task for the air force's battleground readiness.

The PLA Navy (PLAN) too, has formulated its own priorities in constructing the predetermined battle areas. While construction for improving existing destroyer and submarine bases is continuing, preparation is under way to build a strategic naval base that can support the navy's deep ocean combat missions. The construction efforts are especially related to the navy's bluewater explorations. The navy believes that due to the long-term emphasis on inshore defence in the past, China has done very little in collecting crucial information in the sea areas where the PLAN may initiate actions, especially the sea areas beyond the first island chain in the West Pacific. For instance, the PLAN's knowledge is quite limited on the meteorology and geography in those key sea-lanes of communications within 1000 nautical miles from China's maritime borders. These are important items in the PLAN's efforts to familiarise itself with the sea areas where combat actions may be taken.

Logistical supply has always been the PLA's weak point. According to PLA researchers, the military commanders like to spend money on complete weapons but neglect the supporting measures such as repair facilities and storage of spare parts. For instance, the air force has imported a number of advanced aircraft in recent years but it has not created sufficient service and repair equipment to ensure the aircraft work well.[48] To address this persistent problem, the PLA has worked out a number of measures to improve logistical conditions:

1   Creating a united supply system of all services (*sanjun lianqin*). Currently each service has its independent logistical supply system. This results in a lot of duplication and waste. For instance, the navy's petrol station in Shanghai may have enough supply but the ground force units in the Nanjing Military Area Command are short of oil. The Nanjing MAC cannot take the navy's petrol but has to ask the GLD to transport it from other MACs. This may cause delays and ruin a good combat opportunity. The GLD is experimenting with a united supply system that caters for all the services in each MAC. This system is computerised and can show very quickly where the supply is available.

2   Creating a mobile supply system (*dongtai gongying*). The high-tech war will be fought in a very fluid situation and involves PLA fast response units transferred from a long distance. This will stretch to the limit the PLA's current static supply mechanisms. Therefore, there is a great need in the strategic war directions to set up a number of emergency supply stations. These stations will be equipped to provide and receive airlift supply. According to the predetermined war plans they may store special weapons systems and parts for specific fast

response units of all services. In this way fast response units coming from afar in a rush will not face the difficulties of logistical support. Moreover, more transportation networks are being constructed to connect these supply stations.

3   Creating a civilian/military dual supply system (*tongyong wuzi baozhang*). Since the early 1990s the Shenyang, Nanjing and Jinan war zones have implemented a civilian/military supply system of dual-use materials. This system requires the civilian government to incorporate PLA units in the locality in the civilian supply network of petrol, medical equipment, transportation vehicles, and foodstuff. In times of crisis the military enjoys priority in receiving these strategic materials and services, thus shortening the transportation time and raising the reliability of supply if the enemy tries to conceal the transportation routes.[49]

In sum, battleground construction in the PLA's vocabulary is equivalent to war preparation. The PLA has an enormous task to do in this regard in order to reach a minimum level of readiness. Both the fast technological development and the changing Asia–Pacific security landscape have imposed higher requirements on construction. Although the PLA high command has placed an emphasis on this effort, there will be a long way to go for the PLA to build a proper infrastructure for combat engagement. Moreover, there is evidence that PLA commanders at various levels have not fully appreciated the importance of such an infrastructure, which will slow down the pace of its battleground construction.

3

In search of high-tech military power

Although the PLA's new defence strategy provides doctrinal guidance for the modernisation of China's armed forces in the new millennium, a great deal of concrete effort is required to translate an ambition into reality. These efforts are long-term and need to be carefully executed. The Chinese military leadership is fully aware that the country's armed forces are backward in almost all aspects as compared with the advanced military powers. Therefore the PLA's modernisation has to be highly selective and entails a lot of balancing and sequencing. This chapter picks up a few major programs through which the PLA searches for high-tech military power, including its efforts to formulate practical R&D and weapons programs; to gain the largest possible increase in state funding for hardware upgrading; and to tackle some of its weakest links in force modernisation. It also uses the PLA's space program as an example to analyse the PLA's long-term developmental trend.

FINANCING HIGH-TECH MILITARY POWER

While ambitious, China's overall approach to military modernisation is quite prudent, reflecting the pragmatic personality of PLA leaders such as Admiral Liu Huaqing and General Zhang Zhen and their full grasp of China's economic and technological backwardness. The PLA is very anxious to obtain high-tech equipment, as it anticipates a future war with high-tech powers. Yet it is ordered to be patient by both its top brass and its civilian party leaders. As a consequence, it has had to adopt a middle course weapons program since the late 1980s which will very likely continue well into the new century.

The middle course weapons program

Generally speaking, the middle course weapons program reflects the PLA's two crucial evaluations bearing on the issue of modernisation requirements. The first is more fundamental, namely, what kind of financial commitment is necessary for China to prepare for a future war. The second is more specific: what kind of weapons programs are appropriate.

According to an influential financial expert in the PLA, as a major world player, China has to prepare financially for whatever kind of war exists on earth. In peacetime, however, there has to be a priority list.[1] As mentioned earlier, the PLA has reached a conclusion that any limited war involving itself may likely drag in the US and thus quickly escalate. The line between an all-out war and a limited regional war is fine for a major world power. The middle course weapons program attempts to bridge the gap between preparing for an all-out war and a limited regional war. The guiding principle is to plan for a small-to-medium level limited regional war under the consideration of it being escalated into a major war. In other words, through persistent preparation for a limited war with major power involvement, the PLA will gradually possess capabilities suitable for all types of wars.[2] More concretely, the middle course policy specifies giving funding priority to key combat capabilities: enlargement of fast response units and the improvement of the hardware of the navy and the air force.[3] This policy choice is conducive to preparation for both immediate regional conflict and long-term global threat.

In terms of weapons development, this middle course policy can be characterised as a cross between a strategy of steady generational upgrading and a strategy of generational leap. It has been spelled out by the CMC as 'concentrated research on key items, selected production for "fist" units, coordinated retrofitting of some current equipment and co-existence of both old and new weapons'.[4] Under this guiding principle the PLA's long-term weapons development program sets out three concrete goals. The first goal targets R&D for the weapons systems designated for the defence of Chinese peripheral areas, in which low-level conflicts are envisaged. The second targets R&D for advanced conventional weapons systems, for conflicts with high-tech powers within or beyond the country's territories. The third targets R&D for strategic high-tech weapons systems, such as space weapons systems. Under each category, detailed technological criteria have been worked out for prototypes based on similar weapons systems of the major powers.[5]

Generational development may provide the PLA with a level of technology adequate to cope with the demands of immediate and low intensity conflict. But as the Soviet experience indicated, such a 'tortoise' strategy also suggested a growing gap with the west. Nevertheless, this was the basis of Chinese military R&D policy until the late 1980s.[6] The generational leap strategy, on the other hand, aims at the frontier of world technology, but involves a great deal of risk for a military whose R&D program rests on a weak industrial base. The long acquisition intervals and less than adequate level of scientific expertise may mean a waste of time and funds. The middle course policy has been designed to overcome weaknesses of both strategies: the PLA is to receive a limited amount of advanced hardware for its elite units as quickly as possible, but the major R&D efforts are directed towards long-term goals. In the meantime slow general upgrading is continuing for the armed forces as a whole. By positing that normal generational modernisation is not to be disrupted by a costly and uncertain high-tech weapons R&D program, the PLA hopes to minimise the effect of the transitional vacuum it is now encountering.[7] In monetary terms this means that fluctuations in budget do not serve as a portent of major changes in defence strategy. When the budget goes down, this may indicate that more efforts are geared towards long-term technological achievement at the expense of spending on conventional weapons. A budget increase may point to a diversified spawning of new weapons being rushed into service.[8]

In order to narrow the gap with the western powers, the PLA has selected a number of military technologies deemed appropriate for the 21st century.[9] Generally speaking, progress in the following areas is now seen as crucial to the raising of the PLA's technological level: electronic warfare, precision-guided missile technology, high speed computers, powerful laser facilities and the application of artificial intelligence in military facilities. Concentrated funding and personnel resources have been injected into the R&D of such equipment.[10] State-of-the-art weapons systems so developed will be used to equip the PLA's elite units. At the same time generational upgrading of weaponry will continue. The funding balance has, however, leaned toward the latter, indicating an expectation of a long period of peace.[11]

In a way the middle course policy represents a progressive evolution from the PLA's traditional mentality of 'fighting whatever kind of war in accordance with whatever weaponry is available to the PLA'.[12] For four decades until the 1990s this mentality underscored an outdated weapons program closely associated with China's defensive people's war strategy. As a result the country's weapons program produced large quantities of defensive weaponry at the expense of developing any effective power projection capabilities. For instance, when the USSR was identified as the chief military threat, the hierarchy of importance in military R&D was, according to former defence minister General Zhang Aiping, the second-strike capability of the Strategic Missile Force (SMF), followed by the conventional weapons of the army, and then the hardware of the air force and navy. More concretely, priority was given to anti-tank weapons (missiles and guns), anti-air attack weapons, and long-range artillery. The army was preferred to the air force and the air force to the navy in this priority ranking.[13] The serious problem with this priority sequence is that while the nuclear missiles are largely unusable, the low-tech conventional weapons, mainly for the ground force, have left the PLA out of touch with the information era and hampered the PLA's modernisation. During most of the 1980s, the Chinese military budget continued to decline even though China attained a robust economic growth during the same period of time. By 1989, the PLA's share of the state budget had dropped 7 per cent from the proportion in 1980.[14] As a result, the PLA was repeatedly instructed by Deng Xiaoping to exercise patience (rennai). The shrinking budget could hardly meet the cost of personnel maintenance and basic training, let alone significant upgrading of weaponry, causing enormous resentment among rank and file military personnel.[15] Moreover, the weak scientific and technological foundation had slowed down a number of key military high-tech projects, such as the development of a new generation of aircraft.

The middle course guiding principle in the 1990s may represent a visible change in direction, but it also reflects the PLA's financial difficulties. According to Lieutenant-General Mi Zhengyu, the PLA's 1997 budget was US$9.7 billion, or US$7 per capita across the whole population, and just below US$3000 per soldier. This was in sharp contrast to the US military budget in the same year which was US$996 per capita, and US$178 300 per soldier; and to Japan, which budgeted US$360 per capita, and US$188 000 per soldier.[16] The PLA is poorly funded even compared with other Asian countries. In 1993 South Korea spent US$17 000 on every soldier, and India US$5424, in contrast to China's US$2238.[17] If we multiply China's 1997 military budget (US$9.7 billion) by three, a common western practice to establish a rough basis for comparison, the amount of money per head was still well below US$10 000, which can achieve very little in the high-tech era.

Although the Chinese economy is likely to expand at a high rate well into the early decades of the 21st century, a quickly expanding economy will absorb more resources to sustain its developmental vigour.[18] One fundamental constraint on increasing the military budget is the steadily declining proportion of central revenue, about 736.6 billion *yuan* in 1996, in the national income structure, which dropped from 34 per cent in 1979 to only a little over 10 per cent in 1996. According to China's deputy science minister Zhang Yutai, education, family planning (excluding medicine) and science have already taken the bulk of this shrinking budget (7 per cent).[19] And since the military is solely the responsibility of the central government in financial terms, no matter how fast its budget is increasing, its growth will always be affected by the fact that the central government is slowly being impoverished.[20]

This means that the PLA will be forced for a long time to strike a difficult balance between an increasingly ambitious weapons program (the US experience has shown that an ever-rising demand for advanced weapons may take on a life of its own) and a limited budget allocation. According to PLA strategists, the lack of military spending has greatly inhibited the introduction of high-tech equipment in the PLA, which is at the root of its unbalanced force structure in general (weak navy and air force), and its unbalanced army structure in particular (for example, a very weak aviation component).[21] Politically, this presents a challenge to the post-Deng civilian leadership: whether it can resist the PLA's pressure for more funding. To generate the resources to maintain a fair balance between the four services and fund its priority weapons programs, the PLA has adopted a number of measures, some of which are discussed below.

Enlarging defence allocations

The state budget is the largest source of the PLA's financial resources. Officially the PLA has consumed around 10 per cent of the revenue and 1.7 per cent of GNP for most of the PRC's history. The military has asked that its budget be raised to about 15 per cent of the state budget and 2.5–3 per cent of GNP, which it contends would not put too heavy a burden on the national economy. This benchmark of 15 per cent would be reached in gradual steps and remain the guide for state funding thereafter.[22] In fact the PLA has been successful in obtaining an enlarged share of the state budget since 1989, with a double-digit growth in military allocations—1995 alone registered an increase of 22 per cent. It is highly likely that this trend will continue into the first decade of the new century. One reason is that civilian authorities, under pressure from the military, have repeatedly promised to make the growth in military spending parallel the growth in the national economy, which, according to Zhu Rongji, China's new Premier, may sustain another decade or two of near double-digit growth. In 1997 this linkage was written into the Law of National Defence, the first of its kind in the PRC's history. The potential for growth is also reflected in the fact that military allocations are still well below the 15 per cent target requested by the PLA.[23]

The NDU estimated three possible levels of future funding: high, medium and low. On the high side every serviceman would receive US$6080 in funding by the year 2000.[24] When this is multiplied by three, it may at least put the PLA on a level with South Korea in the early 1990s. When this projection was made in 1988, the analysts did not anticipate that the military budget's downward trend would soon be reversed. It was expected that the PLA's budget would remain at the same low level until the end of the seventh five-year plan period, which was 1990. As it turned out, even their generous estimate became conservative. If China's high economic growth rate can be sustained continuously, the military budget is likely to treble about every six to seven years, as was the case between 1989 and 1995 (see Figure 3.1).

The enlarged state allocation for the PLA forms only part of the increase in China's defence expenditure, which also includes indirect military spending. Established in 1962, the indirect state defence budget covers defence-related R&D programs; transportation and communication construction that is dedicated to military use or dual use; and the costs of national mobilisation by civilian sectors. More concretely, this indirect budget finances basic theoretical scientific research for military purposes; high-tech research projects that have a significant military content; militia and national reserves; and national and local civil defence construction. This secondary part of the defence budget is controlled predominantly by the civilian financial department and government agencies, but the PLA is consulted over spending on major items.[25] Like the direct military budget, the indirect part has seen a significant increase since the 1990s.

This trend is clearly reflected by the gradual growth in China's military R&D expenditure in the indirect defence budget, which is divided into two parts. The first is the state's budgetary allocation

Figure 3.1 China's official defence budgets, 1978–95

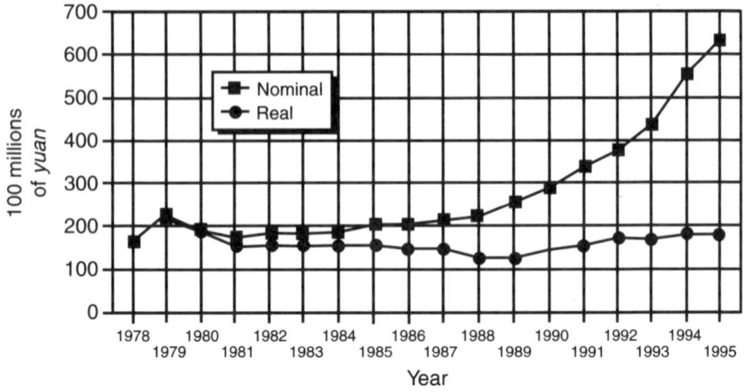

Source: Wang Shaoguang 1996, p. 894.

for the Commission of Science, Technology and Industry for National Defence (COSTIND), a small professional body of a few hundred people. The chief task of this agency is to coordinate military R&D projects and weapons production. It evaluates, approves and oversees the plans for defence-related R&D programs presented by central ministries and provincial governments. Much of these functions have now been taken over by the newly established General Equipment Department, as mentioned in the last chapter. The exact amount of Chinese defence-related R&D is not clear. According to one of the key experts in the PLA's General Logistical Department, the country's entire spending between 1950 and 1990 on defence-related scientific and technological research was about the same as the US's one-year spending on military R&D in the late 1980s.[26] However, considering the difference in labour and material costs, PLA strategists argue that every *yuan* China uses in the research of weapons systems yields the same level of result as every US dollar spent on similar research in the US.[27]

Other analysts have come up with different findings. In the 1980s, for instance, the State Council allocated about two to two and a half billion *yuan* to COSTIND, equivalent to about 10 per cent of the direct budgetary allocations to the PLA. Some experts on China's defence spending have uncovered evidence that after the Gulf War the level of allocation for COSTIND has been visibly raised. In 1993, for instance, military R&D amounted to an estimated 6.4 billion *yuan* on the high side, or one-third of China's national R&D expenditure (19.6 billion *yuan*).[28]

The second part of the indirect defence budget concerns state allocation for civilian R&D programs that can be converted to military usage. Most noticeable in this area is China's hard push for a series of national high-tech projects. The 863 Project and the *Xinghuo* Project are the most important ones.[29] The former brings together the best scientists in the country to concentrate on eight frontier research areas in the hope that these may give China a scientific edge in the 21st century. Among these research areas are space technology, micro-electronics, microbiology, new materials and computer science. Each of these has significant military application value and the government has commissioned enormous human and financial resources to advance this project. In the meantime, the *Xinghuo* Project aims to translate the laboratory results quickly into commercial production.

Restructuring the military budget

While the ratio of military outlay in the overall state budget increases, the share of military funding devoted to equipment and R&D expenditure will also increase. In broad terms this budget consists of three principal components: personnel costs, operation and maintenance (O&M), and equipment. For each of the three there are further subdivisions. Under O&M, for instance, there are allocations for education and training and for the storage of strategic military materials. Under the heading of equipment, there are items such as weapons procurement and R&D for immediate application.[30] From these basic ingredients, PLA strategists have worked out a formula to determine the minimum level of military expenditure (ME):

> The minimum ME = (equipment R&D + procurement + education and training + maintenance + research for military science + personnel + daily management and public affairs + stockpiling strategic materials + miscellaneous) × (1 + *n* per cent)

Here *n* per cent refers to the growth rate of military expenditure. It is important to note that this minimum ME does not include the costs of unexpected combat operations (for example, the series of military exercises close to the Taiwan Strait in 1996), repair costs for major natural disasters and salary adjustments according to the unified national wage increases.[31]

The ratio between all these items is very important for the PLA in its efforts to improve real capabilities. More money available for equipment upgrading and R&D may mean enhanced combat strength. This is especially true in the present situation, where the PLA can only meet 70 per cent of its minimum budgetary requirement despite the increase in its overall budget.[32] Market-oriented economic reform has made the funding shortage even more serious, as the PLA has had to pay rising costs for equipment.[33] Indeed, up to the 1990s the state's equipment allocation had remained as low as 10 per cent of the PLA's budget. The PLA has therefore endeavoured to squeeze as much funding for equipment modernisation as possible, and at the same time, to lower personnel expenditure, which used to be three times higher than equipment spending. Towards the end of 1991, the equipment budget was finally raised to about 20 per cent of the PLA budget and personnel spending dropped to about 30 per cent.[34] In November 1995 China published its first *Defence White Paper*, which presented a rough picture of the ratio between the three major components in the state's direct military budget for 1995. According to the *Defence White Paper*, each of the three took about one-third of all state allocations, with personnel costs making up 34 per cent, operation and maintenance another 34 per cent, and equipment 32 per cent. Most notably, the equipment outlay has reached a new height.[35]

There are a number of ways to readjust the ratio between different budgetary items in order to raise the proportion for weapons upgrading and the introduction of new equipment. The most effective, as mentioned in previous sections, is reduction of the standing armed forces, which lowers personnel costs. Another important method is to reduce the proportion allocated to maintenance. This strategy has great potential for the PLA. At present, maintenance consumes over half of the PLA's operation and maintenance spending. For instance, of the total lifetime cost of a fighter jet, including R&D and production, the maintenance cost constitutes 50 to 70 per cent; for tanks, 70 to 80 per cent; and for major naval vessels, 60 to 70 per cent.[36] It is well known that the PLA's inventory contains huge quantities of obsolete aircraft, tanks and warships. Even eliminating only a small proportion of them will free up a large amount of funding for purchasing new equipment. The air force provides a fine example of this. If the air force, for example, de-activates the bulk of its obsolete J–6/MiG–19 fighter jets, which make up the majority of its inventory, it will not only reduce large contingents of personnel but also save in maintenance costs. This could make much more funding available to accelerate the development of new aircraft and to purchase more advanced foreign jets, without committing additional allocations to the modernisation of the air force. In the last five years, the PLAAF has moved to establish a huge plane storage depot in central China, which is now the largest in Asia and the second largest in the world. Among the over 1000 planes that are stored there, some are still considered as having practical value and are being saved for possible future use. The majority of them, however, will be gradually scrapped.[37]

Opening up new resources

As mentioned earlier, the direct state military budget, at whatever growth rate, can only meet 70 per cent of the cost that the PLA calculates is needed for its annual activities. Therefore the PLA has had to engage in various forms of 'earnings generation' by itself, a tradition that can be traced back to the very day of its founding in 1927. In essence, this self-generated funding is not meant so much to accelerate equipment upgrading as to reduce the proportion in the direct state military budget spent on the everyday upkeep of regular servicemen. Hence the budget allocation to operation and equipment can be enlarged. Funding generation has become a crucial ingredient for the running of the Chinese armed forces as it guarantees a decent standard of living for all personnel. For instance, each group army could generate 100–200 million *yuan* in extra income in the late 1980s, which may have doubled in the late 1990s. This alone may save the PLA about five billion *yuan* a year. Moreover, the farms established for every regiment and brigade have made most of the PLA units self-sufficient in supplies of vegetables and meat. This saved expenditure has been of great assistance for enlarging the 'slice of the cake' for other purposes, such as military training. By the end of the 1980s there were already over 10 000 'economic entities' run by PLA units at various levels which created extra income equivalent to 10 per cent of the national military budget.[38]

The PLA's self-generated income has become a major financial resource it can no longer do without. The profits from this income are reaped simultaneously on four fronts. First, it cuts personnel costs by engaging PLA units in food production, as mentioned above. This is basically a non-profit endeavour engaged in most heavily by garrison units. The national strategic troops, which spend less time on agriculture, are granted higher levels of budgetary allocations.

The second front involves profits that are generated by regular army units. These activities range from running hotels to selling clothes made by the units' logistics departments. Theoretically, these activities are rigidly constrained—according to the CMC regulations only units at the army level can establish such a business—yet under the huge social and budgetary pressures many businesses are created at regiment and brigade levels. Two common profit-seeking efforts are: converting military research and industrial capacities for the production of civilian commodities; and leasing military facilities such as naval ports or air force airfields to civilian users.[39]

The third front involves the commercial enterprises set up by the dependents of servicemen. The PLA provides business licences, some funding and other privileges (for example, lower state tax) to these enterprises, the earnings of which can help support some PLA officers. This indirectly lowers PLA personnel costs.

The bulk of the PLA's self-generated funding, however, comes from the fourth front of activities: the conversion of the national defence industrial complex to civilian production. This complex can be further divided into two categories: enterprises directly run by the PLA, and those managed by civilian defence industries. The former category consists of over 200 research institutes, about 1000 defence-related enterprises and nearly one million personnel (including more than 120 000 technicians). Eighty per cent of these are now engaged in civilian research and production in order to generate more financial resources for military R&D.[40] For instance, Factory 3507 under the GLD is the largest clothing factory in Asia. It is involved substantially in exporting textile products to international markets. The GLD submits profit from its firms to the CMC's General Production Bureau. A large proportion of the profit is used to lessen the CMC's budgetary shortages. According to the director of the Bureau for National Defence in the State Planning Commission, PLA factories can produce 15 000 kinds of civilian goods. More than 30 000 military research findings have been applied to civilian use and over half of China's exported technological items have been products of the country's defence research and industry complex. The Changhong Enterprise Group, which once produced military electronic tubes, now sells colour TV sets and other civilian electronic products. In 1996 it realised 10.7 billion *yuan* in sales and 2.2 billion *yuan* in profit.[41] By 1995 the national defence industrial complex had created enormous returns to the PLA and its industries nation-wide, an estimated 60 billion *yuan* in total, which is about equal to the state military budget for a year.[42] Consequently a major financial burden on the state treasury and the PLA has been greatly reduced, in that the less money spent on bailing out loss-making defence enterprises, the more money can be allocated to upgrading the country's defence

Table 3.1 Volume of Chinese arms exports, 1986–95 (SIPRI trend indicator values, expressed in constant 1990 US$ millions)

1986	1987	1988	1989	1990	1991	1992	1993	1994	1995
1760	3214	2212	1414	1222	1103	1159	1284	744	868

Note: SIPRI arms transfer data are an index which indicate trends in deliveries of major conventional weapons. SIPRI arms trade statistics do not reflect purchase prices and are not comparable with economic statistics such as national accounts or foreign trade statistics. Sources and methods used in development of SIPRI arms trade figures are explained in the SIPRI *Yearbook* (Oxford University Press: Oxford, annual) and in *Sources and Methods for SIPRI Research on Military Expenditure, Arms Transfers and Arms Production*, SIPRI Fact Sheet, January 1995.

Source: SIPRI arms transfer database 1996.

capabilities. What is particularly worth mentioning about the fourth front activities is the export of conventional arms. The profits generated in the form of foreign currency have been important for the PLA, which is increasingly dependent on foreign procurement (see Table 3.1).

According to some analysts the PLA is demanding at least 50 per cent of the earnings from these export deals. For instance, China Xinxing Corporation, one of the largest arms exporting firms directly under the PLA, submits over 70 per cent of its annual profits to the GLD.[43] A large proportion of this remittance is redistributed to subsidise the PLA's weapons program.[44]

Foreign acquisition: addressing the transitional vacuum

A key prerequisite for a middle course weapons development program to work is procurement of advanced weapons from abroad. Deng Xiaoping regarded the importation of advanced technology to be strategically important: 'It serves as the starting point for China's own high-tech development'.[45] In practical terms, the purchase of advanced weapons has several functions. First, it provides hardware for reverse technology, thus reducing the lag time for the PLA's own R&D.[46] Second, citing the US experience of the upgrading of the B–52 as an example, PLA analysts often argue that it is desirable and workable to extend the service life of old equipment by improving its key parts. This has motivated the PLA Air Force to retrofit several types of its aircraft with western technologies of the 1970s. From this, we see the third function of buying foreign arms, which is to alleviate the negative effects of the PLA's transitional hardware vacuum. Indeed the PLA is at a dangerous transitional stage where many obsolete weapons systems need to be replaced but it may take years for new designs to be finalised and put into series production.

Beyond this, there are several concrete reasons why the PLA cannot do without foreign procurement. First of all, it helps the PLA tackle its weakest link in war preparation. The best example is the strengthening of air control and air defence with the purchase of the Su–27 and SAM S300 missiles. Concentrated use of the Su–27s may help obtain air control over a limited area, while the deployment of S300 surface-to-air missiles enhances China's air defence and serves as the starting point for building a missile defence system. To the PLA, air control and missile defence are two preconditions for winning a high-tech war. However, given the fairly long period it takes to make the Su–27s operational, the significance of the aircraft deal lies less in obtaining better attack capabilities in the short run than in the unprecedented opportunity for the PLA to practise with high-tech military equipment. This is the second reason behind China's enthusiastic entry into the international arms market.

The third rationale for buying foreign high-tech weaponry is that it may shorten the time it takes the PLA to get ready for limited actions under international pressure. An example of this is China's purchase of four Kilo class submarines (some analysts suspect that the actual number could be as high as 22).[47] China's own submarines are so obsolete that their deterrence value is dubious at best. For instance, as soon as China's conventional submarines enter the high seas, their movements can be detected by the Japanese Maritime Defence Force.[48] Whether this also applies to the Kilo class is a question yet to be answered. However, Russian submarines will certainly put the PLA in a better position to blockade the SLOCs in the West Pacific, especially around the Taiwan Strait. The fourth consideration for the PLA in buying foreign hardware is to fulfil the strategic need for the navy and air force to establish an elite component for limited, regional conflicts. These elite units will be trained to cope with specific crises. In this way, the PLA tries to reconcile the dilemma of not being able to afford the modernisation of the bulk of its forces with the uncertainties in the post–Cold War Asia–Pacific, which present several conflict scenarios requiring the immediate upgrading of PLA readiness. Foreign acquisitions therefore enable the PRC to continue to rely on a breathing period during which it may concentrate on building a powerful economic and technological foundation for its future overall military modernisation. The Japanese approach of incremental military build-up seems to fit the

Table 3.2 China's purchase of Russian arms, 1990–95

Weapon type	Year(s) of delivery	Number	Comments
Actual transfers			
Mi–17 helicopter	1990–91	24	For transport
Su–27 fighter	1992	26	An additional 26 on order
AA–8 missile	1991–92	96	For Su–27s
AA–10 missile	1991–92	144	For Su–27s
SA–10 SAM	1993	100	With 4 launching systems
Il–76 transport	1992–93	10	For troop transport
Il–28 bomber	1993	1	Exchanged for canned fruit
RD–33 engine	1993	100	For Super–7 fighters
Kilo Class submarine	1995	1	3 more on delivery with more transfers possible
Potential transfers			
Combat aircraft	..	..	Under negotiation for possible co-production
Avionics, engines, airframes	..	..	Under negotiation
T–72 MBT	..	..	Under negotiation
Submarine and ASW technology	..	..	Under negotiation

Source: Gill & Kim 1995, p. 68.

Chinese design: it will not hurt the economy, and in due time the military will become modernised through augmented input. As long as the PLA's dangerous transitional vacuum lingers on, the PLA will be under pressure to buy more foreign weapons, especially from Russia. This need has recently been highlighted by the tensions across the Taiwan Strait, and explains why in five years since the early 1990s China has bought Russian weapons worth US$6 billion (see Table 3.2).[49]

ADDRESSING THE WEAKEST LINK: THE C³I SYSTEM

The adoption of the post-Deng defence strategy has established much higher quality standard for China's C³I system, which the PLA regards as the sinews of any high-tech war but also as the weakest link in its preparation for future warfare. The PLA understands that in both theory and practice, planning for C³I upgrading must precede other weapons improvement programs, and the construction of the C³I projects must keep at least one step ahead of the planned growth in all other sectors. For instance, given China's geographic features, it is difficult to construct a sophisticated telecommunications network of extended landlines and a terrestrial radio-relay link system. To cater to the significant changes in China's defence strategy, the fixed and mobile communications structures must be capable of absorbing a sudden surge of military needs and dealing with all kinds of disruptions caused by high-tech warfare. The PLA also realises that it takes a lengthy period of time for it to provide auxiliary networks, factories to produce new equipment, and laboratories to invent new devices. As the whole process entails intensive preparation and reconstruction, the development of the advanced C³I systems has received special attention from the PLA high command.

During the Sino–Soviet border conflicts in 1969, China's frontline C³I centres were badly jammed, causing repeated disruptions in their communications with the forward units. This prompted Lieutenant-General Kong Congzhou, a close relative of Mao Zedong and a former deputy commander-in-chief of the PLA Artillery Forces, to report to Mao that in a major war with big powers, there was little chance for the PLA's C³I systems to survive the enemy's conventional and electronic bombardment. The consequences would be dire.[50] Mao and other Party and military leaders paid serious attention to the report and ordered the PLA to remedy the situation. In the next three decades, the PLA invested tremendously in establishing a sophisticated C³I network that could endure large-scale electronic warfare. The development can be divided into three stages.

The first stage was launched in the early 1970s and was basically completed at the beginning of the 1980s. Its main purpose was to construct a national strategic C³I system that could connect all PLA commands at the corps level, and it involved a number of large-scale projects. First, a country-wide underground defence electric cable telecommunications network was constructed, with a total length of 53 000 kilometres, linking Beijing and 29 provinces. The network was initially made of balance cables and small coaxial cables but was subsequently upgraded with larger coaxial cables. Second, 86 underground telecommunications command centres were created throughout the country. In order to connect these centres 14 000 kilometres of electric cables were laid through in the early 1970s, in addition to 5000 kilometres of underwater electric cables. At the same time 10 000 kilometres of double open electric wires were installed. The main aim of this project was to connect all key defence outposts in north China, north-east China, and north-west China.

The third project was dedicated to improving the reliability of the national defence communications system, by upgrading the existing underground cables into wave-carrier channels with up to 300 lines. During this period of time, the PLA started to construct maritime communications networks, which was the fourth major task in this area. Two priority projects were commissioned. The first one was to build an extra-long-wave telecommunication centre that could provide Chinese submarines with C³I transmissions. The second was launched following the capture of the Xisha (Paracel) Islands in 1974. It concerned the construction on Hainan Island of one of the PLA's largest signal intelligence (SIGINT) stations, which coordinated Chinese naval activities in the South China Sea. Moreover, in the 1970s 1500 kilometres of seabed electric cables and 8000 kilometres of open wire were laid, as well as 5700 kilometres of microwave trunk lines. By the end of the decade all islands with a PLA presence were linked to the national defence telecommunications system.[51]

In the 1980s the PLA's C³I modernisation program moved on to the second stage. After the first launch of a primitive electronic intelligence (ELINT) satellite in 1976, the PLA launched a few more in the 1980s, enabling it to enhance significantly its mobile battlefield ELINT capabilities. For the first time, ELINT units were deployed in the newly combined group armies. In the 1980s China also developed a satellite communications (SATCOM) SIGINT capability for monitoring international satellite communications together with an associated deception capability. Once a few SATCOM SIGINT stations had been established, the PLA was able to intercept signals transmitted via the US and Russian communications satellite systems.[52]

In this stage Chinese engineers have laid three strategic coaxial cables for long-distance telecommunications. The first one extends from Beijing to Hangzhou, connecting Nanjing and Shanghai; the second from Beijing to Guangzhou; and the third from Chengdu/Chongqing to Shanghai. The second cable represents a major improvement of China's communications network, providing 7200 wave-carrier telephone channels between Beijing and Wuhan and 3600 such channels between Wuhan, Changsha, and Guangzhou. Underground and underwater cables have gradually replaced open-wire lines in handling sensitive information.[53]

Most notably a number of fairly sophisticated SIGINT stations were created throughout the country, particularly in the 'three norths'. At the highest level of command a large scale C³I complex was completed in the Western Hills, a north-west suburb of Beijing.

This centre was satellite-linked and strengthened with effective indigenously-designed counter-electronic warfare (CEW) measures. Benefiting from the Cold War superpower confrontation, the PLA solicited US assistance in improving its C³I capabilities. Two large SIGINT stations were built along the Sino–Soviet borders with the supply of US EW systems and personnel assistance from the CIA's Office of SIGINT Operations (OSO), which trained the PLA operators of the stations.[54] In 1986 the construction of a satellite information processing centre was completed in Beijing. The centre was a Cold War gift to Deng Xiaoping when he visited the US in 1979. One of the purposes of the centre was to receive US satellite imagery information. According to Wang Dayan, the top Chinese scientist who was the chief designer of the centre, the cooperation with the US also helped fill a blank in the Chinese space and remote sensing technology, and proved of enormous scientific and military value. From the huge directional antenna installed in Miyun County, 40 kilometres from Beijing, the centre is able to receive and track satellite information within a 2,600 kilometre radius, and thus covers 80 per cent of Chinese land territory. And even today it remains China's only civilian satellite information processing centre.[55]

In the 1990s the PLA's third stage of C³I modernisation was launched and it is still continuing today. One of the most important tasks at this stage is to establish a large-scale and reliable national strategic early warning system in the PLA's C³I network that is capable of detecting, identifying and tracking air and space targets from long range.[56] According to PLA strategists the PLA's existing tactical early warning network is primarily based on radar installations belonging to the PLAAF and the navy, and it can no longer satisfy the national security demands in the high-tech era. For instance, these installations cannot be used as a strategic early warning system. Without such a system it is impossible for the PLA to provide effective defence against a long-range missile attack, a key feature of a high-tech war in the 21st century. Hence China's national defence system will be full of holes.[57]

The construction of an effective early warning system requires both organisational and technological innovations. For the former, it has been suggested that a national defence early warning headquarters be established under the CMC's National Air Defence Leadership Group. Its chief mission will be to coordinate other early warning subsystems such as border defence, aviation, maritime, low altitude, guidance intelligence, airborne and shipborne early warning networks. In the technological sphere, efforts are to be directed toward overcoming shortfalls in the following areas: satellite-borne radar, space laser sensors, large-scale phased-array radar, beyond vision surveillance radar and airborne early warning systems.[58]

Another chief objective for the C³I upgrading initiative at the third stage is to automate the existing defence communications system through more advanced computer technology. This endeavour can be divided into two categories: development of hardware and development of software. For the former, the PLA developed the Yinghe and Shuguang series of military computer systems. Yinghe is China's first indigenous super-computer system. In 1987 it achieved a speed of 100 million bytes per second. Ten years later its operating speed exceeded ten billion bytes per second.[59] The Yinghe series machines, however, are huge, which makes them very difficult to install in weapons delivery platforms: aircraft, warships, satellites and especially missiles. Hence the Shuguang system, a major endeavour to minimise the size of the computer and at the same time maximise its speed. When the first Shuguang system became operational in 1994 it achieved one billion bytes per second. Each Shuguang computer system is as small as a suitcase, and there is room for further improvement. This makes it suitable for a wide range of applications in China's weapons programs, space, ship-building and other defence-related industries. In 1997 a much improved version of the Shuguang series, the Shuguang–1000A system, was developed, which can calculate over four billion bytes per second. The next Shuguang series, expected in 1998, is designed to increase the speed to ten billion bytes per second.[60] A few sets have even been exported, the first time China has sold super-computers in the international market. According to Chinese sources the R&D for the Shuguang–2000 series has achieved major technological breakthroughs.

Software development is seen as the weakest area in the PLA's C³I modernisation. The problem is particularly serious when one considers the fact that the majority of the PLA's super-computers are imported, and that their software programs tend to be commercial designs purchased from the international market.[61] The PLA observed during the Gulf War that Iraq's C³I system was easily paralysed because Iraq's computer systems were bought from the west.[62] Another telling example is that the US Department of Defense testified in 1998 that US-made communications satellites, which China has bought, have helped the US intelligence agencies to collect information of the PLA's movements and deployments.[63]

Since the early 1990s the PLA has developed a software 'safety net' to protect its C³I system from hackers. For instance, the software program *The Military Practical Operation System* was a national priority and it took the PLA University of Science and Technology five years to complete. The software can be widely used in the C³I systems in the military R&D programs and in airborne and shipborne C³I systems. Another important software program was created by the PLA's missile and space agencies in 1990. Named the 'automatic measurement and control system for missile and spacecraft computers', the system was seen as matching the international technological standards of the 1980s.[64]

At the same time, new telecommunications materials have been introduced to replace the outdated ones. For instance, optical fibre communications systems have been extensively used to enlarge transmission capabilities. In the early 1990s the PLA began a *'baheng bazong'* program, namely to set up an optical fibre communications network composed of eight trunk lines covering the country from east to west and another eight from north to south. By the end of 1995 the country had laid an optical fibre cable network of 10 000 kilometres. The dual-use fibre cable project in Hainan Province is capable of providing 30 000 lines per pair. And it has been announced that by the year 2000 China will be able to develop 120 000 line fibre cables and produce one million kilometres of fibre cable a year.[65] In 1998 the last two of the eight-trunk network were launched between Chengdu, the capital of Sichuan Province to Guangzhou, the capital of Guangdong Province; and between Chengdu and Lanzhou, the capital of Gansu Province. The two trunk lines are 5700 kilometres in total length. Since the beginning of the year over 60 000 soldiers from Chengdu, Guangzhou and Lanzhou Military Areas Commands have been engaged in the project. After these two trunk lines are completed before the end of the decade, the country's national telecommunication network that has linked all Chinese major capital cities will be greatly upgraded.[66] The quality of telephone transmission and the transmission of colour television will also be improved significantly through long-wave optical fibre. During this decade China's defence C³I system is indeed moving towards communications based mainly on fibre cables, digitalised microwaves and satellites.[67]

The PLA now possesses the largest and most comprehensive computerised network in the country. Once this system had been switched to automated operation in the 1980s, it saved 30 per cent of the personnel in the CMC headquarters and improved work efficiency by several dozen times.[68] During a training contest on 4 April 1993, for instance, using newly equipped computerised transmission systems, one female soldier sent out 88 groups of data per minute, which was 2.6 times more than the amount of information dispatched manually.[69]

On the whole, however, the transition has been slow. This is largely due to the fact that the military commanders' attention is focused more on the development of hardware such as guns or missiles than the development of software. The vulnerability of the PLA's C³I system is multi-fold. The first fatal weakness is its structure, which can be characterised as being too thinly deployed along vertical lines. The command and information flow is transferred mainly through the administrative hierarchy at different levels—for instance, from the army down to the divisions and regiments. At each level, the C³I centre is fairly closed, responsible only to the superior above it. The PLA has now recognised that this simple vertical system can no longer cope with the needs of a high-tech war. According to Lieutenant-General Liu Tongzu, former commander of the Telecommunications Department of the GSD: it overburdens the information processing channel and causes delay in information analysis; it lacks capability to withstand electronic warfare, since the thin structure can easily be thrown into chaos; compartmentalisation prevents efficient horizontal information flow; and it is unable to cope with a sudden change in the C³I structure and de-centralised circumstances.[70]

The PLA's C³I system particularly suffers from obsolete command and communication links and lacks anti-electronic warfare measures. As regards the former, the PLA's tactical C³I system is still largely handled manually, which seriously impairs its ability to process the explosion of information in the high-tech era. The system is still heavily reliant on wire communication equipment and is easily jammed. The PLA has not yet been equipped with high-quality mobile systems and airborne C³I systems. The central command has effective coverage of the PLA ground forces only to the divisional level, and this coverage is heavily dependent on radio and security telephones, although the quality of coverage has been improved by relay and carrier technology such as facsimile machines and electronic mail.[71] The C³I system of the basic units is mainly carried by semi-conductor radios of extra-short-wave modulation, such as the T–708 and T–709 extra-short-wave amplitude (15 V and 150 V). These provide only a limited communication capability, usually within a range of 2.5–10 kilometres, and can be easily disrupted through electronic warfare. One typical example is the poor command of and communication with the PLA's martial law troops when they tried to enter Tiananmen Square in May/June 1989.

At the strategic level, the PLA has only recently set up satellite communications channels for the group armies, and computerised links for the divisions. As mentioned earlier, however, the majority of its computers and software programs are imported from foreign countries. This may render the PLA's C³I systems quite vulnerable to virus attack and intelligence penetration.[72] For example, the computer system of the PLA's Command and Communications Centre at Nanyuan, a suburb of Beijing, was imported from northern Europe. Although PLA computer experts have re-established the codes for its operation, they cannot entirely guarantee its secure operation during a war, as the fundamentals of the system are known to the enemy. Moreover, the PLA's strategic C³I system is not yet integrated across different services and units under different regional commands.[73]

These represent urgent tasks for the PLA if it is to adapt its C³I system to the requirements of a high-tech future war. Structurally, the PLA has made it a top priority to create war-zone-based integrated C³I systems under the direct control of the CMC. The key reform concerns enhancement of horizontal links across the services and units. As each war zone has a specified potential war scenario, the C³I system should have specific mission priorities. Concretely, the modernisation plans specify that at the war zone and group army levels the C³I should be more horizontally arranged, and extended below divisional levels. The vertical structure should remain but be reduced in relay layers. For instance, the intelligence system within various services should be placed under a more unified command. According to Lieutenant-General Liu the restructuring should achieve three shifts in transmission method, communication network and deployment: a shift from voice to digital communication; a shift from separate axis (vertical) channels to regional functional channels; and a shift from the land-based C³I systems to multidimensional systems (land, air and space).[74]

At the tactical level, the PLA has made concentrated efforts to develop satellite-based communication networks, digital communication equipment and comprehensive field C³I systems. Among these measures one priority is to establish space-based communications centres. By the middle of the 1980s China had established over 2000 stations to receive satellite signals. Each of them was equipped with an antenna 6–7.5 metres in diameter.[75]

By 1998 China's eleven communication satellites had allocated only limited channels to the PLA. To rectify the situation, it has been proposed that a network of defence satellite communications be created. In this network, emphasis would be given to the development of small mobile stations with an antenna smaller than 3 metres in diameter. In addition to expanding strategic communication channels and reception points, the mobile stations would be deployed particularly in the sensitive border areas and in the rapid response units to meet the needs of high-tech regional wars.[76]

China's launch of its third-generation telecommunications satellite in May 1997 and again in May 1998 has provided new hope for the network to be established in the coming decade. This series of satellites, nicknamed Dongfanghong–3, has 28 C-wave bands and contains 24 transponders, four times more than its predecessor Dongfanghong–2. This may mean that the CMC can request more for the PLA, as its need for more communication channels has been greatly increased. Parallel to the development of a satellite communication network, R&D has been stepped up to develop a military Global Positioning System (GPS) in order to improve the PLA's strategic and tactical communications capabilities.

At the technical level the PLA has worked hard to enhance its electronic countermeasures in order to raise the survivability of its C³I systems. The Fourth Department of the GSD has identified three tasks for improving the PLA's C³I system for the conduct of electronic warfare at the tactical united campaign level. First, in any given war zone, key networks should be duplicated. The whole system should be structured with distributive modules so the system can be reorganised with ease. It is essential that the manual system is always in place in order to continue communication when the automatic system is badly disrupted. The second task is to strengthen the fast response capabilities of the system in order to cope with fluid combat situations. To this end the PLA will deploy more mobile systems. Even with permanent communication stations in place, small-scale mobile equipment has to be made available as backups. Fast response communication units should be created and deployed in key strategic areas. The third task is to introduce more electronic warfare countermeasures into the national defence communication network. At the same time the whole C³I system should be dispersed and well hidden, and fake facilities should be built to distract the enemy.[77] In sum, the PLA's C³I system will be heavily upgraded in the next decade or so, but whether China can reduce its C³I system's vulnerability will be a critical factor in determining whether the PLA can fulfil its ambitious plan to become a high-tech military power.

THE PLA'S SPACE PROGRAM

After three decades of painstaking effort, China's space program has made impressive progress. As one of very few foreign visitors to the secret Chinese Academy of Aerospace Technology under COSTIND, a French space expert concluded that China should be able to launch its first space shuttle by the beginning of the 21st century.[78] This was confirmed by Professor Zhang Qingwei, deputy president of the Chinese Academy of Aerospace Technology, who announced in October 1996 that China had achieved major breakthroughs in developing spacecraft carriers. In the early 21st century China will be capable of accurately positioning 20-tonne spacecraft in low- to medium-altitude orbit.[79] In March 1998 China has publicly announced that it is now able to place a payload of 15 tonnes in earth orbit and up to 5 tonnes in solar orbit.[80] There is no doubt that the Chinese have made impressive progress in the area of space exploration.

An integral part of the PLA's long-term R&D of strategic weapons systems for the new century has been its space program, which is a chief beneficiary of the PLA's quest for high-tech military power. A reliable and substantial space capability is now viewed not only as a multiplier of military power, but also as an indispensable factor in organising united operations and a crucial deterrent to potential adversaries.[81] As early as the beginning of the 1980s some senior PLA strategists advocated the establishment of a comprehensive space program, which they viewed as a potential driving force for China's over-all high-tech development and its defence R&D in particular. As one researcher from the PLA National Defence University pointed out:

> China should make its space program the overriding one in relation to other high-tech development programs. In developing space technology we can push information technology, biological technology, technology of new materials and new sources of energy and other high-tech areas to new frontiers. Space weapons programs are especially crucial for our country's defence. For every *yuan* we invest in the space program now we may obtain 29 *yuan* in return a decade later. China has invested only 13 billion *yuan* in the last 30 years to achieve such impressive progress. We are much more affluent now and can put in a lot more resources. More importantly we already have the capabili-

ties to design and implement a comprehensive space program to launch manned satellites, space shuttles and space stations.[82]

According to Major-General Pin Fan, deputy president of the Commanding Academy of the Commission on Science, Technology and Industries of National Defence, China's space program has entered a new phase of application after decades of experimentation. As a logical development the PLA will soon change its single function in China's space program, supporting scientific experiments, to a dual function: supporting scientific experiments *and* military operations.[83]

The evolving space shuttle initiative

Space shuttle R&D occupies a high priority in China's 863 high-tech project. A number of programs for China's first space shuttle had been vigorously pursued throughout the 1980s. The basic design was finally approved in 1989, and the project was formally launched in 1992. In 1994 Beijing Aerospace Technological Centre was completed and formally launched by Admiral Liu Huaqing. This aerospace centre specialised in testing the over-all systems of a spacecraft and at training cosmonauts.[84] According to the chief engineer in the Chinese Academy of Aerospace Technology, Chinese researchers have theoretically resolved the difficulties in developing a two-stage-to-orbit space transportation system (TSTO, multiple landing technology), and two manned spacecraft can be expected to be launched around the year 2000. These two spaceships are designed to be capable of being connected together to form a temporary space station.[85]

To facilitate this ambitious project, China has signed a comprehensive cooperation agreement with Russia. A group of PLA doctors and astronauts took an intensive course at the astronaut training base near Moscow in 1997. The purpose was to learn how to select and train the first contingent of China's astronauts who would staff China's first space station in the early 21st century.[85] The Russians will offer Chinese astronauts training in the basics of space navigation. The Chinese may also be allowed to visit Russia's Mir Space Station. Negotiations are under way between China and Russia over the transfer of the technology of the Proton rocket, which is capable of placing a payload of 20 tonnes into earth orbit. Russia has agreed to sell China the Kristal plug-on modules, similar to those used by the Union orbital complex. At the same time China is discussing with the Russian Space Energy Company the purchase of the plug-on modules employed by the

Peace Space Station.[87] If this plan materialises, it will greatly assist China's building of its first manned spacecraft, to be launched in the first decade of the new century.

In the summer of 1987, Chinese scientists initiated a heated debate over whether to develop a US-style space shuttle or to continue in the Soviet tradition of the manned spaceship. The former view was supported by the 1st Institute of the China Academy of Aerospace Technology and the latter by the 5th Institute, which was under strong Soviet influence. Toward the end of 1988, Premier Li Peng intervened in the debate. He pointed out that China's space program should proceed in an incremental fashion. Given the high risk in the building of a space shuttle and the country's financial difficulties, more time was needed to re-search and develop the details of a Chinese space shuttle. At present, he said, spaceships may prove a more realistic option.[88] It is understandable that Li Peng made such a decision given his Soviet training. Thus, parallel R&D programs for both a manned spaceship and a space shuttle were undertaken.

Chinese experts reached a consensus in 1988 that the shuttle project should follow France's example: the Chinese space shuttle should be small in size compared to the US's *Columbia*. However, in developing their own software for the design, the Chinese made extensive use of the published material on the *Columbia* shuttle. By using this software the Chinese were able to infer a number of important structural, pneumatic and other data associated with the design of the shuttle. They then proposed a basic blueprint for China's first-generation space shuttle: a three-person crew, a pay-load of 3–3.5 tonnes, an overall weight of 22 tonnes, a maximum usage of 30 times, and a stay in earth orbit of three to five days.[89]

A detailed timetable has also been worked out: finalisation of the initial design of the orbiter and rocket carrier in 1998; the first manned trial on the ground in 2000; launch of the first trial flight into space in 2002; launch of the first manned flight in 2005; and the space shuttle's formal entry into service in 2008.

In 1989 the State Council convened a joint meeting to evaluate the various designs put forward by the Chinese Academy of Aerospace Technology. The conference decided to make the space program an overriding project for upgrading China's level of sci-ence and technology. An organisation was created to coordinate research and construction conducted by different ministries and localities, and to mobilise all the human and scientific resources in China's space industry. Implementation of foreign space tech-nology was given priority. In 1991 another national conference was convened to hammer out the specific features of the space shuttle. The military purposes of the shuttle were highlighted and the missions formulated. These included transportation of people and equipment, space rescue, scientific experimentation and earth observation. The shuttle would be smaller than the Hermes Space Shuttle currently developed by European countries, and would have a cool structure with heat absorption. The flight control system would be compact-structured, employing 1553B Central Data Line, CAD and data base support computers. Three existing launching sites were also proposed: Dongfeng, Kefeng and Xicang, situated at 41, 38 and 29 degrees northern latitude, respectively. Xicang, with its existing launching facilities, was regarded as the best option for the short term. In the long run, however, it was suggested that, in view of atmospheric gravity, Sanya and Wencang in Hainan Province, which are closest to the Equator (19 degrees northern latitude), are the best places in China for a vertical lift-off. The experts also made some estimate of the funding requirements for the program. It was agreed that for the initial R&D and the prototype shuttle a budget of 11 billion *yuan* should be allocated over a period of eight years.[90]

Establishing a satellite network

China has a very ambitious satellite program. As of August 1998 China has had 53 launches since the Changzheng rocket sent the country's first spacecraft into orbit in 1970. Toward the end of the decade China has turned its eyes to planets in the solar system. On 20 March 1998, Mr Yuan Jiajun, deputy president of the Chinese Academy of Aerospace Technology, revealed that his academy has formulated detailed plans to launch a number of spacecraft to study Mars and the moon. The plan even has a landing-on-the-moon component. According to his revelation, the decade between 2000 and 2010 will be the period for human beings to provide a detailed map of the moon's surface, find out its internal structure and establish some research laboratories. And in the two decades that follow, living bases should be created on the moon to further scientific research, and process and transport precious marterials.[91] The message he sent out is clear—the Chinese will not allow themselves to be left too far behind in the human exploration of the universe.

Among China's 53 launches, 19 launches have been for international commercial clients. Generally speaking, the Chinese launching record has been fairly impressive. So far six failures have been registered according to Chinese official statitsics, although there may be others that are not known to the outside world. If we accept this figure, China has achieved a success rate of about 90 per cent. Compared with the first 50 launches by the US and Russia, this is good. For the US, its success rate for the first 50 launches was 66.7 per cent and for Russia, 62 per cent. Yet China's record is inferior to the Euro Rocket, which achieved over a 90 per cent successful rate in its first 50 launches.[92] After China took a share in the international launching market, it has planned to enter the international satellite market. According to the Chinese Aerospace Industrial Corporation, it will strive to export its satellites by the year 2000. Then it can offer a whole discount deal to the client from building the satellite, to its launching and orbit service.[93]

Like all pathbreaking high-tech endeavours, China's space program is unlikely to unfold in a smooth manner. In recent years it has experienced a number of setbacks in these launches. The worst incident took place on 15 February 1996, when a Changzheng–3C exploded only 22 seconds after lift-off, ruining an American communication satellite and killing six people on the ground.[94] In fact, the launch success and failure ratio hit 1 to 1 in 1995–96, temporarily casting doubt over whether China would be able to carry through its ambitious space program. The series of failures has somewhat slowed down China's efforts to capture the international commercial launching market. The CMC has ordered China's space industry and the PLA launching units to give top priority to improving the success rate. It was not until the PLA accomplished thirteen consecutive successful launches in 1997–98 that international confidence began to rebuild, leading to several long-term cooperative agreements with some major clients in the world market. Significant among these launches were China's second-generation communication satellite and two military intelligence satellites. The successful launch of an Asian communication satellite of about five tonnes in July 1997 by the Changzheng–3C has been hailed as a landmark for China's space program. Had that launch failed again, it would have thrown China's space program for heavy satellite launches into complete chaos. Changzheng–3C is so far the largest vehicle carrier in China's rocket family. It can send satellites of five tonnes into solar synchronous orbit and a payload of twelve tonnes into earth-synchronous orbit. It is regarded as the prototype for the Changzheng–4 series, the likely carrier that will assume the task of sending China's manned spacecraft into orbit.[95]

Despite its setbacks with commercial launches, the PLA has never wavered in its determination to implement a military space agenda. The PLA has required its officers and men to establish a sense of space, which is considered of strategic value to China's national defence. In the 21st century, according to some senior PLA officers, a star war might become inevitable because space will have been highly militarised. The PLA has to be prepared, some officers say, for the day when the control of space will acquire the same importance as is attached today to controlling the skies.[96]

A defence-related aerospace program that parallelled the civilian one was formally proposed to the CMC in 1987. During the 1990s, enormous efforts were devoted to improving the PLA's space monitoring and communication systems, to selecting and training space personnel, and to launching various military satellites in order to set up the network. In the first two decades of the next century, the PLA intends to launch defence space stations. More specifically, the air force, army, Strategic Missile Force and navy should have all established separate space command units. PLA strategists have suggested that it is urgent for a temporary space force command to be created to coordinate various military space units in the PLA. This command should be set up in the air force headquarters responsible to the CMC.

At the same time a system of space monitoring and surveillance, similar to Western Europe's limited space defence program (the Small Star War Initiative), should become operational as soon as possible. To this end, R&D efforts should be directed along two parallel lines. The first is to build various kinds of military satellites, such as attack satellites, reconnaissance satellites, communications satellites, and early warning satellites. This network of military satellites should be capable both of self-defence and supporting operations carried out by the four services on the earth. The second step is to construct land-based systems earmarked for space warfare, including missile interception systems, early warning systems, information processing systems and logistical supply systems.[97] By the year 2040 China's space force is set to have become fully operational as an independent service directly under the national military command.[98]

Despite an ambitious development plan, however, China does have a realistic assessment of the current financial and technological difficulties of climbing into space. The PLA has defined the mission of its military space program to be of two types: information supporting and battlefield combating. Recognising the enormous technological difficulties in achieving any combat capabilities in space, China has confined its short-to-medium goal in space within the first category, and it does believe that its path to space will be long and tough. To be more concrete, the PLA has specified three tasks for its space units: observation/intelligence; navigation/positioning; and communication. To cater for these new missions in the country's military modernisation, the PLA has proposed creating a small but effective and practical space force.[99] Given the fact that the PLA has seen its potential opponents to be those which either possess space weapons systems or can expect effective assistance from space powers, it has decided that China has no choice but to promote a carefully designed military space program. Furthermore, such a program will be an indispensable part of RMA, as the combination of space information support and operations on the ground (the air and sea) will represent the essence of a high-tech war in the future.

4

Sharpening the nuclear sword

Formally established on 1 July 1965, the Strategic Missile Force (SMF) comprises China's surface-to-surface ballistic missile systems, which range from short to intercontinental. Its official Chinese name is Dier Paobing (the Second Artillery), given by Zhou Enlai, China's first premier, in 1965. This confusing name probably reveals the leader's less than sophisticated understanding of the strategic importance of missiles at the time: he considered the functions of missiles as an extension of artillery. Even so, the SMF was given priority treatment in all respects from the very beginning. Its importance is reflected in the fact that, despite its small number of personnel (about 4 per cent of the PLA total), the SMF has always been allocated the highest percentage of military outlays in the PLA. For instance, the SMF receives 12 to 15 per cent of the total defence expenditure and about 20 per cent of the PLA's total procurement budget.[1] In 1985, when other services were adversely affected by the cut of one million personnel, the SMF actually expanded. Now it is almost certain that the PLA's nuclear arm will be further strengthened, even though other nuclear powers have begun to trim their nuclear arsenals and force levels. In a way this move is in keeping with China's realism-based foreign policy. The leadership and the public alike believe that a sufficient nuclear capability will give the nation not only a sense of security against other nuclear countries but, more importantly, a solid foundation for exercising influence as a major power. Nothing illustrates more vividly how the Chinese leadership understands the nature of nuclear weapons than the pronouncement of Marshal Chen Yi, the Chinese minister for foreign affairs in the 1960s, that 'without that bomb, I cannot be very firm at the negotiating tables'.[2] It is a matter of debate whether this perception of nuclear weapons has changed in the post–Cold War era. What is certain is that as long as China bases its foreign policy and national security on military capability, the importance of nuclear weapons will not be de-emphasised and, as a result, the PLA's SMF will remain the top priority in the PLA's modernisation drive.

THE EVOLUTION OF THE SMF

With about 100 000 officers and men, the SMF is the smallest service in the PLA.[3] Yet it assumes a disproportionate share of the burden of military deterrence through its capability to launch a second strike, nuclear or conventional, against the major powers. Generally speaking, between the 1960s and 1980s the Chinese nuclear strategy was minimum deterrence. The Chinese notion of deterrence could be characterised as the belief that by emphasising the defensive component, victory can be denied the enemy. The usefulness of the strategy relies on China's ability to show that it can fight and not lose a nuclear war: the high cost would convince the initiator that a nuclear exchange would be fruitless. Nuclear deterrence is a part of China's overall defence posture, which consists of three tiers of forces: passive civil defence, in keeping with the Clausewitizian notion that the social and political dimensions of war must be coordinated; active defence to help minimise the potential damage; and offensive forces able to take the war to the enemy.[4] China maintains only a minimum nuclear arsenal due to financial constraints, shortage of key materials and technological inadequacies. It is closely linked to China's no-first-use policy, which was formulated in the 1960s on the understanding that an insufficient nuclear capability could be inviting a surgical strike by more advanced nuclear powers rather than assuring the Chinese a desirable level of national security. In accordance with the guiding principle of minimum deterrence, the Chinese nuclear strategy between the 1960s and 1980s designated a two-stage development process to attain readiness for a nuclear war. The first stage aimed to resolve the problem of survivability, or how to hide; and the second, the problems of missile range and accuracy, or how to fight.

The improvement of survivability, and of launching range and accuracy have been the primary objectives of the PLA SMF since the outset of its nuclear program. After twenty years of development the SMF has basically accomplished these goals. Its first ICBM was launched in 1980, with a range of nearly 10 000 kilometres. This enabled the PLA to target key American cities on the west coast. A year later, China demonstrated its multiple independently-targeted re-entry vehicle (MIRV) capability by simultaneously sending three satellites into orbit. In 1982 the PLA fired its first sea-based missile. All these efforts gradually gave the SMF a triad system of second-strike capability. China's impressive progress in developing nuclear weapons has caught the attention of many western analysts who point out that sometime during the early 1980s, China had unobtrusively surpassed both the UK and France to become the world's third most powerful nuclear power. In essence the PRC took less time than any of its four predecessors to acquire the various nuclear-energy, ballistic missile, satellite and MIRV technologies necessary to form a nuclear triad and a survivable strategic retaliatory force.[5]

How to hide: mobility and survivability

Throughout the 1970s and the 1980s, the emphasis of the Chinese SMF had been more on 'force consolidation' (*heliliang de zhunbei* or survivability) than on practical operation (*heliliang de yunyong* or the employment of the weaponry).[6] To be more concrete, 'force consolidation' was dependent on two crucial factors: the survivability of launching sites and the mobility of the launching units. China's nuclear policy is to use nuclear weapons only after being attacked by nuclear weapons. This puts great demands on the SMF, as it must be able to perform its mission after absorbing a nuclear strike. For a long time all China's long-range and intercontinental missiles were stored in permanent launching silos.[7] Therefore, the efforts of 'consolidation' entailed, first of all, the secrecy of the launching sites, because the design of the launching silos for China's DF–4 and DF–5 ICBMs are fairly primitive. They are buried much shallower than those of the Russian SS–18s and have relatively low resistance against pressure.[8] As the PLA had to rely mainly on such land-based nuclear weapons for launching intercontinental missiles, the 'consolidation' of the silos constituted the key to survival of the key units of the SMF. The following requirements have been prescribed by the PLA central command for deploying the missile units with a high level of secrecy:

1 Silos have to be isolated from each other to prevent the destruction of two silos by one nuclear missile strike.
2 The nuclear missile units should be deployed in China's deep rear. Once deployed their launching sites should remain relatively permanent. Fake facilities should be constructed nearby in order to make identification of the real ones difficult.

3   All the mobile units should be provided with secret alternative
    launching sites.
4   Transfers of ICBM units should be minimised to reduce the
    likelihood of detection.
5   Sufficient numbers of SAM batteries and AA guns should be
    deployed in the surrounding areas to frustrate enemy air raids,
    missile strikes or surprise attack by airborne troops.[9]

In order to hide its strategic missiles, the SMF kept them stored
in deep caves most of the time. When they are to be fired, they
are driven outside the caves to the pre-planned launching sites,
where they are erected and filled with fuel. The PLA's missile units
have built several hundred underground tunnels, living quarters
and storage facilities in the most inaccessible areas in China.[10] The
construction of hardened silos, however, presented the Chinese
with a major technological difficulty. According to a research report
of 1992, China built two silos in the first years of the 1980s, but
by 1992 only four D–5s had been deployed in the silos.[11]

Long-range capabilities are regarded as a key factor of deterrence value. Without long-range missiles the SMF cannot target
potential enemies beyond a certain distance, and then China's
deterrence is neither reliable nor credible. From the very beginning
of the *Dongfeng* program, political leaders strictly instructed engineers to increase the reach of the missiles stage by stage, which
was not only a military imperative but also served as an important
political task. The aim was to extend missile range to reach
potential targets, from US bases in Japan and Korea to the Philippines, to Guam, to Moscow and finally to continental America
(see Table 4.1).

As far as mobility is concerned, the SMF is required by the CMC
to be able to wage a kind of nuclear 'guerrilla warfare', a mobile
operation similar to what people saw in the Gulf War where the
Allied forces engaged the Iraqi Scud missiles in a cat-and-mouse
game.[12] To this end, the SMF has tested various methods since the
late 1970s to improve the rapid response capabilities of the units
equipped with long- and intermediate-range missiles. The most
important of these methods has been to have the launching units and
facilities on the move all the time. In the last decade or so, launching
roads of thousands of miles have been constructed to link an
increasing number of launching sites with the centrally controlled
C³I networks. Every launching unit has several re-usable launching sites. In each of these it accumulates the launching data for its
fixed targets and practises different launching protocols. In wartime

Table 4.1 The evolution of China's missile program

Chinese designation	Western designation	Range (km)/ payload (kg)	Technical description	Comments
DF–3 (DF–3A)	CSS–2	2650/2150 2800/2150	Single stage; 24 m length, 2.25 m diameter, 64-tonne lift-off weight; storable liquid; AK–27/UDMH; fully inertial strap-down guidance.	Was DF–1; R&D started in Apr. 1964; first successful flight on Dec. 26, 1966; deployed since May 1971; used as the first stage for DF–4; sold to Saudi Arabia.
DF–4	CSS–3	4750/2200	Two-stage; 28 m length, 2.25 m diameter, 80-tonne lift-off weight; same propellant and guidance as DF–3s.	R&D started in Mar. 1965; first successful flight on Jan. 30, 1970; deployed since 1980; used as booster for satellite launcher CZ–1.
DF–5 (DF–5A)	CSS–4	12 000/3200 13 000/3200	Two-stage; 32.6 m length, 3.35 m diameter, 183-tonne lift-off weight; storable liquid; N_2O_4/UDMH; gyro-platform inertial guidance with on-board computer.	R&D started in Mar. 1965; first successful flight on Sept. 10, 1971; deployed since Aug. 1981; used as booster for satellite launchers CZ–2, CZ–3 and CZ–4.
DF–6	None	FOBS/3200	Three-stage; same propellant and guidance as DF–5s.	R&D started in July 1966; discontinued in Oct. 1973.
DF–14	None	8000/700	Two-stage; storable liquid: AK–40/UDMH; computer-digitised strap-down inertial guidance.	Land-mobile IRBM; R&D began in Oct. 1973 and stopped in Sept. 1975; resumed in Aug. 1978 and renamed DF–22.
DF–22	None	8000/700	As above (DF–14).	Was DF–14; R&D discontinued in Jan. 1985.

Table 4.1 cont.

Chinese designation	Western designation	Range (km)/ payload (kg)	Technical description	Comments
JL–1/DF–21 (DF–21A)	CSS–N–3	1700/600 1800/600	Two-stage; solid propellant; 1.4 m diameter, 10.7 m length, 14.7-tonne lift-off weight; gyro-platform inertial guidance with on-board computer.	R&D started in Mar. 1967; DF–21 is land-mobile, JL–1 is submarine-launched; JL–1's first successful flight test was on Oct. 12, 1982; DF–21's first successful flight test was on May 20, 1985; both are operational.
JL–2/DF–23	None	6000/800	Three-stage; solid propellant.	R&D started in Aug. 1970; became DF–31/JL–2 in Jan. 1985 with extended range.
DF–31/JL–2	None	8000/700	Three-stage; solid propellant.	DF–31 is land mobile, JL–2 is SLBM; both are expected to be operational in mid-1990s.
DF–41	None	12 000/800	Three-stage; solid propellant.	Preliminary research began in early 1986; expected to be operational in late 1990s.
DF–25	None	1700/2000	Two-stage; solid propellant.	Land-mobile conventional modification based on DF–31's first two stages; expected to be operational in mid-1990s.
China-designed Tactical Ballistic Missiles				
DF–41/DF–61	None	N/A	Single-stage; solid propellant.	Land-based short-range missile; R&D started in June 1966 but soon abandoned.

Table 4.1 cont.

Chinese designation	Western designation	Range (km)/ payload (kg)	Technical description	Comments
DF–61	None	1000/500	Single-stage; pre-packed storable.	R&D started in 1976 but discontinued in 1977.
M–9/DF–15	None	600/500	Single-stage; 1 m diameter, 9.1 m length, 6200 kg lift-off weight; solid propellant; strap-down inertial computer-digitised guidance with terminal control.	R&D started in Apr. 1984; exhibited in Nov. 1986; successfully passed first flight test in June 1988; DF–15 is the code-name for domestic use, and M–9 is the code-name for export.
M–11/DF–11	None	300/500	Two-stage; solid propellant; same guidance system as M–9s.	R&D started in 1985; a photograph was displayed at an exhibition in 1988.
8610	None	300/500	Two-stage: solid propellant booster and storable liquid propellant main engine.	Modification from HQ–2 surface-to-air missile; R&D began in April 1986.

Source: Lewis & Hua Di 1992, pp. 10–11.

these data and continuous on-spot training could save precious response time.

In order to raise the SMF's survivability, R&D priorities have been given to the development of a solid fuel propellant, miniaturised warheads and a sophisticated C³I system. The solid fuels are of particular importance because most of the SMF's early missiles (mainly DF–3 IRBMs) are propelled by liquid fuel, which needs two hours to get ready for launch. Fuelling a ballistic missile is a long and dangerous process. The first step is transferring the liquid propellant from railway storage into a container carried by a road transporter. The second step is to pour the fuel from the transporter into a huge pot at the launching site. The third step is to pump the liquid from the pot into the missile fuel tank through an underground tunnel. All these steps have to be carried out in the open air and soldiers are exposed to highly toxic chemicals during the whole process.[13] The PLA sees this as out of step with the requirements of a high-tech war in the future. Solid fuel is therefore regarded as the key to any improvement in response time. It is especially important for the mobile missiles and submarine-based missiles. Since 1985, when the PLA launched its first solid-fuelled mobile missile, China has also invested heavily in improving its missile transportation vehicles and launching platforms.[14]

How to fight: getting ready for action

Minimum deterrence is an awkward nuclear strategy: it is too defensive, concerned mainly with how to hide. It is awkward also because it is not applicable to any foreseeable scenarios of a nuclear or conventional war. Considering China's superior conventional forces vis-a-vis its Asian neighbours, it is unnecessary to employ the SMF. The political price would be too high. Neither is the SMF supposed to initiate an attack on the military superpowers, given their overwhelming nuclear superiority, which could wipe out the bulk of China's urban industrial centres. What, then, is the use of the SMF, which receives so much investment but manages only to hide? This doctrine of minimum deterrence has fatal flaws but it is an unavoidable transitional guideline for deterring an all-out war. In essence it is a 'buying-time' strategy, as the Chinese military commanders believe that more time will allow the SMF to develop the necessary technology and arsenal so that the SMF will not need to hide too much any more.

China's rapid rise in economic power since the 1980s has gradually encouraged PLA generals to think more in terms of fighting rather than hiding. In 1984 the CMC officially ordered the SMF to formally assume offensive retaliatory missions.[15] Parallel to this transition from 'hide' to 'fight' in war preparation is the PLA's changing attitude toward nuclear weapons, from viewing them more as an unusable means of mass destruction to recognising their practical use for battlefield conflicts.[16] With the improvement of China's nuclear technology, particularly that related to accuracy, longer range and mobility, the PLA's confidence in its ability to successfully wage nuclear warfare is being enhanced. Indeed, younger PLA generals have gradually broken the psychological shackles imposed by the long-lasting strategy of minimum deterrence, which was the logical root-cause for the mentality of hiding. When designing 'war game' plans, these generals are tempted to formulate scenarios in which they fire nuclear missiles in high-tech wars.[17]

It is the post-Deng CMC's shift to a high-tech defence strategy, however, that has had the greatest effect on the PLA's nuclear programs. This shift may have pushed the SMF to move beyond the stage of 'force consolidation', even though the problem of survivability remains pressing. A key to understanding the PLA's transition toward 'practical operation' is that it is gradually breaking away from its passive defence of 'hiding its missiles and increasing its number of warheads' to assuming a more forward posture. In 1991 Jiang Zemin, accompanied by other CMC leaders, paid a visit to the headquarters of the SMF. During the inspection he was assured that the SMF had acquired all-weather and all-situation operational capabilities. Every launching brigade is assuming missions of strategic duty, missions assigned by the CMC. This meant that the SMF had transcended a historical developmental stage.[18]

China's increasing emphasis on the war-fighting aspect of its nuclear strategy is also reflected in the goal-specific exercises of the SMF. Simulation and live ammunition launches in remote mountainous areas are given concrete targets and proceed in pre-determined circumstances of nuclear exchanges. During the mid-1980s the SMF conducted 120 exercises. The majority of these were designed to assist the PLA's defensive warfare at the divisional level or above against the situations of a Sino–USSR war.[19] One key item in the exercises was group launch, whereby up to four DF series missiles were launched one after another from different locations to test the SMF's rapid response and retaliatory capabilities.[20] When China staged its 'war games' in 1995 and 1996, group launch became the standard exercise. It is believed that group launches will be one of the chief means to affect a blockade of Taiwan's waterways. Since the Gulf War in 1991, the SMF has placed particular emphasis on designing various situations where its missile units are trained to respond quickly in a real nuclear exchange. These situations include retaliation after a nuclear surgical strike, biochemical warfare, and maritime warfare. Most of these are mobile launches. Reducing pre-launch time is one of the key aims in training. China's ICBM units rarely have the opportunity to launch a real missile. For instance, one brigade proposed a new time reduction experiment in 1990. However, it was only two years after the plan had won an all-army award that the brigade had a chance to turn the plan into a live ammunition launch.[21] In addition to worst case scenario preparation, the following important features are also indicative of the SMF's conceptual shift towards 'how to fight'.

Contemplating tactical nuclear battles

The transition in mentality from 'hiding' to 'fighting' may stimulate revisions of China's decades-old minimum deterrence strategy. Numbers of nuclear missiles may have to remain minimal, but war game plans can be formulated on the premise of retaliation without being first hit by a nuclear bomb. After achieving a second-strike capability some military planners are now tempted to contemplate the use of nuclear weapons in an escalation of conventional war, which they believe may place a nation's survival at stake just as much as nuclear attack.[22] PLA researchers often cite the example of the former USSR's plan to initiate a nuclear attack against China to illustrate that the use of nuclear weapons is not inconceivable. They are particularly impressed by Russia's new national defence doctrine, which has deleted the provision of not employing nuclear weapons first in an all-out war.[23]

Generally speaking, the SMF's war-fighting preparations begin with its efforts to grasp the nature, process and consequences of a tactical nuclear war. In the last decade or so the PLA has accorded new emphasis to tactical nuclear weapons due to several concerns. First, it accepted the idea that even in an all-out war in the future, tactical nuclear weapons would be preferred to strategic ones. This led PLA strategists to eagerly embrace the concept of a theatre nuclear conflict, while in the past most of them had not seen such a boundary in a nuclear exchange. In their old mind-set, any nuclear fight was mass destruction. Moreover they would argue that if a missile landed on the Bolshoi Theatre instead of the Kremlin it would be equally effective and that, even if every missile had pinpoint accuracy, the limited number in the PRC's small arsenal could destroy only a small fraction of the enemy's silos, leaving China disarmed before the enemy's remaining missiles.[24]

PLA strategists now agree with their western colleagues that in the future nuclear warfare would most likely be used at the theatre level and against military targets. PLA war games are therefore played for achieving battlefield victory rather than the destruction of the world.[25] While ICBMs can hold urban centres hostage at the strategic deterrence level, tactical nuclear weapons have to be deployed to serve as the second level of deterrence. This can be of particular value for a combatant that is inferior in conventional weapons. A weak navy, for instance, might be left with little choice but to use tactical nuclear means to deal with the superpower's nuclear-armed aircraft carrier battle groups.

Chinese analysts found NATO's Cold War nuclear strategy very attractive. This strategy was designed against a massive Soviet land attack on Western Europe. Under the circumstances it seemed to NATO that tactical nuclear weapons offered the only option to frustrate such a strong conventional offensive. Similarly, the initial proposal for the PLA to develop tactical nuclear weapons originated from the calculation of the PLA high command in the 1970s that they had no conventional weapons effective enough to hold back a large-scale tank invasion by the Soviets in north and north-east China, where the land is flat and the distance between Beijing and Mongolia is only 600 to 700 kilometres. Against such an invasion no weapons other than neutron bombs or 105 mm nuclear shells would be more effective in putting up a desperate defence.[26] In September 1988 when the PLA exploded a nuclear bomb, it claimed that the test successfully produced China's third-generation nuclear warhead. Most western analysts, however, believed that the explosion was meant to test China's first neutron bomb. Indeed, western intelligence agencies discovered that China possessed tactical nuclear weapons with a yield below 30 000 tonnes as early as the beginning of the 1970s.[27]

The fundamental reason for PLA planners to contemplate the use of tactical nuclear weapons is to fill a gap in China's nuclear deterrence strategy. As a weak nuclear power, China was long subject to the nuclear blackmail of the superpowers, which could choose whether to wage a nuclear war, what kind of nuclear war to wage, and when to start such a war. China's deterrence can be effective only when it has the means to deal with all kinds of nuclear threats. By the PLA's assessment, if China were forced into a nuclear war, it is most likely that it would face a tactical nuclear attack, such as a nuclear surgical strike. This would make it very difficult for the SMF to respond with strategic nuclear weapons that target only urban centres. So if China did not possess effective tactical nuclear weapons, it would be deprived of a crucial means for deterrence, both politically and militarily.[28]

Therefore, immediately after the PLA shifted its strategy from people's war to people's war under modern conditions in the late 1970s, the SMF set out to practise the concept of tactical nuclear warfare. It conducted a tactical nuclear war exercise along the Sino–Soviet border in the middle of 1982. This exercise simulated a situation where the PLA ground forces and the SMF jointly obstructed a massive tank invasion by using a tactical nuclear explosive. But the concept of tactical nuclear warfare had never been elevated to any great theoretical heights. Nor had there been any systematic attempts to improve tactical nuclear capability. This situation lingered on until Lieutenant-General Li Xuge was appointed commander-in-chief of the SMF in 1985. He was the first to question why the SMF had not developed a campaign (theatre) theory, and he ordered systematic theatre nuclear missile exercises. In subsequent years repeated exercises were carried out under all kinds of war contingencies. According to the PLA united campaign guidelines, the function of tactical nuclear missiles parallels that of the air force and the navy, although the use of missiles should be under much tighter central control.[29] It is important to note that among the different situations where the PLA was forced to use nuclear weapons, simulation of major operations at sea was given special attention.[30]

Emphasis on sea-based launching platforms

Most of China's nuclear weapons are land-based, which means they are vulnerable to an enemy first strike. Although these weapons are well hidden, the SMF headquarters are fully aware that the latest developments in satellite technology enable China's potential opponents to identify the whereabouts of the silos and mobile missiles by following the tracks of the vehicles that travel to those otherwise inaccessible areas. One countermeasure adopted by the SMF was to put up as many fake launching sites as possible. However, western analysts quoted Admiral Liu Huaqing as saying that after a first strike, only about 10 per cent of China's nuclear arsenal would survive.[31] By PLA estimates, up to two-thirds of the SMF's nuclear weapons might survive, leaving it a sufficient number of warheads to hit back.[32]

However, PLA leaders cannot be sure how many land-based nuclear weapons would actually survive a precision first strike and subsequent attacks. Following the US approach to countering the USSR's nuclear threat, the Chinese place increasing importance on sea-based nuclear launching platforms, which were among China's three top R&D projects in the 1970s.[33] (The other two projects concerned intercontinental nuclear missiles and communication satellites). Chinese strategists have studied and accepted the US's nuclear strategy, which gives prominence to nuclear submarines as the safest basing mode for a second-strike capability. Admiral Liu Huaqing summarised the new thinking in China's nuclear strategy as follows:

In the face of a large-scale nuclear attack, only less than 10 per cent of the coastal launching silos will survive, whereas submarines armed with ballistic missiles can use the surface of the sea to protect and cover themselves, preserve the nuclear offensive force, and play a deterrent and containment role.[34]

According to a long-term development plan, China has decided to gradually move a significant proportion of its land-based nuclear capabilities into submarines.[35] This plan is at the top of China's wish-list, although it is more easily talked about than put into practice. The huge cost and tough technological requirements for developing nuclear submarines may prevent the PLA's long-term plan from becoming reality for a long time to come. Rapid industrial development has compelled the civilian sectors to compete with the PLA for nuclear facilities that supply energy and other economic purposes. Morever, the PLA has been confronted with serious accuracy problems with missiles launched from under water. The submarine-based Hailong–1 (HL–1) missiles (remade from the land-mobile Dongfeng–21) also suffer from other technological weaknesses, such as being relatively short in range (about 2000 kilometres), large in size and unsophisticated in their guidance systems. Its successor version HL–2, scheduled to enter service around 2003, has been on trial for a number of years. Although it has improved on all these three weak points, it is still regarded as inadequate by the PLA. Its active service has therefore been delayed several times. The PLA will, however, continue to give top priority to the development of submarine-based missile launching platforms. By early next century the new submarine-based missile systems will, according to a senior PLA officer, be able to reach a target over 10 000 kilometres away, far enough to cover the US.[36]

By the mid-1990s China has developed a relatively reliable nuclear submarine fleet. Nicknamed the 09 Unit and with a ranking equivalent to a group army in military bureaucratic ranking, the PLA Navy's nuclear submarine fleet is gradually expanding. By the year 2010 it may comprise over a dozen nuclear-powered submarines.[37] However, for the time being most of these nuclear submarines are Han class tactical attack boats, which have a displacement of 5000 tonnes and a crew of 73. Some of these tactical submarines can launch twelve C801 cruise missiles with a range of about 50 kilometres. The C801 is fairly accurate, with terminal guidance measures. The missile is conventional but it can be equipped with a nuclear warhead. The only strategic missile submarine, Xia class SSBN, is more of an experimental boat.

Manned by 104 officers and sailors, it is 120 metres in length, with a displacement of 8000 tonnes. It is said to carry twelve HL–1 nuclear missiles, each propelled by solid fuel and deployed with a single two-megaton (MT) nuclear warhead.[38] Although its everyday running is the responsibility of the navy, the control over the nuclear button is certainly not. There have been no detailed accounts of how the command, control and communications are channelled between the CMC, the naval headquarters and the 09 Fleet.

The PLA high command is well aware that a single Xia class nuclear submarine will not make China's second-strike capability reliable. Recently some Chinese sources have revealed that the PLA has undertaken programs to equip its navy with a new much-improved generation of nuclear submarines, nicknamed 093, with technology similar to Russia's Victor III SSN. Indeed, the PLA has reportedly received Russian help in coating 093's hulls to improve noise insulation. It is said that once in service, in three to five years, the noise level of the 093 submarines may reach that of the US's and Japan's in the early 1990s, a remarkable progress.[39]

At the same time it is said that China is constructing a second but modified version of Xia class submarine (094 type SSBN) in the Huludao Naval Ship Plant. This boat has an enlarged displacement of over 10 000 tonnes and carries HL–2 nuclear missiles with multiple, independently-targetable re-entry vehicle nuclear warheads. With a much more sophisticated terminal guidance system and enlarged range of 8000 kilometres, this new type will represent a greater deterrence to China's potential opponents. Western analysts have raised their doubts regarding the level of technology of these new SSBNs, Moreover, funding difficulties have slowed down the development considerably. Nevertheless, given the importance of nuclear submarines in China's overall nuclear strategy, there is reason to believe the number of sea-based launching platforms will continue to increase, as will their reliability.

Emphasis on conventional missile warfare

International study of the SMF in the past neglected one important aspect of its development, namely its conventional missile forces. In the post–Cold War era the value of conventional missiles is that they are much more usable than nuclear ones. Nuclear warheads are not useful in most of the PLA's war plans, for example a war of any scale across the Taiwan Strait. The PLA now defines high-tech warfare very much in line with missile warfare. Accordingly, it regards the conventional missiles of the SMF to be among the few effective high-tech weapons that it possesses in dealing with its high-tech opponents. Achieving a high level of readiness for the conventional missile units has thus become an urgent mission in the SMF's transition from hiding to fighting.[40]

As a result, the SMF has in the past few years made serious efforts to formulate a new set of guidelines and concepts for future missile warfare. This includes research on improving the terminal accuracy and on countering the tactics and style of a potential enemy attack. The importance of these efforts is elaborated in a research report of the PLA National Defence University:

> The PLA's conventional missiles will be used exclusively against the enemy's key military targets which the weapons of other services cannot reach. These targets include the communications hubs, weapons delivery platforms, and most practically the aircraft carrier battle groups. Since these systems are under heavy protection, the demand for the conventional missiles is thus very high. Moreover, how to use these missiles is a matter of military art involving the optimum timing and smart selection of targets.[41]

Second, the use of conventional missile units of the SMF has been highlighted by the PLA's emphasis on united warfare. Traditionally, however, the SMF has largely confined its war doctrines and training programs to itself, given the nature of nuclear weapons and warfare. United campaigns involving the SMF with other services have never been a priority in the PLA's war preparation. Technological improvement of conventional missiles has made the SMF a highly useful tactical offensive force and thus made it possible for it to join other services in likely war scenarios. For instance, the SMF's conventional missiles are considered as useful weapons against enemy. airfields and thus conducive to the air force's efforts to achieve air superiority. Since training for united campaigns is currently prioritised for the joint exercises of the army, the navy and the air force, the SMF has been ordered by the CMC to formulate protocols for its participation. In effect the officers from the SMF are required to join the headquarters of united campaigns in each war zone, a departure from past practice. Now the SMF's coordination in such war efforts is seen as crucial to whether a war can be won.

The missile firing by the conventional missile units of the SMF in the March 1996 military demonstration against Taiwan, codenamed 'Strait 96 Number One', was the first known case of the SMF's active participation in a large united campaign exercise at the level of group army corps (the level of several group army units, including those of the air force, the navy and the SMF, in

Chinese it is called *Bingtuan*). The early timing of missile firing in relation to other services in the exercise seems to indicate that ballistic missiles would be used in the initial stage of a conflict in preparation for air strikes and amphibious landings. Moreover, during the exercise the missiles were fired from at least two widely dispersed units. This may be a deliberate design by the SMF to test its command, control and communication effectiveness.[42]

The Gulf War demonstrated that high-tech conventional weapons could generate enormous deterring power. At this stage China particularly needs a high level of non-nuclear deterrence in order to cope with any potential crisis in China's periphery and across the Taiwan Strait. The SMF will therefore introduce more 'smart conventional missiles' for the blockade of the airfields, C³I centres and transportation hubs of its adversaries. Medium- to long-range smart conventional missiles are also useful for China in tackling potential threats from its peripheral countries, mainly concerning territorial disputes. Therefore new missile units will be created in the SMF for this purpose.

Currently the SMF has a number of conventional missiles in its inventory. All of them are dual-capable, as they can carry conventional and nuclear warheads weighing from a few hundred kilograms to one tonne (with the nuclear yield of 90 kilotons). The M–9 and M–11 missiles are the two types most discussed in the west. The Chinese name for the former is Dongfeng–15 and the latter Dongfeng–11. Both were developed at the same time and are modern short-range ballistic missiles. DF–15 has an effective range of 600 kilometres but DF–11 has only half of that range. They were reportedly first put into service at the beginning of the 1990s. The two missiles use an inertial guidance package, although the package is being upgraded with the Kalman filter-based Global Positioning System. This may have helped the SMF to improve the accuracy of these two missiles, which is believed to be within the range of 150 to 600 metres. In fact the missile firing in Strait 96 Number One was very precise, as commented Rear Admiral Rod Rempt, the US Navy's Program Executive Officer for Theater Air Defence: 'The missile landed right in the middle of the closure areas'.[43] Recently it was reported that the guidance systems for the two types of missiles have been further upgraded, using a radar-based terminal guidance system which is similar to that on board the former US Pershing II missile, namely the Radar Assisted Digital Area Guidance (RADAG) system.[44]

These two missiles are solid-fuelled missiles, deployed on a mobile transporter-erector-launcher and take less than an hour to

Table 4.2 The SMF's conventional missiles

System	Alternative name	Missile type	Supplier	Maximum range (km)	Payload (kg)
CSS–6	DF–15/M–9	SRBM	Domestic	600	950
CSS–7	DF–11/M–11	SRBM	Domestic	300	800
CSS–8	M–7	SRBM	Domestic	160	190
CSS–N–3	JL–1	SLBM	Domestic	1700	1 RV
DF–25		MRBM	Domestic	1700	2000

Notes: RV = re-entry vehicle.

get ready for launch. China's recent improvement of the missile technology has enabled the missile carriers to install a separating warhead with its own miniature propulsion system, which means that the warhead is able to change its trajectory and range at the final stage of flight. In addition to DF–15 and DF–11, China has also converted other missiles initially intended for nuclear use into conventional ones. This includes DF–21 and DF–25 intermediate range ballistic missiles (IRBMs). Carrying a warhead of 2000 kilograms, DF–25 can reach a target 1700 kilometres away. These two missiles have enriched the SMF's conventional missile family (see Table 4.2).

THE COMMAND AND CONTROL OF THE SMF

China's nuclear command is one of the toughest in the world. The highest authority to issue launching orders rests in the hands of Chairman of the CMC, a position equivalent to commander-in-chief of the country's armed forces. Currently, the CMC's chairman is Jiang Zemin, who is also concurrently the Party's General Secretary and head of state. In deciding whether to use nuclear weapons, Jiang certainly has to consult other powerful figures in the Party, particularly the seven members of the Politburo Standing Committee and the two vice-chairmen of the CMC, namely Zhang Wannian and Chi Haotian. The CMC's two former deputy chairs, Admiral Liu Huaqing, who sat in the Politburo Standing Committee as the highest ranking military officer until September 1997, and General Zhang Zhen, who is now the most senior PLA elder and attracts high respect from all major commanders in the PLA, would very likely be consulted.[45]

Theoretically, the use of nuclear weapons has to be discussed in the joint meetings of the seven-member Politburo Standing

Committee and the eight-member CMC. The membership of the CCP's Politburo Standing Committee is:

Jiang Zemin (Party general secretary, state president, CMC chair),
Li Peng (President of the NPC Standing Committee),
Zhu Rongji (premier),
Li Ruihuan (chair of the National Political Consultative Conference),
Hu Jintao (vice state president and Jiang's designated heir),
Li Lanqing (executive vice premier),
Wei Jianxing (chair of the Party's Discipline and Inspection Commission).

The number of people who have any access to the final decision is small and probably fewer than four people will have the crucial say. These include Jiang Zemin; Li Peng, as the second highest ranking party leader, and president of the Standing Committee of the National People's Congress; Zhu Rongji, the premier, and a representative from the PLA. Jiang, as the commander-in-chief, will certainly have the final veto power.

Outside this small club of top political and military leaders, the headquarters of the SMF normally just implements the decisions relayed to it. Yet they are the people in practical control of the nuclear button. The workings of the SMF command have remained a mystery up to now, although some analysts have described its C³I in some detail. According to Michael Swaine, the PLA C³I system is highly centralised, vertically structured and very personalised. The last point means that some top decisions are transmitted only verbally to military units by the commander-in-chief and his major designated aides. Although a written order may follow, his very voice can serve the function of a formalised authorisation.[46] This was true when Deng was commander-in-chief; whether Jiang Zemin has the same level of authority remains to be tested. Yet it seems that he is now in control of the nuclear button, although any decision on using nuclear weapons would most likely bear the name of a group rather than an individual, for example, the CMC or the Politburo's Standing Committee, which functions as the supreme national security council.

In terms of force structure, the SMF can be characterised as lean and mean. There are only four layers of command between the headquarters of the SMF and the basic launching units: the headquarters, the regional base command, the brigades and the battalions (see Figure 4.1).

Figure 4.1 The command and control structure of the SMF

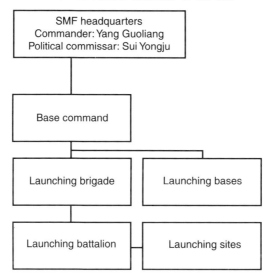

The SMF's headquarters are situated in Qinghe, a north-western suburb of Beijing, and serve as the central relaying point connecting every basic launching unit and site to the CMC through direct communication 'hot lines'. The regional base commands are half a grade higher than a group army in hierarchical ranking. They assume both strategic and tactical missions, the coverage of the command of these bases extending over a whole war zone, which may not coincide with the geographic area of a MAC. The exact number of regional base commands is unknown, but some sources put the figure at six.[47] In addition to these regional command bases there is a major experimental base: China's first nuclear test site, widely known as Lop Nur. For most Chinese who hear about it, it is called Base Malan or Base Number 21. These regional base commands have a number of sub-bases, each of which may have a clear division of labour in terms of warhead targeting. The Xian Base assumes the regional command for the SMF units in north-west China. Its sub-bases—Bases 23 and 27 for instance—command launching units in the region which traditionally have aimed at targets in the USSR. The Liu Qingzhou Base takes control over launching units in north-east China. In south-west China the Tianwei Base, located about 100 kilometres from Kunming, the capital city of Yunnan Province, most likely houses IRBMs that can strike Taiwan, all of South-east Asia, and half of India. The regional base commands in East China take care of the targets in east Asia. They may also target North America, since the covering distance is shorter than for the major launching bases in the north.[48] The regional commands in Jiangxi and Fujian have been specially commissioned with targeting Taiwan; it was they who conducted the Taiwan Strait missile tests of 1995. Politically, firing missiles into sensitive areas is a kind of muscle-flexing designed to inhibit undesired developments without real attack.[49]

Some bases command a number of intercontinental missiles, while others are more responsible for launching tactical missiles, both nuclear and conventional. According to a Russian military expert on China's nuclear programs, China's ten strategic missile launching bases/sites (DF–5s) are located throughout the country, which means they may be under different regional base commands.[50]

Below the regional base commands, there are about fifteen missile brigades, which are the tactical units that would conduct missile firing missions in the event of a conflict. Each brigade commands a number of permanent launching sites scattered over a vast area. Its basic units repeatedly carry out manoeuvres at designated launching sites to familiarise themselves with the key firing data, such as the landscape of the area, atmospheric pressure and gravity, local weather, and re-entry information. Regular exercises and selective training help these launching units to reduce response time and thus enhance their survivability in action. From time to time, other brigades under the same base command (sometimes from other base commands) also exercise at the sites to acquire the necessary launching data.

The majority of the SMF's launching sites were constructed in north, north-east and north-west China. This was intended to counter the nuclear threat from the USSR during the Sino–Soviet confrontation. In the post–Cold War era the threat from the north is no longer imminent, but the new threats have loomed large from the perceived 'containment number two' strategy and from Taiwan's quest for independence. To cater to changed world politics and regional uncertainty, new launching sites have been constructed in south and east China. Training in east China has been particularly tightened up.

The launching sites vary in rank according to their functions, that is, whether they are designed to launch strategic nuclear missiles or tactical conventional missiles. All of them are located far away from urban areas, very often in the most inaccessible mountain ranges. This was a rational reaction to the constant threat of 'surgical operations' by the superpowers in the 1970s. So the guiding principle for base construction was *shan, dong* and *sang,* namely, hiding missiles in mountainous areas, in deep caves and as dispersed as possible. Although this principle has increased the difficulties of command, communication and logistical supply, it has effectively enhanced the secrecy and survivability of the SMF's launching units.

The next level below the brigade is the launching battalion. Each brigade is made up of a number of battalions that are equipped with different types of missiles.[51] Normally, a battalion possesses one strategic missile carrier, or several tactical missile systems. It consists of several companies, each of which has a specialised function. There are C^{3}I companies equipped with computerised satellite-based information systems and connected to the national communications network of the SMF; companies of launching units; logistical supply companies; security companies; and engineering companies. What makes a battalion in the SMF distinctive from one in other services is that over half of its officers have higher education qualifications. Therefore the battalions in the SMF are easily the best equipped, funded and educated basic units in the PLA, although they have to endure extremely harsh conditions that an army battalion would seldom encounter.

The relationship between the launching sites and launching units is an interesting one. Each brigade (and also each battalion) has its permanent 'home', but it is constantly on the move, except for those personnel who take care of the fixed silos for intercontinental missiles. As mentioned earlier, most launching brigades are required not only to familiarise themselves with all the launching sites within their own territories but also with the launching sites belonging to other regional commands. This is designed to increase their survivability in all types of difficult situations, such as tough transportation and field living conditions. These mobile brigades carry missiles of all ranges with them when they are travelling and they always remain in a posture of readiness.

The launching sites of the SMF can be classified into different categories: permanent silos for intercontinental missiles, pre-constructed launching sites (*yushezhendi*), potential launching sites and fake sites. The second type provides shelter for the mobile missile units. Although they do not permanently store strategic missiles, they are equipped with all the necessary C^{3}I systems and supplies. In fact, they represent an important link in China's nuclear guerrilla-war strategy, as they greatly enhance the mobility and response time of the missile units. The potential sites are not fully equipped as category-two launching sites as yet, but can be easily converted into real sites. Carefully chosen, they are difficult to detect from a distance. Since they are reserve sites, their construction is less than complete and they are visited less frequently. The whole set of sites with different grades of readiness has helped increase the secrecy of the SMF's launching activities, and has thus enhanced its second-strike capability.

Despite its advantages, the multi-layered structure has caused some problems in command, control and communication. According to one report by the SMF, access to the nuclear button is extremely restricted but the process of relaying a launching order is cumbersome. It comes down through the four levels through various departments (seven or eight) and usually takes several hours. The problem is particularly acute at the levels below the regional bases, whose C³I systems are still largely operated manually. This obsolete force structure and C³I system cannot fully incorporate modern information techniques and seriously hampers the rapid response capability of the SMF. This has led to a new round of restructuring in the SMF which is intended to remedy this fatal defect.[52]

THE POTENTIAL CAPABILITY OF THE SMF

It is very difficult to determine the real capability of the PLA's SMF. On the one hand, it comprises only a fraction of the size of the strategic missile forces of the US and Russia. Within the world's nuclear club, China has conducted the smallest number of test explosions and generated a relatively small volume of nuclear waste. The technology of its launching vehicles and warheads is still at least one generation behind that of the other nuclear powers. On the other hand, it has great resolve to modernise its nuclear arsenal, at the same time as other nuclear powers may have scaled down their nuclear programs. This could potentially help the PLA to catch up or at least narrow the gap with the other nuclear powers. Therefore, any analysis of China's nuclear capability should start with an analysis of its developmental potential. This book will concentrate on two crucial factors that lay the foundations for China's nuclear potential: nuclear warheads and carrier vehicles.

During the SMF's 'force consolidation' period, two priority construction programs ensured that the number of nuclear warheads and carriers was boosted, since they were seen as two critical factors for the SMF's survival. China conducted a series of nuclear

tests with large payloads in the 1970s and 1980s. It was reported
in the west that these tests were aimed at doubling the number
of warheads.[53] At the same time, the PLA visibly improved its
carrier capability. Driven by a sophisticated space program and
assisted by foreign technology, China's delivering capability can be
expected to increase even further (more on this in a later section).

The potential for producing nuclear warheads

Western estimates of the number of China's nuclear warheads vary
from a couple of hundred to over one thousand, but some recent
studies reveal a general tendency of underestimation in the west.
The lower end of estimates, 200, is certainly too low.[54] According
to a 1972 report by the US Defence Intelligence Agency, the PLA
may have had as many as 120 thermonuclear warheads and 260
fission nuclear weapons in the stockpile by 1972.[55] By another US
intelligence account, the number of China's nuclear warheads
exceeded France's in 1975 and the UK's in 1980. In 1989 the PLA
may already have accumulated over 1455 warheads.[56] A Rand
report also claims that by 2003 China will possess between 600
and 1500 nuclear warheads.[57] This higher end of estimates may be
as unrealistic as the lower end, especially if one thinks in terms
of warheads deliverable after first strike. One difficulty in confirming any of these estimates is the lack of reliable information about
China's capability to produce nuclear materials, such as U235 or
Pu239. Unless we reach some understanding of China's capabilities
in this respect, we will remain unable to achieve a sensible
assessment of the SMF's inventory of nuclear warheads.

The production of U235 and Pu239

China managed to produce enriched uranium for nuclear weapons
as early as the 1960s, but it took almost ten years for it to produce
quality nuclear fuels on a large scale. The Chinese constructed six
nuclear fuel plants in the 1960s and 1970s, all situated in north
and north-west China. The plants that first produced uranium
were Lanzhou (1962), and No. 1 (1969) and No. 2 (1975) Helanshan
Complex. The first two each had an annual production capacity
of 400 kilograms of enriched uranium. It is not known how many
kilograms of U235 the third plant could produce, but it is larger
and more advanced in technology. From this relatively inadequate
information we might infer that by 1991, probably the cut-off year
for China to produce nuclear materials for weapons, the first two
plants could have turned out over 25 tonnes of enriched uranium.

This quantity is enough to build over 1500 nuclear bombs with a yield more powerful than that dropped on Hiroshima by the US in 1945 (20 kilotons, using about 17 kilograms of nuclear fuel).[58]

China possesses several dozen nuclear reactors and the majority of them can produce plutonium (Pu239). The Yumen (Jiuquan) Atomic Engergy Complex (operational from 1966) in Gansu Province and the Baotou/Yibin Plants (1963) in the Inner Mongolian Autonomous Region were China's early fuel fabrication plants specialising in the production of Pu239. Until recent years, when they were converted to produce civilian nuclear fuel, they had been in continuous operation for the production of military nuclear fuel since the early 1960s. The Baotou Factory has two reactors. Each is under 100 MW with an annual yield of 40 kilograms. By the end of the 1980s, it may have produced over 1000 kilograms of fissile material. The two plutonium production lines at Yumen/Jiuquan possess reactors of over 600 MW and have an annual production capacity of 200 kilograms. Therefore their annual output is likely to be considerably larger than that of the Baotou Factory. According to one report, the Yumen reactors produced over 200 kilograms of Pu239 in the first year they became operational. Since then they may already have produced over 6000 kilograms. Some western analysts believe China has about 3.5 tonnes of plutonium in storage, which may expand its warhead stockpile to two or three times its present size.[59] Given the fact that an atomic bomb of 20 kilotons uses only 5 kilograms of Pu239, the Chinese could easily build another thousand nuclear warheads should they feel a need to do so. Indeed, China may have the potential capacity to build over 2000 nuclear warheads.[60] Therefore, this analysis of the Chinese production of fissile material suggests that China may be a lot more capable of constructing nuclear warheads than people have generally thought.

This issue can also be approached from another angle: the stockpiling of nuclear material. China has announced that it is no longer producing fissile material for nuclear weapons, and has no plan of resuming production in the future.[61] This suggests that China may already have a large stockpile on hand, which can satisfy the needs of its future nuclear weapons program. Some western specialists have arrived at estimates that China's stockpile could contain at least three tonnes of weapons-grade highly-enriched uranium and one tonne of separated plutonium, which would be large enough to add 200 nuclear weapons to its current arsenal. However, if China does sign a convention that prohibits production indefinitely, it may demonstrate a high level of confidence that future production will not be required.[62]

On the other hand, China's growing nuclear electricity industry will use an increasing amount of nuclear resources. Thermal power generates 75 per cent of China's electricity, and hydropower 24 per cent. China depends overwhelmingly on coal for generating thermal power, which is found mostly in north and north-west China. The demand for more electricity, however, comes largely from south and east China, where neither coal nor hydroelectric resources are adequate. This has made the development of nuclear power a very attractive option. In 1994 China's two nuclear plants, Qinshan and Dayawan, produced 13.05 billion KW/h, using about 60 tonnes of nuclear material. And in 1997 Chinese experts projected that nuclear power should meet at least 25 per cent of the country's electricity needs in the early decades of the next century. The growing demand for nuclear power may mean that the civilian power industries will increasingly compete with the PLA for nuclear resources in the years to come.[63]

The potential for producing carrier vehicles

When China forced itself into the international market of commercial satellite launches, the world was initially surprised by its achievements in the development of carrier technology. By the end of 1998 China has established a complete rocket family containing seven types of rockets in this Dongfang/Changzheng series: CZ–1D (payload 750 kg); CZ–2C (2800 kg); CZ–2E (9000 kg); CZ–3 (1450 kg); CZ–3A (2500 kg); CZ–3C/HO (5000 kg); CZ–4 (over 5000 kg). These missile carriers can serve a diverse range of launching purposes, as each of them is designed for launching satellites of different weight to different orbits. Among these rockets the Changzheng–2 series are earmarked for launching spacecraft into lower orbits, and it can send a satellite of up to 9000 kilograms into earth orbit. The Changzheng–3 series is capable of positioning spacecraft weighing up to five tonnes in high altitude orbits. According to one top Chinese aerospace engineer, these carriers have been close to the rocket families of Europe's ARIANE and the US's Delta in terms of weight-throwing power, the ratio between the rockets' length and perimeter, and their positioning accuracy. The Changzheng–4 series will be a great improvement on the Changzheng–2 and Changzheng–3.

Up to 1995 China could carry out only four or five launches of foreign or domestic commercial satellites a year, a fairly small number compared to the US, Russia and the EU. One reason for this was the lack of satellites to be launched, commercial or military. Moreover the launching of international commercial satellites requires a great deal of additional technological preparation. The small number of launches each year thus does not automatically mean that China does not have a large potential for building carrier vehicles. On the commercial side, China proclaims that it will achieve the capability for up to a dozen annual launches at the turn of the century. Even this is a relatively small number, which exposes the problem of facility insufficiencies: before 1997 China could use only two locations for launching international commercial satellites, one in Jiuqun, Gansu Province and another in Sichang, Sichuan Province. And very often the launches are constrained by the weather conditions in these places. There are a few more launching sites in north and north-east China that are not open to civilian use as yet. Discussions have been under way in the Party and the CMC for making some of them available for commercial launches.[64] In 1997 China opened another launching site for international commercial launches, namely, the Taiyuan Satellite Launching Centre in Shanxi Province. In March 1998 the Chengzheng–2C successfully sent two American satellites into earth orbit from this location. Moreover since 1997 China has increased its annual launches. In 1997 seven commercial launches were recorded, including four international ones. Eight launches have been scheduled for 1998. Gradually, it is approaching the target it has set for itself: about a dozen launches per annum around the turn of the century.

The fairly successful Changzheng missile family originated from China's strategic missile program *Dongfeng* (East Wind), which was initiated in the 1950s. The DF–5 and DF–4 were designated as China's main rockets for delivering intercontinental missiles. They could reach targets between 8000 and 13 000 kilometres away. The design of the three-staged DF–5 had already achieved impressive technological breakthroughs in the late 1960s:

1   large rocket engines (four 70-tonne thrust engines clustered for the first stage) using a new oxidiser of 100 per cent nitrogen tetroxide, swivelling engines on the first stage and vernier combustion chambers on the second stage for the missile's altitude control;

2   a gyro-stabilised platform and on-board computer for flight control;

3   a large body of difficult-to-weld aluminium-copper alloy.[65]

Its 3.35 metre diameter was larger than that of the similar US Titan II. Although this reflected a degree of its backwardness in technology, the fact that the Chinese mastered a highly demanding task showed their potential capability.[66]

According to some unconfirmed Chinese sources, China has been able to assemble over a dozen launching vehicles for ICBMs per year since the 1980s. Adding up this figure on a continuing basis, China might theoretically have put together about 200 intercontinental missiles by now if it had chosen to do so.[67] The Chinese claim that they will be able to launch over a dozen commercial satellites by the turn of the century suggests that the assembly of vehicles for long-range missiles has become a mature technology for the PLA. One vivid example is that less than a month after China's two full-range test flights into the Pacific on 18 and 21 May 1980, the new ICBMs were delivered to the SMF for 'operational training'. And in December of the same year, they were assigned to 'trial operational deployment' in experimental silos.[68] Another example is that after the first failed launch of the second Australian communication satellite on 22 March 1992, 27 000 people in the Chinese Academy of Aerospace Technology worked frenetically to construct another carrier vehicle for the second launch scheduled within 100 days and the second launch was successful.[69] These examples have testified that China does have the capability to put the desirable number of missiles in its inventory. According to *SIPRI Yearbook* and *The Military Balance* compiled annually by IISS, the number of DF–4s and DF–5s has remained virtually unchanged since the 1980s. But according to a detailed book on the SMF, at least one brigade, probably more, upgraded its equipment at the turn of this decade from medium-range missiles to intercontinental missiles.[70] It appears again that either the estimates of western analysts are a bit too conservative or the Chinese do not feel urgently compelled to increase the number of their intercontinental missiles. Another possibility is that the number of silos has remained unchanged, but that some ICBMs which have been deployed in deep caves are unaccounted for.

NEW MODERNISATION PROGRAMS

The modernisation of the SMF has speeded up since the PLA reoriented its national defence strategy and R&D toward becoming a high-tech power in 1992. One very realistic but unpleasant prospect for the SMF to face in the near future is that the rapid high-tech advance of the major powers may help translate a star wars initiative from imagination into reality. Once an effective missile defence system, both strategic and theatre, is established, the bulk of China's nuclear arsenal may be rendered impotent. The PLA has no other choice but to improve its strategic missile force in terms of survivability, penetrability and accuracy. This underlies China's tenacious efforts to continue with its nuclear test program until the last minute.

Nuclear tests and new generation warheads

The key to smooth progress in China's second generation of strategic missiles is the deployment of smaller and lighter nuclear warheads. Theoretically, China has mastered the required MIRV technology, but the practical difficulties in building sufficiently small warheads have been obstacles to deployment. The smaller throw weight of China's solid-propellant missiles also represents a stumbling block for the JL–2 submarine-based missiles. Compared with the first generation of nuclear warheads, designs for the second are considerably smaller. For instance, the warheads for the DF–31 and HL–2 weigh about 700 kilograms compared to the DF–4's 1500 kilograms. The payload for the DF–41 is about 800 kilograms, 2400 kilograms less than the comparable first-generation ICBM, the DF–5. If China really wants to deploy MIRVs, it has to further lighten the payload.

The modernisation of China's nuclear arsenal requires the PLA to improve the yield-to-weight ratio and to find a configuration that satisfies both missile weights and volume restrictions. This cannot be done without a series of nuclear tests. The series of nuclear tests up to 1996 served as proof that the SMF was designing a new generation of warheads for ICBMs and IRBMs. In the post–Cold War era China was the last member of the nuclear club to terminate nuclear tests. Before China formally ratified the Comprehensive Test Ban Treaty (CTBT) in 1996 it rushed through a series of nuclear tests that were regarded as essential for the miniaturisation of warheads, especially for submarine-launched missiles. For instance, on 21 May 1992, China ignited its largest ever underground nuclear test with a yield of one megaton. This was 70 times the size of the bomb dropped on Hiroshima in 1945 and considerably exceeded the US's self-imposed test limit of 150 kilotons. Some western analysts believed that this test was designed to develop a new generation of nuclear warheads that can be delivered by China's long-range missiles aimed at the US.[71] Although China has conducted the smallest number of nuclear tests of the five nuclear powers, its backwardness in nuclear technology dictates it has to continue such tests as part of a catch-up strategy. In the last four decades China has tested at least fifteen distinct warhead types—four with yields of less than 20 KT, four with yields between 20 and 150 KT, and seven with yields beyond 150 KT (up to 4000 KT). But because China has conducted fewer than 40 nuclear tests, it is reasonable to infer that the warhead types derive from a small family of basic designs, that only a fraction of the warhead types has been developed for practical usage, and that still fewer warheads have been deployed.[72]

Upgrading carrier vehicles

New models of carrier vehicles are now being introduced to the launching units of the SMF, including the DF–31 and DF–41 for land-based launching platforms and Hailong–2 (HL–2) for sea-based launching platforms. These prototypes are more reliable, easy-to-handle, solid-fuel ballistic missiles. Launch preparation times will thus be meaningfully reduced. The DF–31 is an intercontinental missile with a range over 8000 kilometres, which effectively brings Alaska, Hawaii, and the Pacific Northwest as far as San Francisco within its reach. The SMF will store the mobile DF–31 in caves during peacetime and in training, and in crisis situations will move it on a triple-purpose truck to pre-selected launching sites for rapid launching. Its flight tests were completed in 1995 and it is believed to be close to series production. This means that the SMF will begin to replace its liquid-propellant DF–4s soon and complete the replacement early next century.

At the same time, design and development is under way for an even more advanced second-generation nuclear weapon, the DF–41 mobile, three-stage solid-propellant intercontinental ballistic missile. Its basing mode is still unknown at this stage. With a range of 12 000 kilometres, it can reach almost anywhere in the world. As the largest missile in the SMF's inventory, this system will replace the DF–5A missiles in the first decade of the next century.[73] Once deployed, the missile will represent a leap forward for China's war-fighting deterrence strategy. There have been reports that the Chinese are incorporating advanced Russian rocket technology into the design of the DF–41. For instance, China is learning how to improve cryogenic rocket engines from Russian technology associated with the Kosmos, Tsyklon, and heavy-lift

Zenit rockets, and indirectly the technology associated with the SS–18/19 ICBMs.[74]

The navy will install the HL–2 on its second-generation nuclear submarines (09–4 class). It is reported that the first ship in this class has been sailing since 1994 on an experimental basis. Series production may be well under way, although this is difficult to confirm.[75] The HL–2, a sea-based version of the DF–31, is a huge improvement on the HL–1, currently in service. Its range, between 6000 and 8000 kilometres, is three or four times the range of the HL–1. More importantly, this new missile will substantially reduce the onus on the PLA Navy vessels to approach targets far away from the mainland.[76] Confronting very sophisticated anti-submarine warfare measures of the Americans, there is little chance for the PLA's nuclear submarine safely to reach within 2000 kilometres of the US continent to launch nuclear missiles against targets within US territories.

Currently, about 14 per cent of China's strategic missiles can reach North America. In the long run, the PLA will proportionally augment this percentage as a key goal of development. According to one PLA calculation, if this ratio can be raised to 70 per cent, it will effectively strengthen China's national security vis-a-vis western powers. Therefore, the first readjustment of the SMF's force structure concerns the increase of longer-range missiles in comparison with short-range missiles.[77]

Improving targeting accuracy

One current priority in the SMF's modernisation program is to improve the precision of missile targeting. The guidance and flight control system has long been a serious technological barrier for the SMF in its attempts to raise its battlefield readiness. Using a fairly crude inertial guidance system, the circular error probability (CEP) of the DF–4 and the DF–5 is about 1.5 kilometres and 2 kilometres respectively, according to Chinese and western experts on Chinese missiles.[78] Their improved versions, the DF–5As, have brought the radius of the circle to within 1 kilometre. Within this relatively small scope of CEP a nuclear or biological warhead may destroy or at least disable even a reinforced military target. The Chinese have tried, with some success, to employ stellar-aided guidance and terrain-matching terminal guidance systems. However, this is still far from good enough for battlefield tactical purposes. Pinpoint first-strike capability is now regarded as necessary to make even minimum deterrence work in the high-tech era. Consequently, a more sophisticated computerised measuring and control system has been installed in the SMF's long-range and intercontinental missiles in recent years. According to US specialist Richard Fisher of the Heritage Foundation, the updated global positioning system (GPS) technology has been incorporated into the SMF's missile guidance system. He also learned from Chinese missile engineers that China is experimenting with a new radar-based terminal guidance system, which is similar to that employed on the highly accurate US Pershing II. Potentially, this may give the Chinese missiles an accuracy in the 50-metre CEP range.[79] An article in *The PLA Daily* reported that all launching units in the SMF were ordered to place the improvement of CEP at the top of their agenda in training. Using the latest technology available to the SMF, some brigades were able to improve the CEP by 45 per cent.[80] A sophisticated simulation system which the SMF has developed in recent years, named the Supporting System for Assessing the Launching and Flight Control of ICBMs, can display on a monitor screen the whole process of missile flight control and terminal guidance. With the advance information provided by this system, SMF units achieved an unprecedented level of precision in a live missile test in mid-1997.[81]

There have been other modernisation efforts that are transforming the SMF from a 'hiding' power to a 'fighting' power. By the year 2000, for instance, all DF–4 and DF–5 ICBMs will be placed in new-generation launching silos. Most DF–3 IRBMs have been converted to solid fuel use, which will substantially reduce the preparation time for launches. Early warning, anti-missile-attack and space monitoring systems are being upgraded to improve the SMF's readiness for crisis situations.[82] It is rumoured that a defence satellite network will be established within the next decade or so. This will not only speed up rapid response time and the general effectiveness of the SMF's C³I systems but also improve the reconnaissance, multi-targeting, and final stage guidance for the strategic missiles that are launched.

In order to catch up to the technology of third-generation nuclear weapons of the other nuclear powers, the SMF has identified a number of areas for improvement:

1   To improve the security of nuclear weapons by expanding the coverage of the protective membrane and permissive action link to the entire stockpile.
2   To improve the effectiveness of nuclear weapons through the development and presumably the deployment of an earth-penetrating strategic warhead to target deep-underground

hardened shelters. Even earth penetration of a few metres will substantially increase the effectiveness of the thermonuclear weapon by coupling the energy output with ground shock, thus increasing the depth to which a warhead of a given yield can destroy an underground silo.

3   To improve the effectiveness of nuclear warheads by using the X-ray laser, enhanced electromagnetic pulse production, intense particle beams, and low-yield weapons for accelerating large numbers of small pellets as a type of nuclear howitzer.

4   To improve the accuracy of a new generation ballistic-missile system that can combine the missile's final stage (the bus) and its guidance system with a single warhead, and carry it to re-entry. Alternatively, such buses could be used in multiple warhead systems to allow near-instantaneous deployment of warheads from the missile.[83]

In the 1990s and beyond, the SMF will continue to give priority to two traditional missions: to maximise its survivability and to improve its reach and launching accuracy. More emphasis will probably be accorded to the latter. As regards the former, the PLA will gradually stabilise the number of its permanent launching silos that currently house liquid-fuel intercontinental missiles. In the meantime, research will be intensified to upgrade the current solid-fuel propelled missiles so as to make them truly mobile rather than merely movable. The SMF is pressured by the potential enemy's powerful reconnaissance capability (land-, sea- and space-based equipment) and high strike accuracy. According to the researchers in the SMF, China should make technological breakthroughs in the following areas in order to improve its survivability: simulation capability in the areas of electronics and sound; early warning networks at the national level, the war zone level, and the level of missile bases; interception capability of the Chinese air and missile defence system, which should be integrated with similar systems of the other services in the strategic war zones; hardening of launching facilities; penetration and neutralisation of the enhanced missile defence systems of the major powers, which can intercept and electronically disrupt the Chinese missiles; and reconnaissance and target selection.[84]

The PLA will press ahead with its nuclear weapons program, despite opposition from the west and some Asian countries. To the PLA, the need to enhance the SMF is based on the fact that the PLA's conventional weaponry is too backward to serve as a meaningful deterrent to the major powers. The strengthened second-strike capability may provide the PLA with a level of confidence no other weapons can, despite the fact that the PLA's nuclear arsenal is at least one generation behind the major powers. The development of nuclear weapons is also relatively cheap compared to efforts to achieve a similar level of deterrence based on developing high-tech conventional weapons systems. All this indicates that the PLA will continue to build up its nuclear inventory rather than scale it down.

5

The build-up of an offensive air force

Modern technology has fundamentally altered the way modern warfare is conducted. Among all the changes the most visible is the changing function of air power, as demonstrated by the Gulf War. This new development has speeded up the PLA Air Force's transition from its traditional subordinate role in China's armed forces. Now the PLAAF is entrusted with a much wider range of missions than before, from supporting ground force units in their tactical actions to launching independent air campaigns and to projecting power far from home.[1] These new demands have motivated it to achieve the status of an independent strategic force. However, the Chinese air force is still the weakest service in the PLA. Most of its aircraft are two generations behind the technological level of major western military powers. Therefore, the PLAAF has been given developmental priority over the other services.[2] One direct outcome of this special treatment can be seen in the acquisition of air force hardware, which has taken a dominant proportion of China's arms purchases from the international market. In other words, the PLAAF is the major beneficiary of the PLA's shift toward a high-tech oriented defence strategy. This chapter is an attempt to analyse the changes in the PLAAF due to its recent modernisation efforts.

The hardware modernisation has been paralleled by a drive for 'software improvement' which, in the PLAAF's terminology, refers to a better force structure, a better personnel education and a better training program. Since the three-stage pilot education system was established in the 1980s (flying academy, training base, operational units), all the pilots in the PLAAF have acquired university qualifications and all the aviation unit commanders including the air force commander-in-chief can pilot aircraft.[3] And since the PLA's comprehensive training reform was carried out in 1993, the air force has tailored its training program to the scenarios of a high-tech war: it is more target-specific, close to combat situations and integrated into united exercises with other services. More concretely, training for strike and very low altitude flying has increased substantially and night exercises have become a must for all PLAAF units. According to PLA sources, most aviation units have over-fulfilled the annual flying requirement of 122.25 hours.[4] Some elite flying regiments (*jialeituan*) in certain war zones have approached a record-high 200 hours in implementing the *PLAAF's training guideline for united campaigns*. Even the cadets in the PLA Flying Academies have to increase their hours in the air. A cadet now normally flies 200 to 300 hours in his three years of training. This is in sharp contrast with the 1980s, when a cadet could only fly a few dozen hours.[5] The traditional pattern of 'closed door training' (single service training) has been remedied through joint training with the army, the navy, and the SMF.[6] One particular theme in the training reform has been the change in emphasis from defensive to offensive missions. This was the central design of the largest live ammunition exercise the PLAAF ever staged, in north-west China in September 1996, which was a follow-up to the war games close to the Taiwan Strait in March of the same year.[7] By the mid-1990s the PLAAF had achieved visible improvement in 'software' development, even though it was still left far behind the other major powers in terms of 'hardware modernisation'.

THE PLAAF COMMAND AND CONTROL STRUCTURE

With over 470 000 officers and men and about 5000 aircraft, the PLAAF is one of the largest in the world. Its basic structure can be analysed from two different angles: administrative structure and combat force structure. The former describes the chain of command organised top-down into five layers: the central headquarters (*junwei kongjun*), the Military Area Air Force Command (*junqu kongjun*), air corps/command outposts (*zhihuisuo*), divisions and brigades, and basic operational units (regiments). The latter comprise three main service arms (*bingzhong*) in the air force: aviation, air defence (AA guns and SAM missiles) and airborne forces. This book, while analysing briefly the administrative structure, will concentrate on the combat structure, within which each of the three elements has its own subdivisions. For instance, the aviation wing consists of four major divisions: interception, ground attack, bombardment and supporting units. Air defence troops assume three specialised missions: field air defence, air defence for strategic points, and air defence for cities and population centres. Airborne troops are being transformed into highly mobile, combined army corps that serve as central strategic fast response units. There are other types of branches in the combat structure, such as radar units, communications units and logistical units. Yet in the PLAAF's terminology they are regarded as supporting elements which service the combat units directly involved in action.[8] Before proceeding with more detailed analysis on these three major components, it is necessary to analyse first the recent restructuring of the PLAAF's command and control structure under the PLA's new high-tech defence strategy.

Located on Outer Fuxingmen Street, Beijing, the central headquarters of the PLAAF is under direct command of the CMC, and constitutes the highest executive organ of the Chinese Communist Party over the air force. Its principal missions include monitoring daily movements of air force units throughout the country, formulating the air force's strategic long-term development plans, directing the training programs of each air force regional command, coordinating intra-service cooperation between different departments and regions, and extra-service affairs with other services. One important task of the headquarters is to recommend personnel changes involving senior officers (above the divisional level) to the CMC and appoint them on the CMC's behalf. Composing and re-allocation of the air force budget is one of its crucial powers.

Within the central headquarters in Beijing there are four 'big departments': Headquarters Department (silingbu); Political Affairs Department (zhengzhibu); Logistics Department (houqinbu); and Aero-Engineering Department (hangkong gongchengbu) (see Figure 5.1).[9]

Each is one grade above the group army level in the PLA's bureaucratic ranking and carries general administrative affairs in the primary areas of operations, training, political affairs/personnel, logistics, and aircraft maintenance/R&D. Among these departments the Headquarters Department has the largest number of personnel and is responsible for keeping the PLAAF in good combat order. Headed by the chief of staff of the PLAAF, it has about a dozen second-grade divisions (erjibu) at the group army level. The most important of them include the departments of operations, training, educational institutions, electronic warfare and radar, military administrative affairs (junwubu), and AA and SAM command posts (gaopao zhihuibu). Each of these departments has

Figure 5.1 PLAAF headquarters administrative structure

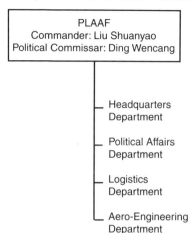

corresponding subordinate agencies in the regional bureaucracies and in operational units. In functional terms a tight network of administration and supervision is thus formed according to the responsibilities and specific tasks of the PLAAF.

The PLAAF has seven regional headquarters, each established under the seven military area commands of the PLA. These are called Military Area Air Force Command (MAAFC or *junqu kongjun*). This structure implies dual command and control over the regional air force units by the air force central command and the PLA's regional command. The design of such a command and control system reflects the missions of local air force units, which are oriented toward supporting the local ground force in its united campaigns. Therefore, in peacetime the PLA military area commands have heavy responsibility for monitoring both the training and maintenance of air force units stationed in the region. In wartime, local air force units are often put under direct command of the regional ground force headquarters and carry out supporting air attack and defence operations within major united campaigns sponsored by the MACs.

The next level in the administrative rank are the air force's regional command posts (*zhihuisuo*), which at an administrative level are equivalent to an air force corps, and which form an intermediate linkage of control between the central air force command in Beijing and local air force units. Currently nine such posts are established in Shanghai, Xian, Tangshan, Wulumuqi, Dalian, Wuhan, Kunming, Chengdu, and Lhasa. Most of these command posts were formerly the headquarters of air force corps. For instance, the Shanghai Command Post was transformed from the 4th Air Corps; Xian, the 11th Air Corps; Wulumuqi, the 9th Air Corps; Tangshan, the 6th Air Corps; and Dalian, the 3rd Air Corps.[10] Wuhan and Kunming Command Posts were formerly Wuhan and Kunming MAAFCs, which were downgraded when the two MACs were abolished. The initial purpose for the change was to reduce the command layers between Beijing and the divisional units, since these posts are regarded as the outpost commands for the air force headquarters but do not have a direct command relationship with the flying divisions until they are entrusted with such missions. They are generally charged with the tasks of maintaining military airports, deploying civil air defence and providing logistical supply to the units in their prescribed areas. Now their responsibility has been potentially enhanced. With the status of the air force elevated in the united campaigns, these outposts are supposed to form the basic command structure of air force units in a major battle direction of a war zone. In time of war they may be granted combat commanding duties over one or more air force corps and thus serve as the headquarters for the group air force corps (kongjun jituanjun).

It should be pointed out that not every province has such an outpost. Some provinces do not have heavy air force deployment, for example Qinghai Muslim Autonomous Region. The seven provinces that house the headquarters of the MAAFCs are saved from establishing a concurrent command post. For some localities where large numbers of air force basic units are located, however, these air force command posts maintain very heavy working agendas. For instance, until the tension along the Sino–Soviet border was eased in the late 1980s, the Air Force Wulumuqi Command Post (in the Xinjiang Uygur Autonomous Region) had the tremendous task of coordinating air force activities in the region.

Air force corps and divisions are the main units assuming operational (tactical) air defence and air strike campaigns at the war zone level. Before the restructuring of the air force in the early 1980s, there were 12 corps and 36 fighter divisions. In addition there were seven bomber divisions, six attack aircraft divisions and two transport aircraft divisions.[11] The round of restructuring in the 1980s saw the majority of air corps headquarters abolished. Five of them were transformed into regional air force commands, as mentioned above. Some were removed altogether, such as the 5th Air Corps in Hangzhou and the 2nd in Dandong. Now in those

Figure 5.2 PLAAF command and control structure

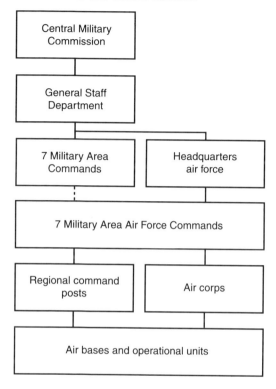

most important Military Area Air Force Commands, where more air force divisions are deployed than other MAAFCs, a few air corps headquarters are reserved to serve the purpose of concentrated command and control over their subordinate units, and they serve as the strategic combat units on duty in peacetime. For instance, as in the Beijing MAAFC, the 10th Air Corps is deployed in Datong; in the Nanjing MAAFC, the 8th in Fuzhou; and in the Shenyang MAAFC, the 1st in Changchun. During a war they carry out strategic air strike or defence missions as integrated units in a large-scale united campaign. On the other hand, the 7th Air Corps in Nanning has been retained because the Corps Headquarters fulfil the function of the Guangxi command outpost for the Guangzhou MAAFC, which is geographically fairly remote from the basic tactical units.[12] Now a new round of restructuring is under way. This time the air force corps that survived the previous round of restructuring may not be so lucky as to escape the merger with the regional air force commands, a measure to further trim the leading agencies in the PLA.[13]

In order to highlight the need for united campaigns, the PLAAF has been required to have a force administrative structure consistent with those of the ground force and the navy. This current command and control hierarchy is downward extended as follows: the General Staff Department under the CMC (the air force Headquarters and the naval headquarters); the seven Military Area Commands (the Area Air Force Commands and the navy's three fleets); group armies (the air force regional outposts/air force corps and the naval bases/sub-fleets); and the ground force divisions (the air force divisions and the naval specialised fleets or task units). In time of war this administrative structure can be quickly transformed into a three-layered unified command chain capable of conducting major air campaigns. In this chain the Area Air Force Commands and air force group corps form the first-grade commanding agency. It coordinates the actions by various air corps in the war zone. The air corps and air force command posts are the second level. They directly command the air strike and defence formations. The first-line command posts may be established at the levels of air corps, divisions or independent regiments.[14] See Figure 5.2 for the air force command and control structure.

THE PLA AIR FORCE'S WAR FIGHTING DOCTRINE

Since the late 1980s the PLAAF has undergone considerable reforms in terms of its combat doctrine, force structure and weapons programs. Changes in war-fighting guidelines have involved all these three areas of the air force modernisation. At the strategic level, as the PLAAF is urged to transform its traditionally defensive nature, the air force doctrine prescribes the fundamental principles of employing air power in a pro-offensive manner. At the operational level, the PLAAF is required to develop better offensive capabilities in air control, air strike and air defence. Tactically, proper use of specific weapons systems has been highlighted in order to accomplish specific missions. Never before has the PLAAF's role been formulated with such a level of clarity. For instance, at the operational level it is now regarded as the key link in fulfilling the CMC's strategic goal for joint operations and theatre campaigns. At the tactical level, standard procedures are written for a given unit, for example a regiment, to conduct a formation strike against a target.

Transforming itself into an offensive force required the PLAAF to put forward a series of new air power concepts, which have absorbed the main features of the American air–land doctrine and other western military ideas. Prominent among these borrowed ideas is that of air deterrence, which is now deemed as even more practical and applicable in contemporary warfare than the concept of nuclear deterrence.[15] Another western concept that has influenced greatly the PLAAF's long-term development plan is that of beyond-vision air combat which is regarded as a key form of future air wars. As mentioned in Chapter 1, after a comprehensive review of the international armed conflicts in the 1980s, the PLA high command has realised that any future warfare would have to be multi-dimensional: land/sea, air and space. As a result, air superiority is so crucial that without it no strategic objectives of the PLA can be achieved in any of its future operations.[16]

The new thinking: the air force as an independent force

Given the backwardness of the Chinese air force, the PLA identifies air attack by a potential enemy as the gravest threat in its future involvement in high-tech wars, both total and limited. Chief Air Marshal Wang Hai, a former commander-in-chief of the PLAAF, has identified three factors in demonstrating how the development of new technology has changed the role of the air force in modern warfare: firepower, manoeuvrability and control of electronic means. In terms of firepower, he pointed out that the traditional role of the air force qualitatively changed in the US–Vietnam War as early as the 1970s. The US Air Force inflicted as much as 70 per cent of total casualties in the communist Vietnamese army, much more than the number killed on the ground. This probably set up the first precedent in the military history of world, and forced PLA generals to think hard of the plight of the PLA in similar situations. To them the largest obstacle for the PLA's organisation of large-scale united campaigns comes from the air. The multiplied payload, pin-point targeting and long-distance bombing of the enemy's aircraft would easily frustrate the movements of the PLA's ground troops. In contrast the PLAAF's air support capability is very weak, often leaving the ground force units unprotected from the air.[17]

Wang Hai is particularly concerned about the rapid troop mobility of China's potential opponents, which is made possible primarily by their airlift capability. He warned the PLA that the wide use of attack helicopters in foreign ground forces has multiplied their capability of breaking through opponents' defence lines. In a potential armed conflict, he continued to analyse, China's enemy could, thanks to superior airlift capability, concentrate massive airborne forces and drop them in China's strategic areas before the PLA even had time to respond. This 'time lag' would immediately put the Chinese ground force in a very difficult situation. To a large extent, the outcome of the war would have been decided before the ground forces of the two sides actually met on the battlefield.[18]

In the area of electronic warfare, aircraft are recognised as the best carriers of electronic warfare measures. According to PLA researchers, contemporary warfare is first of all electronic warfare to win control over information. Aircraft platforms for information and intelligence gathering can help to expose the enemy's strategic intentions and troop deployments and movements. The PLA has painfully realised that its traditional tactics of hiding movement in the darkness will no longer be viable since the enemy's electronic aircraft can easily find targets at night. If it does not acquire sophisticated means of electronic warfare, the PLAAF could not provide timely information for the organisation of united campaigns. The PLA will then become deaf and mute. To a considerable extent, acquisition of advanced platforms for information and intelligence is seen as a matter of life and death for China's armed forces.[19]

Wang Hai was among the first PLA top brass to recognise in the second half of the 1980s that application of information technology has revolutionised contemporary warfare. As mentioned in Chapter 1, the Gulf War further stimulated the new thinking of the PLAAF and helped lay the groundwork for the transition from conceptual change to practical change (as demonstrated by changes in war plans, force restructuring and deployment).[20] For instance, in the 1980s, the role of the PLAAF in the PLA's defence strategy was still that of weakening the enemy's effectiveness in an air offensive campaign, a role generally regarded as no more than supplementary. Now the air force has been elevated to the position of an independent combat force. An air war may have become an independent process without involvement of the other services, and it is so crucial that the outcome of the entire war may hinge on the war in the air.[21] Jiang Zemin and the CMC instructed the air force that it must dare to wage independent air strike campaigns as a means to secure victory in a war.[22]

The theory of offensive air campaigns

The ascenscion of the PLAAF to the status of an independent combat force, as required by the PLA's post-Deng defence strategy, has paved the way for a number of innovative concepts to emerge in the air force's campaign theories. To some extent, these new developments are also politically important because they reject the PLA's traditional emphasis on men rather than weapons and its emphasis on ground force battles over the role played by other specialised services.

Traditionally, the chief mission of the Chinese air force was defensive, largely confined to territorial defence. This was due mainly to the low level of its technology, which restricted its aircraft to a short flight radius (200–500 kilometres), dogs-of-war combat (short range combat), and reliance on interceptors (passive defence). With the application of high-tech in aircraft development, the offensive aspect of air power has been greatly highlighted. As a result, there has emerged a general consensus among China's top air force commanders that the PLAAF's strategy and tactics must be primarily offensive.[23]

This indicates that the PLAAF has accepted the idea of air strike in the enemy's defence depth as its primary mission. This is a visible departure from its traditional practice of engaging enemy aircraft at the front lines. In other words the PLAAF is learning to conduct major air battles far away from home. Therefore, it has substantially enlarged the size of air war zones to the extent that the distinction between the air defence front line and the in-depth strike zone becomes less clear. Seeing itself as an independent offensive service, the PLAAF has required its troops to prepare simultaneously for attack on strategic targets in the enemy's rear and for defence against the opponent's aircraft or missiles strikes from a long distance. Accordingly, medium- to long-distance air attack and defence have been emphasised in recent years as operations decisive to the establishment of air superiority. Moreover, the traditional focus on high-altitude intercepting has now been at least paralleled by low-altitude strike missions, and control over medium-altitude combat is seen as linking the two.

Since future air war is understood as a war of high technology and information, the result of the offensive campaigns will largely depend on the quality of the offensive aircraft and supporting aircraft. In contrast, the number of aircraft will relatively decrease in importance. The application of AWACs and medium- to long-range missiles can conveniently destroy a large number of aircraft of the weaker side beyond the vision of its pilots. Precision and guided missiles and smart bombs reduce the need for large bomber formations. Aircraft battle wings, both offensive and defensive, will thus become smaller. Moreover, the PLA's future offensive air operations will particularly depend on effective electronic warfare measures and countermeasures, as these are crucial for the survivability of its aircraft and for achieving air superiority over its opponents.[24]

To cater to the development of an offensive air force, the PLAAF has revised its campaign theories and combat principles. It has also established its own rapid response strategies, particularly for limited regional high-tech wars under different circumstances.[25] Behind these developments is the recognition of the functions of the air force in the new era: without control of the air nothing can be achieved in modern warfare. Similarly, without a long-range strike capability it is very difficult to achieve a minimum level of deterrence. This is especially essential for guaranteeing the country's maritime security.[26]

According to the PLAAF, the development of its offensive air force will proceed through several stages. As the PLAAF cannot expect to introduce enough aircraft of the third generation in the near future, its offensive capability will remain limited. So will its campaign objective, which during the next decade will be basically defensive in nature and confined to the task of weakening the enemy's offensive air capability. Most operations will be conducted within China's land borders. This self-imposed limit is necessary because without sufficient support from home bases any large-scale air operation would result in heavy losses. This limit also reflects the fact that the PLAAF is unable to secure air superiority over its potential adversaries for a fairly long time to come.[27] In the early decades of the 21st century, however, when the PLAAF deploys more third- or fourth-generation aircraft and receives more sophisticated C³I and early warning support, it will be able to project air power much more effectively. The PLAAF is well aware that only hardware modernisation will bridge the gap between the doctrinal design and application.

The following are some of the new features of the PLAAF's operational and tactical concepts.

1 Pre-emptive and surgical strike

The need for the PLA to conduct pre-emptive strikes lies in the fact that as the inferior side, once the initiative is lost, it is difficult for the PLA to recover and reposition itself to take the offensive. Therefore the PLA should not be prevented from making plans for pre-declared actions.[28] These actions include bombing the enemy's key political and military targets, such as nuclear missile sites, defence headquarters, telecommunications hubs and air bases, especially those for strategic bombers. As soon as a political decision is reached, the air force should, according to Lieutenant-General Cheng Shenxia, commander-in-chief of the PLAAF's Shengyang Area Command, attack first; otherwise the PLA will be left in a no-win situation.[29] One thing the PLA learned from the Gulf War was that if Iraq started to attack before the majority of Allied troops were in combat readiness, it would not have lost in such a shameful manner. The opportunity for pre-emptive strike is always available, since the enemy inevitably requires time to deploy to a forward position. Yet the opportunity is brief, given the awesome airlift capability of some potential opponents. When such an action becomes unavoidable, such as in the hypothetical case of Taiwan's independence declaration, the PLAAF will have to implement pre-emptive strikes to block the take-off of Taiwan's advanced aircraft. While recognising the difficulties in achieving this objective, bombing Taiwan's air bases can at least disrupt the sorties of its sophisticated jet fighters, and thus somewhat reduce pressure on the PLA's inferior planes. Such pre-emptive strikes will also help give PLA aircraft crucial time for a short-distance engagement in which numbers may compensate for technological weakness. In the final analysis, as argued by PLA strategists, the PLAAF must accept the principle of pre-emptive and decisive use of its forces. Under this principle it should make its front- and second-line units constantly in readiness so as to lay a solid foundation for a united campaign with the army and the navy.[30]

2 Securing air control in selected battle directions

Given the large gap between China's air power and that of its potential opponents, it is not possible for the PLAAF to obtain absolute air control in a major air war with a regional opponent if the war is conducted beyond a certain range. The PLAAF believes, however, that if it concentrates enough of its advanced aircraft and air defence weapons in a selected battle direction, it may achieve temporary tactical air superiority against even a major power and, in doing so, it would be able to win limited offensive air campaigns.[31] This is possible because post–Cold War international politics will not involve China in multiple war directions at the same time. Therefore, this allows the PLA to deploy its main attack capabilities in the war zone where actions are most likely to take place. Quoted below is one case analysis by a PLAAF officer:

> In future wars the air force must concentrate enough strength to neutralise airports or aircraft carriers in its front. For instance, an aircraft carrier battle group has strong defences that can be extended over 400 kilometres in five layers. To tackle this target the PLAAF should mobilise enough aircraft to launch a continuous strike, even at a high cost. It should also be supported by land-based, airborne and shipborne tactical missiles. In one battle direction the PLA is able to achieve limited air superiority if it makes coordinated efforts.[32]

Here the number of aircraft is a significant factor. For instance, by the PLAAF's calculation, if the enemy has 400 aircraft, the PLAAF will have to concentrate enough aircraft to outnumber the enemy's four to one. This should be done through regrouping the PLAAF's best aircraft located in different air force regional commands.[33] Again, it is interesting to note that this figure of 400 aircraft is the current force strength of Taiwan. And the idea of concentrating the PLAAF's best aircraft from its different regional commands is also important. At present the number of the PLA's first-line aircraft across the Taiwan Strait is fairly small due to the small number of military airports, now standing at thirteen. This scenario, therefore, also dictates a major redeployment of the PLAAF's best units.

However, concentration in strength may not be executed as easily as it sounds. Take Taiwan's case as an example. Each of the PLAAF's thirteen first-line airports, within 400 kilometres from Taiwan, can normally deploy one regiment, which has about 30–35 aircraft in its battle array. Therefore, there are only about 400–500 aircraft available for the first-wave attack. This number is too small in dealing with the advanced fighter jets in Taiwan. The offensive cannot be sustained over a given period of time. Even if more than one regiment is stationed in these airports, risking the danger of overcrowding, and doubles the figure cited above, there is another problem of limit in combat air scope over the key political and military targets in Taiwan. By the estimates of Taiwan air force generals, the air space limit restricts combat activities to 168 aircraft at any given time. Therefore, even if the PLAAF can concentrate a large number of aircraft, these cannot be employed in the way it theoretically designs.[34]

Another important factor is how to deploy enough strength for a credible first-strike capability. Traditionally, the PLAAF's defensive nature prescribed a principle of 'front light, rear heavy' to guide its deployment. This is the chief reason why the number of first-line airports targeting Taiwan is so small. This is now impeding the PLAAF's switch toward an offensive-oriented posture in some anticipated contingencies. Yet the PLAAF also opposes positioning too much strength in the front line, as its capabilities of early warning and air defence are weak. To overcome this contradiction the PLAAF has proposed new deployment plans. Under the precondition of no substantial increase in the number of front-line air bases, the PLAAF will have to adjust the types of its aircraft in the first ring in order to make it more offensive-oriented. This means more ground strike aircraft will be deployed in the front than before, supported by some interceptors and specialised aircraft. The main purpose is to pre-emptively destroy the enemy's jet fighters, early warning aircraft, and air defence hubs on the ground. At the second line there should be sufficient bomber and jet bomber regiments. Their deployment is decided by their specific missions in an offensive action. Due to the lack of air bases, coordination by fixed deployment on the ground and mobile deployment in the air is necessary. The overall posture should serve the ultimate objective of active air strike.[35]

3 In a united campaign with the army and navy

The PLAAF has been designated to play a key role in a united campaign with the army and navy in any future wars. Specifically, it assumes the missions of air reconnaissance, air control, bombing before and during the charge by the ground force, transporting troops and supplies, and airlift of casualties. Recently the PLAAF has particularly studied its role in a theatre (war zone) campaign participated in by a number of army groups and navy sub-fleets. The PLAAF has also formulated detailed campaign designs for likely borders wars and conflicts with different landscapes (countries). Moreover, it has planned for various kinds of smaller-scale actions, including how to employ the air force in a maritime operation 1000 kilometres away from home, the air force's role in a surgical strike against a terrorist state that damages China's vital interests, and the procedures of the air force in a tactical nuclear war.

One special project is planning the air force's missions in a large-scale landing operation involving 100 000 personnel or more, again with an action across the Taiwan Strait in mind. This is a strategic campaign joined by several army groups. At least one air force corps and a number of air defence divisions would be deployed. If necessary, a few airborne divisions would also join the campaign. The forces involved are organised into three formations. The first is the strike formation, intended to destroy prescribed enemy targets. It is composed mainly of bombers and ground strike divisions, plus some jet fighter regiments. The SMF's tactical missile units should be an important additional component of this formation. The second and third formations are deployed for the purpose of protection of the first. The second comprises jet fighter divisions and surface-to-air missile divisions. They provide not only a shield for the strike formation in the air, but also air defence for the major political and military targets on the mainland. The third formation is made up of specialised aircraft with duties such as electronic warfare, early warning and surveillance, and transportation.[36] Throughout the whole process they should keep close contact with the landing forces, as they assume specific tasks such as providing air cover for land forces boarding ships, navigation, landing and consolidation of landing platforms.[37]

In such a large-scale united campaign, the formation of the air wing should give more emphasis to attack aircraft. In the stage of establishing air control prior to landing operations, while 10–15 per cent of the aircraft should be used for providing air cover for shipping the troops, only 35–40 per cent of all aircraft should be employed in paralysing the enemy's air power by attacking its airfields and C^{3}I centres. In the stage of landing and consolidating landing platforms, at least 50 per cent of the sorties should be devoted to protecting the ground force landing units. During this stage, the air force provides crucial support for the PLA Navy to secure sea control, a precondition for shipping the landing troops. Bombing operations should be carried on throughout, although fighter jets play the decisive role of intercepting the enemy's aircraft, which is essential for the ground force to create and consolidate landing platforms at the third stage.[38]

RESTRUCTURING FOR AN OFFENSIVE AIR FORCE

Since the early 1990s the PLAAF's preparation for action has been characterised by three parallel initiatives: restructuring, enhanced training (mentioned at the beginning of the chapter) and hardware upgrading (see the next section), each of which is regarded as critical to the PLAAF's modernisation and readiness. So far no initiative has made the desired progress in meeting the demand of a high-tech air war, largely due to the fact that the PLAAF cannot provide enough advanced aircraft to make the transition from a defensive force to an offensive force. The long-term guideline for the three tasks is that the PLA should create an air force capable of conducting both a high-tech air warfare and of exerting credible deterrence against China's potential threats from the air; that is, it should be powerful enough not only to win a limited regional conflict but an all-out war; and that it should be effective both in its supporting role in a united campaign organised by a military area command and in an independent operation initiated directly by PLA headquarters.[39]

The PLAAF went through a deep restructuring in the mid-1980s in an effort to make it leaner. By 1988 its total personnel was cut back by one-fourth.[40] The on-going restructuring efforts of the PLAAF have been guided by one fundamental objective: transforming it into an independent and multi-role air force, in order to serve as a strategic arm of the PLA central command. The key to the multi-role force is to create an air force that should, according to its deputy commander-in-chief, Vice Admiral Jing Xueqin, transform its force structure from one that is mainly defensive to one that is a combination of credible defensive and offensive capabilities. As an offensive force it should perform not only its traditional missions of air attack and defence but also of space attack and defence. It should also develop nuclear and missile defence capabilities.[41] To be more concrete, the following restructuring measures are being implemented.

First, the whole air force should be divided into two parts: strategic and regional units. The former are placed directly under the control of the CMC (through the air force central command in Beijing) and should primarily be offensive-oriented, while the latter should be under the control of the seven military regions, assuming tactical missions. The priority in force development is accorded to the former, including funding, training, equipment and personnel allocation.[42]

The defensive nature of the PLAAF is reflected in the fact that it has disproportionately too many fighter divisions in the overall force structure. PLA analysts have noticed that since the late 1980s the former USSR reduced its fighter jets by 55 per cent, and the US by 24 per cent. They concluded that under high-tech conditions simple-function fighters could neither establish air superiority nor a level of deterrence. Therefore, the on-going restructuring aims at cuts in the number of fighters and the enhancement of the bomber/attack units. According to the first *Defence White Paper*, the PLA scrapped over 6000 old aircraft in the 1980s. J–5s and J–6s made

Figure 5.3 PLAAF fighter force projection

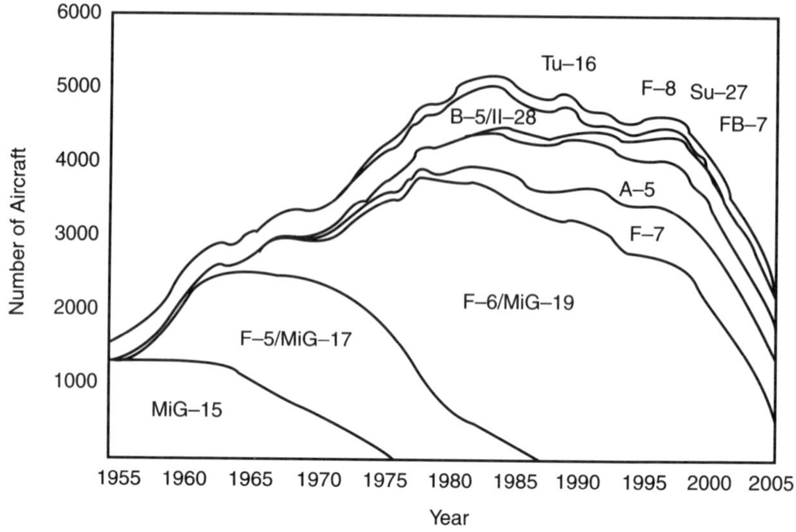

Source: Allen, Krumel and Pollack 1995.

up a large proportion of them.[43] And there is further room for scrapping fighter jets in the PLAAF.

Now the biggest challenge to the PLAAF is how to get rid of the ageing J–6s, which comprise over 50 per cent of the air force's fighter jets, and how soon. The PLAAF has proposed that the number of J–6s should be at least halved before the end of the 1990s, and gradually they should be phased out altogether in the first decade of the new century when reaching the end of their service life. This will profoundly affect the PLAAF's overall size and strength, cutting its entire inventory from 4297 in 1994 to about 2344 in the year 2005 (see Figure 5.3).

The number in 2005 may be even smaller, as China may stop producing the J–7s at the turn of the century. It is likely that the PLA will acquire more Su–27s than the 70 listed in the table through domestic production of the aircraft. Yet this will be unlikely to compensate for the loss of J–7s. As the J–8II is only a transitional aircraft and no new follow-up to it has been planned to enter the service in fairly large numbers, the pace of decommissioning the J–6s has to be slowed down to allow the PLAAF to maintain a force level of at least twenty fighter jet divisions.

As an alternative to removing the J–6s substantially in the

short run, the PLAAF put forward a restructuring plan of establishing combined divisions composed of jet fighters and attack aircraft in order to enhance the strike capability of the air force.[44] The restructuring resulted in mergers of a number of fighter and ground attack/bomber divisions. Therefore, some of the first-rate fighter divisions now have regiments of bombers and attack aircraft. For instance, some elite jet fighter divisions have two interceptor regiments and one ground strike aircraft regiment. Each of the interceptor regiments is equipped with 32 jet fighters, mainly J–7s and J–8IIs but with a small number of Su–27s and J–6s. The strike regiment is equipped with about 25 A–5s. In some cases a ground attack division can also be injected with fighter jet regiments. The PLAAF's elite divisions have already begun this experiment.[45] This mixed structure is aimed at creating an all-altitude defence/strike capability, with the Su–27s, the J–7s and the J–8IIs performing high–medium-altitude missions and the J–6s and the A–5s the low-altitude missions. Here the J–6s assume the mission of strike aircraft in relatively large formations, utilising their low-altitude and close-range combat capabilities.[46] In what is defined by the PLAAF as the *yijian daiqian* (using interceptors as attack aircraft) program, the J–6s and J–7s can have some extended life. Although both of them have limited radius in air combat, they are still regarded as suitable for large-scale air war above the Taiwan Strait because of the short distance the aircraft have to cover. In recent years these types of aircraft have been engaged in ground attack training.[47] This experimental effort has been designed to strengthen the offensive function of the jet fighter divisions at the tactical level. It is prescribed that following the principle of the *yijian daiqian* program strike capability should make up at least 40 per cent of the force structure's overall strength.[48] More concretely, this is designed to counter the air force formations of Taiwan. In a way the S–27s will be deployed against the Mirage–2000 for long-range and high-altitude strike missions; the J–8IIs against the F–16s for medium-range and medium-altitude missions; and the improved versions of J–6s and J–7s against the IDFs (the indigenous developed fighters) for short-range and low-altitude missions.

Second, the establishment of fast response units has been listed as a top priority in the new round of restructuring. These units include a few air force corps as the national strategic reserve force (*zhanlie yubeidui*); the elite fast response units (*zhanlie zhiban budui* or those units on 24-hour strategic duties); air defence corps that are entrusted with defence of sensitive areas; airborne corps;

perhaps in a decade or so, strategic transportation corps; and other special units such as the electronic warfare and early warning aircraft.[49] The need for these fast response units can be seen from the fact that until the second decade of the next century no Military Area Air Force Command except for Beijing will be able to organise independent air campaigns. In such an event it would need reinforcement by the centrally controlled national strategic reserve force. Therefore, all elite air force units in military regions may take the mission of supporting other MAAFCs in an emergency situation.[50] This endeavour of forging fast response units is now being pursued on the following three fronts:

1 Concentration of the troops which are responsible for strategic missions but are currently under separate regional commands. They are to be reorganised into an independent force. For instance, the PLAAF's medium bomber Hong–6s (Tu–16s) are designated as carriers of nuclear weapons, although they represent the weakest link in China's nuclear triad. The H–6s are, nevertheless, the only strategic aircraft available to the PLAAF for supporting united campaign operations with the PLA's ground force and the navy. H–6 units are now dispersed in several military regions, but the restructuring will see them concentrated within a single command and control system, similar in function to the US Strategic Air Command.[51]

2 Direct central command of the elite jet fighter units. These are highly mobile 'fist' units equipped with the PLA's best aircraft. They are to be deployed reasonably close to 'flash point' areas in order to assume the functions of deterrence and 'containment'. They should be exercised, however, in all potential major battle directions.[52] These units are centrally controlled but may be placed under the normal daily management of a war zone command. For the time being, there are no air defence units directly under the control of the headquarters of the MAAFCs. The most urgent restructuring task in this regard is, therefore, to create fast response air defence units at the war zone level, as suggested by senior PLA officers. Each war zone should organise at least one fast response air defence division vis-a-vis air defence brigades in the normal force structure, and each division should have regiments responsible for high-, middle- and low-altitude defence. It should be highly mobile and equipped mainly with the most advanced surface-to-air missiles in the PLA's arsenal.[53] They should also be

capable of getting airborne and arriving at any potential battle-field on short notice.

3   Strengthening the PLAAF with sufficient aircraft with specialised functions such as early warning and control, aerial refuelling, electronic warfare, large transport, surveillance and reconnaissance. One proposed ratio is that fighter jets consist of no more than 55 per cent of the total aircraft of the PLAAF (down from the current over 70 per cent), bomber/attack air-craft 35 per cent and others 10 per cent.[54] This proposal was tabled in the late 1980s. It is likely that the percentage of the simple-function interceptors is to be further reduced as a long-term developmental trend, while the specialised aircraft units are strengthened. Many PLA reports of the Gulf War noted that the percentage of supporting aircraft was larger than that of aircraft directly involved in the attack. This is under-stood as a key feature of modern high-tech warfare.[55] Moreover, preparation has been made for the establishment of 'arms of specialised functions' in the air force, for example a space force to deal with the increasingly intense threat from space and an independent anti-electronic warfare command in the PLAAF.[56] This need has been highlighted by the fact that two Chinese meteorological satellites suddenly became dysfunctional in early 1998. Although the real causes have not been made known, some sources say that the satellites did encounter a great deal of abnormal 'disruptions' from space.

As briefly mentioned earlier, restructuring and redeployment for future air wars require modification of the PLAAF's traditional 'light front, heavy rear' principle, which is meant to prevent unnecessary losses of planes if the enemy launches a surprise strike at the PLAAF's airfields. Under this guiding principle the PLAAF divides the battle area into three tiers, using the front line of enemy airfields as the baseline. The first tier extends to a radius of 500 kilometres from the baseline, the second another 500 kilometres, and the third extends beyond 1000 kilometres. This, however, creates a major problem for air force deployment, as most of China's military aircraft are deployed at least 200 kilometres away from the national borders. As a result the majority of China's aircraft do not have the capability to fly to the border from their home bases, loiter for any length of time, conduct an intercept, and return home again.[57]

This problem is especially serious in the major war direction across the Taiwan Strait. In the 500-kilometre radius on the mainland side, the first line is short of airfields, the airfields in the second are too sparsely located, and the airfields in the third are too distant. Therefore, while the force level in the first line is abnormally low, the limited space across the Strait restricts a high concentration of force strength, as mentioned previously. In order to overcome this difficulty, the PLAAF has formulated a new tactic: combining pre-deployment and mobile concentration. According to Senior Colonel Zhang Cangzhi, a senior researcher in the PLAAF's Commanding Academy in Beijing, pre-deployment refers to the principle for allocating forces for offensive air campaigns. Normally, the SAM and AA units should be pre-deployed to provide a shield for aviation units and the C^{3}I centres. Combat aviation units should be deployed in sequence: first fighters, then fighter bombers, and finally bombers. At the deployment stage the 'light front, heavy rear' principle is still applied, but immediately before the start of the campaign, transfer of 'fast response' and 'fist' units should be completed as quickly and secretly as possible. This moves the pre-deployment to the stage of mobile concentration. There will be little timelag between force concentration and the first attack. Units in transit form attack posture while in the air. Under a unified campaign plan, different types of aircraft enter the action from different directions and at different times. Some get into engagement directly after leaving their air bases. Others add fuel at the front-line airfields and take off immediately. With different echelons of formations thus planned and employed, the PLAAF's overall static superiority can be transformed into regional dynamic superiority.[58]

AIR DEFENCE

China's air defence system comprises five subsystems: the C^{3}I system (the headquarters at various levels), the early warning system (the radar and communications units), the interceptive system (the aviation wings), the logistical supply system and the civil defence system. Generally speaking, air defence is the most backward arm in the PLAAF. According to one PLA air defence expert, qualitatively China's air defence weaponry is two generations behind that of the major powers and the gap is now widening. In terms of the numbers of aircraft and anti-aircraft weaponry the PLAAF has deployed, China's territorial air defence is at least five times sparser than that of the former USSR, leaving large numbers of key political and military targets inadequately protected.[59] The lessons of the Gulf War also demonstrated the importance of air defence in the overall national defence. Gravely worried, CMC leaders have in recent years allocated large sums of funding for upgrading the air defence system, as seen from purchases of foreign hardware. High on the agenda is the R&D of a sophisticated missile defence system.[60]

Operational air defence concepts

The guiding principle of China's air defence for a long time was point defence, a form of passive defence that requires positioning of air defence weapons around sites in need of protection. Air defence weapons are separately deployed for defending their specific targets and do not function as an integrated system. Now the PLAAF has proposed a new kind of air defence theory, which can be termed 'large area defence' (quyu yanhu).[61] According to this concept, defence should be effectively extended to the whole area within which those points are located. Each point is just part of a whole network, and the weapons around it can be employed to support the defence of other points. Sometimes this enlarged area covers a region large enough for a theatre campaign. Each area as such is a major battle direction within a war zone. The PLAAF's early warning system is thus required to extend well into the enemy's territories. From there the multi-layered defence is divided into three lines: outer ring, medium ring and inner ring. The outer ring is mainly the responsibility of the jet fighters, which should stop a major proportion of intruders. The medium ring includes both aircraft and SAMs. The inner ring, composed of short-range SAMs and AA guns, is the last defence line for the key targets and must wipe out the remaining invaders.[62] This in-depth area defence dictates improvements in early warning, multi-layered interception and four-dimensional defence (underground, land, air and space), and therefore represents a kind of integrated defence with combined combat units from different services.[63]

Transforming air defence from passive to active defence is another new trend in the PLAAF's operational strategy. The PLAAF has recognised that with the greatly improved penetrating capability of fourth-generation aircraft, passive defence can no longer protect targets effectively. In a high-tech era, comprehensive measures are needed to combine different defence systems: interceptors, surface-to-air missiles, anti-air artillery, and civil construction to augment the survivability of the protected installations.[64] Among these, the first one is most preferred. Therefore, large-area air defence is closely linked to pre-emptive strike and long-range interception. Nothing would bolster air defence more than neutralisation of the enemy's air bases or aircraft carriers.[65]

An effective modern air defence must proceed from developing countermeasures to 'soft kill'. The PLAAF has raised the issue of anti-electronic warfare as the key link in a successful air defence. It believes a contemporary air defence system is based on high-tech-intensive electronic equipment. Air defence is first of all anti-electronic warfare. Without the means to deal with electronic bombardment, 80 per cent or more of military hardware can be rendered ineffective, and many vital facilities paralysed. The PLAAF has therefore broadened the concept of air defence from defending against the enemy's aircraft and missiles to include electronic warfare in the air. It believes that only when the PLA can defend itself against electronic warfare, which is the prelude to offensive air campaigns, can it win the real air war.[66]

The three missions in air defence

As mentioned earlier, the air defence force of the PLAAF is entrusted with three major missions: territory air defence (*guotu fangkong*); defence for key political, economic and military targets (*zhongdian fangkong*); and battlefield defence (*yezhan fangkong*). Therefore, the components of the PLAAF's air defence systems are structured accordingly. For territorial air defence, the main force is a combination of regular air force defence units and civil air defence networks. The regular air defence system is largely equipped with anti-aircraft artillery and surface-to-air missile batteries. The civil air defence system involves millions of militia personnel. The backbone of the system is the air force reserve AA units, which are organised into a division/regiment structure and commanded by active and reserve air force officers. These divisions are normally positioned around the major civil targets.

The key-points air defence and battlefield air defence systems are now undergoing a transition from relying on AA artillery to surface-to-air missile systems. For the key-points air defence, a national missile defence command centre has been set up at the headquarters of the PLAAF. It is linked to a national surveillance system composed of large numbers of early warning radars of all ranges.[67] On the eve of the PLA Founding Day in 1997, Chief Air Marshal Liu Shungyao, the PLAAF's new commander-in-chief, announced that China now has a complete air defence network composed of all types of surface-to-air missiles, including long-range missiles.[68] As the construction of the network is still at its initial stage, however, it suffers from, among other things, slow response time, normally taking a few hours to become fully operational nation-wide. The most heavily guarded city is the country's capital, Beijing. The first few SAM units were deployed around Beijing in the 1960s. In 1996–97 a special air defence missile division was established in the Beijing Military Area Air Force Command, and was equipped with China's latest types of SAMs. Its regiment/division force structure is quite unique. In contrast to most other air defence units, which are organised in brigade/battalion formation, its deployment follows the principle of grouping short-, medium- and long-range missiles together to build a three-ring network of interception. Soon after the division's new equipment became operational, General Zhang Zhen visited the division and watched its live ammunition exercises. He spoke highly of the division's readiness for action.[69]

Battlefield air defence is mainly the responsibility of the ground force anti-air defence brigades at the group army level, and battalions at the division/regiment level. One chief task of these ground force air defence units is to defend the infantry and tank troops against enemy helicopters. Normally, however, the group army's air defence is strengthened by the PLAAF's air defence units in the major combat directions. These units are mobile and equipped with surface-to-air missile batteries, most of which are short- and medium-altitude missiles. And they are better trained as well, specialising in battlefield air defence missions (for instance, in dealing with different types of aircraft).

Currently field air defence is based mainly on AA artillery guns and surface-to-air missiles, which are combined within air defence units in the PLA ground force. This mixture is designed to meet the needs of providing an air defence shield for the army units against enemy aircraft flying at both high and low altitudes. In their division of labour the surface-to-air missile systems mainly cope with fixed-wing medium-to-high-altitude aircraft, and the AA artillery is still considered effective against low-altitude aircraft, especially paratrooper transports and attack helicopters. This is the reason why a fairly large number of AA artilleries still remain in service in the PLA and are mixed with SAMs.[70] The most advanced type of these artilleries has been equipped with an effective fire control system which has substantially raised its rapid response capability. The PLA reportedly copied it from a similar system used by the Israeli armed forces. The system aims to reduce human losses through separation of personnel from the guns, relying on its computerised automation procedures. On the other hand, however, the pace of transition toward missile systems is accelerating. This will lead to decommissioning a large number of AA artillery currently in service. At the same time, more and more short-range air defence missile systems have been introduced, mainly for the purpose of dealing with tank-killer helicopters.

The territory and key-points air defence systems will increasingly move toward missile systems as well. The PLAAF began to build up SAM units in the early 1960s and now possesses over two dozen missile divisions/brigades. However, the quantity in personnel is compromised by the lack of quality in hardware. The bulk of the missiles are updated versions of Soviet prototypes of the 1950s and 1960s. Their reliability is questionable in the high-tech era. Even though the number of air defence units is large, the density of air-defence coverage is still limited. The big 'holes' in air defence have made strategic cities and military facilities extremely vulnerable to a 'Desert Storm' type air attack. This may be the major reason the PLA included the purchase of S300 surface-to-air missiles in the first Sino–Russian military deal.[71] S300PMU–1, the version the Chinese have bought, is said to be the world's most advanced surface-to-air interceptive missile system.

For the time being, the aspect of air defence most worrying to the PLA high command is battlefield air defence. The threat to PLAAF ground force units comes from two sources, attack aircraft and tactical missiles, but the former is the more serious danger. One senior PLA army officer calculated a battalion of 44 A–10 helicopters could fly five times a day and each helicopter could destroy one or two tanks on each sortie. This could wipe out one PLA tank division within a day. Furthermore, the air defence capability of the PLA's tank divisions is weak. All its air defence weapons put together could only cover one-tenth of the area into which its tanks are deployed. The protection is even weaker when the division is on the move. In addition to its low speed, the division's anti-aircraft guns and a small number of infantry surface-to-air missiles could only cope with a limited number of sorties flown by low-altitude aircraft. According to this analyst, the long-range guns of the division could reach targets no more than 27 kilometres away and its artillery battalion could merely cover a space of 1.4 square kilometres. One such division normally had no more than three air defence battalions, which could only be used to protect the command posts in the main battle direction.[72] At the group army level the situation is even worse. According to

Lieutenant-General Huang Xinsheng, former commander of the 27th Group Army, when the army is positioning for an offensive campaign, its troops cover an area of 40–60 kilometres in width and over 100 kilometres in length, a total of 5000 square kilometres.[73] The current anti-air weaponry available to a group army is grossly inadequate to provide protection for this large area. Lieutenant-General Li Jijun, deputy president of the PLA Academy of Military Science, estimates that, if a group army cannot destroy 24 per cent of the enemy's attacking aircraft, it cannot get through the battle zones. Even if it can, it may have suffered unbearable losses.[74] The PLA is trying to address this fatal weakness, as it constitutes a matter of life and death in any high-tech war. Among other things, more anti-air attack weaponry will be introduced to the ground force AA units and basic-level companies in the coming years. Moreover, when a group army is in forward movement, measures will be taken to make it sparsely deployed. The objective is to prevent the situations where in any given enemy air strikes one wing can simultaneously threaten more than one division/ regiment, or an enemy missile or bomb can damage more than one company.[75]

AIRBORNE TROOPS

Departing from most of the world's major military powers, which place airborne troops under the command of the ground force, the Chinese paratroop units belong to the PLAAF. Their campaign missions, according to the PLAAF's war regulations, include occupying strategic points in the enemy's rear, preventing its supporting forces from reaching the front, destroying its key communication hubs, and especially helping the PLA main offensive units to achieve their campaign objective.[76] At the moment the 15th Corps is the PLA's only airborne unit at the army level. Formerly an infantry army in Deng Xiaoping's Second Field Army, it obtained a special place in the PLA for its toughness in positional defence during the Shangganling defence campaign in the Korean War. In the 1960s Mao Zedong personally allowed it to maintain a force level of over 30 000 soldiers.[77]

In the PLA's 1985 restructuring its three divisions were reduced to three brigades, causing serious concern among PLA analysts who calculated that China's airborne force was only about a quarter of the US's in terms of its percentage of the armed forces. Many PLA analysts believe it should be substantially expanded to suit the changing nature of regional limited wars.[78] One of the PLA's recent efforts toward building up a high-tech military power has been the reinforcement of the 15th Corps, which was restored to its former army/division/regiment structure in 1992. Thus its overall force level may have been enlarged by 25 per cent.[79] Even so the PLA high command believes China's airborne troops are still far too small given that they constitute a key component of the national rapid response force. One proposed remedy is to establish additional airborne units in those military regions where war actions may be most likely to occur. The expansion plans were repeatedly discussed in the 1980s but did not eventuate. Largely this has been due to budget constraints. Now that the PLA has accepted the air–land strategy as the basic pattern of future wars, the enhancement of the PLAAF's airborne units has been given a renewed emphasis in the PLAAF's over-all force restructuring initiative.[80]

Pending creation of new airborne units in the PLAAF, efforts have been made to strengthen the 15th Corps through internal restructuring aimed at readjusting the proportion between its ordinary and specialised paratroopers. The duties of specialised paratroop units include communications and reconnaissance. They are especially supposed to engage in electronic, tank, missile and chemical warfare. In contrast, ordinary paratroopers are trained to carry out general supporting duties in a combined army campaign. In 1985 only 17 per cent of soldiers were specialised paratroopers. Now the percentage of the latter has been raised to 43 per cent, while the percentage of ordinary paratroopers dropped from 53 per cent to 23 per cent.[81] The purpose of increasing these specialised branches was to turn the corps into a combined force from just a mobile infantry. This will make it more capable of carrying out independent combat missions in high-tech limited wars. In the PLA's post-Deng war-fighting doctrine the status of the airborne troops has been elevated to that of a strategic force. Among other missions, it will be employed for power projection and deep strike manoeuvrability. This theory has to some extent broadened the original role of the corps.[82]

Doctrinal modernisation has elevated China's airborne troops to the role of the principal force employed for independent campaign missions in future wars. It is now accepted that the airborne troops should be used for pre-emptive attack on the enemy's key military targets in the rear in order to paralyse or disrupt its preparation for an offensive. Previously this was considered as a tactical campaign task. It may now be regarded as a strategic campaign involving large numbers of soldiers.[83] As a priority development force, the former commander of the corps, Major-General Li Yuliang, proposed that by the beginning of the next century, China be capable of paradropping 100 000 soldiers at one time. If this capability cannot be achieved that soon, he believed dropping 50 000 personnel at any given time would be the minimum needed to achieve its strategic missions. This 'fist force' could make a major difference in the outcome of a war.[84] Apparently this projection has a strong Taiwan overtone, for only an invasion of Taiwan would require such a massive paratroop operation.

Therefore, preparing for a major war means attaining the capability to paradrop at least at the divisional level. Moreover, the airborne concept is no longer restricted to parachuting, but includes the landing of troops through transport aircraft and helicopters in combat. Although the PLAAF is restricted in this area because of technological limits such as the short range of its helicopters, it has detailed procedures for landing one divisional airborne force in the enemy's rear. During an airlift the division should be flown in two or three routes, each separated by 30 kilometres and each in several formations such as the main combat force and supporting units. The main force should be divided into a number of echelons, each composed of no more than twenty aircraft. One battalion normally uses one landing zone; for the whole division six to ten of them should be predetermined. If it is a helicopter landing, there should be two to three landing platforms per battalion, each 300 × 200 metres.[85] The PLA has already planned for landing operations at the group army level in the early decades of the new century. It foresees revolutionary change in the form of airborne operations in the high-tech era, such as employing large numbers of giant ground strike helicopters that can transport soldiers as well as attack land targets.[86]

To elevate the 15th Corps to the status of a strategic force has been a departure from the PLA's traditional airborne force concept. The 15th Corps is now evaluating its role in united operations of different scales. As pointed out by its current commander Major-General Ma Diansheng, the application of information technology has created a five-dimension battleground. No single service can win a high-tech war. Therefore, the corps must train its officers and men about the strategic importance of their action in a future war.[87] When the airborne troops were basically considered as tactical in the past, their training programs followed those of small-scale commodore units, normally at or below regiment levels. This doctrinal deficiency was largely the result of the PLA's inadequate airlift capabilities. Conceptual and technical backwardness joined hands to deprive the PLA airborne force of any deterrence power. Since the late 1980s the PLAAF airborne troops have conducted a series of exercises in difficult locations to simulate campaigns in regional flashpoint conflicts. These included paradropping in the South China Sea (at the level of a brigade) and in the Himalayan mountain area (at the level of a division).[88] For the first time, however, these exercises were also designed to carry out strategic or campaign objectives, which demanded the level of paradropping increase from its normal scale of battalion to that of division. Each occasion involved over 100 aircraft. The 15th Corps claims to have acquired the capability of airdropping at one time with more than 10 000 soldiers with light tanks and self-propelled guns.[89] It is the most useful rapid response unit in the PLA for both internal and external missions. Therefore, it will continue to enjoy priority in funding and equipment allocations. This has been reflected in the PLA's purchase of a number of large transport planes from Russia. These planes, including the Il–76, will further enhance the corps' airlift capability for rapid reaction.

THE AIR FORCE'S NEW WEAPONS MODERNISATION PROGRAMS

Over the past four decades, China has built up a formidable research and production base for the aviation industry which employs 556 000 staff and workers. The number of personnel directly involved in aviation R&D is 120 000, making it one of the largest in the world.[90] China has developed or redesigned 27 types and 60 models of aircraft and constructed over 14 000 planes.[91] Since the 1970s, the development of new weapons systems for the air force has always been a priority in China's over-all military modernisation programs. On 5 July 1979 Deng Xiaoping personally decided that the air force should be the key area of investment in the country's aviation industry and should be the priority service over the ground force and the navy. He specifically singled out the attainment of air superiority as the strategic objective of the PLAAF's modernisation.[92] In the following year the air force formulated two weapons R&D programs for the next five and ten years, namely, *The R&D of Major Air Force Equipment During 1981–1985* and *The PLAAF's Ten-Year Development Program*. Both documents identified the R&D for new types of aircraft and surface-to-air missiles as top priorities. These new aircraft included the J–7III, J–8II, Yun–8, A–5, H–7 and their improved versions.[93]

Under these long-term development plans, China has made slow but steady progress in the modernisation of its military aviation industries. According to the report that was presented to the third national conference of China's aviation industries in December 1995, Admiral Liu Huaqing announced that between 1991 and 1995, Chinese defence industries conducted trial flights for ten types of various military aircraft, finalised designs for fourteen types, and thoroughly assessed and tested designs for seven types. In these five years 156 aircraft rolled off the production lines. A large number of these were transportation planes that would improve the PLAAF's airlift capability.[94] With financial inputs constantly augmented and more foreign assistance available, China's aviation industries may have entered the best period of its existence. It may be anticipated that the pace of development for new military aircraft will accelerate in the coming decades.

The guiding principle for new designs

The PLA's high-tech strategy has provided new impetus to the air force's hardware upgrading. The guiding principle for China's airpower build-up is now quality instead of quantity. Therefore, the PLAAF has been required to enhance the survivability, manoeuvrability and avionics capabilities for any aircraft currently in development. This is a visible departure from the past design emphasis on speed and altitude.[95] The new generation fighter jets have to fulfil the requirements of multi-functional air superiority, including sophisticated fire control systems, electronics, beyond-vision combat capabilities, and effective air–ground assault systems.[96]

In the late 1980s, the PLAAF formulated a new weapons program: *The research and development of the PLAAF's weaponry and equipment to the year 2000*. It contained six special reports covering R&D of new generation aircraft, air and missile defence and the upgrading of a number of existing weapons systems. The new aircraft and other major air force weapons systems include new fighter jets and bombers, such as the F–10, high- and medium-altitude surface-to-air missiles, powerful long-range early warning and control radar and sophisticated C³I systems. The program targeted the western technological level of the late 1980s and prescribed that the new weapons should become operational in the second half of the 1990s and remain combat effective through the beginning of the 21st century.

Since the adoption of the post-Deng military strategy a thorough review of the existing R&D programs has been carried out. This has given a greater push to the development of the weapons systems that the air force does not have at present but are essential in future high-tech air battles. The medium- and long-term development plans were reassessed against the specific technologies that China's potential opponents had already possessed or would soon possess. For instance, the operational capability requirement of the PLAAF's new jet fighter projects under development was re-evaluated against the F–16s and the M–2000s that would enter Taiwan's inventory in the late 1990s. This involved a series of technical analyses that dictated revisions of the basic standards for the aircraft, the number required, dates for delivery, and additional financial inputs. As a result some major weaponry projects were scrapped, such as the A–9 ground-attack aircraft which was supposed to replace the A–5 but was thought far short of high-tech power, while others have been stepped up, such as the early warning and surveillance aircraft. The central theme for the review is retrenchment: reducing the number of aircraft development projects but concentrating on a few key ones.[97]

The key technologies under development

A number of high-tech research projects are currently under way to address the PLAAF's serious transitional problems. Among 350 items of new equipment that were approved for intensive R&D and trial production in 1995, a large percentage was related to the aviation and aerospace industries.[98] Among various key projects the air force has specified three crucial technologies as most urgently needed in the short- to medium-term: airborne early warning and control systems (AWACS), inflight refuelling, and an anti-missile defence system.

AWACS

China's R&D for AWACS was launched as early as the 1960s. However, deployment has been delayed repeatedly due to many frustrated trials. Since the Gulf War the PLA has placed greater emphasis on the development of AWACS technology, which is now regarded as indispensable in winning a high-tech air war. A publication on high-tech military weapons systems, jointly edited by the PLA General Staff Department and the General Political

Department and issued free of charge to all senior PLA officers, says that the AWACS technology may raise China's air defence efficiency by 15–55 times, increase the interception rate by 35–150 per cent, and prevent the enemy's deep-strike sorties by 15–50 per cent. Therefore, a small number of AWACS may streamline a large number of ground-based radars which are not effective for detecting low-flying aircraft exploiting terrain masking and radar blind areas. Moreover, the number of aircraft deployed in the front line could also be reduced by a significant margin.[99] Driven by an unprecedented recognition of the role to be played by AWACs in future wars, the PLA has made enormous efforts to acquire AWACS technology, which are pursued simultaneously from two separate channels: domestic R&D and foreign purchase. For the former, a national leadership office has been set up in the air force headquarters in Beijing. It coordinates various sectors in the civilian aviation industries and military research institutes in developing the electronic kits that can be installed in the Y–8 military transport.[100]

There have been many reports regarding China's procurement of foreign AWACS technology. The Chinese purchase of UK Searchwater AEW systems (which will be mounted on the Y–8) and the Russian Il–76 Mainstay AWACS has repeatedly appeared in western newspapers and scholarly works.[101] Additionally, there is photographic evidence of an Il–76 carrying AWACS flying in China bearing the PLA's emblem.[102] Other sources also reveal that the Russians and Israelis are helping the PLA to develop anti-electronic warfare (AEW) technology. According to a recent report IAI Elta Electronics has signed a contract with the Chinese to install its Phalcon system (using solid phased-array technology) in the Il–76s. Some UK-sourced components will be incorporated into the package following a successful PLA mission to GEC Marconi in 1996. The whole project has been scheduled for 1998 and up to eight AEW aircraft will be assembled.[103] There seems to be little doubt that the PLAAF has by now acquired the basic AWACS technology. What remains to be seen is how soon it will become deployable and how well it is operated.

Aerial refuelling projects

Inflight refuelling is especially crucial for the PLAAF because of its current force deployment posture. The 'front light' principle in the past has, as mentioned earlier, restricted the numbers of first-line airports, which will require large-scale reinforcement from the rear in a major air war involving PLAAF group corps.

However, as most of China's aircraft fly within a very limited radius, the planes from the second and third echelon formations have to depend on refuelling in the air in order to assist front air battles in a timely manner. More importantly, since the PLAAF has been given offensive missions such as in-depth strike beyond its current area of air defence, inflight refuelling is the technology it has to have to achieve a meaningful level of deterrence.

Since the beginning of the 1990s analysts in the west have repeatedly reported that China has acquired aerial refuelling technology. Sources of kits included Iran's stocks purchased from the US by the Shah (Beech refuelling pods and bolt-on probes), Israel's Bedek Aviation, and some samples obtained from a UK firm.[104] The Chinese have also revealed many times that they have achieved breakthroughs in applying the technology to transform some of their aircraft into refuelling tankers. According to one book about the PLA's modernisation, the air force has converted a number of H–6s into refuelling tankers and adapted some J–8IIs as receivers. Numerous refuelling experiments have been conducted and most of these were successful. As a result, the radius of the J–8IIs has been expanded by a big margin. Despite the fact that the inflight refuelling technology can be made operational any time if the air force so chooses, the PLA high command has not been satisfied with the level of the technology, which was developed by the US in the 1960s. While the experiments have provided good practice for the PLA, it is still exploring improved technology via its own R&D.[105] On the other hand, the PLAAF already counts on refuelling its second-line interceptors to reach the front as part of its war preparation plans,[106] and its flying academies and 'top-gun' units have listed air refuelling as a compulsory item in their simulations and practical training.[107]

Surface-to-air missiles

China's development of SAM missiles can be traced to the 1960s, when it reversed the technology of the Soviet SA–2 into the Chinese Hongqi–1 (HQ–1), which was later modified into the HQ–2 with an enlarged range and the capability of engaging more than one target. The HQ–2 is guided by the SJ–202 radar, reportedly stolen from the USSR in the late 1960s. It is a large, liquid-fuelled missile.[108] China's indigenous SAM program also began in the 1960s and produced the HQ–61. Lack of target planes for shooting trials and sophistication of computerised radar control systems subsequently delayed completion of the project, and it was not until the end of the 1980s that the HQ–61 system became operational. The system has different versions deployable in mobile vehicles, in aircraft and in warships. The fire control system is fairly advanced. Each system uses target acquisition radar capable of identifying and tracking multiple targets. Its truck-mounted continuous-wave illuminating radar can provide semi-active homing and anti-jam guidance.

The Gulf War has shown the PLA high command the devastating effects of air and missile assaults. At stake is not only a country's political prestige and economic wellbeing but also its perceived survival. The pace of research for a new generation of SAMs and anti-missile systems has thus been accelerated. According to the PLAAF's Missile Technology Academy, the PLA has identified three 'big research directions' and ten specific technologies as high priorities for short- to medium-term R&D. The 'big three' concern anti-jamming, anti-stealth, and anti-radiation missile technologies. Among the ten key research projects are low-altitude capability, accuracy in locking and tailing the target, an effective explosive 'kill area', a simulation system for comprehensive surveillance and measuring of SAM missiles, and a simulation system for the SAM missile/aircraft engagement process.[109] The construction of a modern national air defence system, including a missile defence component, has also been stepped up. At the same time the PLA has been experimenting with using aircraft to shoot down long-range cruise missiles. The PLAN 'Sea Eagle Regiment' was reportedly successful in shooting down missiles with J–7IIIs.[110]

The short-range SAM systems, normally within a range of 15 kilometres, are mainly based on the HQ–61 and its improved versions, for example the HQ–62. The latest class of low-altitude surface-to-air missile, the BM–80, has just entered the PLAAF, although little is known about this class of missiles. According to PLA sources, the HQ–61 is a medium- and low-altitude, all-weather missile propelled by solid fuel and guided by a semi-active radar system.[111] Now the PLA is trying to use the HQ–61 as the trial prototype for developing a more sophisticated surface-to-air missile defence system, something similar to the US Patriot. Chinese researchers have made significant progress in their R&D. For instance, the missile has reached a speed four to six times that of sound and is controlled by a miniaturised super-computer system. Laser and infra-red end-guidance and electronic measures have been incorporated into the system. The technological co-operation between China and Russia in the missile R&D, and to a lesser extent between China and other countries such as Israel in the program of the Python, may have improved these crucial military technologies.¹¹² Moreover, the Chinese researchers have also devoted enormous efforts to developing various types of short-range portable SAMs for close-in air defence, especially for ground force field air defence. It was reported that when an unspecified type of short-range SAM was finalised in 1992, it achieved three technological breakthroughs, which normally refers to speed, guidance, and firepower.¹¹³

The PLAAF's current medium-range SAM systems are the HQ–2 and KS–1. The latter is a significant improvement over the latter, and was first unveiled in 1991. It is a large (900 kilograms), single-stage, solid-fuel command-guided missile with a maximum range of 42 kilometres.¹¹⁴ The fire control system for the KS–1 is an indigenously developed phased-array system with absorption of foreign technology.

China's efforts to develop long-range SAMs have not been very successful until recently. This constituted one of the reasons why the PLA negotiated hard with the Russians to acquire the SA–10b and SA–12. The former can reach a target at 90 kilometres and the latter at 150. It is not known whether the PLA has acquired these two versions in the S–300 series among the six batteries it purchased from Russia in 1993. A recent report has revealed, however, that China has successfully launched a high-tech long-range surface-to-air missile. It is indigenously developed and capable of chasing both high-altitude and low-altitude targets over an extended range. It is equipped with sophisticated electronic warfare measures, and more important, it has achieved a high level of stealth.¹¹⁵ Given its stealth and electronic warfare capability, the missile enables the PLAAF to attack the enemy's AWACS from a distance, which will be a primary target in time of war. And the technology can be easily applied to other types of missiles such as long-range cruise missiles and land-based anti-ship missiles.

Other key projects

There are other priority projects currently under intensive development. The R&D of the advanced avionics systems is one. Enormous efforts have been devoted to creating more advanced fire control and radar systems for the PLAAF's new generation aircraft and air defence systems. Among these are airborne or land-based phased-array, pulse-Doppler and millimetre-wave radar networks, satellite-guided navigation and positioning systems for air force attack weaponry, and electronic countermeasures in the air and missile defence systems. The R&D emphasis is particularly placed on the development of airborne platforms for these systems in the air force's Year 2000 program.[116]

Long-range transport aircraft is another priority area. Since the early 1980s, China has devoted tremendous efforts to developing the Yun–8, which is an improved version of the Russian An–12 and is similar to the American C–130 transport plane. This aircraft has now entered service and visibly elevated the PLAAF's airlift capability. The An–26, formerly the mainstay of the 15th Airborne Corps, can carry only up to one platoon of soldiers (about 36). The Yun–8 has increased this capacity to 86. By world standards, the cost of building such aircraft is very low, allowing the PLA to afford fairly large orders. The Yun–8's cargo capability of 20 tonnes is also a significant improvement on previous Chinese transport planes. With increased numbers of Yun–8s entering service, the rapid response capability of the PLA can be expected to increase. Almost at the same time the Yun–8 entered the service in the 1980s, a new project was launched to construct another type of large transport aircraft able to carry a cargo of over 30 tonnes.

The new project for multiple role fighter jets

Since the 1980s, China has implemented a program of retrofitting aircraft such as J–7IIIs and A–5s with new technology as a transitional measure. The goal is to multiply the capability of the PLAAF's existing aircraft through incorporating the west's advanced avionics and fire control systems. Yet none of these retrofitting programs has been successful in narrowing the gap with the third-generation aircraft of the western powers. In the early 1980s the PLAAF designated the modified version of the J–8, the J–8II, to be China's backbone jet fighter until more sophisticated aircraft could be developed. It even set up a high-powered office in its Beijing headquarters to coordinate the national effort in R&D of this fighter jet. According to PLA analysts, the J–8II is regarded as quite advanced, comparable to the F–16 in speed, altitude and manoeuvrability, and better than Taiwan's interceptor, the Jingguo (IDF). The average speed of the J–8II is 1300 km/hr and the maximum range 2200 kilometres. Its radius is 800 kilometres and can be extended considerably with aerial refuelling. It is equipped with the indigenously developed fire control systems which give it look-down shoot-down capability.

The J–8II is relatively weak, however, in avionics.[117] To address this defect China simultaneously carried out two upgrading programs. The main one was to modernise the aircraft's avionics through domestic R&D. This included a pulse-Doppler radar system that was capable of detecting and tracking at least five targets at the same time and providing active home guidance to short- and medium-range AA missiles.[118] In the 1980s these domestic efforts were supposed to be supported by a joint development plan with the US Grumman Corporation to install avionics-upgrade kits in the J–8IIs, the so-called 'peace pearl' program, which was worth over US$500 million. The Chinese, however, cancelled the deal in 1990. The initial Chinese hope was that acquiring western electronics would increase the relative capability of the PLAAF vis-a-vis the USSR. However, the US may have emerged as the PLA's chief potential adversary after 1989, and militarily it would be very dangerous for the PLAAF to use the US's second-hand technology, which amounted to exposing its soft underbelly to the enemy's punch in the event of a confrontation with the US Air Force. More importantly, after seriously studying the developmental trend of military aircraft, the CMC concluded that the PLAAF's future mainstay jet fighter had to be multi-functional, with the capabilities of beyond-vision interception, ground attack and superior dog-fight manoeuvrability. Furthermore it should have stealthy features and a high level of survivability in deep-strike missions. Apparently the J–8II could not meet these criteria. Therefore, as soon as the prototype plane was flown in 1984 and its finalisation was given central permission in 1987, doubts were raised as to whether it was desirable to pour in enormous national resources to develop a type of aircraft whose technology fell far behind that of its potential opponent. The CMC eventually decided in the early 1990s that the J–8II project would continue but only as a transitional aircraft.

This means that the J–8IIs will not be produced in large numbers. By some estimates, production by the Shenyang Aviation Corporation is maintained at a rate of only two aircraft each month in contrast to its monthly output of over 50 for J–6s in the past.[119] Sadly, after twenty years of intensive efforts, China's indigenous defence aircraft industries have failed to produce what is badly needed, and the 'transitional vacuum' in the PLAAF's hardware inventory will remain an acute problem at the beginning of the new century. To tackle this problem, since the 1990s the Chinese aviation industry has stepped up its efforts to produce a successor aircraft to the J–8II. There has been a lot of speculation that this new fighter, named the J–10, is being developed in the Chengdu Aviation Corporation with the help of all domestic aircraft producers and international technology. According to western analysts the plane's design has absorbed features analogous to those found in the F–16, and its appearance resembles the Israeli Lavi.[120] However, some Chinese sources revealed that it is much larger and heavier than the Lavi. It is an all-weather, all-altitude and multi-role aircraft with the capability for ground attack.[121] The prototype of the plane has been fully developed and the aircraft can reach initial operating capability in ten years.[122] On the other hand, even though the project has taken many features of the F–16 or other advanced aircraft, many of these will be 40 years old when the Chinese are able to make it operational in fairly large numbers in the first decade of the next century. It lacks crucial technologies found in fourth-generation aircraft, for example, stealth. At the end of the day, it is still questionable whether it is simply another transitional aircraft for the PLAAF, filling a gap left by the J–8II and the Su–27 (due to the latter's fairly small number in service).

Therefore, simultaneous to the J–10 program, the CMC has organised a national initiative to design a new military aircraft that can be used as the PLAAF's mainstay jet fighter in the early decades of the next century. According to the US Office of Naval Intelligence, China has launched a new aircraft project to produce a jet fighter with technology comparable to that of the superpower's fourth-generation aircraft. Nicknamed the XXJ fighter, the aircraft is large and stealthy. It can perform in multiple roles, including air combat at different ranges. By the ONI's estimate the aircraft can enter service with the PLAAF around 2015.[123]

The Russian connection

As mentioned earlier, the PLAAF is in a risky transition phase in that more and more old aircraft have to be de-commissioned but their replacements are not suitable for the wars designed in the minds of PLA generals. In this sense the sudden demise of the Cold War and the collapse of the PRC's most threatening enemy, the USSR, was fortuitous. The implications for China are profound: the need to equip the PLAAF with large numbers of advanced aircraft is no longer urgently biting, as the PLA need only to prepare for wars on much smaller scales. The former enemy has now turned out to be an indispensable source of supply of advanced military technology, something no less than a sudden windfall presented at China's door.

For the PLAAF, the availability of Russian air defence weapons is most welcome since they serve perfectly as a 'quick fix' to lessen the pressure of the 'transitional vacuum'. The 'quick fix' refers to an immediate partial solution to the PLAAF's zero stock of sophisticated aircraft against a background of its potential opponents in the region acquiring such aircraft. Although it cannot remedy the basic causes of the PLAAF's impotence in an all-out war, it offers the capacity for China to conduct a limited regional war, and it buys time for China's aviation development to gear up for an eventual take-off in the not too distant future. The quick fix is best understood from a number of air-defence-related foreign purchases, with the Su–27 as the best example.

The purchase of Russian Su–27 Flanker long-range fighter jets has been a topic keenly discussed among strategic analysts in the west and Asia since early 1991 because no other purchase could so quickly raise China's military aviation capability. The PLAAF has never before operated any heavy, long-range fighter jets of the third generation. The Su–27s are very powerful aircraft capable of various air superiority functions: long-range bomber escort, ground attack in depth, combat trainer, carrier-based interceptor, theatre bomber, electronic warfare jamming aircraft and future multi-role combat aircraft. Its powerful twin AL31F afterburning turbofans, each rated at 122.6 kilonewtons (kN), can provide a maximum speed of Mach 2.35 at height, and Mach 1.1 at sea level.[124] The aircraft's long range of 4000 kilometres, despite the lack of provision of external tanks or in-flight refuelling, is particularly useful for the PLAAF, whose duties have been extended to 2000 kilometres away from home. This was one of the reasons why the CMC finally preferred the Su–27 over the Mirage–29, although it had to pay a significantly higher price.

Second, the aircraft's sophisticated search and fire control radar systems are the best high-tech the PLA can acquire. Its Phazotron NO–01 'Slotback' coherent pulse-Doppler radar can provide multiple target searching at a range of 240 kilometres and tracking at a range of 170 kilometres. Its avionics package also includes an infra-red search and track (IRST) sensor with a range of 50 kilometres and a laser rangefinder with a range of 8 kilometres. These can be used with the radar switched off, conferring a degree of stealth as the target is approached. Its radar, IRST and rangefinder are integrated with display data on the pilot's head-up display and are slaved to his helmet-mounted target designator, enabling sensors and air-to-air missiles to be pointed at a target towards which the pilot turns his head, within an off-foresight angle of +60°.[125] The plane is equipped with a variety of missiles capable of attacking targets simultaneously in different directions.

Its six IR and radar-homing R–27 (AA–10 Alamo) missiles can reach a target over 70 kilometres away.

The first batch of 24 entered the PLAAF in 1994, and the total number of the planes purchased seems to have been fixed at 72.[126] The issue of quantity does make a difference in evaluating the outcome of the deal. Seventy-two aircraft, which form two regiments, may or may not alter China's defence posture qualitatively, depending on where they are located and against whom they are supposed to be used. Mixed with a number of supporting aircraft, 72 Su–27s may form the core of an entire division of the elite units in the PLAAF. It is certainly a considerable force in small-scale regional wars.

It was reported that a likely base for the aircraft is on Hainan Island, since the planes have to be stationed away from north and north-west China, the areas close to the Russian Far East, under the conditions of the sale.[127] However, there is little possibility of locating the aircraft on the island at this stage. It is against the PLAAF's principle of 'front light' in deploying strategic aircraft. Some sources reported that the first batch of 22 is stationed at the air force's Wuhu base, Anhui Province, and the second batch of 22 is in Suixi, Guangdong Province, with some unaccounted for.[128] The air force division in Wuhu has the best safety record in the PLAAF and it is the only division that is equipped entirely with China's best fighter aircraft, such as the J–7III and J–8II. In other words, the division is well qualified to be the CMC's national strategic reserve unit. Even though the planes have to be allocated far away from the Sino–Russian borders, they undertake flying exercises throughout the country. However, their location in eastern or south-eastern China will likely affect the military balance across the Taiwan Strait and in the South China Sea. This is logical because these two directions are currently designated as likely action spots.

The Su–27 deal included a joint production agreement between China and Russia. The commander-in-chief of the Russian air force announced in Moscow in February 1996 that the two sides had concluded the transfer deal which cost US$2 billion. The agreement prescribed that in addition to the technology transfer, Russia would provide parts, especially engines, for assembling a fairly large number of aircraft (about 200 over a ten-year period), plus training of Chinese pilots and servicing the aircraft already delivered.[129] What is not officially confirmed are details such as the exact quantity, the version of the plane, the weapons and avionics systems fitted to the plane, and what version China is allowed to assemble. The latest variant, the Su–27IB, has a strong air–surface attack capacity and has been earmarked for naval use. If China acquired this type, it would boost air coverage for its ocean-going fleet. If the deal includes a certain number of Su–27IBs that can be used on aircraft carriers, it will reduce the time required for China to develop its carrier aircraft, or at least provide useful clues for China's aircraft designers. What is clear is that China is so far the only country outside Russia that has acquired Su–27s. In fact the Russians have upgraded the technology of the exported version of the Su–27. For instance, a major shortcoming of the aircraft is that its radar systems can track ten targets simultaneously but engage only one at a time. The upgraded version for export has doubled this. In fact such an emphasis on export has led to a departure from a long Russian tradition of not selling weapons systems with technology that is not yet available to their own service.[130]

The long-term significance of this transfer deal lies in China's acquisition of a fairly large number of third-generation warplanes under production licence from Russia. Since 1996 tremendous national efforts have been coordinated to lay the groundwork for local production of the Su–27s, including the establishment of a national leadership office. Admiral Liu Huaqing has taken personal charge of the project. In order to assemble these planes as soon as possible, he has instructed all the factories in the Chinese General Corporation of Aviation Industries to contribute their best personnel and equipment to the initiative. In 1995 and 1996 he visited all of the major aircraft producers more than once and issued strict orders to these producers to fulfil the CMC plan that the initial assembly should be achieved before the end of the Ninth Five-Year Plan period and the series production in the Tenth. Although technology reversing is challenging, the prospect of this alone will influence the war planners of countries in the region. Given China's previous rich experience in reversing Soviet aviation technology and active Russian support, Liu's prescribed time framework for series production should not be taken lightly. A senior western defence analyst pointed out that the first Su–27 could be produced as early as 1999.[131] One Chinese aviation expert also estimates that mass production can be expected in the next decade.

The PLAAF can significantly benefit from the aircraft's weapons systems in three ways:

1   for the first time it can engage an over-the-horizon air battle. Without the Su–27s its own planes will only serve as targets for long-distance attacks, unable to counter-attack;

2   although the aircraft's ground attack role is weak, it still represents something significantly better than the PLAAF's current inventory, especially against a major target at sea;

3   the joint production of the Su–27s will elevate the PLA into a new frontier of aircraft design and production: China will have a lot to learn from the Su–27's advanced mechanics and avionics. The result may be a qualitative change in the whole concept of China's military aircraft R&D. For instance, under the Russian licence sold to China, the latter is acquiring unique technologies for manufacturing titanium structural elements, an essential feature of fourth-generation fighter aircraft.[132]

If the PLAAF indeed receives about 300 Su–27s (72 purchased plus 200 or more manufactured at home), in about ten years the PLAAF may take on a new look. Three hundred aircraft can well equip a reinforced air force group corps. In any limited regional war, it represents a significant platform for power projection. Although even then the PLAAF still would not represent any challenge to American air power in the Far East, the calculations of small and medium powers along the Chinese borders will be greatly affected. Once the PLA is able to deploy a fairly large number of Su–27s, China may have overcome its technical weakness in a major air war with Taiwan, whose security depends heavily on a technological edge. This will certainly increase military pressure on the island and compel it to seek more foreign weapons.[133] For Chinese military planners, the acquisition of the Su–27 serves well their strategic purpose of establishing an elite force as the 'fist' for limited, low-intensity regional flash point conflicts. This is probably the reason why a number of Asian countries used the deal to justify their search for advanced western and Russian aircraft.

Despite all this, as a quick-fix measure, the procurement of Su–27s can only modernise a very narrow part of the PLAAF's overall structure. In terms of overall capability, even if China is able to produce a fairly large number of the aircraft, the generally weak state of its inventory will continue to linger on in the early decades of the new century. From the western point of view the deal may mainly represent a generational patching up rather than a great leap forward in China's technological development.[134] Unless China is capable of producing its own fourth-generation warplanes, its fundamentally inferior position vis-a-vis the major air powers will not change decisively.

6

The ambition for a bluewater navy

The PLA Navy's modernisation has been slow, but gradually it has begun to produce visible results. The PLA recognises that in order to achieve a reliable defence depth the navy must be able keep the enemy's warships far beyond China's coastal waters. At the same time, to deal with maritime territorial conflicts that involve China and a number of its neighbouring countries, the PLA Navy (PLAN) must be capable of projecting power into oceans far from the continent. Gradually, this recognition evolved into a complete set of new naval theories, including bluewater combat tactics, bluewater weapons programs, and above all a sea power mentality (*haiyang yishi*). Vice Admiral Cheng Mingshang, vice commander-in-chief of the navy, set this out in clear terms in 1991:

> The navy is the tool of big powers' foreign policy. Compared with the army and air force, which cannot go beyond the national boundaries, an international navy can project its presence far away from home. It can even appear in the sea close to the coastlines of potential opponents. While this demonstration of power constitutes a high level of deterrence, it does not provide any formal excuse for the target countries to protest. Such a function of projecting power has made the navy a most active strategic force in peace time, a pillar for foreign policy initiatives and an embodiment of a country's will and power.[1]

CHINA'S MARITIME INTERESTS

According to Zhang Xusan, former vice-commander-in-chief of the PLAN, China's naval modernisation has entered a new era and so has the development of its maritime strategy. The design of this strategy runs parallel with China's new appreciation of its maritime interests.[2] The PLA has realised that in the era of information technology which has substantially extended the attack distance of aircraft and missiles, any effective maritime defence has to be deployed with great depth. Only when China is capable of engaging the enemy in blue waters will its national security be better protected. In Deng Xiaoping's words, China's naval activities should not be confined to coastal areas. This has been China's new approach toward the oceans since the early 1980s.[3] In a textbook for an advanced course on national defence strategy at the National Defence University, the PLA's motivation for deep sea exploration has been summarised as the following:

> Except for the Antarctic Pole, the global continental spheres of ownership have by now been fixed. While the land strategic structure is difficult to alter, there are vast oceanic waters yet to be developed. These oceans will not only have tremendous military value, as seen from the fact that they encircle all the continents, but also tremendous economic value, as seen from the fact that resources under the seabed represent the future of mankind. Therefore all major powers have shifted their strategic focus from land to the sea. This will inevitably pave the way for more maritime conflicts and thus pose a serious challenge to China's rise. To achieve the proper status in international waters is a goal that has to be incorporated into planning for the PLA's long-term development.[4]

More concretely, the PLA considers the following five maritime interests to be crucial for the country's national security and economic security.

The first maritime interest is China's worry about encroachment into its territorial waters by other states. China lays claim to a coastline of 18 000 kilometres and a vast expanse of ocean spanning some 3.6 million square kilometres. Two-thirds of its territorial waters, however, are subject to dispute. A large number of the Spratly (Nansha) Islands claimed by China have been occupied by Vietnam, the Philippines, Malaysia and Brunei. In 1985 alone, 100 million tonnes of oil was extracted from the islands by these countries in defiance of China's repeated protests.[5] This issue has aroused grave concern in the Party and military leadership. When the UN Convention on the Law of the Sea is formally adopted, according to Commodore Liu Zhenhuan, director of the navy's Military Academic Research Institute, China can expand its territorial waters from 12 nautical miles to 200 nautical miles, and thus legitimise its claims to about 3 million out of a total of 4.7 million square kilometres in the East and South China Seas and in the Yellow Sea. Such an increase of territorial waters will require a corresponding expansion of naval power for effective control over the area in order to make the claim meaningful.[6] This is reflected in Admiral Liu Huaqing's remarks that to secure China's sovereignty at sea in terms of its maritime rights and interests is the primary goal of the Chinese navy's future development.[7] Exercising sovereignty in the South China Sea through naval activities has remained high on the CMC's daily agenda. With the return of Hong Kong to PRC sovereignty after 1 July 1997, recovering Taiwan has become a major task for the navy to contemplate in the years to come. It has become increasingly clear that the navy has to build a credible capability to deter any crisis that might otherwise be triggered by the trend toward independence on the island. Given this long-term possibility, a blockade or invasion does not sound forever unthinkable. Indeed, how to conquer the Taiwan Strait, which is three times wider than the British Channel, and how to overpower Taiwan's enlarged arsenals of high-tech weaponry represent serious challenges for the navy's strategic plans and hardware development.[8]

A second interest is the exploitation of the sea for its mineral resources. Chinese geologists have reported that the country's offshore mineral resources may amount to eight billion tonnes. The oil deposits in the South China Sea form one of the world's largest; the area has been called the 'second North Sea'. China's known extractable inland oil deposits are gradually diminishing, and its current production level cannot sustain rapid economic expansion. Since 1994 China has become a net importer of oil. This has made seabed oil extraction ever more urgent. Chinese geologists have reported that soon in the new century, China's production of crude oil from the sea will approach 40 per cent of its gross yield. The deep-water basin in the South China Sea also has a rich concentration of manganese nodules. In addition, China has the potential to generate 110 million kilowatts of tidal electric power, of which only 0.3 per cent is being exploited and used at present.[9] For China, overpopulated and relatively poor in land-based resources, the prospect of ocean exploitation is a lasting attraction. In 1996 China derived directly from the sea an economic value of 220 billion *yuan*, which was 34 times more than its 1979 figure of 6.4 billion *yuan*.[10] This well expressed the country's interest in ocean exploration. Such a spirit is captured by Commodores Yan Youqian and Chen Rongxing, two senior staffers in the navy headquarters: 'The 21st century is a century of conquering the sea, as maritime resources will become the major resources for mankind.'[11]

A third maritime interest is China's fast-growing coastal economy.

Since 1979, the date China commenced its policy of opening to the outside world, the economic expansion of China's thirteen coastal provinces has been impressive. With an area of 14 per cent of the national territory, they now contribute over 60 per cent of China's GNP. The importance of industrial bases along the coast has prompted calls for better protection in times of war.[12] Additionally, as Hong Kong and Taiwan have played a crucial part in China's economic development, the navy has made it a priority to create an effective capability to deter any crisis over either of these areas.[13]

A fourth maritime interest is China's foreign trade, which has been growing at an annual rate of 12 per cent since 1979 and ranks within the top ten largest trading nations in the world. China relies heavily on sea-borne freight, which consists of 40 per cent of its overall volume of goods transported and 97 per cent of export and import shipment. Now China has about 3700 ships (totalling over 22 million tonnes) travelling around the world's oceans, many of them passing through the South China Sea.[14] The volume of goods shipped by Chinese vessels has reached 500 million tonnes a year.[15] This has placed an increasingly heavy onus on the navy to protect sea lines of communication.

A fifth maritime interest is China's burgeoning ocean fishing. In 1985, for the first time in the history of the PRC, a fleet of thirteen fishing ships was sent by China's National Aquatic Company to fish off the coast of West Africa. Since then numerous teams have gone to various oceans. Many Chinese fishermen are now provided with new ships, either imported from Germany or Poland or made at home. These include a large number of retired military vessels.[16] China's ambitious goal is to reach the catch-level of South Korea and Taiwan in the near future and ultimately to surpass the catch-level of Russia.

THE EVOLUTION OF THE PLAN'S WAR FIGHTING DOCTRINE

Given the demanding task of protecting these maritime interests, China's naval commanders are becoming more aware of acute inadequacies, both of the navy's war fighting doctrine and of its equipment. For example, all the land-based naval aircraft are capable of only a very limited flight radius. This exposes the navy's surface ships to enemy air attack. Furthermore, in a major conflict, a navy incapable of defence in depth could not protect the key coastal cities from bombardment by enemy warships. As the navy has accumulated more knowledge about foreign navies and its own vulnerability, the demand for stepping up modernisation has been growing. A commander in the navy's East Sea Fleet even called for the building of a 'usable navy' to cope with the new economic requirements placed on 'this stagnant coastal force'.[17]

The plight of the navy largely stems from its doctrinal deficiencies. Until the early 1980s the PLA maritime doctrine was centred on coastal defence. Formulated by the former navy commander-in-chief Admiral Xiao Jingguang in 1950, the doctrine was a copy of the Soviet 'small battle' theory, which prescribed naval warfare conducted by light warships, shore-based planes and submarines. Nothing is more revealing about the Navy in its formative years than Xiao's following instructions:

> The navy should be a light type navy, capable of coastal defence. Its key mission is to accompany the ground forces in war actions. The basic characteristic of this navy is fast deployment, based on its lightness.[18]

In step with this doctrine, the navy established the 'three-point pillars' of its forces, namely, the torpedo boats, land-based naval aircraft and submarines. Of these, the submarine fleet enjoyed priority in development.[19] Over the next 30 years, the navy built a large number of small vessels. Designed for 'guerrilla skirmishes against invaders at sea', few of them were capable of modern warfare. Consequently the Chinese navy remained 'light' for a good part of its history.

Liu Huaqing's appointment as the navy's commander-in-chief in 1982 marked a turning point in the PLAN's development. Although a veteran Long Marcher, Liu was one of four high-ranking naval commanders trained in the USSR in the 1950s. In the 1960s and 1970s he was first put in charge of naval R&D and then of national military research. This experience made him a major campaigner in the PLA for a modernised navy and a corresponding maritime strategy.[20]

Some foreign and domestic naval experts have dubbed Admiral Liu 'China's Gorshkov'.[21] The term can be substantiated, given the fact that both of these naval commanders regard high-tech and modern equipment as essential. The way Liu changed the Xiao Jingguang doctrine reflects the influence of Soviet training on his military thinking. It was in the mid-1950s, when Liu studied in the Voroshilov Naval Academy, that the Soviet maritime strategy for greenwater power took shape under the command of Gorshkov.

The Soviet prescriptions could not have failed to make an impact on Liu. When the Chinese navy took similar steps under Liu's command, the Soviet example became relevant in China's build-up. This is probably behind Liu's advice to his colleagues that they should read carefully Gorshkov's book, *Sea Power of the State*.[22]

As soon as Liu assumed office in 1982, he organised a forum in which ranking commanders and experts discussed naval development for the rest of the century. This forum later became the Navy Equipment Assessment Centre, the first of its kind among all services in the PLA. The reports from this centre and other 'think tanks' in the navy served as useful inputs in the formulation of the navy's new maritime strategy, characterised as the 'active greenwater defence strategy' (*jijide jinhai fangyu zhanlie*).[23]

A NEW BLUEWATER STRATEGY

Admiral Liu's new maritime strategy addresses two key areas of the PLA Navy's modernisation. First, it offers guidelines for the navy's long-term development program, aiming clearly at bluewater power status. It also specifies not only the key links in each phase in this long-term program but concrete steps for realising the goals set for each phase. Constant equipment upgrading will be the key link for the whole process. Two elements are crucial to an understanding of this strategy, namely the meanings of 'active defence' and 'green water'. The first prescribes a model of future war fighting for the navy; and the second draws the geographic scope for naval activities. Together they provide a strategic guide for a forward naval defence that will gradually transform the PLA Navy in the new millennium.

Creating a pro-active and offensive navy

According to naval strategists, active defence encompasses both defence against invasion and offence after a period of defence. What this means is that the PLAN is now more inclined to take initiative in waging war actions. This markedly distinguishes its current doctrine from the one in the pre-Deng era, which was fundamentally responsive by nature. For instance, in coping with the designated enemy in the 1970s China's maritime strategy was designed to lure the enemy deep into Chinese territorial waters for the purpose of engaging it in a 'people's guerrilla war'.[24] Under Liu's new strategy, the PLAN would confront the enemy in the outer approaches and stop its advance well before it reached coastal waters. The navy may make a tactical withdrawal, but only after weakening the enemy's initial offensive, and only as a prelude to a later retaliatory strike. Therefore, to some extent, active defence is an offensive-oriented strategy.[25]

The PLA's recognition that the navy should take an offensive posture in future high-tech warfare is an important lesson it has learned from the experience of contemporary maritime warfare in the world. The navy now sees itself as a fundamentally attack-oriented service, for without fixed defence lines and depth at sea, only through offensive actions can naval fleets survive a high-tech war. Furthermore, it is almost impossible for a defensive-oriented navy to fulfil its strategic missions.[26]

According to a report by the PLAN headquarters, towards the end of the 20th century naval operations will most likely be offensive campaigns on a limited scale, such as attacking the enemy's fleets, blockading its islands, ports and naval bases, disrupting its SLOCs and landing troops on islands. These operations will be launched toward and beyond China's maritime territories.[27]

One crucial component for an offensive navy is its determination to launch pre-emptive campaigns. According to a former naval chief of staff, the PLAN should wage pre-emptive actions when it regards the situation to be critical, such as when foreign navies intrude into China's territorial waters, seriously violate its maritime interests and threaten its national security.[28] The intensified China–Taiwan conflict and the brazen show of force in 1996 by the US Navy close to the Taiwan Strait might have met these criteria, had exchange of fire accidentally occurred and escalation of tension reached a high level. Such recent events may have forced the PLAN to adjust its war theory. The offensive guidelines remain as before, but the navy has to simulate actions on a larger scale, involving operations at the fleet level and above. A military action across the Taiwan Strait will likely be a PLA initiative of massive proportions, at least as far as troop mobilisation is concerned.[29]

Enlarging space for naval defence

Admiral Liu's concept of *jinhai* or green water is more than a simple geographic term. It spells out a new geopolitical and strategic consideration. It is similar to Japan's 1000 nautical miles defence line. It may even be motivated by this idea. By Chinese interpretation, green waters embrace a large proportion of the East and South China Seas. As specified by Admiral Zhang Xusan, former deputy commander-in-chief and naval chief of staff, this

concept covers China's entire sea territories and the islands scattered in these waters, such as the Spratly and Paracel (Xisha)
Islands.[30] Geographically, this area stretches from the Chinese
waters adjacent to Vladivostok in the north to the Straits of
Malacca in the south and continues to the first island chain of the
West Pacific in the east. Obviously, this incorporates a vast area
of the Pacific including Japan, the Liuqiu (Ryukyu) Islands and the
Philippines. Militarily, the concept creates an enlarged space for
actions. One commander observed that the navy must project a
sea control capability beyond the second chain of islands, which
lie a few hundred nautical miles east of the first island chain.[31]
Given the long distances between these areas and the Chinese
mainland, some as far as over 1000 nautical miles, the concept
constitutes a leap in Chinese naval strategic thinking.

Therefore, the projected distance for Chinese naval activities
entails a crucial feature of a forward defence. To the navy this is
a matter of life or death. Conditioned by China's coastal geographic
make-up, the majority of the PLAN's forces have to be stationed
in first-line ports, whose defence depth is very shallow. As these
ports can easily be blockaded, the navy must deploy some of its
combat units elsewhere to broaden the defence depth in order to
give the central high command more warning time.[32] Emphasising
defence in great depth in turn dictates that the PLAN create as
large a space for fleet manoeuvrability as possible. As reasoned by
Admiral Zhang Xusan, compared with the army, the navy has no
rear line. The cushion of the country's 12-nautical-miles territorial
seas is so thin that it cannot shield the key coastal political and
economic targets from the enemy's bombardment from inshore
waters. Defence in depth is essential to the navy's survival, not to
mention fulfilment of its strategic missions. Therefore, the PLAN
should extend its defence as far forward as it best can, disregarding
the limit of the maritime borders. Only when this is achieved can
the country's defence for coastal cities and the navy's rear bases
be relieved from the enemy's direct attack.[33]

To achieve its objective of forward defence, the PLAN must
redress a number of legacies left by the era of the coastal naval
doctrine. As pointed out by Zhang Xusan, due to its obsession with
defensive missions in the past, the navy had constructed very few
forward bases away from the continent. Naval forward airports and
navigation facilities were especially scant. Preparations for action
in deep seas, such as information about marine meteorology,
magnetic field intensity and nautical charts for the likely battle
areas, were largely neglected.[34] These have now become priority

targets for the navy's battlefield reconstruction efforts since the early 1990s. Indeed, the navy has adopted an even longer view for forward defence, seeking potential sites for facilities in areas its ships cannot yet reach. The PLAN desires to establish footholds in areas that may be important for its future movements and even deployment. The observation stations which Burma constructed with China's help in the early 1990s may give the PLAN vital access to the Indian Ocean.[35] China's heavy investment in South Pacific islands may also pave the way for its naval port calls when needed in the future.

A navy assuming independent combating tasks

The active greenwater strategy reflects such a recognition that actions in the sea have changed from being an integral part of a land war to being independent means to achieve strategic and campaign objectives. The significance of this change is that the navy has to be prepared for high-tech warfare with the major powers, independently or in a combined action. The PLAN's two new basic defence guidelines, namely, pro-active initiatives taken in waters fairly distant from home, as mentioned previously, resulted in a developmental trend that the navy will be empowered to assume independent combat missions, both at the strategic and tactical levels.[36] Politically, a navy as such acts as a big power's foreign policy tool.

Militarily, the navy as an independent fighting force is changing its traditional role as a subordinate service to the ground force. In future warfare it will launch independent campaigns which require forward deployment of its units in areas subject to sovereignty disputes. Very often this forward deployment is carried out without the support of the other services, such as in actions of sea control or denial, blockade of SLOCs and second nuclear strikes.

In fulfilling the new requirements, Admiral Liu Huaqing required the PLAN to attain four basic capabilities in planning independent campaigns in safeguarding China's maritime interests:

1   securing sea control in the major battle directions in China's offshore waters;
2   blockading major SLOCs effectively and within a required span of time, in the waters encompassing China's maritime territories;

3   initiating major sea battles in waters adjacent to China's mari-
    time territories; and
4   waging reliable nuclear retaliatory strikes.

Aggregating the four fundamental missions, the navy was
instructed to acquire the capabilities of rapid response, independent
campaigns, offensive orientation and long-range power projection.[37]

The navy's developmental stages

In quest of high-tech naval power, the PLAN has worked out
detailed short-, medium- and long-term plans. Based on the aware-
ness that naval build-up is a long, cumulative process, the navy
has realistically set up three evolutionary phases. Each has clearly-
defined goals and tasks.

The first phase is expected to take to the end of the 1990s. By
the turn of the century, the navy will still remain a light-type navy,
lacking capabilities to fulfil many important missions China deems
necessary to carry out. On the other hand there are always possibilities for a crisis situation to emerge along China's maritime
peripheries. To cater for this need, the navy is required to develop
rapid response task forces capable of operations and deterrence in
the waters beyond its traditional areas of activity. Its goal is to
deter regional threats (mainly small powers) without fighting or to
win a limited regional maritime conflict with quick, low-cost
strikes. Accordingly, the first phase build-up is to concentrate
efforts for selective upgrading of key equipment so as to quickly
raise the navy's fighting capability in certain areas. By the end of
this first phase the navy should possess:

1   a relatively large radius of action, reaching the first island chain
    of the East and South China Seas;
2   a strong rapid response capability;
3   a reasonably effective amphibious capability;
4   a reasonably complete air wing for self-protection and offence;
    and
5   a credible second-strike nuclear deterrence capability.[38]

In the first phase, the naval attack forces are to be composed
mainly of land-based medium-range bombers and fleets of attack
submarines. Medium-sized surface ships equipped with helicopters
will serve as command and escort forces. In other words the
navy will try to avoid sea-battles involving its main surface combatants. However, each of the navy's three fleets will establish one
task force capable of ocean navigation. Once these task forces are

set up, they will be trained intensively and continuously in blue waters. To meet the basic requirements of the first phase force development, the current land-based C³I and logistic systems will be supplemented by air- and sea-based systems.³⁹

In the second phase of evolution, which should extend over the first two to three decades of the 21st century, the navy will gradually break away from the West Pacific. For instance, its bluewater fleets may exercise in the Indian Ocean or enter the Atlantic Ocean or pay a port call in the Mediterranean Sea. Major efforts should be devoted to developing capabilities for sustained deep ocean warfare. By then, the task forces set up in the first phase should be evolved into large sea-battle combined fleets, which should be headed either by aircraft carriers or large missile cruisers. These fleets should possess various kinds of warships to form a three-dimensional system of attack and defence with air, surface and submarine attachments.⁴⁰ The key to achieving this goal is the development of advanced equipment. Apart from aircraft carriers, new nuclear ballistic missile submarines and new-generation surface ships will join the PLAN. The third phase would go beyond the year 2030 and assumes China's naval capability to be that of an international sea power.⁴¹

THE RISE OF THE NAVY AND THE PERCEPTION OF POTENTIAL THREAT

The navy's new strategy is ambitious and costly. The long-term effect of a navy assuming an independent strategic role vis-a-vis its traditional subordinate position to the army constitutes one important feature in the PLA modernisation: the rise in the navy's status within the armed forces. In the last decade or so the PLAN has received unprecedented leadership attention, budgetary allocations and increased human and natural resources. With the strong personal push of Admiral Liu Huaqing, naval strategists led the other services in calling for change in the PLA's traditional thinking and in proposing new strategies and tactics to suit high-tech warfare. For the first time in the PLA's history, a naval commander, Admiral Liu, acted as the de facto commander-in-chief of China's armed forces for a number of years (1992–97). And he was the first professional soldier since Marshal Ye Jianying to sit in the Politburo Standing Committee, the top policy decision body in the country.⁴² One of the outcomes of this rise in status is that naval allocations have in recent years climbed to close to one-third of China's defence budget.[43] Similarly, its manpower strength has risen from 8 per cent to about 10 per cent of the PLA's total, in contrast to the reduction of the army from 81 per cent to 70 per cent.[44] In October 1995 Jiang Zemin led all CMC members in a review of a naval exercise in South China, during which each one of them committed himself to supporting the development of the navy as an urgent priority.[45] Another reason for the rise of the navy in the PLA stems from China's immediate security concerns due to territorial and sovereignty disputes. Conflicting claims in the South China Sea are a constant threat to trigger armed actions. The PLAN will bear the initial brunt of any military actions against Taiwan if independence is declared by Taiwan's future authorities. Under these circumstances the PLAN may even confront the powerful US navy, if the US carries out its promise of intervention to help the Philippines in the South China Sea and the Taiwanese over an action across the Strait. Indeed, threats from the seas have far exceeded those from land borders, thus giving the navy the strongest reasons for receiving priority attention from the leadership.

The rise of the navy, therefore, has simply mirrored China's changed perception of possible external threats in the current strategic environment. As a result the PLAN has been called to be better prepared for both regional conflicts that may disrupt its modernisation program and long-term potential threats posed to it by major powers. Even minor or potential threats can become a major headache for China to deal with, as the PLAN's modernisation is entering a dangerous transition. As Vice Admiral Lin Zhiye pointed out:

> Towards the end of this century and early in the next, the major political and economic conflicts between our country and other countries will focus on the sea. The threats to our development and security also come from the sea. To be more exact, they lie in the areas within the first island chain in the North and South China Seas.[46]

According to the navy's dominant view, China's principal adversaries are the major naval powers, with which a war may not be avoidable eventually.[47] At the same time the low-level conflicts related to territorial and sovereignty disputes have also loomed large as a likely scenario. On the basis of this two-front assumption, the new naval strategy is an important component of the PLA's two-tiered high-tech defence strategy, as analysed in Chapter 1. The PLA's ultimate answer to the two-tiered threat is to develop high-tech armament. As pointed out by a PLA strategist:

> Once we are fully prepared for a war with major powers in terms of weapons development, it would be much easier for us to cope with threats on a smaller scale.[48]

Recently, voices from different services have been loud in sanctioning a speedy naval expansion. To some extent these views reflect the formal position of the top leadership and the way these views have been articulated is unprecedented. For instance, an article was published in the PLA's journal, *Junshi jingjixue* (The study of military economics), calling on the state to give a priority slice of the limited national defence budget to the naval build-up.[49] A group of senior naval planners went even further in suggesting that 'we should cut a few mechanised divisions so as to allocate more funds to the navy'.[50] This clearly carries implications for the equipment upgrading of the group armies. Considering the cost of modernising one army corps, which stands at several billion *yuan*,[51] the impact of such a decision would be far-reaching for naval development.

THE NAVY'S ADMINISTRATIVE AND OPERATIONAL STRUCTURE

There are four levels of naval administrative structure from Beijing down to the tactical campaign units: the navy's central head-quarters, the three fleets, the naval bases, and the naval ship brigade/naval garrison/naval fortress. Under each of the units at the fourth level there are also basic combat units, which will be analysed in later sections. This administrative structure can be observed also from the establishments of the navy's arms of services (*bingzhong*): the naval aviation/fleet aviation units, marines, land-based missile and artillery commands, research and educational institutions. Altogether they form a gigantic and expensive war machine (see Figure 6.1).

The central command

Situated across the road from the headquarters of the PLAAF on Outer Fuxingmen Avenue, the headquarters of the navy is the highest organ of command for the PLAN, assuming everyday administrative and operational duties on behalf of the CMC. The current navy commander-in-chief is Admiral Shi Yunsheng, a former naval pilot and a member of the CCP's 15th Central Party Committee. The navy headquarters' principal tasks include monitoring daily movements and training of the naval units under the

Figure 6.1 PLAN command and control structure

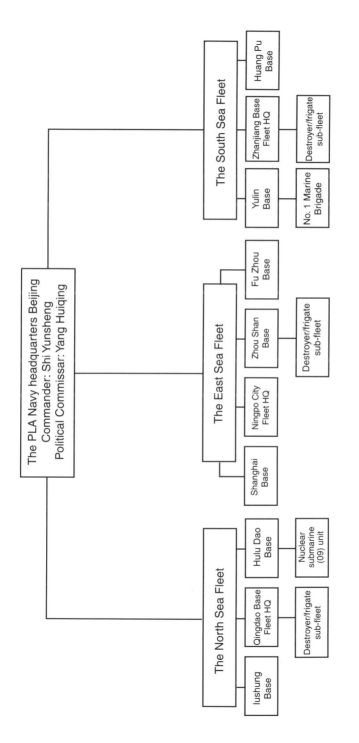

three fleets, formulating strategic long-term development plans for the CMC, coordinating the activities of the different branches within the navy and between different fleets, and cooperating with other services (for example, the PLAAF and SMF) and the seven Military Area Commands. One important task of the navy head-quarters is to recommend the personnel changes of senior naval officers (above divisional levels) to the CMC and appoint them on the CMC's behalf. Formulating the annual naval budget and appro-priating the central naval funding to the subordinating units are also among its key missions.

Within the headquarters there are six major departments (*yijibu*): the Headquarters Department, the Political Affairs Depart-ment, the Logistics Department, the Aviation Command, the Equipment and Technological Research Department (*zhuangbei jishubu*) and the Equipment Maintenance Department (*zhuangbei xiulibu*) (see Figure 6.2).

Each of these departments enjoys the same administrative ranking, but the relationship between the Headquarters Depart-ment and the other three specialised departments (excluding the Political Affairs Department) are fairly complicated. According to the Navy Administrative Regulations (*Haijun xingzheng tiaolie*) the Headquarters Department provides guidelines to the four departments in their everyday work regarding matters of supply and maintenance, but on matters of combat operations it is the command organ over them. Under the Headquarters Department there are a number of high-powered offices. For instance, the General Office serves as the hub of the administrative communi-cation chain of the navy, yet the most important office is the Headquarters of the Naval Staff, which is responsible for combat operations, training, intelligence gathering, deployment and re-deployment of fleet units and war game plans. Other second-level departments (*erjibu*) include the Coast Defence Department, Communications Department, Signal and Intelligence Department, and so on.

The Naval Equipment and Technological Research Department is the overriding authority for naval R&D. Within the department there are six second-level departments and two research institutes. Its main tasks include formulating the PLAN's annual and medium-to-long-term development plans; monitoring the procure-ment procedures; organising key national R&D projects; assessing, testing and finalising specific weapons systems (for example, new classes of warships, aircraft, missile systems and electronic hard-ware); proposing items to be purchased from overseas and their

Figure 6.2 PLAN headquarters administrative structure

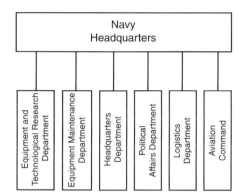

standardisation at home; technological intelligence gathering; and promoting technological innovations by all naval units. It is a powerful body, as it controls the bulk of the naval equipment research budget and state procurement funds for naval hardware.

The Naval Equipment Maintenance Department is responsible for maintenance and repair of all naval equipment. Its second-level departments include the warship technological department, enterprise management department, equipment department and warehouse department. Under its control are numerous repair factories, storage and procurement stations. The department is also involved in assessing and finalising new weapons prototypes, mainly from the tactical and technical angle. Its opinion on the equipment's reliability, maintainability and the length of warranty carries a lot of weight in selecting weapons systems. It has large sums of maintenance funds under its control. It is rich also in the sense that many of its factories are engaged in civilian 'moonlighting' activities.

The fleets

Currently the PLA Navy has three fleets: the North Sea Fleet, the East Sea Fleet and the South Sea Fleet, each of them equivalent to a joint army group (*bingtuanji*) in administrative ranking. According to the Navy Regulations, in organisational terms, these fleets are both a naval administrative agency and an operational command. Formerly they were called naval military area commands (*junqu haijun*), similar to the air force area commands.[52]

As such they were under dual leadership of the navy headquarters in Beijing and the local military area command. In 1955 they changed to the present name, partly to tighten administrative control (*junzheng*) between the central naval command and the regional naval units. The CMC believed that in peacetime administrative relations were the main chain of command. From then on the dual leadership started to move in favour of the naval top command.

However, the influence of the Military Area Commands (MACs) over the fleets remains considerable because of several factors. First, the fleet headquarters are physically much closer to the MAC headquarters. Second, the fleet commander-in-chief is a deputy to the commander-in-chief of the MAC. Against this background, each time the navy headquarters is selecting the fleet commander-in-chief, it normally consults the opinion of the commander-in-chief of the MAC where the fleet headquarters is located. Most importantly, with the current emphasis on united warfare, the MAC headquarters are jointly responsible for the fleets' military operations (*junling*). Their preparedness has been incorporated into the construction of the war zones under the leadership of the MACs. The fleets' war zone may incorporate areas of a number of the ground force's MACs or may constitute only part of one MAC. The North Sea Fleet covers an area that embraces three MACs: Shengyang, Beijing and Jinan. The East and South Sea Fleets only cover the area of the Nanjing and Guangzhou MACs.

Each fleet headquarters is also the operational superior to all naval units deployed in a naval war zone. Administratively each fleet has a number of bases at the group army level under it. These bases are located in the strategic waterways linking China's inner waters to its oceanic territories. Together they form the Chinese maritime defence line from the Sino–Korean border to the South China Sea (see Figure 6.1).

North Sea Fleet (Beihai jiandui) This fleet is responsible for the maritime security of the Yellow Sea and the Bo Sea (from the Yalu River to Lianyungang Port), which is the most important maritime defence line for China. First, the Bo Sea is the oceanic gateway to the country's capital, Beijing. It is only a few dozen kilometres away from Tianjin, the third largest city in China and a little over 100 kilometres away from Beijing. In China's modern history, whenever the defence of the Bo Sea was broken, the fall of Beijing soon followed. Second, across the Yellow Sea are China's two traditional foes: the Russians and Japanese. For these two reasons the North Sea area was the cradle of China's modern navy and a number of sea battles were fought there. The PLA has also devoted enormous resources to building its North Sea Fleet and has made it the strongest among the three: it has the largest number of warships in the navy, over 400 in total, and the largest number of major surface combatants. It is also the home of China's nuclear submarine fleet and boasts the largest naval ports in the Far East. Although this was originally designed to cope with the real threat from the USSR, now the North Sea Fleet is still a priority in the navy's long-term force development, because of the security uncertainties posed to China by the tension in the Korean Peninsula and the potential challenges from Russia and Japan.

East Sea Fleet (*Donghai jiandui*) The defence responsibility of this fleet is the East China Sea, which covers the coastal provinces of Zhejiang, Jiangsu, Shanghai and part of Fujian (from Lianyungang Port to Dongshan Island). It embraces the northern part of the Taiwan Strait. Traditionally this is the area from which foreign navies intruded into the Chinese territories. After 1949 the area registered almost all Chinese naval actions, mainly with Taiwan's navy. In recent years the fast economic growth of the area has increased the onus on the fleet in safeguarding the East China Sea. For a protracted period of time, the fleet's principal combat strength was in its large numbers of speed boats of various sizes (torpedo and missile craft). Partly this was because Taiwan, the chief opponent of the fleet, did not possess many large and modern surface combatants. This is in contrast to the North Sea Fleet, whose potential enemy, the USSR's Pacific Fleet, was heavily equipped. However, since Taiwan's naval modernisation has accelerated and the threat from Russia has faded in recent years, there has been a readjustment of forces between the North Sea and East Sea Fleets.

South Sea Fleet (*Nanhai jiandui*) The defence area of this fleet begins at Shantou, Guangdong Province, in the east and ends in Beihai, Guangxi Zhuang Autonomous Region, and Yulin, Hainan Province, in the west. Its maritime defence line is the longest due to its responsibility for the huge expanse of waters in the South China Sea. Since 1 July 1997 its control has extended to include the Hong Kong maritime areas. Before the territorial disputes over the Spratly and Paracel Islands surfaced in the mid-1970s, the South Sea Fleet was the weakest in the PLAN. Since then it has been constantly strengthened, although it is still the smallest, with about 300 ships. The reinforcement of the fleet has stepped up since the 1980s, when the disputes in the South China Sea intensified. And in the 1990s the stand-off across the Taiwan Strait has added additional reasons for the expansion of the fleet, as it assumes the task of dealing with Taiwan from the southern part of the Strait, Indeed, the PLA has initiated a number of efforts to enhance the fleet, including an increase in the number of submarines available for a possible sea blockade, and further reinforcement of its amphibious strength—for instance, enlarging the units of marines and increasing the sealift capabilities.

The bases

The forces immediately under the fleets are naval bases and special combat units. The former are at the group army level and assume administrative and sometimes operational command duties over a prescribed maritime area. There are nine such bases in the PLAN. The latter are specialised sub-fleets consisting of the major surface combatants: destroyer, frigate and submarine brigades. Normally each of the three fleets has one destroyer/frigate brigade and one submarine brigade. Each brigade has a number of warship groups under it and is equivalent to an army division in ranking. These brigades are administratively attached to one of the bases in the fleet where they are anchored. However, as China's main mobile maritime forces assume strategic and tactical missions far away from home waters, they are operationally commanded by the fleet headquarters as well.

Naval bases have a number of everyday missions. One of the most important is to provide logistical and other supplies to the mobile sub-fleets of the major combatants. As the PLAN is moving further and further into deep oceans, this task is becoming more and more demanding. Other missions include ensuring the security of the base headquarters and the military ports under its command; supporting air defence units in the area; equipment maintenance; and offering medical treatment and recreational activities. The PLAN bases also have large numbers of combat units, which can be divided into two groups: coastal surface combatants and coastal defence corps. The former refers to light missile and torpedo craft, transport ships, minesweepers and speed patrol boats. The latter refers to shore-to-shore missile and artillery troops and combat support for coastal defence corps, including engineering units, radar and electronic warfare units, ammunition storage, and others.

Almost all of these units are under the command of the naval garrisons (*shuijingqu*). A standard divisional garrison may have a service ship group (sometimes a salvage and rescue ship group), a submarine chaser group, a torpedo/missile boat group, a landing ship group, a minesweeper squadron, and an engineering ship squadron. Under the naval garrison there are also non-combat supporting units such as ammunition storages, hospitals, communications units and meteorological stations. Among China's most important naval garrisons is a special one, the Paracel Islands Naval Garrison, which also has jurisdiction over the Spratly Islands and faces the possibility of naval clashes there. For commanders in this garrison, sometimes political judgement is more important than military judgement. There is therefore a direct communication line with navy headquarters in Beijing.

Parallel in administrative ranking to naval garrisons are naval fortresses, which are established in key water passages. The PLA Navy has set up seven such fortresses along China's coastal defence line. Within each fortress permanent bunkers are built for shore-based anti-ship missile and artillery units, naval infantry regiments, and logistical and ammunition supplies. It is an independent defence system designed to prevent enemy warships from entering the country's inland rivers. For instance, the Wusong Naval Fortress and the Jiangyin Naval Fortress guard the Yangtze delta, the industrial powerhouse of China.

The strategic naval base

One key task of naval modernisation is the construction of strategic naval bases for the three fleets. For the North Sea Fleet, after the first-phase nuclear submarine base was completed in Huludao in the middle of the 1970s, the navy launched the project of a major base for destroyers and frigates in Qingdao in 1977. Consisting of four deep-water docks, shipyards and three anti-wave banks, covering approximately four kilometres, and capable of berthing aircraft carriers, the base is now the largest naval base in the Far East.[53] In Zhoushan and Zhanjiang, similar efforts have been launched for the East and South Sea Fleets, although on a smaller scale. None of these naval bases, however, can be defined as a strategic naval base. The PLAN is worried that its naval operations will be severely limited by the absence of any strategic base, especially in the most likely war direction in the East and South China Seas.[54]

The construction of a strategic naval base is a project of enormous complexity, requiring systems of docking, defence, C³I, logistical supply, repair and management. Since the navy's warship visit to Pearl Harbor, many articles have been published highlighting lessons to be learned from the American experience. Some naval officers argue that the building of an aircraft carrier would take more than a decade, as would the construction of a strategic naval base. Therefore, it is important for the base to be planned soon and launched at the same time as the carrier, if not earlier.[55]

One of the proposed sites for the strategic base is in the Zhoushan/Ninpo area, adjacent to Shanghai, the headquarters of the navy's East Sea Fleet. The aircraft carrier task force could enter the East China Sea as soon as it leaves the harbour, and the Pacific is only 500 nautical miles to the east. Land-based air cover for the carrier battle group could be extended to most of the areas in the Yellow Sea, East and South China Seas. This would greatly enlarge China's ocean defence in length and breadth. Zhoushan is also a deep, warm-water harbour, with a number of entrances and a spacious interior. The depth of the navigation lanes is more than 15 metres, deeper than the canals of Amsterdam. Its deep-water coastline stretches about 100 kilometres, longer than Antwerp, and the space for deep-water anchorage is 82 square kilometres, an area larger than Vladivostok. It has the capacity to berth 500 ships of 10 000 tonnes and 100 of 100 000 tonnes, and may serve as a convenient home for one or more major surface fleets. Within the harbour area, Zhoushan can be used to station aircraft carriers, Qitojia can serve as the base for nuclear submarines and Beilun for cruiser and destroyer sub-fleets. The whole area is covered by numerous islands and mountains, where the PLA Air Force's airfields, the navy's land-based missile batteries and the army's AA troops are heavily concentrated, providing effective protection.[56]

THE CHIEF MISSIONS OF THE NAVY

Naval missions are closely related to the securing of China's maritime interests. In the short-to-medium future they are designed to carry out the principles of limited warfare. In other words, although the long-term naval development plan is quite ambitious, the scope in naval activities is fairly limited. Specifically the missions are independent and mobile campaigns for defending China's crucial sealanes of communications (SLOCs) and disrupting the enemy's; waging limited sea battles against non-major maritime powers in the region; landing operations; blockading the enemy's military/civilian ports or its transportation routes; and exercising a level of deterrence (sometimes even war brinkmanship).

Campaigns for defending or disrupting the SLOCs

These campaigns are regarded as a new challenge to the PLAN, as it has not had any real experience in such an action. Moreover, the navy is aware that it lacks crucial capabilities to wage such sustained campaigns. Nevertheless, the navy believes that it must be prepared for them because safety of SLOCs means China's economic survival.[57]

By the analysis of the PLAN, defending or disruption SLOCs is a new challenge because of the following factors:

1   Long distance. The naval escort has to be projected over the whole navigation of civilian ships which may take a few thousand nautical miles. This long distance will force the navy to shift its preparation for sea actions from 'points' to 'long lines' and this will stretch the PLAN's current strength to the very limit, for as a 'light type navy' it does not have enough ocean-going warships.
2   Unpredictability. In implementing a campaign of defending SLOCs, the PLAN will have to face the problem of being the passive side in the warfare—it is the object of attack by advanced enemy aircraft and submarines. It is difficult for the escort fleet to decide when and where to engage opponents. This compounds the navy's inadequacy in general capabilities.
3   The escort fleets' combat preparation is highly restricted by the civilian transportation ships. For instance, they have to set the speed, route and time according to the escorted ships. These greatly narrow the choices of engagement with the enemy navy.

Thanks to these difficulties the navy have formulated some basic guidelines for the defence of SLOCs. First, the inshore escort should proceed using China's territorial islands and land-based aircraft. Second, a special fleet should be established for the deep ocean escort. It is made up of major surface combatants and submarines. The nuclear submarines can be deployed. The fleet should have strong anti-submarine warfare capabilities. Third, the enemy's long-distance missiles have increased the navy's escort difficulties. This may force the escort fleets to enlarge surveillance scope and enhance their capabilities for air/missile defence. Fourth, the fleet should work out the priority defence areas and take concrete measures for preparation for any possible actions there. Fifth, some large civilian ships may be transformed into defence platforms, for example, to be used as helicopter carriers.

Closely related to the defence of the SLOCs is the mission of the navy to disrupt the adversaries' SLOCs. This is regarded as an important form of the navy's future war action. According to PLA analysts no matter how powerful the superpower's navy is, its forward deployment has to depend on long-distance logistical supply. Blockade of Taiwan's SLOCs is of practical significance in China's anti-independence campaign regarding the island.

In projecting campaigns for disrupting SLOCs, the PLAN has formulated a number of principles:

1   Because of the navy's limited offensive capabilities, it should launch selective attacks on the enemy's priority SLOCs, which can be either in deep oceans or in its inshore areas.
2   In order to avoid the enemy's intensified anti-attack, the choice of targets and employment of PLAN units should be dispersed. At the same time concentration of major combatants should be supplemented by small-scale disruptive activities in the whole process of the campaign.
3   Because the PLAN is still a light-type navy and its normal radius of action is quite limited, anti-SLOCs campaigns should be mainly conducted within the scope of 'green water'. This may make it possible for the campaign to be supported by the land-based air power of the air force.
4   Due to lack of sufficient numbers of major combatants, there should be a carefully planned limit for targets. There should also be restrictions on the times of using main attack units.
5   Anti-SLOCs campaigns should include assault on the enemy's ports.

Actions to capture, occupy and defend islands

These are regarded as the likely form of China's engagement in the near future.[58] Campaigns for capturing islands can be further classified into two scenarios. First, they concern recovering the lost islands in the South China Sea. China is unhappy about the fact that most of the South China Sea islands under dispute are now occupied by foreign countries. The last action the PLAN took in the South China Sea was 1995, when it seized Meiji (Mischief) islet, which is also claimed by the Philippines. For the time being China realises that it cannot afford an irredentist agenda regarding these islands. Yet neither can it afford to give up altogether its claims in the South China Sea and military preparations.

The second dimension to the mission of capturing islands is related to attacks on some offshore islands currently occupied by the Nationalists in Taiwan, islands such as Jingmen and Mazu. In a way an attack in this category is more politically motivated, as it is designed to send signals across the Strait that Taiwan's declaration of independence will certainly lead to war. Militarily, however, recapturing these islands places formidable demands on the navy. Some of these islands are heavily occupied by Nationalist troops, and they can expect reinforcement from Taiwan at short notice. Indeed if the PLA takes a few islands of no consequence, the war signal may not be well received. But if the mission involves Jingmen, for instance, it means that the PLA has to launch a landing campaign involving all PLA services and more than 100 000 personnel. And the campaign may be long. This requires a much higher level of readiness than now exists, including the make-up of task forces, necessary equipment, training, logistic supply and an effective C³I system.

Deterrence

The concept of deterrence constitutes the core of the navy's maritime strategy driven by the concept of sea power. The former navy commander-in-chief Admiral Zhang Liangzhong commented: 'A peacetime navy is the symbol of power of a country'.[59] As a weak sea power, China suffers from a lack of credibility in carrying out its political and diplomatic objectives. Wang Dongpo, a key naval researcher, presented several frustrated sentiments that are shared by most officers in the Chinese armed forces. Although China is a big nuclear power, he said, its powerful conventional ground forces cannot exert due deterrence even against small countries such as Vietnam, the Philippines, Malaysia, and Brunei, which have occupied large parts of the South China Sea and challenged China's image in Asia and the world.[60]

Even at the regional level, the PLA Navy's deterrence is limited so far. Although its DDGs (destroyer with area SAM) outnumber those of most navies in Asia and the Pacific, the weak air and logistic support may place the surface ships in difficult situations, whereby victory would be likely but costly. In addition, most of the countries with which China has territorial disputes have entered security arrangements with outside powers. This particularly makes it necessary for the Chinese navy to devote more

Table 6.1 Comparison of Pacific fleets, 1995

	US	Russia	China	Japan
SSBN	8	16	1	0
SSGN	20	28	5	0
SSG	–	–	1	0
SSK	–	17	44	16
CVN	3	0	0	0
CV	3	1	0	0
Cruisers	13	9	0	0
DD/DDG	18	11	17	42
FFG	20	10	39	20
FF	–	23	–	–
Amphibious	18	15	74	8
MCM	1	67	184	37

Sources: Compiled from *Jane's Fighting Ships*, Richard Sharpe, ed. (Coulsdon, Surrey: Jane's Data Division, annual), *The Military Balance* (London: International Institute for Strategic Studies, annual), *The Almanac of Seapower* (Arlington, VA: Navy League of the United States, annual); quoted from Woolley, Marks & Woolley, 1996, p. 54.

resources to increasing its deterrence, to deter not only the small regional navies but also the outside powers behind them. However, the ultimate goal is deterring the major powers. As pointed by one senior naval officer:

> Given the strategic interests of the US and other major powers in this region [the South China Sea], the presence and growth of our navy should create more strategic pressure. Therefore, the two superpowers will not be able to do whatever they want with no regard to our country.[61]

China is resolved to increase its naval combat capabilities to inflict great damage on a major-power navy, but this is a long-term goal rather than a practical policy to follow in the near future. See Table 6.1 for a comparison of the major naval powers in the Asia and Pacific region.

THE PLA'S NAVAL BUILD-UP IN THE 1990s

Under the new naval strategy and the three-phased development plan, the Chinese navy has expanded steadily in the last two decades. By the end of the 1980s it had grown into a large force that was formidable by regional standards.[62] For instance, the PLAN is already capable of conducting sea actions with its potential regional adversaries in the high seas around the Spratly Islands. In terms of military equipment, however, the navy's capabilities are uneven and, as a result, it could not achieve its objectives without horrendous cost. Each of the navy's five branches—submarines, surface combatants, aircraft, marines and shore-based defence systems—has a long way to go before it can confidently engage in a major action. According to Vice Admiral Cheng Ming, head of the navy's equipment department, the development of new generations of major surface combatants, larger submarines and long-range aircraft will be the priority in the years to come.[63]

Force restructuring

Since the second half of the 1980s the navy has initiated a restructuring program designed to make it 'leaner and meaner'. It has been conducted simultaneously on several fronts. First, the restructuring deeply affects the traditional naval base command system. A few first-grade naval bases (at the group army level) were removed. The Yantai Base under the North Sea Fleet, for instance, was merged with the Qingdao Base. When the Yantai Base was established in 1969, it was meant to strengthen the maritime defence line of the Shangdong Peninsula, especially against a Soviet landing from the Bo Sea. As the Soviet threat diminished, the navy decided the Yantai Base's functions could be taken up by the Qingdao Base.

At the lower levels, the specialised naval bases and the patrol and defence areas (xunfangqu) were also removed. The former refers to those bases designated to house certain specific types of warships, such as the submarine base, the speed boat base and the destroyer base. These bases used to be a level of administrative structure and each had a fairly large number of subdivisions. For instance, a submarine base normally had a base command, a technological unit, a unit of service ships, a communications station, a maintenance station, a clinic, and a training centre. Now it has been transformed into a comprehensive service department (anqinbu) with a smaller number of personnel. Its functions are simpler, namely providing logistical support to ships in transit.

The patrol and defence area was set up in the early 1950s and there were dozens of them in the PLAN force structure. Each was an intermediate body between the basic combat units and the naval garrison, assuming the functions of area patrol and logistical supply for the units within the area. Under its command there were light craft units, land-based anti-ship artillery and AA gun units, and observation and communications companies. When these patrol and defence areas were dismantled, their attachments were regrouped and placed directly under the naval garrisons. However, their previous functions of sea control for the safety of civilian ships have been taken over by the Maritime Branch of the People's Armed Police (PAP), which has set up fourteen security areas along China's 18 000 kilometres of coastline. On top of their everyday agenda are anti-smuggling and anti-piracy patrols. Sometimes the maritime units of the PAP are confused with regular naval units by foreign correspondents, who report that the Chinese naval soldiers are involved in 'piracy activities'. More often than not these activities are actually anti-smuggling efforts by the PAP.

The second major task of the restructuring has been to mothball or scrap a large number of warships that were considered to be either obsolete or incapable of bluewater navigation. For instance, the PLAN has retired all four of its first-generation destroyers: *Anshan, Lushuang, Changchuan* and *Taiyuan*.[64] About the same time it decommissioned most of its early Romeo class submarines and thus cut its submarine force considerably. At the moment only 42 submarines of this class are still in service, as compared to about 100 at the beginning of the 1990s.[65] Large numbers of speed boats, torpedo boats, missile boats and small or old landing boats were also decommissioned. Interestingly the navy has sold several of these landing ships (the larger ones, made by the US in the 1940s) to civilian users, who have converted them into tourist ships.

The third restructuring task was to scrap weapons systems and naval units that were regarded as of little use in high-tech warfare. Among these weapons systems were almost all the J–5s, a large proportion of the J–6s, and a large number of land-based anti-ship artillery units. There was also a major reform of the naval tertiary education system. The Navy Commanding Academy (Nanjing), the Navy Academy of Political Affairs (Dalian), and the Navy Academy of Logistics were downgraded in administrative rank in order to reduce the officer corps. Curricula in the naval academies were thoroughly reviewed and many obsolete courses were dropped from the teaching programs. In terms of software, strategies and mentality, the efforts of the restructuring have resulted in the navy's moving closer to the contemporary developmental trend of major naval powers. In terms of 'hardware', it is still far behind.

Force expansion and modernisation

The PLA Navy's ambitious long-term goal involves the modernisation of its existing ocean-going fleet, composed of 18 DDGs and a small number of nuclear attack and missile submarines. Supported by a number of the latest models of frigates (FF), the PLAN can now be employed relatively effectively to maintain surveillance and protection of offshore resources in the Yellow and East China Seas. It has maintained active engagement in the South China Seas. Yet the navy's 'light composition' (lack of large surface combatants) places a visible restriction on its activities around the first island chains. In order to extend its operations beyond the second island chains in the new century, the navy has put forward its force modernisation plans:

> In the build-up of a credible naval power, we must give priority to the development of deep ocean capabilities. This means that the navy has to establish one or several combined rapid response fleets. These fleets should be supported by long-range aircraft and nuclear attack submarines. When the conditions become ripe, they should be incorporated into aircraft carrier (or large cruiser) battle groups.[66]

The surface combatants

The main components of China's surface combatants are the Luda class destroyers (15), Jianghu class frigates (29) and their improved versions (two Luhu DDG and one modified Luda DDG, a number of other classes of frigates). They constitute the mainstay of the PLA's ocean-going fleet. The technology of these warships is obsolete by western standards and is of little value in extended operations in deep waters.[67] For instance, the hulls of both the Luda class DDG and Jianghu class FF were designed with high sides, reflecting a rationale that the major surface combatants were to engage the enemy at a short distance with their big guns. The legacy of the PLAN as a 'brownwater' navy can still be seen from the fact that no sufficient SAM systems are deployed on board most major warships. Technology has been a major factor. However, as the navy restricted its activities within inshore waters, the fleets developed a mentality that their combat operations would be brought under the protection of the land-based air defence. Related to this are poor ASW and electronic warfare capabilities. Due to their many weaknesses, the Luda class destroyers do not make the PLAN a bluewater navy.[68] Another factor that may have slowed down the navy's hardware modernisation is that in comparison with other claimants to the Spratly Islands the Chinese fleet still has a clear edge and has been fairly effective in limited power projection.[69] This may have convinced the Chinese civilian leadership that there is no urgency in spending large sums of money on naval modernisation. Probably this short-sightedness was finally rectified in the early 1990s when suddenly China's neighbours acquired high-tech naval equipment. The fast modernisation of the Taiwanese navy has been particularly alarming to the PLA high command.

China has made enormous efforts to rectify these deficiencies so as to meet the requirements of its bluewater strategy. These efforts have led the PLAN to a slow generational modernisation with a fundamental goal of enhancing the PLAN's strike capabilities and manoeuvring space. In the process, reliance on big guns has been substituted by long-range precision-guided over-the-horizon anti-ship missiles. The displacement has been raised by one-third for both DDGs and FFs. Fire and navigation control systems have been upgraded through installing indigenously developed equipment and Russian and western technology. For instance, in the early 1990s the Luda class destroyer *Dalian* acquired sophisticated radar systems including the 'Rice Screen' planar array, air surveillance 'Bean Sticks' radar, and 'Eye Shield' antenna, which serves for both surface search/acquisition and target data radar. The deployment of foreign-designed helicopters on board the ships and upgraded ASW warfare facilities have improved the navy's ASW capability. The Italian Whitehead Moto-Fidi 324 ASW launchers are found in a number of Luda class destroyers and Jianghu FFGs.[70]

Since the late 1980s, a number of new DDGs and FFs have entered service. The PLA calls the Luda class destroyer its second-generation destroyer. Its modified version, namely, the Zhanjiang class (named after the city of Zhanjiang, the headquarters of the South China Sea Fleet), entered service in 1991. Powered by combined diesel and gas (CODAG), Zhanjiang has an enlarged displacement of 4200 tonnes versus Luda class's 3200. This version is an embodiment of many foreign technologies—US LM–2500 gas turbines, Crotale naval octuple SAM launchers, Z–9A (Daupin II) helicopters and MK 46 2 ASW torpedoes.[71] With the Thomson CSF combat system and two helicopters, Zhanjiang is said to have a strong surface warfare and anti-submarine capability, but is limited to short-range point-defence anti-aircraft missiles.[72]

China's third-generation missile destroyers *Harbin* and *Qingdao* became operational in 1995 and 1996.[73] *Harbin* is so far the heaviest warship in the PLAN, with a displacement of 5300 tonnes. It is fitted with four C–802 anti-ship missile launchers, one octuple Crotale anti-aircraft missile system, one twin 100 mm gun, two triple anti-submarine torpedo tubes and a hangar for two Z–9 helicopters. According to *Harbin* Captain Wu Hongle, this class of destroyer encompasses China's latest technology from shipbuilding to electronics to weapons systems. As the first ship in this series, it is an all-sealed ship equipped with a computerised C^3I system and a satellite-guided navigation system. Since its maiden voyage in 1995, Jiang Zemin has twice inspected the ship, unique treatment for a naval unit only at the regimental level.[74] Although it is still unknown how many ships are to be produced in this series, it is expected that no fewer than six will be ordered for the navy, which normally assigns at least two ships in a class to each of its three fleets.[75] Reportedly Ukraine has agreed to supply China with four gas turbine engines with which the PLA will build four more destroyers in the *Harbin* class. The four new warships will have a displacement of 6000 tonnes, making them the largest China has ever produced.[76] In this way China has circumvented the US embargo on providing the General Electric LM–2500 originally intended for the new class. However, as the production process may take a long time, China has bought the Russian Sovremenny class missile destroyers for the transition.

Indeed it is quite fortunate for the Chinese that the St Petersburg Shipyard was also desperate to sell, as it was in huge need of new orders which the Russian military cannot place. This made it easier for a deal to be struck in 1996: the PLA will acquire two Sovremenny destroyers at US$400 million apiece.[77] Sovremenny, with a displacement of 7900 tonnes, is a specialist surface warfare ship comparable to the US Navy's Arleigh Burke-class (8300 tonnes) and the Japanese Kongo-class (8400 tonnes). As described by the US Department of Defense, it is the best destroyer the USSR has ever made. Its impressive firepower includes eight supersonic, active-homing, medium-range SS-N–22 Sunburn anti-ship missiles (speed mach 2.5, range 90–120 kilometres), which have a downlink terminal seeker that can be programmed to manoeuvre and select a carrier in a naval battle group, and can evade the US Aegis/ Standard RIM–67-equipped cruisers and destroyers that protect US carriers. Sovremenny is very attractive also because of its Aegis-type integrated air defence system, which is the weakest point in the PLAN major surface combatants. The system can deal with multiple air threats simultaneously, with a digital fire control system and 44 short-to-medium range SA-N–7 Gadfly SAM missiles and two fast-reload launchers.[78]

In the meantime, at least three types of new frigates have joined the PLAN in the last decade. These include three ships (535, 536 and 537) of the Kaifeng class, China's first all-sealed missile frigates with a capability for anti-nuclear, chemical and biological warfare.[79] Powered by CODOG and equipped with eight C–801 missiles, this series is a transitional design, pending a more advanced class to replace the Jianghu class as the mainstay of China's attack frigates.[80] The navy's AA capacity was enhanced by the introduction of Jiangdong class FF with China's first vertical launch system: HQ61 SAM, which is controlled by an indigenous phased-array radar system. Jiangwei is the latest series of China's missile frigates, and two ships from the series have been commissioned. With an enlarged displacement of 2250 tonnes, its sea-going capability has been improved. Similar to the Jiangdong class, they carry the HQ61 SAM system with six canister-launched missiles with a reported effective altitude of 8000 metres and a speed of Mach 3.[81]

Submarines

The navy's nuclear submarine fleet (09 Unit) consists of six or seven nuclear submarines, all capable of bluewater navigation. China's possession of nuclear submarines dates back to the early 1970s, although the development of the fleet has been extremely slow. The oldest boat, which has been in service for more than twenty years, conducted an up-to-the-limit submergence test lasting for three months in late 1985 and early 1986. It covered a distance of 20 000 nautical miles and set a new record for sea endurance.[82] This 09 fleet is the third submarine force in the world that is capable of launching submarine-based ballistic missiles (SLBMs).[83] However, much of this capability cannot be translated into power projection in war actions in the West Pacific.

The navy continues to place the development of its submarine fleet as top priority. At the tactical level it believes its submarines can help achieve a degree of a combat edge over its neighbours, which do not possess sophisticated ASW capabilities. At the strategic level, its nuclear submarines will assume the role of being China's most reliable second-strike deterrent. So the plan to modernise submarines has a dual focus: inventing new models of conventional submarines and expanding the nuclear submarine fleet. New conventional designs which have been put on trial since 1990 have larger displacement and are quieter than the existing classes, while China is also making efforts to increase both the quality and quantity of its nuclear submarines. It has been projected that the number of nuclear submarines will reach over a dozen early next century.[84]

Although long-term development still gives priority to nuclear submarines,[85] the short-term focus has been on the build-up of new models of conventional boats for possible conflicts in the East and the South China Seas. To this end, according to high-ranking navy commanders, new and larger conventional attack submarines will join the service continuously, and will form the underwater component in ocean-going task forces in the 1990s and beyond. In the R&D of these submarines, reduction of noise level, improvement in the accuracy and firepower of weapon systems and modernisation of communications and navigation technology, such as using satellite guidance, are high on the agenda of submarine upgrading. At the moment two new Song class SSK diesel-electric submarines are under construction at the Wuhan Shipyard after the first Song class submarine entered service in early 1997. This class is relatively high-tech and will eventually replace the obsolete Romeo and Ming class submarines. The technological criteria for the new class have been formulated to allow the PLAN's submarine fleet to change its traditional operational guidelines. Since the 1990s the naval submarine commanders have been ordered to reform their attack tactics. For instance, they are required to launch missiles and torpedos from auto command log rather than using an attack periscope, the traditional practice. This requires them to attack from unspecified positions, from deep waters, from a relatively long distance, and at targets that are moving at medium and high speed.[86]

As mentioned earlier, China's conventional submarine force has been in a major restructuring process. Most Romeo class submarines built before the 1980s were decommissioned. The current make-up of the force is much leaner but stronger than before. About twelve improved Ming class and 36 Romeo class submarines, based on a Soviet prototype, remain in service as transitional warships pending the arrival of new classes. In the meantime the four newly acquired Kilo class submarines will play a significant role in bridging the gap. The fundamental line of thinking is that submarines are not the force that should operate in shallow coastal waters. As attack platforms they must be capable of hiding in deep seas. Therefore they need to be powerful and heavily equipped. Any submarine not suitable for these requirements will have to be decommissioned.[87]

China's submarine units will constitute a major naval fighting element in possible future wars. For instance, they will be able to form an ambush platform at the strategic chokepoints in the West Pacific such as around the Bashi Channel and the Taiwan Strait. With the growing strength of the 09 nuclear submarine unit and modernised conventional attack submarines, the Chinese will be able to provide a second echelon to support the 'wolf pack' of patrol submarines. The PLAN's conventional submarines are vulnerable, however, to modern ASW.[88] While they frequently exercise in coastal waters, only a small number of them, mainly the Ming or Wuhan class boats, may be granted greenwater missions. This has been the case since the mid-1980s, when a Chinese submarine was lured into the waters of a foreign country (probably Korea, although the source does not reveal the country's name) and sealed there for more than 500 hours. Due to the long submergence, seven of the vessel's 28 sailors died.[89] This highlights the serious problem of the survivability of the old-type submarines, and the navy has realised how vulnerable its submarines (both nuclear and conventional) will be if they are not substantially improved.

A combat-effective structure in the making

These new destroyers, frigates and submarines are meant to fulfil the following missions of force restructuring:

1   Forming battle groups through concentrating major surface combatants. These groups will be used as rapid response units and specially trained for deep ocean combat missions.
2   Specialisation. Specialised warships have been designed from the existing classes of destroyers and frigates in order to enhance the fast response battle group's anti-air and anti-submarine capabilities. They cater to different tasks required by bluewater missions and are potential escort ships for aircraft carrier groups.
3   Increasing the numbers of ocean-going warships. The navy is to equip all three fleets with a sufficient number of major combatants. The objective is to allow each fleet to conduct independent warfare at certain high levels so as to avoid trading off strength in other strategic directions. Numbers are considered also as making up for the insufficient quality of PLAN weapons.[90]

For the PLAN, a sufficient number of warships is of vital importance, as was shown in the naval clashes with Vietnam in 1974: the navy had to hurriedly dispatch warships from the East and North Sea Fleets to the South, weakening the strength in these key areas at a time when the Sino–Soviet conflict might have triggered some action in the North. After the South Sea Fleet had been reinforced in the 1980s, it was able to plan the incident in the Spratly Islands with great ease in 1988.

Following these guidelines each of the battle groups that is being created in the next few years will be probably centred on one Sovremenny, reinforced by one or two third-generation destroyers and a few second-generation destroyers and frigates. In carrying out deep ocean tasks it will also be joined by a number of nuclear or conventional submarines and large supply ships.

The navy's amphibious units

The PLAN's development of amphibious forces has followed a zigzag course in the last 40 years. In the early 1950s, when an assault on Taiwan was seriously contemplated, there were as many as eight naval infantry divisions. When the plan was aborted later in the decade, the marines disappeared altogether in the Chinese force structure[91] until 1979, when the PLAN started to rebuild a marine unit in its South Sea Fleet. This later became the First Marine Brigade.[92] Although the PLAN planned to set up marine units in other two fleets, this has not come to fruition.[93] This partly reflects the opinion of the PLA leadership that the unit should be trained as a commodore team with the best equipment and personnel. With a tight budget, it was thought better to have a small number of 'commodore troops' than a massive marine structure. This formation underlined the emphasis on flashpoint conflict rather than a large-scale landing operation. This is why the training of the brigade has been heavily influenced by the US and Israeli marine programs.[94] It stresses high mobility and long-distance independent fighting such as island capture, lightning assault on the enemy's transportation and communication hubs in the rear, establishing landing theatres and airborne missions. In recent years one of the priorities in training has been survivability in various challenging situations, such as beach assault and defending a remote island.

The unit has a brigade/battalion/company structure with about 5000 soldiers. As a combined unit, it has three mechanised infantry battalions and battalions of artillery, armour, amphibious tanks and communications. The combat troops are supported by aviation (both fixed-wing and rotary aircraft), anti-chemical and anti-electronic warfare, and engineering units. This is a unique formation in the PLA and the marines call themselves the 'elite of elites'.

Among the brigade's equipment are Z–9 helicopters with two anti-tank missiles and rockets, T–63 amphibious tanks (18.7 tonnes with an 85 mm gun), LVTs (T77–1, based on the Soviet BTR–50, 15.5 tonnes, 16 persons), and T–83 122 mm howitzers. The company weapons include T–71 mortars and T–78, T–82 and T–73 portable anti-tank missiles. One main weak point of the marines is their limited amphibious lift capabilities. The majority of their 700 landing craft are small and incapable of open-ocean navigation. Many of 55 large and medium ships are more than 40 years old, left behind by the Nationalist navy in 1949. Only since the late 1980s has China made the effort to build LSTs and LSMs with displacement of more than 2200 tonnes. But the number is so small that it is far from adequate to support sustained open-ocean operations.[95]

The Chinese military leadership has in recent years tried to address the problem of inadequate transportation. Since the mid-1990s a number of landing ships and supply ships have been under construction. These ships have much larger displacement than the ones currently in service. Another transitional measure that the PLA has taken is to invest large sums of money for the development of ground-effect aircraft (GEA), which it considers to be a cost-effective means of expanding the navy's sealift capability in the future. Jointly designed by the air force and the Seventh Academy of the National Defence Science and Technology Commission, China's first ground-effect aircraft was successfully flown in 1990. In 1997 it was announced that China's GEA technology had become operational. One of the prototypes is the Xintianweng 4, which can carry a load of six tonnes and twenty people. It flies three or four metres above the water (maximum altitude: over 100 metres) and can reach a maximum speed of 180 km/h. Such a high speed is believed to be very useful for landing actions as it will greatly quicken the navigation time. Now concentrated efforts are being made to increase the GEA's lifting capability up to a few dozen tonnes.[96] In addition China has solicited technological assistance from Russians to speed up the development of GEAs.

In the short to medium term it is likely that China will strengthen the marines, which is now viewed as a strategic force suitable for dealing with regional conflicts.[97] Development of better amphibious lift capability has been enhanced. The implementation of the planned formation of two more marine brigades under the command of the East and North Sea Fleets will be high on the agenda, and some marine units may soon appear in the East Fleet.[98]

AIRCRAFT CARRIER: A POWER BOOSTER IN 2000 AND BEYOND

Talk that China is to build an aircraft carrier has persisted since the mid-1980s, but the PLA openly denied the existence of such a plan in 1987. In recent years, however, China's popular journals have carried an increasing number of articles reasoning why China should acquire an aircraft carrier, and these have received a warm response from the readership country-wide. In March 1993, for the first time, Vice Admiral Zhang Yuanhai, political commissar of the East Sea Fleet, admitted in a news conference that the R&D for a carrier was under way, although construction had not yet begun.[99] As recently as 1996 Jiang Zemin visited the Daliang Ship Building Complex, the largest ship producer in China, and told its leaders that the task to construct China's first aircraft carrier would be given to their factory. This was one of the most important national projects in the Ninth Five-Year economic plan.[100]

The R&D for the carriers was gradually unveiled in the 1980s. Selective training for aircraft personnel was also put into real practice. In 1985, Admiral Liu Huaqing personally ordered the establishment of a pilot warship captain's course in Guangzhou Naval Academy for Command of Surface Combatants. Nothing can more clearly reveal the purpose of the course than the remarks made by the academy's president, Rear Admiral Yao:

> Since the Second World War, aircraft carriers as the symbol of a country's important deterrent power have been accorded more attention. For some historical reasons, China has not yet built aircraft carriers. But the academy must look forward and train experts needed for the carriers. As the building process is long, we simply cannot afford to dig wells after becoming thirsty.[101]

According to these trainee captains, their courses are intimately linked to the command of an aircraft carrier. Obviously, the Chinese navy intends to follow the American tradition of promoting aircraft carriers' commanders from amongst pilots rather than from amongst captains of surface warships. Many articles have been published in recent years about the technology of US carriers, and they are being seriously studied by these navy elites. One of them confidently remarked that he was sure Chinese aircraft carriers would navigate in the blue waters with him on board.[102] After four years of systematic studies these pilots have been allocated to the navy's destroyer and frigate fleets; 70 per cent of them have become commanding officers of frigates and the remainder deputy commanding officers of destroyers.[103]

In April 1987 the Navy Air Force (NAF) conducted the first take-off and landing trial on a simulated deck at a naval base of the North Sea Fleet. Chinese sources have revealed quite detailed information about the trial. Officer Li Guoqiang successfully piloted a J–8II in a take-off from the 70 metre-long deck. Using a catapult, Li reached 80 km/h at 20 metres, 110 km/h at 30, 160 km/h at 40, and 250 km/h at 60 metres. Then he landed at the second arrester wire, of which there were four, and continued another 30 metres before stopping steadily. According to this source this simulated deck was said to be modelled on the Australian carrier, HMAS *Melbourne*, which China bought for scrapping. Since then several dozen pilots have been trained intensively on the deck.[104]

The R&D on carriers has been accelerating in recent years. In November 1990 a model of China's first-generation carrier was displayed at a highly classified weaponry exhibition in Beijing. According to the information available about the display, the carrier had a displacement of 40 000–50 000 tonnes and carried twenty fixed-wing planes on deck and another twenty in the hangar. The deck was over 70 metres in length and made use of catapults and arrester wires. The navy reportedly plans to establish two battle groups centred on such carriers in the early years of the 21st century.[105] The design is a generational leap from the navy's initial consideration, which envisaged a lighter carrier with only STOVL aircraft on board.[106] The navy calculated that if it had a carrier with 40 aircraft on board, it could achieve the combat effectiveness of 200 to 800 coastal-based fighters in air support functions. Further, the sea area under control of a convoy headed by a carrier would be fifty times as large as that controlled by a convoy of destroyers.[107]

PLA leaders see the construction of carriers as a major boost to the general level of naval technology, as it will stimulate R&D on effective AA and anti-missile systems, early warning and electronic counter-measure technology, the development of carrier aircraft, and a sophisticated C³I system. Western analysts view China's planned first generation of carriers to be more of symbolic significance than posing any real threat to regional security.[108] Yet to the Chinese it represents a prerequisite for achieving the navy's long-term modernisation ambitions. Despite the inevitable deficiencies associated with the Navy's first aircraft carrier, the navy needs to begin with whatever it can build so as to develop more sophisticated carriers at a later date.[109]

According to some naval planners, the acquisition of an aircraft carrier is the crux and symbol of the navy's bluewater strategy.[110] Obviously, the point they raise is important. Without air cover provided by an aircraft carrier, an ocean-going task force of medium-sized ships cannot be confident of a mission to secure sea territories 500 nautical miles beyond the mainland. At 25 knots per hour, a carrier task force may extend the combat radius to 500 kilometres and effectively cover 200 kilometres a day. The navy only needs one such task force to control the entire sea and air space around the Spratly Islands.[111] Therefore, the building of aircraft carriers has been regarded as the key to the realisation of the second-stage naval development program, as mentioned earlier, and to the fulfilment of the second level of China's national defence strategy, which aims to deter any threat to China from major world powers.

The plan to build aircraft carriers is not without controversy. Diplomatically, it will exert a profound impact on China's foreign relations, especially with the ASEAN countries, Japan and Australia. ASEAN leaders would fear that 'China may seek to play a role in the region similar to that played by the US in Central America'.[112] Japan has openly linked its economic aid to China and the PLA's construction of an aircraft carrier. All this could not have failed to arouse concern in the Ministry of Foreign Affairs. China's vice premier Qian Qichen has stated several times that China would not build aircraft carriers.

Militarily, there are growing voices of doubt for such a project from within the PLA. A small but increasing number of futurists have questioned the value of aircraft carriers in future high-tech limited wars. To this RMA school of thought the future sea battle may not be dominated by aircraft carriers but by missile carriers, which are much smaller and much more survivable. When a missile carrier launches large numbers of over-the-horizon precision missiles from afar, it can better perform the missions of an aircraft carrier and it is more cost-effective.

Technologically, there are bottle-neck difficulties for the navy to tackle. If the technology of developing special equipment such as catapults, arrester wires and elevators presented an insurmountable obstacle for the USSR, it would be a larger obstacle for the Chinese. The PLA has certainly placed considerable emphasis on the need for western expertise in these areas. It is fully aware how difficult it would be to obtain related software and hardware. Another key block facing the navy is the advanced technology needed for protecting carriers from enemy attacks, particularly missiles. Without sufficient anti-air and anti-surface missile defence systems, an aircraft carrier would present itself as a 'floating corpse' in a sea battle with the superpower. Therefore early warning and electronic countermeasure technology are essential for the defence of carriers. Given the current stage of China's research in these two areas, enormous efforts are required if China is to bridge the gap in technology. Other obstacles include the design and development of aircraft suitable for operating from the carrier, an effective C³I system, and the training of the carrier's crew.

Additionally, the astronomical cost of building the carriers is particularly prohibitive when China is struggling with its economic transformation: even by cheap Chinese standards, calculated in the mid-1980s, it would cost the state treasury over four billion *yuan*. If other costs are included, for example aircraft and electronic warfare systems, the figure would at least double. This was probably the major factor in the cancellation of the project in 1987. Under the circumstances, naval commanders have been advised that for the time being having more H–6IVs in service, which would strengthen their regular surveillance over disputed waters far away from the mainland, may prove to be more cost-effective. The argument can be further reinforced by the fact that China has acquired aerial refuelling kits, which can greatly extend the combat radius of the NAF.

Yet the naval leadership has never wavered in its determination to build aircraft carriers. Admiral Liu Huaqing once said with a lot of passion about his carrier dream: 'I will not die with my eyes closed if I do not see a Chinese aircraft carrier in front of me'.[113] He also questioned the argument that using inflight refuelling to extend the radius of naval aircraft can technically make up for the lack of an aircraft carrier in the South China Sea, in terms of surveillance. He asked, 'Who would protect the refuelling aircraft? And would the refuelling aircraft need to be refuelled? Without an aircraft carrier, how can the operations be sustained?'[114]

Liu Huaqing's resolve has been translated into the navy's practical efforts on two fronts. The first one is the continuing domestic R&D for the aircraft carrier project. The navy's Shanghai Research Institute started the feasibility studies in its 600-metre model pool in the early 1980s. Further tests were conducted in Tai Lake in Jiangsu Province.[115] Some basic designs have been completed and platform experiments are well under way. As far as ship construction is concerned, the navy argued that China already has rich experience in building large ocean-going surface ships, including construction of a 120 000-tonne oil tanker for Norway in 1986.

Since the early 1980s both civilian and naval institutes have undertaken comprehensive experiments on ships of extra width.[116] In the meantime, an alternative plan has been proposed to retrofit a large civilian ship to provide a training platform.[117]

The second front of the PLAN's aircraft carrier initiative has been reflected by its persistent shopping trips around the world since the beginning of the 1990s. There are numerous media reports about China's attempts to purchase one or two aircraft carriers. First the world focused its attention on a possible Sino–Russian or Sino–Ukrainian deal on one second-hand Soviet carrier such as the *Varyag*. Then it was shifted a few years later to Spain, where the Chinese officers were seen discussing a possible purchase of a brand new carrier design. Finally, Liu Huaqing was said to have raised a request to buy the French carrier *Clemenceau*, which was scheduled for scrapping in 1998, during his last official trip to France as an active officer in September 1996. This time the deal may not be 'crying wolf', as the senior French officials embraced the idea enthusiastically. They reportedly stated that France would like to give *Clemenceau* to the Chinese for nothing, provided that France was allowed to do the retrofitting of the vessel. Although France needs to find ways to circumvent the EU's arms embargo on China imposed since 1989, the abiding effect of the embargo has already been losing ground for some time.[118]

If the deal is to come through, it will give the PLAN a major boost not only in realising its decades-old aircraft carrier ambition but also in uplifting the war capability that the Chinese have planned for its first carrier. Although more than 30 years old, *Clemenceau* can launch highly capable fighter jets. This represents a sharp contrast to either *Varyag* or the Spanish carrier, which are capable only of launching short take-off/vertical landing fighters, which have a relatively short range and payload. The PLAN would really prefer to have a fairly high starting point in mastering aircraft carrier technology and combat capabilities. In this respect, *Clemenceau* is an ideal choice.

The navy has also disputed the opinion that the lack of funding is the biggest impediment for the project. One naval officer argued that China spent 13 billion *yuan* on its space program when it was much poorer. If the decision is taken at a sufficiently high political level, and national support can be mobilised, budgetary constraints should not be too difficult to resolve. Indeed, if the state could concentrate its strength on one project, there is no obstacle that could not be removed.[119] Moreover, the lengthy process associated with the development of a carrier means that the cost breakdown for each year will not be unbearably high. Adjustments may be made in the overall military budget to increase the naval share. And the navy, too, can allocate more money from its new weapon research fund. Ultimately the carrier project relies on political determination.[120] Increasingly the question to be or not to be seems related to when China feels its economy is strong enough to build an aircraft carrier.[121]

In the final analysis the Chinese leadership is seriously assessing the pros and cons of the carrier initiative. However, the current CMC leadership centred around two infantry solders Generals Zhang Wannian and Chi Haotian, may not be as enthusiastic as their predecessor in considering such a project. As pointed out by a research group in the PLA National Defence University,

> whether or not we should go ahead with the construction of an aircraft carrier is not a naval question. It is related to the question of how to adjust the overall force posture and national defence policy. Inevitably this will cause wide domestic and international concerns.[122]

7

The PLA and regional security

The end of the Cold War has left a fluid situation in the Asia–Pacific region. The 'rise of China' question, which centres on its fast growth in economic and military power, seems to have made the situation even more unpredictable.[1] While some Asian countries worry about China's long-term intentions, China itself has also developed a pessimistic image of the new world order, which, it believes, is overtly dominated by the US and the west, even though the Chinese have acknowledged the fact that for the first time since the nineteenth century China has been relieved of any major military threat. China can no longer take shelter behind bipolarity on many concrete issues such as human rights and weapons sales. The conflict in interests between China and the west has been brought into the open and intensified. This has led to a conspiracy theory popular in China that the west will step up challenges to China's domestic stability and territorial sovereignty in order to slow down China's economic growth. In view of this many PLA strategists have regarded the end of the first Cold War as ushering in a long period of cold peace, and have responded with a call to accelerate the country's military modernisation. On the other hand, they also see that in the era of multipolarity, the lines between friends and potential adversaries are not clear-cut. War can be avoided at least in the short run, giving the PLA a vital breathing space to overcome its dangerous transitional vacuum in hardware development.

A REALPOLITIK PLA?

How does the PLA perceive its strategic security environment? This question has no simple answers. The direction of China's armament policy is not always in tune with its foreign policy orientation, which is non-confrontational by nature.[2] While the latter is designed to prevent a crisis situation from emerging through diplomatic means, the former is more influenced by a worst case scenario based on a comparison of military strength and the order of battle.[3] With such a world outlook the PLA sees potential enemies all around. Asia is now in the midst of an intense military modernisation drive against a backdrop of major power involvement. According to PLA analysts, the protracted Cold War *détente* hinged on a relative balance of power between the two superpowers. The collapse of the USSR removed its foundation, resulting in a lot of uncertainties. Without the balance of the USSR the remaining superpower may be tempted to exercise its hegemonic power more willingly. In the Far East the long-standing insecurity between the two Koreas and across the Taiwan Strait may involve major powers in a sudden confrontation, resulting in a military clash. China's war planners, like those elsewhere, exhibit an obsession with the traditional security dilemma: any relative gains in military power of its potential adversaries are viewed as weakening China's defence capabilities. Obtaining a high-tech edge appears to be the most reliable guarantee for national security. In the words of a PLA officer: 'China's economic construction and peaceful diplomacy can be carried out only when these are backed up by the military's sufficient preparation for action.'[4]

Therefore, from the PLA's perspective, China is under serious threat from the west. The PLA's strategic shift since the 1990s can best be construed as a military readjustment designed to cope with a second Cold War in Asia, as vividly reflected in the PLA's wish-list, which suggests an offensive-oriented defence.[5] As mentioned at the beginning of this book, the PLA's new defence strategy recognises that with the superpower's intervention China may have to face a coalition of potential opponents.[6] Although this has not been a new dimension in the PRC's war preparations since its founding, it generates huge pressure on the PLA, whose capabilities are simply inadequate for dealing with such a development. More concretely, the PLA harbours the following perceptions of each of its potential opponents in the region.

Japan: the long-term rivalry?

The PLA is becoming increasingly sensitive to the growing military power of the countries which may pose long-term security threats.

The rapid growth of the Japanese navy in particular has been seen as a major potential threat to the PLA.[7] To PLA planners, Japan's growing military power is the primary mechanism though which the country is seeking political power. This is reflected in Japan's southward expansion strategy, which was interpreted as attempting to fill the potential power vacuum left by the US's readjustment of its forward deployment.[8] To Chinese commanders the quick growth of the Japanese navy is neither necessary nor desirable: the Russian navy is no longer a threat to Japan, so why proceed with this massive build-up? The PLA believes that Japan is motivated by three considerations: the first is, naturally, to contain China, filling a role as one of the two anchors for US forward deployment in the Far East; the second objective is to place itself in a better strategic position vis-a-vis ASEAN, again to aid US efforts to dominate East Asia; and the third is to monitor India, whose strategic plan to achieve freedom of movement in a vast area between the Malacca Strait and the Suez Canal has caught Japan's attention. Among the three, the first objective appears to be the most important one in the minds of Japan's naval commanders. The outward expansion of the Japanese Maritime Defence Force could be seen as posing a challenge to the Chinese navy. For instance, its 1000 nautical miles sea denial ambition is perceived as aiming at control of the waters around the first island chain in the West Pacific and especially control of the SLOCs near the Diaoyu Islands and Balin and Bashi Straits, and would effectively cut into the eastward movement of the PLAN.[9] Consequently the two navies may encounter in the West Pacific in the future, because they have both identified the first island chain as the gateway into the open oceans.

To some extent, China may regard this evolution as a mixed blessing, since a militaristic Japan's move toward becoming a world class military power may also alarm the Americans and Russians and thus increase the weight of the China 'card'.[10] Indeed, the PLA believes that the post–Cold War era may see rising conflicts among Western powers. Prominent among these conflicts will be worsening trade ties between Japan and the US.[11] Moreover, most Chinese analysts assume that Japan will not emerge as a threat before the turn of the century.[12] Beyond that, the PLA is confident that China's enhanced military capability can eventually match Japan's: it is capable of preventing the Japanese from attempting a repetition of history. The nuclear age has made island countries highly vulnerable. At the same time, PLA officers agree that although the US–Japanese Common Security and Cooperation Treaty is formulated to enhance the US's forward deployment position vis-a-vis China and Russia in the short run, it also functions to keep at bay the tendency of Japan remilitarising itself in the longer run. It is particularly useful in preventing Japan from going nuclear. This constraint imposed upon Japan may explain why China has chosen Japan to be the first country with which to establish limited mechanisms for security transparency.[13] Yet the PLA has also realised that if it does not have sufficient means for self-protection, utilising a militarily strong Japan to balance western pressure may backfire badly. Thus, having to cope with a politically powerful Japan will provide an additional incentive for a faster modernisation of the Chinese military.[14]

However, the new interpretation of the US–Japanese Common Security and Cooperation Treaty in 1996 may have shattered the wishful thinking of these PLA personnel who envisaged playing a 'Japan card' against pressure from the west. Japan's former minister for defence, Seiroku Kajiyama, has openly announced that Japan has expanded its area of security vigilance to cover the Taiwan Strait, and will not lie idle when its allies resort to action in the region. Japan was the only Asian country that openly criticised China for its war games in the Taiwan Strait in March 1996 and offered navigation assistance to the US naval task force. Consequently, the long-term rivalry, as perceived by the PLA, has suddenly become an immediate concern. According to senior colonel Yu Juliang from the PLA National Defence University, the renewed Japan–US alliance has apparently shifted its target from the former USSR to China, which is seen as the potential foe. If Japan functioned as a shield for US forward deployment in the Far East in the past, it is now also assuming the role of a sword.[15] When a major action takes place in the Taiwan Strait with US involvement, Japan, bound to the US–Japan security treaty, would receive an unrefusable request from the US to join its war plans. This was officially confirmed by a classified study made by the Japanese Defence Agency at the instruction of Prime Minister Hashimoto. During such an action Japan would assist US forces in various ways, for example, refuelling US warships, offering military intelligence and providing medical treatment.[16] To the PLA this involvement is an indirect act of war against China, signalling that Japan will definitely side with China's enemy in a Taiwan conflict. This would be a potential turning point in the bilateral relationship. If such a scenario indeed came true, the PLA would have to consider whether to attack Japan or US military bases in Japan.

Russia: long-term uncertainties?

In recent years Chinese and Russian leaders have enjoyed talking about a Sino–Russian strategic partnership in the new century. At least on the surface the bilateral relations are closer than they have ever been since the break-up of the Sino–Russian alliance in the late 1950s. Without Russia's military sales to China, the PLA would still be knocking on the door of the high-tech era. The supply of Chinese consumer goods to the Russians in turn has lessened the Russian government's difficulties in meeting the daily needs of the population. Strategic partners or strange bedfellows, the new cooperative relations between the two major powers have helped their efforts to better position themselves in the emerging post–Cold War multipolarity. Consequently each of them has benefited from this relationship in its dealings with the sole superpower and the whole western camp.

To some Chinese civilian and military analysts, however, Russia still represents a potential threat, not only because it has not yet settled all its territorial disputes with China, but also because its future is uncertain. What is more, this uncertainty is highlighted by a deepening trend of extreme nationalistic strife inside Russia. For example, local governments and residents in the Russian Far East have expressed opposition to the border treaties signed by Moscow. In a worst case scenario, with economic difficulties deepening, the history of Germany in the 1930s may repeat itself in Russia in the first decades of the new century. To compound this uncertainty, a general pro-west stance by the top Russian leadership and intelligentsia may pave the way for anti-Chinese feelings. If Russia gradually stabilises, it may become a strong economic power competing with China and other regional countries in the world market. If the reverse is true, social unrest will spill over the Sino–Russian borders. In both cases, nationalistic tendencies are likely to prevail. Militarily, the number of Russian soldiers along the Sino–Russian borders is still too large to make the Chinese feel comfortable, despite the troop reduction agreement signed by China, Russia and three other central Asian states in early 1997. Since the 1990s Russia has constantly transferred troops from Europe to the east of the Urals. This has not evaded the eyes of PLA analysts. In short, whatever happens in Russia, the PLA may have to work out contingency plans to deal with a powerful Russian military. After all, Russia shares long land borders with China, and the two countries have yet to eliminate completely their unpleasant historical legacies.[17]

A second Sino–US hot war in the 21st century?

One reason for the PLA's adoption of a high-tech defence strategy is the perceived potential threat posed by lethal US weaponry and war strategy, as demonstrated by the Gulf War in 1991. Politically, the PLA's move was a logical response to the US post–4 June sanctions, F–16 sales to Taiwan, the most-favoured-nation (MFN) debate, obstruction of China's Olympic bid and human rights pressure. US-led Western efforts to change China's socialist system through 'peaceful evolution' have been regarded as a grave threat to China's security. PLA analysts often cite US nuclear targeting of China as evidence that Washington views Beijing as a potential military adversary.[18]

Although the PLA generally does not view the increased tension in Sino–US relations as a portent of any imminent military confrontation, incidents such as the forced inspection of the *Yinhe* shipment in 1993 and the USS *Kittyhawk* stalking a Chinese submarine in 1994 crystallised the potential for a serious clash. The PLA Navy's outward stretches have increased encounters with the superpower. This is the reason why the two countries saw the necessity of establishing regular high-level military consultation as a key mechanism for preventing unexpected incidents. It is not surprising that the first such consultation in 1988 between China's deputy chief of general staff Lieutenant-General Xiong Guangkai and his US counterpart, deputy secretary of defence, was about avoidance of naval clashes on the high seas.

In private, however, US Defence Secretary William Perry's statement, 'We have the best damned navy', has convinced the PLA of whom it will have to deal with sooner or later.[19] More seriously, as one senior PLA researcher pointed out, the US Defence Spending Act of August 1996 identified, for the first time in legal terms, China as its potential enemy, which could exert a far-reaching impact on bilateral relations.[20] Indeed, some of these incidents appear serious enough to pose a question: will it trigger small armed exchanges if next time China does not allow US inspection of a Chinese shipment? A large US invasion of China's vast land is most unlikely, but a punitive surgical strike against some of its military targets has to be reckoned with.

The positioning of two aircraft carrier battle groups close to the Taiwan Strait in March 1996 especially stimulated some senior Chinese security analysts to contemplate a second Sino–US hot war.[21] To the PLA, the show of force by the US Navy in waters close to Taiwan clearly indicated changing geo-strategic relations in East Asia. Any plan for military action against Taiwan will now have to factor in US intervention. The possible use of airborne warning and control systems to help coordinate Taiwan's air defence and anti-submarine warfare support to the north, east and south of Taiwan would greatly increase PRC losses with little threat to American lives.[22] Therefore, the possibility of a Sino–US conflict should not be ruled out completely despite the efforts by both sides to avoid such an incident. In a way the US authors of the book *The Coming Conflict with China* have their like-minded colleagues in the PLA.[23]

All this adds validity to a 1987 prediction by Admiral Zhang Xusan that in the next fifteen years or more, a major war involving the PLA may not be entirely avoidable.[24] Events in the late 1980s and early 1990s convinced the PLA's high command that it must be militarily prepared for a sudden crisis.[25] This sense of inevitability of war in the long run has been deeply influenced by a post–Cold War reality where a powerful US anti-China lobby pushes for a confrontation with the PRC.[26] More concretely, for the PLA the reality of war stems from the irreconcilable conflicts between China and Taiwan over the issue of reunification/independence, from the non-negotiable nature of the South China Sea disputes, and from the Americans' lingering Cold War mentality of eliminating ideological foes. Above all, a sense of war inevitability is perceived as the unavoidable outcome of a clash of civilisations based on opposing economic interests and value systems—a clash provoked by 'US neo-interventionism', to use a new PLA term.[27] Therefore, the new uncertainties in Asia and the Pacific have led the Party to put more emphasis on military modernisation in general and high-tech weaponry in particular.

CHINA'S VIEW OF COLLECTIVE SECURITY

The PLA's inferior capabilities vis-a-vis the major powers and its perception of a hostile world after the Cold War have produced a particular set of attitudes towards issues of security cooperation in the region. China's reluctant and belated response to the international call for greater military transparency and confidence-building is one of the indicators of the PLA's position on a multinational security mechanism, which is best characterised as ambivalent. China agrees with the argument that the peace of individual countries cannot be separated from that of the international system. Security can only be maintained through dialogue between adversaries, so there is a need for establishing a forum for such communications.[28] This is why China has engaged some major powers in the region, among them the US, Japan, Russia and Australia, in bilateral security dialogues. China has also explored the concept of security cooperation with major powers to reduce the level of nuclear threat in Northeast Asia. At a conference at the Georgia Institute of Technology in 1995, the four major players in Northeast Asia—Russia, China, Japan and South Korea—reached an understanding to work for a limited nuclear-free zone in the area. 'Limited' here refers to a decision to relinquish certain types of nuclear weapons, such as tactical ones. The PLA was strongly opposed to this idea at the beginning but eventually accepted it, as a goodwill gesture to rectify the non-proliferation treaty (NPT).[29] Military transparency has also been placed on the agenda of China's bilateral talks with its neighbouring countries, although China has placed strict limitations on the level of transparency. The PLA has thus slowly come to realise that in the post–Cold War era it cannot reject the idea of multilateral security without a negative reaction from the region. This has been the chief reason why China published its first *Defence White Paper* in 1995, and another in 1998.

However, China is more ambivalent on the question of how to take part in these bilateral and multilateral security dialogues and how far to go. In other words, the key to China's ambivalence is that China is reluctant to place itself under the constraints of such a mechanism. Generally speaking, China is more in favour of bilateral dialogue. As far as multilateral security arrangements are concerned, it has serious reservations for a number of reasons. The most obvious one is its fear of US domination of these regimes. One leading Chinese international relations analyst has this to say about such a development:

> China is sensitive towards a collective security system or mechanism initiated by the big powers, out of fear that China might be put under the control of the big powers and that its national interests might be injured.[30]

He adds another reason why China is reluctant to join these collective security dialogues. One objective of these mechanisms is an arms control agenda for the region, and often the forums are led by big powers which already possess advanced military capabilities. China will be under pressure to reduce its armaments. However,

> China is a late-comer to defence modernisation. Its defence buildup was restricted by its economic underdevelopment for

decades, and was started not long ago thanks to the progress in economic reform . . . This is the kind of mentality the western countries have to understand.[31]

In his view, therefore, it is unfair and unreasonable for regional security arrangements to pressure China in this regard.

The PLA's basic assessment of the post–Cold War Asia–Pacific region can be characterised as an emerging multipolarity represented by the interaction of the US, Russia, China, Japan and the ASEAN countries. The nature of this multipolarity is a kind of balance of power in geopolitical terms. To the PLA it is very difficult, if not impossible, to aggregate these multiple poles in a mutually acceptable security framework. Indeed, there will be a long way to go before the five major poles can truly talk about interdependent relations. In other words, all of these powers have their own strategic interests to pursue and sometimes these interests clash. Very often competition rather than cooperation is an appropriate term to describe the situation.[32] Outside these major powers, Asian countries have not yet developed to the stage where, as in Europe, interdependent relations foster a unified market. In Asia, most countries are still concerned about their internal stability and political legitimacy. Economic cooperation is deepening among these countries, but so is competition for obtaining more resources and investment. Under the circumstances, it is too early to think of any feasible formula to bring the region together.[33]

Functionally, the PLA does not have enough confidence that multilateral security mechanisms are an effective means to solve regional conflicts. Asia is still troubled by many Cold War legacies. 'Sitting war' in the Korean peninsula can evolve into a shooting war. Some potential conflicts, such as those across the Taiwan Strait, in the South China Sea, and around the Northern Territories, may develop into confrontation. These have made the continuation of bilateral alliance arrangements a necessity. For the countries that may be involved in a major conflict, while multilateral security dialogue is conducive to regional stability, bilateral alliances are more reliable in dealing with any potential wars, as the US security umbrella serves as a deterrent no other security arrangement can substitute for. In the Chinese view these bilateral security relationships are a barrier to the development of an effective multilateral security forum.[34] Largely, this is because if the countries concerned do not enjoy equal guarantees of security, for instance, North Korea versus South Korea, they have to think of enhancing their military capabilities themselves. As the limitations for any formal or informal multilateral security mechanisms are both logical and obvious, it will take a long time for the convergent strategy to really work.[35]

What is China's position on the issue of collective security? In a research report published by the State Council's International Research Centre, one senior Chinese analyst, Xu Jian, recommended to the Chinese leadership several foreign policy options regarding regional multinational security frameworks. The report examines the pros and cons of the four collective mechanisms likely to be created in Asia and the Pacific (formal multilateralism, security concert, loose concert arcs and concentric arcs). According to Xu's report, formal multilateralism is the model put forward in 1990 by Gareth Evans, then Australian minister of foreign affairs, and is based on the Council for Security Cooperation in Europe (CSCE). Security concert is a concept similar to that of a concert of powers, which stresses the role of major powers in resolving world conflicts. Loose concert arcs describes the halfway house between alliance security and collective security, which is based on the concept of balance of power, recognises the importance of collective security and interdependence, and involves bilateral dialogue plus institutionalisation, for example Post-Ministerial Conference (PMC), ASEAN Regional Forum (ARF), and Asia-Pacific Economic Cooperation (APEC). Concentric arcs denotes a collective Asian security mechanism, with only limited involvement of outside powers. It is a copy of the CSCE, but with less abiding power.

Xu's report concluded that the first and the last were not feasible now, if not entirely impossible. China could make use of the second and the third, although each contained positive and negative elements. He suggested that China consider the model of security concert in the short-to-medium run, if the balance of power in the region was stable, if Sino–US relations did not deteriorate due to Taiwan or other issues, and if China did not plan to make major concessions in the South China Sea in the near future. Xu believed that if major powers pushed for other models, it would be difficult without China's cooperation. In the long run, he would support the model of loose concert arcs because it had stronger abiding power. However, there needed to be preparations for such an option. For instance, according to him, China needed to propose more specific principles and plans concerning the South China Sea and formulate more comprehensive contingencies in dealing with possible upheavals in Sino–US and mainland–Taiwan relations. Moreover, even if China accepted the loose concert arcs,

'We should still uphold that the bilateral principle was the foundation, and multilateralism was the supplement'.[36]

What is even more interesting is Xu's comment on the role of the regional multilateral security mechanisms as perceived by China. He states:

> Because these mechanisms can only replenish the defence mechanisms, it is very difficult to see any breakthroughs in their implementation. Moreover, the military strategy of some of these powers is potentially targeted at us. Therefore, our defence has to rely on our own capabilities. Whichever model we agree to adopt, we must pay attention to strengthening our national defence. This is the basis for maintaining security for our country.[37]

Xu's remarks vividly reflect a high degree of ambivalence in China's attitudes towards the post–Cold War world order: its distrust of interdependence on the one hand, and its hope to benefit from its increased involvement in international political and economic cooperation on the other.

THE TAIWAN REUNIFICATION IMPASSE: CASE STUDY I

The PLA's missile test in July 1995 marked a turning point in the PRC's Taiwan policy, which has shifted from an emphasis on peaceful inducement to a combination of peaceful inducement and threats of force. Although China has not given up the goal of eventual reunification through negotiations, the emphasis on military deterrence seems to have gained more currency. The question of whether this shift represents a temporary and calculated over-reaction or a long-lasting policy orientation remains unanswered. Given the rising influence of pro-independence forces across the Strait, and the increased policy weight of the PLA at home, China's hardline option will probably hold centre stage in its Taiwan policy for some time, although messages of peace will continue to be sent over.

As a result, a war between China and Taiwan is perceived as looming large in the background of the China–Taiwan relationship.[38] The possibility of war is driven by Taiwan's gradual slide toward declared independence and China's rising nationalist attitudes toward its lost territories. In recent years the PLA has studied the issue of how a sovereign state deals with a situation where part of the country strives for independence, as in the case of Chechnya. They have concluded that a national government must be as firm as possible in suppressing any separatist tendencies. Exerting military pressure is a natural response. When such a separatist tendency first emerges, a political offensive (propaganda) should be launched and military threats should be stepped up. When the banner of independence is openly raised, military action must be taken in order to destroy the armed forces upon which separatism relies.[39] According to Admiral Zhang Xusan, a future war in the China seas will most likely be fought with an aim of securing political and diplomatic interests. Such a war will not be initiated according to the laws of military science. In fact, it may be waged in complete defiance of them. For instance, victory in a sea battle may be easily attained but the navy may have to stop its operations promptly when the state believes a cease-fire is likely to achieve more political and diplomatic benefits (the Nansha Islands scenario). Conversely, upon the order from the state, the navy may have to fight a war which, by military calculations, should never have been fought; the navy has to do it at whatever price (the Taiwan scenario with US support).[40]

Taiwan's strategic value

Behind these obvious political reasons for war, the PLA's recent hard line on Taiwan can also be explored from a military point of view. Taiwan represents a very useful stimulus for the PLA to project a strong naval presence around the Strait. At present the real danger of a war, as perceived by the PLA, lies in the unfavourable tilting of the military balance across the Strait by Taiwan's procurement of advanced weapons from the west. As pointed out by a PLA naval researcher, the partial technological superiority of Taiwan's air force and navy is the principal capital with which Taiwan pushes for independence. According to his analysis, only when the PLA exceeds Taiwan's military capability will its deterrence achieve the desired effect: prevention of independence and thus prevention of war. Air and naval power is indispensable in the struggle for reunification.[41] Apparently, the PLA's new assessment of Taiwan's military power has convinced the civilian leaders that a peaceful offensive can no longer work if Taiwan is militarily more capable than the mainland. This is the background to the series of war games since mid-1995.

To fully understand the PLA's war games in March 1996, one also needs to analyse China's perception of Taiwan's enormous strategic value for a forward PLA posture in the Pacific. Two PLA naval officers offer this insight:

> China is semi-concealed by the first island chain. If it wants to prosper, it has to advance into the Pacific, in which China's future

lies. Taiwan, facing the Pacific in the east, is the only unobstructed exit for China to move into the ocean. If this gateway is opened for China, then it becomes much easier for China to manoeuvre in the West Pacific.[42]

Furthermore, Taiwan's strategic importance has been assessed from its position in the hub of SLOCs in the West Pacific: it is situated conveniently to control the Balin and Bashi Straits in the south, to block the Gonggu and Naguo waterways in the north, and to protect the mainland in the east. As such, it may be used to adversely affect the US's forward deployment, Japan's economic lifeline, and Russia's freedom of movement. So if Taiwan returns to the mainland, this will not only help China's efforts to resolve the South China Sea problem but also disrupt the US's front strategic chain in the Asia–Pacific region.[43] This PLA perspective on Taiwan directly clashes with the US perspective, which appreciates Taiwan's value as an unsinkable aircraft carrier for its forward engagement and access to strategic points in the Far East.[44]

Brinkmanship

Clashing perspectives held by both parties across the Taiwan Strait often perpetuate a war mentality. A war may never break out but, for the PLA, the prospect of a war will always exist. Between peace and war there will be continued tests of force. Sometimes this may just mean loud voices. At other times it may mean a kind of brinkmanship, which is now an important mission of the PLA. This was best demonstrated by the PLA's war games in March 1996. The military is subject to a nation's political and security impulses. Brinkmanship is one response to challenges to China's vital interests. It is seen as risky but necessary in the evolution of 'cold peace'. The danger of this is not just that it sends out belligerent signals; when a military embarks on this path, it is also preparing to fight if left with no other choice.[45] One clear indication of this was that during the exercise the PLA Air Force ordered its aircraft to fly over the middle line of the Strait, purposely breaking a tacit understanding, observed by both sides for years, that each side will keep its warships and planes to its half of the waters. General Ye Jingrong, Taiwan's former deputy commander-in-chief of the army, believes that once the understanding is removed, the PLA may continue to encroach upon the space in the Strait. This could pose a grave threat to Taiwan's military, whose strategic defence depth is shallow.[46]

Therefore, brinkmanship involves both war games and war

avoidance. The pendulum seems likely to sway towards the latter, however, at least in the foreseeable future. Missile firing carries the message 'Do not force our hand'. This disguises the reality that the PLA is not yet ready for any major action. For example, the PLA has to ask itself whether it can achieve reliable air control over the war zone for a fairly protracted time and the required landing capabilities to launch a large-scale invasion. As mentioned in earlier chapters, the PLA is in the midst of a dangerous transition. Until the PLA feels confident, it will be reluctant to be dragged into a war of a certain scale. Militarily, brinkmanship in essence buys time for the PLA to prepare for a real showdown in the future.

On the other hand, however, the PLA's brinkmanship in 1995–96 served as a convincing indicator of the changing mentality among senior officers in both the armed forces and other security establishments (if not yet a real change in policy) toward a more hardline approach to territorial issues. After Clinton granted Li Teng-hui a visa to visit the US in May 1995, the central authority was under increasing pressure to revise the 'one centre, two basic points' guiding principle set by Deng for China's modernisation. In the PLA's view, Deng's 'one centre', economics in command, should be joined by another centre, namely the safeguarding of national sovereignty and territorial integrity, which should always be regarded as the primary task of the Party and the military.[47] Under such a policy guideline, an accelerated military build-up is a foregone conclusion.

For the time being, however, the civilian leadership still faithfully follows Deng's instruction that the peaceful solution of territorial disputes should form the foundation of policy formulation toward Taiwan. And there is a broad consensus among them that an escalation of territorial disputes will hurt China's important foreign relations. The enlarged Politburo's Beidaihe conference in August 1995 decided to persist with Deng's 'one-centre' principle, after Jiang Zemin and Li Peng persuaded the participants that at this moment a non-confrontational policy best served China's interests. The debate itself, however, may have long-term effects, and a shift in mentality among both senior civilian and military leaders may be felt in due time. That the leadership prefers to maintain an ambiguous stance rather than push for a premature solution stems from its realisation that China is now under serious constraints and at the same time cannot afford to make a rash decision. For the PLA this ambiguity may at once mean lying low as well as being assertive.

Assessing the 1996 war games

As the latest round of Chinese military manoeuvres is now over, it may be high time for both sides across the Taiwan Strait to contemplate what to do next. So an initial assessment of what they achieved is in order. A crucial question we need to ask is why this brinkmanship was carried out in the first place. The paradoxical answer is that it was intended to ensure peace across the Strait, no matter how ironic this may have seemed. The logic is as follows: China will have to wage a war against Taiwan if the latter declares independence; military threats will reduce the likelihood of a declaration of independence; therefore military threats will make a war less likely. Even during the live-fire exercise, all analysts pointed out it was highly unlikely a real war would break out. Convincing proof for this was that senior officials from both sides of the Strait were in the US during the exercises, conveying the same message of peace, with the US acting as the messenger.

The three successive live-fire exercises in March 1996 gave the PLA an opportunity to conduct an operation clearly aimed at simulating a seizure of Jinmen, Mazu and the Penghu Islands.[48] Without any pressing political need, it would not have been easy for the PLA to arrange such a costly endeavour—costly not only in terms of the special budget required for it, which is estimated to have taken up about 3 per cent of the PLA's annual allocation, but also in terms of China's international image.[49] However, in terms of arousing domestic support, the exercise can be regarded as well worthwhile. First, it has led to the installation of a semi-civilian-military war preparation system in the coastal areas in Fujian Province. It was not a coincidence that the PLA invited a large number of civilian leaders to observe the exercises. In a sense this spells out a long-term preparation for 'a people's war' against Taiwan's slide toward independence.[50] Second, the extensive television coverage of the exercises displayed all kinds of PLA weapons to the public. For TV watchers, it was a rare opportunity since the Gulf War to witness such a demonstration of military muscle. And since they could not really tell the difference in the firepower displayed by the PLA and the Allied forces, their confidence in the PLA has been greatly boosted. This may in turn help the leadership gain support for hardline policy measures in the future.

In terms of international repercussions, however, the PLA's war games may have altered the existing geopolitics in East Asia to the disadvantage of the PLA. First, the PLA is determined not to be dragged into a two-front battle at the same time with both ASEAN over the South China Sea dispute and Taiwan over the issue of independence. In the new political climate the resolution of the South China Sea dispute is subject to that of the Taiwan problem, which may have forced the PLA to put its southward reorientation plan on the back burner.[51] As a result this has dictated a readjustment of war preparation priorities regarding territorial disputes. Conflicts in the Taiwan Strait and in the South China Sea require different kinds of readiness, and the Taiwan issue apparently dominates the PLA's consideration of troop deployment and weapons programs. Second, the war games in the Taiwan Strait have driven key regional powers to closer military cooperation with the Americans. This is reflected in the response to the war games by the Australians and the Japanese, who are now more willing to serve as the US's two anchors in the Pacific than they were before the war games. Japan has even agreed to participate in collective military action should this be required. This is by far its furthest step toward becoming a 'normal' military power. One senior Chinese security analyst revealed in May 1996 that Japan's swift response to the changing situation across the Taiwan Strait had taken the Chinese government by surprise.[52]

THE SOUTH CHINA SEA AND PLA POWER PROJECTION: CASE STUDY II

The 1980s saw the PLA's power projection extend to the South China Sea. The PLA Navy is clearly charged with the mission to safeguard China's maritime interests centred on China's territorial claims in the area. The PLA has contingency plans to defend the islands that China claims but are occupied by foreign navies.[53] At the same time the navy is not capable of any sustained sea battle far away from home. According to some analysts, technical inadequacies forced the PLAN to confine its 1988 operations to a few small reefs in the South China Sea, because it would have been incapable of conducting a protracted war with Vietnam.[54] This contradiction has dictated some unique behavioural patterns of the Chinese navy in the South China Sea since the mid-1980s.

The enhanced capability for an armed conflict

The preparation for action in the South China Sea has enhanced the navy's South Sea Fleet (SSF), which will bear the first brunt of any hostilities in the area. In the early 1970s the SSF was the

weakest among the three fleets (North, East and South Sea Fleets).
But since the 1974 Sino–Vietnam clash in the Paracel Islands, the
fleet has grown on a par with, if not exceeding, the other two in
terms of force levels. In recent years, for instance, two of the three
Yukang class LSTs, the newest and largest in the navy, have been
transferred to the SSF. The assignment to the fleet of the first ship
of China's modified Luda class destroyers, *Zhanjiang*, indicates the
extent to which naval authorities have recognised its strategic
value. As far as aircraft are concerned, one technical reason why
the PLA opted for the Su–27 over the MiG–29 was that the former
are twin-engined. This is a key factor for survivability over the
sea.[55] Another reason is the Su–27's longer range, which enhances
the capacity for interdiction far from the coastal bases. Although
the distance of about 1400 kilometres from the fleet's nearest base
stretches its flight radius to the limit, it can still make a difference
compared to the MiG–29, especially when China's in-flight refuelling technology becomes operational.

The PLA has launched several military projects in the Paracel
Islands and the reefs it occupies in the South China Sea. Woody
Island, the largest in the Paracel Islands, has become a military
fortress with a naval detachment comprising tank units, AA batteries and high-speed missile and patrol boats. There are also a C³I
centre capable of processing satellite-transferred information, and
a runway capable of landing medium-sized fixed-wing aircraft.[56]
This has reduced the burden of air coverage for a South China Sea
operation from the PLAN's nearest base in Yulin, Hainan Province,
by several hundred kilometres, thus raising the navy's rapid
response capability for a South China Sea incident.

Nevertheless, in the near future, the navy's capability for
coping with a conflict around the South China Sea will remain
less than that of clear superiority. Its main surface combatants are
vulnerable, as they are exposed to land-based air assault. In contrast, China's land-based medium-range bombers cannot sustain an
operation over the ocean due to their small numbers. The same
can be said for China's submarine capability. Although most of the
parties involved in the South China Sea dispute do not have strong
ASW capabilities, the activity of PLAN submarines is restricted
by the problem that most of them can only stay submerged for a
limited period of time. Apart from the political constraints on the
Chinese, which will be analysed in the next section, these hardware deficiencies have dictated the pattern of China's actions in
the area, as can be seen from the following.

Quick occupation and low-intensity clash

China's construction of an observation station on the Yongshu Reef (Fiery Cross) triggered the fighting between the navies of China and Vietnam in March 1988. From the planning stages of the project, China was bent on avoiding a clash, although preparation for a possible battle was more than adequate. The Chinese hoped to achieve occupation without provoking an exchange of fire by seizing the reef before the adversary could respond. The pre-requisite for this was that the reef should not be occupied already, so that the initiative was not an action of capture through assault.[57]

Two aspects of the PLAN's 1988 operation in the South China Sea may give insight into the PLA's planning. First, the reefs taken were not claimed by an ASEAN state with which China wanted to develop good relations. Second, each was submerged at high tide, so the Vietnamese would probably assume the Chinese would not stay permanently, a psychological factor that facilitated quick action.[58] Politically, taking a reef claimed by Vietnam carried the flavour of 'teaching them a lesson' for its continuing occupation of islets in the disputed areas since 1986.

The Chinese geographic survey began in 1987 amid a number of naval exercises in the area. By the end of the year, the naval intelligence ship *Xiangyanghong 5* had obtained all the data needed for the occupation of the Yongshu Reef and the construction to turn it into an artificial islet. Escorted by Frigate 552, a detachment was sent to the reef from Yulin Base in February 1988 and took the reef only a few hours before the arrival of the Vietnamese from nearby. By the time the Vietnamese arrived they could do little but stand offshore.[59] This short difference in time may have signalled what a limited war was all about: careful planning and a quick outcome designed to pre-empt the opponent.

The occupation of the Yongshu Reef triggered domino reactions, with both sides intent on defending their claims. The Chinese sent a destroyer/frigate battle group to the area to reinforce the seizure. Vietnam launched a major initiative to take the unoccupied islets in the southern part of the South China Sea. The battle of 14 March 1988 can be seen as the culmination of this series of actions. Yet no further shots were fired after the 3.14 (14 March) incident. That the clashes were confined to a manage-able level showed the extent to which both sides tried to prevent further escalation. Obviously, neither party considered seesaw war-fare to be in their best interests. The low level of firepower used perfectly served China's purpose of a special kind of limited war in the settling of the South China Sea problem: force was used not as a means to eliminate the opponent's capability but rather to roll back its territorial claims.

Limited objective and tight command and control

The PLA's initiatives in the South China Sea in 1988 and again in 1995 over the Meiji Reef were well calculated and executed.[60] The use of low-level weaponry and only a small number of troops in the South China Sea clash in 1988 reflected the limited tactical objectives sought by the Chinese government as part of its overall political and strategic goals. These can best be characterised as effecting a naval *presence* in military terms, which in turn creates a form of *fait accompli* in legal terms.[61]

Compared with the other claimants—Vietnam, Malaysia, Brunei and the Philippines—China was a latecomer to the South China Sea and has the smallest presence in the South China Sea. By the time China made its first move in 1988, there were only a few reefs left unoccupied among those islets that emerge at low tide. A foothold in the South China Sea was of strategic importance for China. As a semi-enclosed sea linking the Indian and Pacific Oceans, and located between continental Asia and insular South-east Asia, it encompasses important sea lines of communication. For instance, over 70 per cent of Japanese commercial ships go through the South China Sea.[62] A naval presence in this vital sea path would enhance China's strategic position in the West Pacific. There were also economic benefits from such a presence, as China is increasingly dependent on foreign trade, the bulk of which is carried through ocean shipping and through the South China Sea. The sea-bed oil there is another attraction, an even more attractive prospect now that China is a net energy importer.[63] But the most urgent need for China to have a foothold in the South China Sea stemmed from its concern that, without a presence in the South China Sea, it would be either excluded from or marginalised among the group of claimants. Therefore, the presence had to be achieved at any cost.

The PLA may have calculated that, although taking a few uninhabited reefs subject to overlapping claims would cause repercussions from the regional states, to capture them from other countries once they are occupied would have attracted fiercer protests. If China has to have a presence of one sort or another as an expression of sovereignty, it is better to do the former than the latter. Again the question of how large a presence is needed may have mattered less than the presence *per se*. The larger the presence obtained by the use of force, the greater the negative consequences. The PLA's operation in the South China Sea has to be a finely balanced one. The scale of any naval action is thus closely linked to political and diplomatic efforts designed to defuse a subsequent international outcry.[64]

This raises the question of command and control in a low-level regional conflict. According to a PLA strategist:

> Whereas in major wars tactical actions have little influence on the 'overall war situation', in small wars, these may achieve strategic objectives. [So] the objective, location, and timing of an action can be so significant that even tactical actions will require a decision by the highest command, including the head of the state. Thus, those in charge of the strategy for a local war campaign may well have to pass over all intermediate levels of command and communicate directly with the tactical units.[65]

This was especially true of China's action in the South China Sea in 1988. Every detail of the occupation, from the survey in 1987 to the action one year later, was first approved by the highest authority in the Party and the PLA. The firing of the first shot had been prescribed well in advance and was executed, on location, by a rear admiral.[66]

The timing of the initiative was also decided with great care. In 1988, the strike was taken on the eve of the Sino–Soviet rapprochement, which alleviated China's worry about a possible Soviet intervention. The action took place at the time when China's relations with the west had reached the Cold War peak and thus international reaction was deemed to be mild. Added to that was an opportunity offered to China by UNESCO in 1986, when China was asked to establish a weather observation station in the South China Sea.

A dilemma for China's foreign and defence policy

The PLA's power projection in the South China Sea contributes to the perception of a potential Chinese threat in the region. According to many international relations theorists, a big country is automatically considered to be a real or potential threat to its small neighbours. China's occasionally strong rhetoric regarding sovereignty disputes does little to dispel a sense of uneasiness in the minds of its small neighbours. Yet what we hear are always broad generalisations about China's intent. However, there is a large gap between preconception and reality.[67] It is more useful for analysts in the region to provide the concept with substance rather than just perceptions. For instance, empirical study should be conducted on questions such as under what conditions a dispute may turn into a violent conflict and how to find ways to prevent this from happening. Sometimes unsubstantiated preconceptions stand in the way of regional confidence-building and legitimise arms acquisition.[68] This is especially true in Asia, where there is a lack of security mechanisms and transparency.

Moreover, many China specialists in the west believe the long-term socio-economic changes in the country will undercut the foundations of the authoritarian regime and affect its behaviour in world affairs.[69] This clashes with the popular view of a long-term China threat as the 'giant dragon' awakes. So the different perceptions by experts in international relations and by China specialists show a degree of dichotomy in projecting the country's future development.[70] Far too few studies have thus far linked China's internal 'peaceful evolution' and its external behaviour. Even in analysing China's defence and foreign policy, it is important to factor in those constraints that bind China's hands, and incentives that encourage China to become more interdependent.[71] This has been clearly demonstrated by China's handling of the sovereignty disputes over Taiwan and the South China Sea, which represent a dilemma for China's policy makers.

In regard to issues of sovereignty, the Chinese government does not have wide-ranging diplomatic options other than upholding entrenched territorial claims, as indicated by its often-stated position that sovereignty issues are not negotiable.[72] Ever since the first Opium War in 1840, no Chinese government has been able to stand firm in the eyes of the people if it did not uphold the country's claim on its territories. In fact the territorial claims over the South China Sea and Taiwan do not have their origin in the current Chinese government, but were raised by its predecessors, especially the Republicans. Territorial claims are now central to the relegitimisation efforts of the CCP, which is using the current surge of nationalism and patriotism in China as measures to promote national cohesion. It is in this context that China promulgated an Ocean Law in February 1992 that incorporates the entire Spratly Islands group into the map of China. According to Chinese diplomats, however, the law was directed more at an internal than an external audience. The promulgation was meant not to escalate the disputes, but rather to restate the sovereignty claims already put on the map in 1958.[73] However, this popular irredentist pressure on the government does keep alive the *potential* for a South China Sea conflict.

On the other hand, China has realised that it is not able to act alone in the Spratlys. If it adheres to its economy-in-command foreign policy and accepts the benefits of an interdependent world, it has only one choice: a settlement of the dispute through peaceful means. The Chinese leadership's reaction to pressure from these two opposite forces is naturally a policy that exhibits a great deal of ambiguity: conciliatory foreign policy efforts vis-a-vis a forward naval presence. What makes the Spratlys a potential flash point is exactly this ambiguity, which also characterises the position of other claimants. It is a flash point, as the question of sovereignty is non-negotiable due to domestic and economic factors. It is only a *potential* flash point, however, because all the claimants are under real constraints which prevent them from taking any drastic action. This dictates a measure of flexibility in the interactions of the claimants involved.[74] Under the circumstances, China seems to bear a heavy responsibility not to escalate the dispute, for whilst it is the country with the smallest presence in the Spratlys, it has the greatest capability to enlarge that presence. This adds another element of ambiguity to China's foreign and defence policy. For the time being this ambiguity seems to be reconciled by China's plan to maintain the status quo.

China's efforts to maintain the status quo

As far as China is concerned, the status quo allows for a degree of flexibility seen from the major concession China made in the 1995 ASEAN Regional Forum meetings, where it claimed to be ready to base the South China Sea settlement on the United Nations Convention on the Law of the Sea. This was a major departure from China's previous position, which was based on the concept of historical waters.[75] It seems that the PLA has given a measure of support to the current civilian policy of restraint. For instance, the Chinese defence minister Chi Haotian made a public statement during his visit to Malaysia in May 1993 that no military force would be used to settle the South China Sea dispute. On the other hand, observers do see rising nationalism in China. One key component of this nationalism rests on territorial integrity and the PLA is a driving force for the spread of this nationalism based on its traditional view that China's security has to be guaranteed by sufficient military strength rather than diplomatic appeasement. Therefore, maintaining the status quo as a Chinese response to the South China Sea stalemate has taken preference over other solutions. This means that China is reinforcing its existing naval presence but at the same time working for a negotiated settlement.

China's status quo strategy toward the South China Sea is centred on one crucial consideration in the short-to-medium term: maintaining a presence of appropriate size. Although China followed other claimants in involving foreign companies in oil extraction in the disputed waters, the action spelled out a degree of pre-emptiveness. For PLA strategists, China's presence in the South China Sea at the moment is useful only in terms of 'point control'. Yet China intends to achieve 'section control' in the future.[76] The PLA's move on the Meiji Reef in 1995 may be regarded as an important step in this direction. Some Chinese scholars think the reef was chosen because of the Philippines' aggressive attitudes towards the South China Sea settlement: its strong push towards internationalisation of the dispute, its arrest of Chinese fishermen, and its discussion of oil deals with western firms in that part of the South China Sea. Nevertheless, the action has not transcended the limits of the considerations mentioned earlier. In fact, exploration of Chinese relics in the Meiji Reef was planned and made known in 1994 when, at a Taiwan South China Sea conference that year, a Chinese professor, Wang Hengjie, and a Taiwanese professor, Chan Zhongyu, agreed to do collaborative research on the South China Sea.[77] Moreover, while the reef's sovereignty is non-negotiable, the permanence of the structure that was built on the reef may be open for discussion. As a measure to ease tension, the PLA has again allowed Philippine fishermen to enter the reef.

In a sense the Meiji Reef move was similar to tactics in the board game *wei qi* (or *go* in English): laying a piece in an area to be contested later. The structure in the Meiji Reef serves as a sovereignty symbol in the south-eastern section of the South China Sea, where there had not been any Chinese presence before. This presence may or may not be removed in the future, depending on China's perception of its usefulness, but it has also given China a bargaining position in the negotiations, albeit at a high cost.

While China's reluctance to join in regional efforts to increase security transparency contributes to the perceived 'China threat', equating a naval forward posting with an irredentist military policy may be over-simplifying this vital issue. The difference between the two concepts may be explained by the current pattern of China's action in the South China Sea: in practical terms, military force is likely to be employed only as a last resort to defend direct threats to Chinese sovereignty or territorial integrity, and not as a means to expand the Chinese presence.[78]

With the foothold achieved, any preparation for another South China Sea action is less important in the PLA's overall policy hierarchy, as China moves to improve relations with its ASEAN neighbours in the changing world order of the 1990s. What worries the PLA now is how to obtain a measure of deterrence against the pressure from the major powers. Tai Ming Cheung pointed this out in 1991, before the PLA's strategic shift became finalised:

> Although the Spratlys issue is at present the most important naval priority, it is nevertheless of short-term importance. The longer-term priority is to establish China as a major regional sea power with an expanded sphere of influence. To effectively achieve this, it needs to deter competition from other aspiring naval powers, most significantly from India and Japan, as well as better meet the challenges of Soviet and US sea power in the region.[79]

In early 1990, when I conducted a research project on the Chinese navy, I read several dozen papers in the PLA journals which were arguing for a bluewater capability. They inevitably used the South China Sea dispute (mainly with Vietnam) to justify a faster naval modernisation.[80] In 1991, when I returned to China for fieldwork, I found to my surprise that many of the authors were actually much less concerned with the territorial issues of the Spratlys than with the generally poor state of the navy. The impression obtained in discussions was that if their demand for a strong navy was granted, they might not pursue the South China Sea question in the same way. Surely this should be treated with caution, but such a message is useful if we are to arrive at a full understanding of the PLA's intention in the Spratlys. Whether we are dealing with a navy focused on the recovery of claimed territories or one concerned mainly with a general modernisation program can make a crucial difference in the process of settling a dispute, peacefully or otherwise.[81]

This brings us back to the question raised in the last section: how big a naval foothold in the Spratlys does China calculate is enough to serve its strategic needs in the South China Sea? The declared goal of the Chinese government is to recover the entire group of islands, yet in the current world situation it is increasingly unrealistic for China to achieve that goal. Under the circumstances, there is always a balance between diplomatic and defence interests. China seems to have accepted its current size of presence, although reluctantly. How long will the PLAN's forward posture in the South China Sea remain defensive? This is open to speculation, but the fact is that the PLAN has not made any move since 1995. The ultimate answer to this question should reveal the influence of the South China Sea case on the development of China's overall foreign and defence policy. A number of factors can be identified to substantiate an argument against a repetition of the 1988 incident in the near future.

The first is the current weakness of the Chinese navy, which, as mentioned in previous chapters, has a long way to go toward becoming a formidable, offensive-oriented force.[82] Even under an ambitious development plan and extensive preparation for regional conflicts, the major weakness of the Chinese navy, that is, its air force and logistical supply capability, has not substantially improved since 1988. Any Chinese victory in a seesaw South China Sea clash could only be won at a price the PLA would deem exorbitant, especially given its increasing focus on strategic matters such as Sino–US relations and the situation across the Taiwan Strait.

The second factor is the political and diplomatic pressure brought to bear on China in its power projection, which has magnified considerably since 1989. China's relationship with the west has been seriously eroded, not only because of the Tiananmen tragedy, but also because of the loss of its strategic role in opposing the USSR. The favourable conditions under which China initiated the 1988 takeover of Yongshu (Fiery Cross) Reef no longer exist.[83] The enlargement of ASEAN has also increased their influence in world affairs and they have collectively acted to constrain China's new initiatives in the South China Sea. The strong ASEAN response to the Meiji Reef incident in 1995 may have convinced the Chinese government that any further move in this direction could be very expensive.

Third, Vietnam's relations with China have visibly improved. This makes the possibility of repeating a PLA attack on Vietnam very remote. In the successive summit meetings between the two countries since 1990, the issue of sovereignty over the Spratlys has not presented a serious obstacle to the overall agenda of rebuilding a friendly bilateral relationship. Some concrete progress has even been achieved in the expert meetings on the Spratlys dispute settlement. Both sides have made this difficult issue subject to other more immediate concerns troubling the remaining socialist regimes.[84] In fact, the Sino–Vietnam dispute on land territory has traditionally been a stronger irritant than the maritime disputes and has caused more military clashes in the past. The latest

Sino–Vietnam agreement on settling the South China Sea dispute through negotiations has greatly softened China's differentiated South China Sea policies toward Vietnam and ASEAN.

The fourth constraint in China's South China Sea calculations comes from the collective security arrangements that some of the South China Sea claimants have entered into with outside powers.[85] The Philippines would seek US support in a South China Sea conflict involving its claim. The annual joint naval exercises of Australia, Malaysia, Singapore and Indonesia would also affect China's plans in the South China Sea. A major confrontation would definitely induce intervention from major powers. Japan, for example, would be tempted to safeguard the commercial shipping routes. The prospect of sanctions looms large enough to caution China against instigating a major offensive move in the South China Sea.

Despite China's Meiji Reef move in 1995 and its announcement in 1996 that it would extend its maritime territories in the South China Sea by two million square kilometres according to the UN Convention on the Law of the Sea, the PRC has continuously sent conciliatory signals to ASEAN. The PLA believes that, unlike the Taiwan issue, the South China Sea problem does not have any political or military urgency at the moment. This has led the CMC to arrive at an expedient calculation: easing tensions in the South China Sea may help the PLA to overcome its transitional difficulties. Therefore the PLA's intentions in the South China Sea have been hijacked by its lack of both military capability and diplomatic options. And this will remain true for a long time to come.

In summary, the PLA clearly intends to recover what China regards as its legitimate territories, and this intention drives its naval deployment in the South China Sea. In other words, if there is an armed conflict in the area, the intention is the gun, while the naval presence is the trigger. It is, however, neither constructive nor helpful to focus on intention only. One needs to analyse the capabilities and constraints as well. China has other important diplomatic agendas to pursue in Southeast Asia. As pointed out by Michael Leifer, at issue is to what extent China's relations with ASEAN will be allowed to stand in the way of the People's Republic asserting its historical title in the South China Sea.[86]

Conclusion

Since the Party's 14th Congress in 1992, the PLA has increased its influence as a corporate interest in national politics. The final stage of political succession in China has elevated a number of military leaders to the core of the post-Deng leadership. This group of PLA leaders, led by Admiral Liu Huaqing and General Zhang Zhen, is well known for its advocacy of a powerful and professional army. It is they who have campaigned for a military that should be able to fight a high-tech war with any major power in the world. Thanks to the Gulf War and American pressure, since 1992 Liu and his colleagues in the CMC have convinced the Party leadership of what direction the PLA should move in the new century and achieved a consensus among the armed forces to adopt a new national defence strategy centred on preparation for high-tech warfare. Based on this strategic shift, the post-Deng military command has been successful in uniting the previously faction-ridden PLA, much as what Admiral Liu did to the navy in the early 1980s. The CMC of the 14th Central Party Committee has passed control of the PLA's destiny to a younger leadership of military professionals established in the 15th National Party Congress in September 1997. These new top generals are equally committed to the goal of transforming the PLA into a high-tech military power. With this trans-century military leadership in command, it can be expected that the PLA will press ahead with the concepts of forward defence and strategic deterrence. To accomplish this long-term objective the CMC will continue to remedy the doctrinal defects associated with the obsolete 'people's war' theory (both Mao's and Deng's versions), increase financial and material inputs in order to quicken hardware modernisation, and respond to security challenges with whatever means it considers appropriate, including military actions.

As discussed in Chapter 1 the post-Deng military leadership has a clear vision of the PLA's modernisation and steps to achieve it. First it is tackling the doctrinal flaws in the overall strategic guideline. The unprecedented effort of the PLA to study information warfare (IW) has placed it among the top three countries in terms of interest in the Revolution in Military Affairs (RMA). As pointed out by Michael Pillsbury, a senior fellow at the Atlantic Council, the very fact that the RMA is written about in China is an indication of the PLA's advance. This has shaken up some western notions about the backwardness of Chinese strategic planning.[1] In fact the PLA is not only learning RMA but also indigenising it to suit its modernisation efforts: to make it a knowledge-intensive and technology-intensive powerhouse. The second step the Chinese armed forces are taking is to enhance scientific research and address their financial constraints, as mentioned in Chapter 3. For the former, China has launched a national drive to promote research in areas of both basic science and practical technology. For the latter, the PLA has pursued a policy of selective modernisation, which means the PLA has not placed the gun before the butter. Although this may delay the improvement of the PLA's overall capabilities in the short run, it will not cause too much strain to the national economy. As economic growth is sustained in the country, it will eventually provide the financial and industrial basis for fulfilling the PLA's aspirations. At the same time selective domestic development and foreign purchases can elevate the PLA's elite units into forces capable of fighting limited high-tech wars. Given the current low likelihood of the PLA involving itself in a major war, this middle course weapons R&D policy suits China's immediate purposes. With doctrinal and financial deficiencies being remedied gradually, the third step of an overall modernisation will probably take place around 2010 and 2020, based on a much improved economic and technological foundation. The enormous implication of this development to the world is the simple truth that we are indeed witnessing a powerful military in the making, although the pace of it is not to be fast at the beginning. From an organisational perspective a professional and well-equipped military is more awesome than one that is revolutionary and politicised.

As argued in Chapter 1, a high-tech oriented defence strategy is based on the laws and principles governing contemporary warfare in the information age. It is a forward-looking strategy that recognises the revolutionary effect of technological development on military science. Technologically, it will guide the PLA to concentrate on the R&D of urgently needed high-tech weaponry, which increasingly blurs the dividing line between offensive and defensive systems. In military terms, the post-Deng defence strategy will dictate that the PLA create defence in depth, which will greatly broaden the traditional concept of national defence. For instance, some kind of forward deployment may be thought to be inevitable for national security, designed to keep the potential front line as far away as possible from the nation's continental and maritime borders. With high-tech military equipment, this line of defence may not be a manned line, but rather it may be in the form of controllable airspace beyond China's territory, or an area under surveillance from space. However, one concrete form of forward deployment for the PLA is power projection, which has become necessary for coping with sovereignty disputes in the areas subject to overlapping international claims.

Therefore, the PLA's post-Deng strategic shift is not just one of conceptual slogans. It contains concrete measures regarding troop reduction, deployment and redeployment, adjustment of weapons development programs, a fundamental reform of everyday training, reordering budgetary priorities for different services and the establishment of both rapid response units and efficient C^3I structures for limited high-tech regional warfare. One revolutionary change in the PLA is the abandonment of its time-honoured mentality of relying on human numbers to prevail over firepower. As elaborated in Chapter 2, the PLA has finally realised that in high-tech wars quality of hardware is far more important than quantity of infantry soldiers. The size of the Chinese armed forces has been cut continuously since the mid-1980s and the latest round of troop reduction will affect half a million servicemen, as pronounced by CMC chairperson Jiang Zemin in September 1997 when he addressed the CCP's 15th National Congress. Smaller size but increased financial inputs seem to have set the PLA's modernisation on an efficient and speedy course. In the final analysis the new national defence strategy is meant to provide a much more detailed road map for the modernisation of the Chinese military than at any time before.

All these changes introduced to the PLA in recent years have a lot to do with the identification of potential enemies. Since high-tech warfare is seen as the basic type of war China will enter in the future, the PLA logically expects a major power to be its opponent. Therefore, the PLA's two-tiered defence will lean more toward strategic concerns (major powers), although regional conflicts are still given due attention. This new thinking enriches the limited regional war theory that was developed by PLA war planners in the 1980s. Now a limited regional war is not envisioned as a war just between China and its neighbours due to sovereignty and territorial disputes. It may potentially be a military action between China and a major world power on a small scale, for example, in the form of a surgical strike or anti-surgical strike. In a worst case scenario this small-scale action may even escalate to medium level. For instance, a foreign power might assist Taiwan's efforts to break a PLAN blockade. China's accelerated military modernisation in recent years reflects the CMC's worry that the PLA is awkwardly short of the required hardware to deal with military involvement from outside the Asia–Pacific region. Refocusing its modernisation on the major powers is a sensible move in the PLA's calculation of China's security needs in the post–Cold War era. Indeed at the moment, if diplomatic efforts fail to resolve the confrontation with major powers, China has not had the military means to counter threats posed by them to its national security.

What does this mean to the PLA? The immediate outcome of identifying major powers in the PLA's war game planning is to force the state to maintain the current relatively high level of military spending on arms so as to narrow the gap with the west. China's economic boom seems to make this more affordable than before. The PLA has a natural mentality regarding the catching-up policy: it was against logic everywhere in the world that a large country should become an economic power of the 21st century, but leave its military capability behind in the 20th century. General Chi Haotian, China's defence minister, said of the PLA's weapons program, 'We must have whatever the big powers have already had in their inventory'. The question is really what to have first. In recent years China has committed enormous resources to the research of micro-electronics, spacecraft, computer science, new materials and laser technology. In due time these programs may help to produce high-tech weapons that will greatly enhance the PLA's readiness for modern warfare. For instance, some sources have revealed that the PLA has experimented with laser equipment that is close to real application in military operations.

The PLA has stepped up restructuring and redeployment of troops to position itself better for a potential armed conflict in the new century. The specialised services are given priority treatment in funding and access to advanced weapons acquired from the international market. The order of development seems to be the air force, the navy, the SMF and the army. Each of these services is undergoing restructuring to make it more suitable for fighting a high-tech war. The guiding principle is to increase the service's offensive capabilities in order to enlarge China's defence in depth. The PLA's new consensus that a solely defensive posture in the age of information technology will only weaken the country's defence will have far-reaching implications for the PLA's modernisation, and for the global balance of military power.

The PLA has gone through a number of major redeployments, each responding to a change in perceived security threats. The current round of redeployment is to move the defensive centre of gravity from north to east, as the Russian threat has greatly subsided but the Taiwan Strait poses long-term problems. Parallel to the redeployment are efforts to establish a new centre-theatre-campaign command and control system, as seen from the reintroduction of the war zone institution. One prominent feature of the war zone is to prepare PLA units for united operations of all the services at the strategic and tactical levels. This is unprecedented for the PLA, which has until recently only talked about combined operations within each service. Although this great leap forward in military thinking is largely rhetorical at this stage, it has provided a new strategic guideline for the PLA's future war planning, and since 1993 united operations have been incorporated into PLA training.

Each of the PLA services is undergoing a tremendous transition and is gradually improving its capabilities. Hardware modernisation has been slow but is accelerating. It may take years for the service structure to be adjusted to suit a high-tech military power. However, the PLA seems to have got the basics right. As a result a more integrated military is in the making, with each service more focused on its immediate and long-term missions in collaboration with other services.

As analysed in Chapter 4, the PLA's Strategic Missile Force has gradually moved from its previous emphasis on 'how to hide' to 'how to fight'. Although its doctrinal principle remains 'minimum deterrence', the transition has added new elements to the strategy. For instance, the SMF's minimum deterrence has become more pro-active. This can be seen from several new developments of the SMF:

1 With the progress made in tactical nuclear weapons systems, the SMF is studying features of a tactical nuclear war. The employment of battlefield nuclear weapons is attractive to a technologically inferior military whose threat to use nuclear

weapons as the last military resort may exert strong deterrence against enemies vulnerable to large losses of human life.

2   The recent restructuring of the SMF has targeted the enhancement of its conventional missile units as a key mission. Compared to nuclear missiles which have a near-zero chance to be used, the conventional ones are regarded by the PLA as a very effective weapon needed absolutely in any high-tech wars.

3   The SMF has always believed that without a second-strike capability China's nuclear force is unusable. To achieve this end, the SMF has devoted tremendous efforts to shortening its launching time, hardening launching sites, increasing mobility, lengthening missile range, miniaturising warheads and computerising guidance systems. There is no doubt that the SMF will continue to enjoy top-priority status in China's overall military modernisation.

The best lesson China has learned from the Gulf War is the employment of air power in high-tech wars, which significantly influenced the debate within the PLAAF regarding the role of the service in modern warfare. As discussed in Chapter 5, a consensus soon emerged that emphasised the strategic importance of air power in the new age. The air force's traditional role of supporting the ground force has not been discarded, but it is given more independent missions to perform, such as establishing air superiority, launching long-distance strikes, and conducting surgical operations for political purposes. The new thinking concerning the air force's functions in the future has paved the way for a number of key reforms:

1   The PLAAF is being restructured from a fundamentally defensive force to a force capable of both defensive and offensive capabilities. In this combination, however, the orientation of offence is highlighted as representing the nature of the service. As a result the number of jet fighter divisions is to be reduced, while space is being created for the introduction of more multifunctional aircraft to take the leading role in the years to come.

2   This force restructuring has affected the whole weapons program for the air force. Among the top priority projects are strategic airlift, aerial refuelling, and ground-attack capabilities. A new generation of air superiority fighters is being developed.

3   Air defence and missile defence have been listed as the weakest point of the PLA's modernisation and thus received new emphasis for remedy.

4 The PLA Airborne Unit (the 15th Airborne Corps) has been upgraded as a national rapid response force. It is now assuming both strategic and tactical missions both at home for domestic political control and overseas for power projection.

All this is designed to match the PLAAF with the international trend of the revolution in military affairs.

The navy has actually spearheaded the PLA's current transformation into a modern military power. In the first half of the 1980s it redefined its role in national defence and put forward a bluewater maritime strategy as the guide for its ambitious long-term development. The navy is the first service to redress Mao's and Deng's doctrinal deficiencies in the PLA's modernisation drive. It is now more forward-looking and postured in order to compete with the navies of other major world players in the new century. Because the Chinese national leadership sees its future threat coming mainly from the seas in the east, particularly from the necessity of containing Taiwan's independence, it will place naval modernisation on the high-priority list. After all, the PLAN will be the most likely service to bear the first and ultimate brunt if China is involved in any armed conflicts in the future. As shown in Chapter 6, the PLAN has continued to tackle its fundamental weakness: its lack of capability to launch sustained and coordinated operations in waters some distance from home. Admiral Liu Huaqing set four immediate tasks for the navy in the 1980s:

1 Capability to secure sea control in the major battle directions in China's offshore waters.
2 Capability to blockade major SLOCs in the waters containing China's maritime territories.
3 Capability to initiate major sea battles in the waters adjacent to China's maritime territories.
4 Capability to wage reliable nuclear retaliatory strikes.

These will remain the concrete objectives until the navy has the confidence to set higher goals for its modernisation. For instance, some naval officers have formulated a blueprint for the Chinese navy to reach the Atlantic Ocean in the decades ahead.

To build a bluewater navy the PLAN is now patiently laying a solid foundation for its real rise in power in the next twenty years. The efforts for this grand plan include a substantial restructuring of the force and gradual upgrading of its existing equipment. The former is designed to form battle groups through concentrating major surface combatants; to promote specialisation of warships in order to enhance the battle group's anti-air and anti-submarine capabilities; and to enlarge the numbers of ocean-going warships so that strength in the different strategic directions will not have to be traded off. The latter urgently requires the acquisition of large surface warships, powerful submarines, and long-range air-craft. In the final analysis the PLAN has set up a clear vision of development and is determined to realise its ambition.

The PLA indeed has an ambitious modernisation program, and China's strong economic growth will eventually deliver what the PLA wants. The relationship between economic strength and mili-tary power is very clear in the long term. In the short term, however, the PLA will endure a fairly long and painful transition in which, as pointed out in Chapter 3, more and more weapons systems become obsolete but replacements are difficult to come by. This transitional vacuum should be taken seriously in evalu-ating the PLA's capability. It is particularly important not to confuse ambition with capability—the PLA's doctrinal desires at present stand in sharp contrast to its severely limited capabilities.[2]

However, it may be overly simplistic to calculate capabilities solely based on hardware or technological level—'We have stealth bombers but you do not, so you will lose the war'. If the US experience in Vietnam and the Soviet experience in Afghanistan taught us anything, it is the unpredictability of the real battle-ground. The Gulf War showed the general patterns of a high-tech war but it still constituted an exceptional case that may not be applied to other future wars. The problem is that no major powers have encountered the PLA in combat situations for more than four decades. We simply do not know how capable it is. Most western analysts were indifferent to the prediction made by Albert Wohlstetter in 1988 that the PLA would become a world class military power. This indifference was largely due to a general trend in the west to underestimate the PLA's capabilities. In Wohlstetter's opinion, the PLA has been successful in achieving a level of 'pockets of excellence', as reflected by its space programs.[3]

It is not easy to realistically assess the PLA's capabilities. On the one hand, there are large numbers of obsolete weapons such as the J–6 fighter jets and the T–69 tanks. On the other hand, according to Pillsbury, the Chinese have an excellent military laser program and they have made enormous efforts to develop 'new concept weapons systems' such as particle beam guns.[4] Moreover, while the PLA's weapons program is 'more research, less produc-tion', there are few Chinese reports on what they have accom-plished in R&D. Neither do we know exactly how helpful the military technological transfers from Russia and Israel have been to the PLA's weapons program. Russia's technology may have been instrumental in China's 100 per cent successful satellite launching record in 1997 and 1998. In addition, there is a question of what standards are applicable when evaluating China's military build-up. By US standards, the PLA is certainly poorly equipped. Yet as seen from the perspective of countries in Asia and the Pacific, which may have more chances of being in a conflict with China, the PLA has formidable military strength. This is why the spillover of the PLA's efforts of arms catch-up with the big powers may galvanise a response in kind throughout the region.[5]

Chinese military strength will grow steadily not only because of China's economic boom but also through new mechanisms that are stimulating the country's development of science and high technology. The state-directed '863' and 'Touch' high-tech programs, as mentioned in Chapter 3, have injected large sums of money into key technological projects.[6] Moreover, China has impressive human resources in the military-related industrial sector. Among over three million people working in the national defence/industry complex, 14 per cent are scientific and technological personnel. Over one-third of their products are high-tech.[7] More importantly, the market-driven civilian high-tech projects have tapped the country's great scientific potential, which has been long suppressed by the command economy.[8] For instance, the Beijing Electronic Development Zone has developed so rapidly that the science adviser to President Clinton dubbed it a potential Silicon Valley. For the first time the PLAAF has purchased and installed in its aircraft global satellite positioning equipment developed by a civilian firm without its commissioning.[9] This has shown that the civilian and private sectors can provide the PLA with high-tech facilities that the PLA itself is not able to develop due to its limited research funds and personnel. When this is coupled with the state-directed high-tech projects and the PLA priority R&D programs, military modernisation can be expected to accelerate, as it is now more solidly based on market competition.

As far as China's regional foreign and defence policy is concerned, Chapter 7 shows that the PLA's concentration on strategic concerns (the big powers) may in the short run require the PLA to downgrade some of its specific regional foci such as the Spratly Islands, thus extending the space and time for a negotiated settlement of some regional disputes. The PLA has concluded that it is not desirable for the PLA to engage in a two-front confrontation.

The logic behind this strategic shift in the 1990s originated from increased western pressure, not the prospects of China involving itself in an armed conflict with one of its neighbours. The Taiwan issue, which China regards as a domestic affair, has currently preoccupied the minds of Chinese civilian and military leaders. This may somewhat ease the immediate tension in the Spratlys. In the long run, however, the existing flash points in Asia remain a serious concern and produce a great deal of uncertainty. Over time the PLA's identification of major powers as the impetuses for military modernisation may better enable it to flex its muscles in the region and affect the regional balance of power.

A national defence strategy is based on a national defence culture. China's defence culture is firmly built on the nation's historical desire to become economically wealthy and militarily powerful. This desire is often interwoven with popular irredentist sentiments. When the state is pressured externally, these sentiments can be easily aroused, as the people are constantly reminded of the nation's humiliating modern history. When some citizens suggested that everyone in the country donate a few *yuan* to the navy for the construction of an aircraft carrier, the proposal was warmly received from a people still struggling to move out of a subsistence economy.[10] The discord between China's diplomatic efforts to defuse the sovereignty quarrels and the push by PLA planners to acquire more advanced weaponry do not worry the Chinese people, who have demonstrated a high degree of concern about the country's low level of military technology and funding. China's defence culture is thus a driving force for China's military modernisation.

The PLA has a key role to play in China's balancing of international and domestic needs, and its role will become even more decisive in the post-Deng era when the civilian leadership of the younger generation will have to be more mindful of the military's interests in the process of foreign policy formulation.[11] This is one of the reasons why China is at a conjuncture: the contradiction between the continuation of the economy-in-command policy (the emphasis on an interdependent China) and the insistence on an obsolete concept of *realpolitik* may come to a head in the next decade or so. If the post-Deng PLA is directed toward a hardline alternative as a response to domestic and international pressure, this has the potential to affect the regional balance of power.[12] Moreover, events such as the *Yinhe* incident and the deployment of US carrier battle groups close to the Taiwan Strait only enhance the influence of hard-liners. In summary the PLA is, like China itself, at a crossroads. Here we may have two Chinas: a China that is driven by the nationalist impulse and bent on assertive military power and a China that seeks to be fully incorporated into an interdependent world. At this moment China is neither, but it is poised to move decisively in either direction.

Notes

FOREWORD

1 See Desmond Ball (ed.), *The Transformation of Security in the Asia/Pacific Region*, London: Frank Cass, 1996, pp. 6–7.

INTRODUCTION

1 The number of papers dealing with the question of rising China is also rising rapidly. See, for instance, Segal 1995, p. 61; Cable & Ferdinand 1994, pp. 243–61; and Kristof 1993.
2 Yan Xuetong 1998, p. 35.
3 You Ji 1997b, pp. 287–306.
4 Events such as the US Navy's stalking a Chinese nuclear submarine in the Yellow Sea in 1994 and US naval exercises close to Taiwan in March 1996 have alerted the Chinese leadership. Such things did not even occur with the Soviet Union at the height of the Cold War. And the navy believes that as it launches more bluewater activities in the future, it becomes inevitable that such encounters will increase.
5 Together with the warships, Russia agreed to transfer a number of anti-ship missiles specially designed for use against US aircraft carriers.
6 Pillsbury 1997.

1 EMBRACING REVOLUTION IN MILITARY AFFAIRS

1 The CMC has not yet coined an official terminology for this new strategy. This is due largely to a prudent desire to avoid undue political repercussions that may be caused by openly discarding Deng Xiaoping's doctrine of 'people's war under modern conditions' at a

sensitive time of power transition. See General Wu Guoqing 1994, pp. 43–51.

2   Liang Minglun 1993, p. 42; You Ji 1995b, pp. 231–57.

3   Jencks 1984, p. 319.

4   For their views, see *Junshi xueshu* (ed.) 1984.

5   In fact PLA historians unanimously agree that the most forceful impetus for the change was the speech by the former chief of General Staff, Su Yu, at the PLA Academy of Military Science on 11 January 1979 (Su Yu 1979, pp. 1–10).

6   Yang Dezhi 1979, pp. 1–8.

7   Dreyer 1993.

8   Deng Xiaoping 1993, p. 121.

9   Joffe 1987, p. 119.

10   Li Cheng 1992, p. 288.

11   Lan Shuchen 1986, p. 27.

12   According to a survey by James Mulvenon, by the end of 1994 79 per cent of PLA officers received higher education of different types, a remarkable progress compared to the pre-reform era. However, it is still considerably lower than the US's 97 per cent and Russia's 90 per cent (Mulvenon 1997, p. 15).

13   *The PLA Daily*, 8 March 1991.

14   Song Shilun 1984, pp. 42–61.

15   There was a lengthy debate in the 1980s among officers about whether the people's war strategy became obsolete under modern conditions. They argued that if this fundamental question was not resolved, many other key questions could not be answered, such as what weapons programs should be worked out.

16   This leadership is headed by Jiang Zemin, the Party's general secretary but its everyday running was anchored in Admiral Liu Huaqing and General Zhang Zhen, the last two active serving Long March veterans, until their retirement in 1997. In the Fifth Plenum of the 14th Central Committee held in October 1995, General Zhang Wannian and General Chi Haotian were promoted as deputy chairs of the CMC. Their succession to Liu and Zhang was confirmed in the Party's 15th National Congress in September 1997, and they will lead the PLA toward the new century.

17   You Ji 1996a, pp. 1–28.

18   *The PLA Daily*, 20 March 1991.

19   Liu Zuoxin 1995, p. 40.

20   You Ji 1997a, pp. 72–3.

21   Guo Yongjun 1995, pp. 47–9.

22   Chen Baojiang & Huang Xing 1995, pp. 24–8.

23   Zhou Yingcai 1995, pp. 24–8.

24   Ouyang Wei 1995b, p. 20.

25   Gao Jinxi 1995, p. 93.

26 GSD & GPD 1993, pp. 276–82.
27 Pillsbury 1997, Introduction.
28 Zhang Zhen 1987, p. 16.
29 *The PLA Daily*, 29 May 1997.
30 See, for instance, the Decision on Advancing Technological and Sci-
    entific Research by the Central Committee of the CCP, May 1995.
31 You Ji 1997c, p. 158.
32 Yu Huating & Liu Guoyu 1993, Chapter 1.
33 In numerous papers and books published by the PLA concerning
    China's high-tech strategy, the writers simulated a Gulf War situation
    where they played the opposition to the Allied forces. In so doing
    they studied high-tech war and proposed countermeasures.
34 Interviews with people who attended these report sessions in 1991.
35 'Gaojishu tiaojianxia zhanyi de xinfazhan' (The new development of
    campaign operations under high-tech conditions), *Zhongguo junshi
    kexue* (Chinese Military Science), no. 2, 1994, p. 54.
36 *The PLA Daily*, 25 January 1991 and 9 July 1993.
37 Wu Guoqing 1994, p. 49.
38 *The PLA Daily*, 18 June 1993.
39 Liu Jixian 1992, p. 252.
40 *The PLA Daily*, 25 May 1992.
41 *The PLA Daily*, 30 August 1993.
42 *The PLA Daily*, 25 January 1991 and 1 May 1992.
43 *The PLA Daily*, 27 August 1993.
44 Espeland & Curr 1991, pp. 19–27; Cohen 1994, pp. 109–24.
45 *The PLA Daily*, 8 March 1991.
46 Dai Jingyu 1993, pp. 24–7.
47 Munro 1994, pp. 355–73.
48 Pillsbury cited in *Far East Economic Review*, 24 July 1997.
49 Ahrat 1997, p. 472.
50 Chen Youyuan 1997, pp. 37–8.
51 ibid.
52 ibid.
53 Li Qingshan 1995, Chapters 5, 6.
54 Gao Jinxi 1998, p. 32.
55 Wang Gezhen & Li Mindtang 1997, p. 22.
56 Ahrat 1997, p. 473.
57 Wilson & You Ji 1990, p. 40–1.
58 Liu Jishan & Qian Zunde 1988, p. 32.
59 Typical of these younger officers is Major-General Zhu Borong, cur-
    rently deputy commander of the PLA Hong Kong garrison. He received
    a tertiary education, served as an active duty officer and worked in
    western countries as a military attache. When he led the Institute of
    Strategic Studies at the PLA National Defence University, he devel-
    oped good working relations with General Zhang Zhen, as the insti-

tute frequently put forward innovative ideas concerning the PLA's modernisation. All this along with Zhu's experience in England and his fluent English have greatly assisted his selection by Zhang Zhen as a key leader in the Hong Kong garrison.

60 Teng Liangfu & Jiang Fusheng 1990, p. 143.
61 *Economist*, 29 July 1995.
62 Tang Daoshen 1990, p. 249.
63 Yao Zhenyu 1993, p. 2.
64 *The PLA Daily*, 16 February 1990.
65 Huang Yuzhang 1988, p. 89.
66 Mi Zhenyu 1986, pp. 3–7.
67 Mi Zhenyu 1987, pp. 2–10.
68 Min Zengfu 1995, p. 35.
69 Zhu Yingcai 1995, p. 26.
70 The PLA has not failed to notice that since the beginning of the 1990s western military intelligence units have stepped up their operations inside China. High on their agenda are the precise location, surrounding environment and landscape of those key military facilities such as the headquarters of each PLA service, communications hubs and major bases.
71 Xu Fangce 1987, p. 76.
72 Liu Cunzhi 1987, p. 1168.
73 Wang Wenpo 1993, p. 27.
74 Hu Changfa 1997, p. 33.
75 Hu Changfa 1997, p. 34.
76 Wang Qunbo 1994, p. 28.
77 Hu Changfa 1997, p. 34.
78 ibid.
79 The PLA National Defence University 1993, p. 23.
80 Hu Siyuan 1993, p. 72.

2 POSITIONING THE PLA FOR A 21ST-CENTURY WAR

1 Hu Guangzheng 1997, p. 123.
2 You Ji 1996b, pp. 24–7.
3 Hu Guangzheng 1997, pp. 124–6.
4 Guo Qiqiao & Yao Yanjing 1991, pp. 232–3.
5 Zheng Wenhan 1990a, p. 8.
6 Xu Fangting & Liu Hongji 1995, p. 23.
7 You Ji 1998a, p. 32.
8 Guo Qiqiao & Yao Yanjing 1991, p. 202.
9 Hu Wenlong 1990, p. 181.
10 Hu Guangzheng 1997, p. 124.
11 Zhang Liangyu 1993, pp. 24, 52.
12 During this round of reduction the PLA also cut: the field army by

six divisions (mainly those engaged in economic production); garrison troops by one division, two garrison districts and eleven regiments; engineering corps by seven project areas and 27 regiments; railway corps by three divisions and 37 regiments; the navy by one army-level base and six AA artillery battalions; the air force by four headquarters and six AA artillery divisions; the General Logistics Department by four regional commands, ten division-level bases and one army-level base (Li Ke and Hao Shengzhang 1989, pp. 150–8).

13 Wang Pufeng 1986, p. 9.

14 Zheng Wenhan 1990a, p. 7.

15 Liu Qingzhong 1992, p. 4.

16 *People's Daily*, 28 May 1993.

17 An interview with him in Beijing in 1992.

18 *The PLA Daily*, 23 April 1998.

19 There may be interpretations other than this. It is rumoured that the 113th Division of the 38th Group Army is also being converted. If true, this shows that the Party leadership believes the domestic situation to warrant such an initiative. The 113th Division is one of the best divisions in the PLA. It is mostly heavily equipped and, stationed in Gaobeidian, it assumes the duty of defending the Niankou Pass, the last stronghold protecting Beijing against an attack from the north. Its conversion may indicate that the Party leaders might have believed the internal uncertainties after Deng dictated the need to have a few outstanding PLA divisions prepared for any emergent situations.

20 Normally it takes eight people to operate an anti-tank gun in the PLA. When some of the elite group armies were equipped with anti-tank missiles in the mid-1980s, each launching unit comprised only three soldiers, and the number can be further cut in the future. See Hou Shanzhi 1987, p. 145.

21 Zheng Xianli 1988, p. 250.

22 Hu Wenlong & Cha Jinlu 1991, pp. 11–14.

23 Zheng Xianli 1988, pp. 249–51.

24 Liu Beiyi & Yun Qing 1994, p. 149.

25 Wang Jianghuai & Zhu Guolin 1994, p. 82.

26 Ball 1997, p. 368.

27 *Renmin ribao*, 31 July 1995.

28 Li Ke & Hao Shengzhang 1989, p. 255.

29 Xu Fangting & Liu Hongji 1995, p. 26; Ouyang Wei 1995b, p. 42.

30 Ouyang Wei 1995a, p. 20.

31 Xu Fangting & Liu Hongji 1995, p. 23.

32 Wang Zhiyi 1991, p. 133.

33 In private some PLA officers held that Deng made the decision also

because he was a Sichuanese and naturally in favour of his home province.
34 The Research Institute for Strategic Studies, PLA Academy of Military Science 1998, pp. 142–3.
35 Oral sources from PLA officers in Beijing, 1991.
36 Huang Bin 1992, pp. 3–4.
37 Huang Bin 1992, p. 79.
38 Huang Bin 1992, pp. 143–4.
39 Zhang Guangting 1988, p. 281.
40 The other three group armies in this category include the 27th Group Army in the Beijing Military Area Command, the 54th Group Army in the Jinan MAC and possibly the 47th Group Army in Lanzhou MAC.
41 Wang Jianghuai & Zhu Guolin 1994.
42 Zhang Guangting 1988, p. 282.
43 The CMC formulated a number of principles for merging field army units: the history of the unit (for example, whether it was formed in the Red Army period or the 8th Route Army period); merit record (any major achievements in training, the level of its general discipline, and readiness); combat experience (whether it fought in any major wars and how it performed); and political stance (for example, whether it had committed political errors in past political movements; the 43rd Army was dismantled because its former leader General Huang Yongsheng was a close follower of Marshal Lin Biao in the 1960s and 1970s).
44 *Guangmin Ribao*, 13 February 1997.
45 *The PLA Daily*, 27 September 1992.
46 Li Ke & Hao Shengzhang 1989, p. 257.
47 Xu Jian 1995, pp. 363–7.
48 Yu Yongzhe 1997, p. 79.
49 Jiang Tiejun 1997, p. 72.

3 IN SEARCH OF HIGH-TECH MILITARY POWER

1 Xu Xiaojun 1991, p. 53.
2 Xu Xiaojun 1991, p. 55.
3 Hong Shisheng 1995, pp. 24–5.
4 Zheng Wenhan 1990b, p. 10.
5 Writing Group of the PLA NDU 1990, p. 238.
6 Li Jiang 1988, p. 197.
7 You Ji 1996b, p. 27.
8 Godement 1997, p. 96.
9 Wang Yamin 1993, p. 56.
10 Yao Zhenyu 1993, p. 29.

11 Hang Suwei & Yang Zhonghua 1995, pp. 30–2.

12 Reng Xiufeng & Wang Guangxu 1986, pp. 59–60.

13 Zhang Aiping 1984, p. 229.

14 Wilson & You Ji 1990, p. 42.

15 Zhang Feng 1989, pp. 8–11.

16 *Ta Kung Pao*, 19 April 1997.

17 *Bauhinia Magazine*, no. 8, 1993, p. 56.

18 There have been debates about why the growth of the economy is so vigorous. My opinion is that when a vast country like China moves from a subsistence economy to a consumption economy, a huge market demand is generated. If there is sufficiently large initial outside investment to stimulate it, a lasting expansion can be sustained by this demand. For more on this see You Ji, 1997c.

19 *Keji ribao*, 28 April 1997.

20 Central revenue can be used to gauge the PLA's open and hidden budgets. Some western estimates of China's defence spending are way off the mark because they approach or even surpass China's entire government budget. The authors of one controversial book claim that China's annual military spending is about US$87 billion (713 billion *yuan*, or about 90 per cent of China's national revenue). This is wildly inaccurate. If China needs to hide the true figures of its military budget, it does not need to hide its true central revenue, which is under close scrutiny by world financial institutions such as the World Bank and the IMF.

21 Yu Hongmin & Wang Xingwang 1993, p. 20.

22 Writing Group of the PLA NDU 1990, p. 232; Ku Guisheng 1993, p. 46.

23 An interview with a State Council official in 1992.

24 Writing Group of the PLA NDU 1990, p. 147.

25 Writing Group of the PLA NDU 1990, p. 228.

26 Liu Huajin 1991, p. 11.

27 Writing Group of the PLA NDU 1990, p. 225. In November 1998, one US dollar is worth 8.25 *yuan*.

28 Wang Shaoguang 1996, p. 898.

29 China's first national high-tech research project, the 863 Project, aims to keep the PRC abreast of cutting-edge international scientific and technological developments and to specify China's own R&D priorities. It is so named because Deng approved the plan proposed by a number of China's top scientists in March 1986.

30 China's military R&D covers two separate areas of the weapons program. The R&D for new weapons is paid by the indirect military budget mentioned earlier. The R&D for immediate application concerns the improvement of weapons already in the hands of the

servicemen, and is basically financed by the direct military budget. (Yao Yanjin & Liu Jingxian 1994, p. 159.)

31 Writing Group of the PLA NDU 1990, pp. 230–1.

32 Wang Shaoguang 1996, p. 893.

33 *Bauhinia Magazine*, no. 8, 1993, p. 72.

34 Li Jingchun, Li Zimin & Zhou Xie 1993, p. 23.

35 *The PLA Daily*, 17 November 1995.

36 Writing Group of the PLA NDU 1990, p. 244.

37 *Ta Kung Pao*, 18 March 1997.

38 Chou Shi 1989, p. 12.

39 Wang Yamin 1993, p. 56.

40 PLA Academy of Military Science 1988, pp. 177–8. However, by a most radical move the CMC issued a decree in July 1998 that banned all commercial activities conducted by PLA units. They must now surrender all their firms and factories to civilian government for which the latter will allocate an unspecified amount of money to the PLA as compensation funds (*The PLA Daily*, 23 July 1998).

41 *Keji ribao*, 3 April 1997.

42 Yu Zonglin 1996, p. 24.

43 Ding 1996, pp. 432–4.

44 Wang Yamin 1993, p. 56.

45 Yao Yanjin & Liu Jingxian 1994, p. 159.

46 According to a survey in 1991, the PLA has bought a number of single items of state-of-the-art equipment with a view to disassembling them and duplicating them by reverse technology. One example is the Chinese Exocet. See articles by Larry Engelmann, 'China's Arms Business', carried in *Life*, starting in January 1992.

47 Segal 1996, p. 121.

48 A Japanese defence expert revealed this to me in Canberra in 1991.

49 *The Economist*, 20–26 September 1997, p. 38.

50 Kong Congzhou 1991, pp. 320–50.

51 Li Ke & Hao Shengzhang 1989, pp. 258–9.

52 Ball 1993, p. 51.

53 US Defence Intelligence Agency 1984, pp. 45–6.

54 Ball 1993, p. 51.

55 *Keji Ribao*, 6 March 1997.

56 Guo Xilin 1995, p. 26.

57 Guo Xilin 1995, p. 27.

58 Guo Xilin 1995, p. 26.

59 *Liaowang*, no. 30, 1997, p. 4.

60 *Keji Ribao*, 19 April 1997.

61 *The PLA Daily*, 5 December 1990.

62 *The PLA Daily*, 25 May 1992.

63 Voice of America, 2 June 1998.

64 *The PLA Daily*, 10 October 1991.

65 *Keji Ribao*, 11 January 1997.

66　*Renmin Ribao*, 6 April 1998.
67　*The PLA Daily*, 9 August 1993.
68　Huang Bin 1993, pp. 44–5.
69　*The PLA Daily*, 5 May 1993.
70　Liu Tongzu et al. 1987 pp. 1107–30.
71　Some special services, such as the Strategic Missile Forces (SMF) and air force, have admittedly been more thoroughly integrated into satellite-based computerised C³I networks.
72　*The PLA Daily*, 5 December 1990.
73　Liu Tongzu et al. 1987, pp. 1112–21.
74　Liu Tongzu et al. 1987, pp. 1112–15.
75　The NCDSR 1994, pp. 671–6.
76　Yang Jinhua 1993, p. 51.
77　Liu Tongzu et al. 1987, pp. 1117–18.
78　*Cankao xiaoxi*, 13 September 1988.
79　*China Daily*, 9 October 1996.
80　CCTV, Channel 4, Evening News, 26 March 1998.
81　Pin Feng 1996, pp. 26–7.
82　Wu Qinwen 1987, pp. 7–8.
83　Pin Feng 1996, pp. 26–7.
84　*Renmin ribao*, 29 October 1994.
85　*Da Kung Pao*, 20 October 1996.
86　*Chanjing xinwen*, 28 March 1998.
87　ITAR-TASS 18 October 1996.
88　Shi Fei 1993, p. 74
89　Shi Fei 1993, p. 71–2.
90　Shi Fei 1993, p. 74.
91　*Renmin ribao*, 21 March 1998.
92　*Renmin ribao*, 27 March 1998.
93　*Renmin ribao*, 25 August 1993.
94　*Renmin ribao*, 4 March 1996.
95　*Renmin ribao*, 3 April 1994.
96　Hua Renjie 1992, Chapters 8, 9.
97　Bao Zhongxing 1988, p. 358.
98　Bao Zhongxing 1988, p. 359.
99　Pin Fan & Li Qi 1997, pp. 130–1.

4　SHARPENING THE NUCLEAR SWORD

1　Segal 1990, p. 52.
2　Wang Jing 1978, pp. 2–5.
3　One expert on the Chinese armed forces has suggested that the SMF has at least 130 000 personnel. However, logistic, engineering and technological supporting units make up a large proportion of the whole force (Pin Kefu 1993 p. 41).

4 Segal 1984, p. 104; 1990, pp. 189–205.
5 Hahn 1989, p. 42; Lin Chong-pin 1988.
6 Zhang Baotang 1988, p. 412.
7 ibid.
8 Pin Kefu 1993, pp. 40–3.
9 Zhang Jingxi & Zhang Mengliang 1987, p. 1018.
10 Yu Hao et al. 1994 (vol. 2).
11 Lewis & Hua Di 1992, pp. 20–2.
12 Xu Jian 1995, p. 378.
13 Liu Zhongyi 1992, p. 26.
14 Yu Hao et al. 1994 (vol. 1), p. 528.
15 Ling Yu 1995, p. 22.
16 Zhang Baotang 1988, pp. 411–20.
17 Xu Jian 1995.
18 Wang Huangping & Xu Jian 1993, p. 12.
19 Ling Yu 1989, p. 69.
20 Sha Li & Min Li 1992a, p. 257.
21 *The PLA Daily*, 8 September 1992.
22 Xu Zhongde & He Lizhu 1988, p. 192.
23 In private conversations with a number of senior Chinese researchers immediately after the Gulf War, I asked them whether the PLA would consider the use of nuclear weapons as the last resort if it were in the Iraqis' position and deemed that nothing could stop the enemy's advance. They agreed that it would probably be the only option left to the PLA. Some of them cited the Russian example to make the point.
24 Lewis & Hua Di 1992, p. 21.
25 Xu Guangyu, Yang Yufeng & Sang Zhonglin 1987, pp. 1086–106.
26 Xu Guangyu, Yang Yufeng & Sang Zhonglin 1987, p. 1095.
27 US Defence Intelligence Agency 1972, II, p. 25.
28 Xu Guangyu, Yang Yufeng & Sang Zhonglin 1987, p. 1091.
29 Huang Bin 1990, p. 158.
30 Editor Group 1987, pp. 97–8.
31 Downing 1996, p. 189.
32 Zhao Yunshan 1997, p. 95.
33 Yu Hao et al. 1994 (vol. 1).
34 *Liaowang*, no. 33, August 1984, cited in Mohan Malik, 'Chinese Debate on Military Strategy: Trends and Portents', *Journal of Northeast Asian Studies*, Summer 1990, p. 18.
35 Bao Zhongxing 1988, pp. 420–3.
36 Wang Yongzhi 1987, pp. 502–7.
37 Estimates of the number of China's nuclear submarines vary significantly. According to an informant from the Chinese Navy, the number is at least eight. See also Norris et al., 1994.
38 *Liaowang*, no. 46, 1988, p. 4. Yet western analysts believe they are capable of launching fourteen missiles each at most.

39 *Jane's Defence Weekly*, 13 August 1997, p. 21. According to *The Military Balance 1997/98*, published annually by the International Institute for Strategic Studies, the PLA has only one SSBN, five Han class tactical nuclear submarines and one nuclear-powered attack submarine. The 094 and 093 types will enter service in 2000 and 2002 respectively (p. 176).

40 Dong Xuebin 1997, pp. 47–9.

41 ibid.

42 Gerardi & Fisher 1997, p. 127.

43 Gerardi & Fisher 1997, p. 129.

44 ibid.

45 General Zhang Zhen, who retired in September 1997, played a crucial role in the reshuffles of the Chinese military command in 1992, 1993 and 1994. The reason that he is very powerful is threefold. First, he was entrusted by the Party leadership with the job of selecting new military leaders because of his experience as the president of the PLA's National Defence University, which gave him the best opportunity to familiarise himself with the most competent top officers (the university offers an intensive course to train the top brass in modern military science, and Zhang could read their graduation theses). Second, according to some Chinese sources, Zhang was personally chosen by Deng Xiaoping to join the CMC because Deng thought it was necessary to have an army elder from the former Third Field Army to watch the top brass, a large number of whom come from the former Third Field Army. Third, Zhang is the most enthusiastic supporter of Liu Huaqing, who masterminded the PLA's shift to a hi-tech oriented military strategy. In short, Zhang is the second most powerful military leader in the PLA and he is given the right to attend meetings of the Party's Politburo. However, after retirement in 1997 at the age of 84, there will be a question of how long he can remain influential in the PLA.

46 Swaine 1992, p. 123.

47 IISS 1998, p. 176.

48 China has signed an agreement of mutual non-targeting with Russia and the US.

49 You Ji 1997b, pp. 287–306.

50 Pin Kefu 1993, p. 41.

51 Information from a retired officer in the SMF. However, it seems strange that different missiles are operated within a single brigade.

52 Zhu Kunling 1995, p. 59.

53 For instance, both the CIA and the Stockholm International Peace Research Institute believed that the Chinese planned to double their

number of warheads by 1990. Stockholm International Peace Research
Institute, 1988, p. 52.
54 Johnson 1995/96, pp. 548, 558.
55 US Defence Agency 1972, II, p. 35.
56 Pin Kefu 1993, p. 40.
57 Molander & Wilson 1993, p. 78.
58 Zhao Yunshan 1992, p. 53.
59 Johnson 1995/96, p. 37.
60 China has a few more factories specialising in the production of
nuclear material. They include the Henzhong Factory in Shanxi
Province and the Hongyuan Factory and Mianyang Factory in Sichuan
Province. The Huangyuan Factory and the Haiyan Factory in Qinghai
specialise in the production of LiD, the nuclear material used for
building hydrogen warheads.
61 This is what a senior Chinese official told the 1994 Beijing Conference
on arms control, which was jointly sponsored by the International
School on Disarmament and Research on Conflict and the Central
Liaison Department of the CCP. A Chinese participant revealed this
to me in 1996.
62 Gronlund, Wright & Yong Liu 1995/96, p. 151.
63 *Guangming ribao*, 19 March 1997.
64 Information from interviews in Beijing in 1994.
65 Lewis & Hua Di 1992, p. 18.
66 *Guangming ribao*, 13 February 1994.
67 Zhao Yunshan 1992, p. 53.
68 Lewis & Hua Di 1992, p. 18.
69 Li Mingshen 1995, p. 382.
70 Xu Jian 1995, pp. 363–7; *The PLA Daily*, 26 March 1992.
71 Gary Milhollin, director of the Wisconsin Project on Nuclear Arms
Control, quoted by Reuters, 28 May 1992.
72 Gupta 1994, p. 31.
73 Lewis & Hua Di 1992, p. 29.
74 IISS 1997, p. 170
75 Oral information from China's shipbuilding industry in Shanghai in
1995.
76 Lewis & Hua Di 1992, p. 29.
77 Quoted from 'China's Nuclear Missile Strategy', *Independent* (Russian), 14 December 1995.
78 Norris, Burrows & Fieldhouse 1994.
79 http://www.cdiss.org/China-essay.htm
80 *The PLA Daily*, 2 August 1995.
81 *The PLA Daily*, 7 August 1997.
82 Zhang Baotang 1988, pp. 414–15.
83 Zhai Zhihai 1993, p. 171.
84 Jing Weixin 1995, pp. 12–13.

5 THE BUILD-UP OF AN OFFENSIVE AIR FORCE

1 Teng Liangfu & Jiang Fusheng 1990, p. 149.
2 Deng Xiaoping 1993b, p. 57.
3 *The PLA Daily*, 10 November 1994.
4 Yu Hao et al. 1994, p. 78.
5 Yin Changzhi 1994, p. 21.
6 Mao Huangli, Jia Xilin & Li Hiatao 1993, p. 31.
7 *The PLA Daily*, 16 September 1996.
8 In recent years, however, the importance of these branches has also been emphasised, as they are now seen as directly involved in high-tech warfare. Radar and communications units, for instance, are seen as key players in electronic warfare.
9 This is the bureaucratic level of army groups, called *bingtuanji* in Chinese. Each army group commands a few group armies. The rank is equivalent to that of a US army.
10 Latham & Allen 1991, p. 38.
11 Li Ke & Hao Shenzhang 1989, p. 370.
12 *The PLA Daily*, 26 January 1993.
13 Information gathered when talking to air force officers in 1995.
14 Liu Zuoxing 1995, p. 41.
15 Min Zengfu 1995, pp. 31–40.
16 Commanding Academy of the PLAAF 1986, p. 14.
17 Wang Hai 1987, pp. 927–39.
18 ibid.
19 Dai Jingyu 1991, pp. 50–1.
20 Liu Yicang 1993, pp. 22–6.
21 Dong Wenxian & Hu Siyuan 1994, p. 25.
22 Jing Xueqin 1997, p. 41.
23 Ouyang Wei 1995a, p. 20.
24 Fang Lin 1995, pp. 40–2.
25 Teng Lianfu & Jiang Fusheng 1990, chapter 5.
26 Zhang Cangzhi 1988, pp. 239–354.
27 Commanding Academy of the PLAAF 1987, p. 942.
28 Zhang Xusan 1987, pp. 967–77.
29 Cheng Shenxia 1997, p. 45.
30 Wang Qunbo 1994, p. 27.
31 Zhang Cangzhi 1995, p. 37.
32 Yang Zhenggang 1995, p. 37.
33 Liu Zuoxin 1995, p. 40.
34 Fan Li 1995, p. 7.
35 Zhang Cangzhi 1995, p. 36.
36 Yang Zhenggang 1995, p. 37.
37 Dai Jingyu et al. 1991, pp. 291–308.
38 ibid.
39 Dong Wenxian 1995, pp. 77–82.

40 Wang Hai 1989, p. 675.
41 Jing Xueqin 1997, p. 41.
42 Dong Wenxian 1988, pp. 384–410.
43 *Renmin Ribao*, 19 November 1995.
44 Teng Lianfu & Jiang Fusheng 1990, p. 174.
45 *The PLA Daily*, 6 May 1998, p. 2.
46 Ji Rongren 1995, p. 46.
47 *Renmin Ribao*, 2 December 1995.
48 Liu Zuoxin 1995, p. 40.
49 Dong Wenxian 1988, p. 398.
50 Liu Zuoxin 1995, p.41.
51 Dong Wenxian 1988, p. 399.
52 Zhang Cangzhi 1988, pp. 239–354.
53 Cui Longzhu 1994, p. 53.
54 Dong Wenxian 1988, p. 398.
55 Zhang Zhen & Su Qingyi 1993, chapter 2.
56 Jing Xueqin 1997, p. 42.
57 Allen, Krumel & Pollack 1995, p. 115.
58 Zhang Cangzhi 1995, p. 37.
59 Min Zengfu 1992, p. 579; Dong Wenxian 1988, p. 402.
60 Chen Hongyou 1992, pp. 61–9.
61 *The PLA Daily*, 30 April 1993.
62 Hu Wenlong & Cha Jinlu 1991, p. 445.
63 Guo Yongjun 1995, pp. 47–9.
64 Chen Hongyou 1992, p. 64.
65 Chan Fangyou 1991, p. 134.
66 Fang Lin 1995, p. 42.
67 *The PLA Daily*, 11 November 1994.
68 *Ta Kung Pao*, 23 June 1997.
69 *Ta Kung Pao*, 9 July 1997.
70 Hu Wenlong & Cha Jinlu 1991, p. 552.
71 Information gathered from interview in Beijing in 1992.
72 Zhao Ji 1992, pp. 31–2.
73 Huang Xinsheng 1992, p. 104.
74 Li Jijun 1987, p. 882.
75 *Junshi xueshu*, no. 11 1994, p. 51.
76 Dai Jingyu 1991, p. 221.
77 Zhang Songshan 1992, pp. 4–54.
78 Dong Wenxian 1988, p. 400.
79 *Jane's Defence Weekly*, 2 October 1993, p. 12.
80 Information from an active officer in the 15th Corps in Wuhan in 1995.
81 Yu Hao et al. 1994, p. 70.
82 Zhang Songshan 1992, p. 34
83 Ou Jingu 1997, p. 57.
84 Li Yuliang 1987, p. 969.

85 Hu Wenlong & Cha Jinlu 1991, p. 612.
86 Hu Wenlong & Cha Jinlu 1991, p. 622.
87 Ma Diansheng 1997, p. 77.
88 *Zhongguo Qingnianbao*, 27 April 1995.
89 Zhang Songshan 1992, p. 36.
90 *Jingji Ribao*, 18 July 1995.
91 *Renmin Ribao*, 19 November 1994.
92 Yu Hao et al. 1994, p. 476.
93 Sha Li & Min Li 1993, p. 14–15.
94 *Renmin Ribao*, 17 January 1996.
95 Hua Renjie 1992, p. 332.
96 Sha Li & Min Li 1993, p. 17.
97 Jing Xueqin 1997, p. 41; Sha Li & Min Li 1993, p. 14–7.
98 *The PLA Daily*, 9 November 1995.
99 GSD & GDP 1993, pp. 7–8.
100 Ball 1994, p. 14.
101 Menon 1997, p. 112.
102 *Lien Ho Pao*, 29 November 1993.
103 *Jane Defence Weekly*, 4 June 1997, p. 12; Shichor 1998, pp. 76–7.
104 Allen, Krumel & Pollack 1995, p. 170.
105 Shi Fei 1993, p. 17.
106 Liu Zouxin 1995, p. 40.
107 *Ta Kung Pao*, 23 June 1997.
108 Allen, Krumel & Pollack 1995, p. 236.
109 *Guangmin Ribao*, 1 January 1996.
110 *Renmin Ribao*, 2 December 1995.
111 Zhang Xusan 1997, p. 707.
112 Shichor 1998, p. 70.
113 *Renmin Ribao*, 15 May 1996.
114 Allen, Krumel & Pollack 1995, p. 236.
115 *The PLA Daily*, 28 September 1997.
116 *The PLA Daily*, 9 November 1995.
117 Interview with a PLA pilot in 1991.
118 Other modifications included, for instance, composite airframe materials, such as titanium alloy, the FDSX–03 electronic anti-skid brake system and the KJ–12 autopilot.
119 Allen, Krumel & Pollack 1995, p. 164.
120 Allen, Krumel & Pollack 1995, p. 170.
121 Interview with designers in the Chengdu Aviation Corporation in 1995. The upgrading was relatively successful. For example, the employment of titanium alloy material reduced the weight of the aircraft by nearly 10 per cent, and the amount of spare parts by 12 per cent. This increased the design life by three times.
122 Fulghum 1994, p. 26.
123 *Jane's Defence Weekly*, 5 March 1994, p. 3.
124 Taylor 1995, pp. 212–13.

125 Taylor 1995, p. 213.
126 Menon 1997, p. 112.
127 Dantes 1993, p. 43.
128 *Jane's Defence Weekly*, 16 July 1996, p. 15.
129 Menon 1997, p. 112.
130 Taylor 1995, p. 213.
131 Willett 1997, p. 110.
132 ibid.
133 *Central Daily* (Taiwan), 11 February 1996.
134 Skebo, Man, Gregory & Stevens 1992, p. 674.

6 THE AMBITION FOR A BLUEWATER NAVY

1 *Jianchuan zhishi*, no. 11, 1991, p. 2.
2 Huang Caihong 1989a, pp. 2–3.
3 Tang Fuquna, Du Zuoyi & Zhan Xiaoyou 1997, p. 76.
4 Writing Group of the PLA NDU 1990, p. 62.
5 Zhong Su 1989, p. 78.
6 Liu Zhenhuan 1997, p. 95.
7 Liu Huaqing 1986, pp. 17–21.
8 You Ji 1997b, p. 291.
9 *Liaowang*, no. 8, 1984, pp. 8–9.
10 Tang Fuquna, Du Zuoyi & Zhan Xiaoyou 1997, p. 76.
11 Yan Youqian & Chen Rongxing 1997, p. 86.
12 Tang Fuquna, Du Zuoyi & Zhan Xiaoyou 1997, p. 77.
13 Chen Xiaoxing 1989, pp. 39–41.
14 Lin Mu & Jin Yan 1995.
15 *Renmin Ribao*, 16 June 1990.
16 Duan Ruanlin 1989, pp. 26–7.
17 Dong Xingtai 1989, pp. 13–8.
18 Xiao Jingguang 1988, pp. 31–5.
19 Run Bei 1989, pp. 2–3.
20 In the 1960s Liu was president of the 7th Research Academy under the Ministry for National Defence, specialising in naval R&D. In the 1970s he was vice director of the National Defence Commission for Science and Industries.
21 Hahn 1986, p. 119.
22 Zhao Wei 1990, p. 39.
23 A proper translation of the Chinese word *jinhai* is 'green water'. According to Bradley Hahn, the term is used to express a naval capability somewhere between 'brownwater' (coastal defence) and 'bluewater' (full open-ocean fleet) (1986, p. 116). This paper argues that a 'greenwater' capability is not the PLAN's goal. All its efforts point to the direction of becoming a bluewater power.
24 China did take offensive actions against the Nationalist navy in

Taiwan and against Vietnam in the 1960s and 1970s. However, there should be a distinction between preparing a war with major powers and small countries. As China's maritime strategy is formulated mainly for dealing with the major powers, it was dominantly responsive in nature.

25 Xu Shiming 1988, pp. 417–44.

26 Pi Guoyong 1995, p. 8.

27 Yan Youquian, Zhang Dexin & Lei Huajian 1987, p. 1000.

28 Zhang Xusan 1987, p. 977.

29 Zhang Yuliang 1994, p. 25.

30 Huang Caihong 1989b, pp. 2–3.

31 Lu Rucun et al. 1987, p. 477.

32 Chen Fangyou 1991, p. 66.

33 Zhang Xusan 1987, p. 979.

34 Zhang Xusan 1987, p. 980.

35 China denies that it has ever built any military facilities in Burma. Some western experts on Asian military affairs also dispute such an allegation (Ashton 1997, pp. 84–7).

36 Li Dexin et al. 1990, p. 221.

37 Zhang Xusan 1987, p. 984.

38 Xiao Jun 1989, pp. 2–4.

39 ibid.

40 Chen Fangyou & Lu Jianxiu 1991, p. 164; Bai Keming 1988, pp. 2–4.

41 Xiao Jun 1989, pp. 2–4.

42 Ye retired in the early 1980s. Therefore, for about a decade, there was no professional soldier in the Standing Committee of the Politburo. Although Liu retired from the CCP's 15th National Congress in October 1997, he remains the most powerful figure in the PLA. At the moment he is serving as Jiang Zemin's top military adviser. Currently there is no professional soldier in the Standing Committee, although generals Zhang Wannian and Chi Haotian are Politburo members.

43 Wang Shichang 1989, p. 186.

44 Zhang Yihong 1993, p. 879.

45 *The PLA Daily*, 2 November 1995.

46 Wang Chuanyan 1989, pp. 10–11.

47 Zhang Xusan 1987, p. 984.

48 Xu Xiaojun 1991, p. 55.

49 Liao Xinqun & Wu Xuansheng 1989, pp. 4–7.

50 Ye Zhi 1989, pp. 4–6.

51 Wu Qinwen 1987, p. 49.

52 It should be noted that the North Sea Fleet was established only at the beginning of the 1960s, that is, after the naval area commands were abolished.

53 Lu Ruchuan et al. 1989, p. 247.

54 Wang Yongguo & Sun Meisheng 1989, p. 19.
55 Wang Yongguo & Sun Meisheng 1989, pp. 19–20.
56 ibid.
57 Chen Fangyou & Lu Janxiu 1991, p. 158.
58 Xu Shiming 1990, p. 221.
59 Xiao Ping 1989, p. 2.
60 Wang Dongpo 1990, p. 115.
61 ibid.
62 Lee 1989, p. 68.
63 *Jianchuan zhishi*, no. 8, 1991, p. 2.
64 These were purchased from the Soviet Union in 1954.
65 IISS 1998, p. 177.
66 Chen Fangyou & Lu Jianxiu 1991, p. 164; Hu Guangzheng 1997, p. 124.
67 For a detailed analysis of the weakness of Luda class destroyers, see G. Jacobs, 1992, pp. 263–4.
68 ibid.
69 Lee 1989, p. 70.
70 Jacobs 1992, pp. 80–5.
71 *Jane's Defence Weekly*, 18 January 1992, p. 88.
72 *Asia–Pacific Defence Reporter*, 1995 Annual Reference Edition, p. 14.
73 *Guangmin Ribao*, 20 April 1997.
74 ibid.
75 Information from a senior naval academic in Beijing in 1997.
76 *Jane's Defence Weekly*, 9 July 1997, p. 21.
77 Menon 1997, p. 111.
78 Klintworth 1997, p. 6.
79 *Jianchuan zhishi*, no. 3, 1988, p. 32.
80 *Guangjiaojing*, no. 11, 1989, pp. 70–83.
81 *Jane's Defence Weekly*, 11 April 1992.
82 Shen Lijiang 1989b, pp. 2–3.
83 Lin Chong-pin 1988, pp. 57–62.
84 Li Dexin et al. 1990, p. 227.
85 With one Xia class submarine in service, and two or three under construction, a minimum second-strike capability at sea may be achieved in the early decades of the 21st century. From then on the navy may shift the priority from hardware deployment to technology improvement. One other reason for this is that the state cannot afford to provide very many nuclear reactors to the navy.
86 Wu Xiangyun 1994, pp. 17–18.
87 Zhang Xusan 1987, p. 983.
88 According to an informed Japanese researcher, every movement of these submarines can be detected by the Japanese navy.
89 Wang Weixing 1988, pp. 2–14.
90 You Ji 1997a, p. 81.
91 Lu Ruchuan et al. 1989, p. 57.

92 *The New China News Agency*, 7 June 1987.

93 The First Brigade has, however, been structured with a heavy officer formation so it can quickly provide officers for the newly established units. A national marine training centre is attached to the brigade, which is located in the Yu Lin Base in Hainan Island. It is reported that the centre not only trains the personnel from the brigade but also a large number of infantry officers from other naval fleets and the army.

94 *Guangjiaojing*, no. 1, 1993, p. 53.

95 The Chinese have claimed that they could launch an amphibious invasion with 30 000 soldiers at one time. This could only have meant an assault on Taiwan (*Jianchuan zhishi*, no. 9, 1991, p. 6).

96 *Renmin Ribao*, 13 September 1997.

97 *People's Daily* 7 June 1987.

98 Oral sources from officers from the East Sea Fleet.

99 *United Daily News*, 15 March 1993. A Chinese naval officer revealed to a Chinese newspaper that the construction had actually already begun in the Shanghai Ship Building Factory (*Zhongguo gongshang shibao* [The Chinese industrial and commercial times], 14 November 1992).

100 Information from people present in the meeting, 1997.

101 Shen Lijiang 1989a, p. 6.

102 ibid.

103 *The PLA Daily*, 27 September 1995.

104 Shi Fei 1993, pp. 2–22.

105 Shi Fei 1993, pp. 12–13.

106 Ye Zhi 1989, p. 5.

107 *Foreign Broadcast Information Service* (FBIS), CHI–90–106, 1 June 1990, p. 30.

108 If a carrier were used in the Spratly conflict, it would be quite vulnerable to attacks by the MiG–29s based in East Malaysia. Besides, the shallow waters around the Spratlys are not ideal for a carrier and its supporting vessels. See Simon Sheldon, 'Regional issues in Southeast Asian security', a paper prepared for the conference *Enhancing Security in Southeast Asia*, Canberra, 5–6 April 1993, p. 9.

109 Information gathered from an interview with a naval researcher in Beijing in 1992.

110 Ye Zhi 1989, p. 45.

111 Ye Zhi 1989, p. 46.

112 *Pacific Research*, vol. 3, no. 2, May 1990, p. 14.

113 *Far East Economic Review*, 10 October 1996, p. 20.

114 Shi Fei 1993, pp. 10–17.

115 Ye Zhi 1989, p. 46.

116 *Jianchuan zhishi*, no. 5, 1987, p. 17.

117 ibid.

118 *Far East Economic Review*, 10 October 1996, p. 20.
119 Wu Qinwen 1987, pp. 4–8.
120 Liao Xinqun & Wu Xuansheng 1989, pp. 4–7.
121 However, given the long process of constructing a carrier, many unexpected factors exist that may torpedo the project. Moreover, China is under diplomatic pressure from some Asian countries to abort the plan. Japan, for instance, has particularly linked its soft loans to China to its wish that China not acquire a carrier.
122 Writing Group of the PLA NDU 1990, p. 100.

7 THE PLA AND REGIONAL SECURITY

1 Kristof 1993; Goodman & Segal 1997.
2 You Ji & Jia Qinggou 1998, p. 55.
3 The following analysis of the PLA's threat perception is mainly based on the opinions expressed in influential PLA journals and books, although these writings may not be the official policy stated by the Chinese leadership.
4 Jiang Lingfei 1997, p. 44.
5 Pi Guoyong 1995, p. 8.
6 GSD & GPD 1993, pp. 276–82.
7 Wang Yunlan 1995, pp. 7–10.
8 Zhao Hongmei 1994, pp. 44–5.
9 Zhao Hongmei 1994, p. 45.
10 Chanda 1990; Morrison & Oksenberg 1992, pp. 2–5; Olsen 1993, pp. 491–510.
11 He Fang 1993, pp. 78–9.
12 Glaser 1993, p. 257.
13 *Kyodo News Service* and *Japan Economic Newswire*, 21 November 1993.
14 Information gathered from a number of interviews with PLA researchers and officers in Beijing in late 1992.
15 Yu Juliang 1997, p. 58.
16 *Tokyo Shimbun*, 27 July 1997.
17 During the Sino–Russian summit in Beijing in 1992, President Yeltsin explicitly advised China: 'Do not hurt our feelings by capitalising on our current problems. Russia will stand up again in the not too distant future.' This has made a strong impression on the top Chinese leaders, the majority of whom were trained in Russia in the 1950s and know well the Russian potential. After Yeltsin's visit, a circular was issued by the PLA, stating that Russia's weakness was only temporary. (Seminar on Sino–Russian relations at Beijing University by Xing Guangcheng, a researcher from the Russia and East Europe

Institute of the Chinese Academy of Social Science, 20 November 1992.)

18 Glaser 1993, p. 261.
19 Reuters, 20 March 1996.
20 Feng Changhong 1997, p. 36.
21 Chu Shulong 1997, p. 227. The first Sino–US hot war was the Korean War, 1950–53.
22 Lasater 1993, p. 157.
23 Bernstein & Munro 1997.
24 Zhang Xusan 1987, p. 984.
25 Editors 1993, pp. 27–30.
26 Wang Zhenxi 1994, p. 89.
27 Zhao Hongmei 1994, p. 90.
28 Le Renshi 1994, p. 7.
29 *World News*, CNN, 28 February 1995.
30 Ji Guoxing 1994, p. 16.
31 Ji Guoxing 1994, p. 15.
32 Editors 1993, pp. 27–30.
33 Fang Shaolei 1993, pp. 58–9.
34 Xu Jian 1994, p. 21.
35 Interview with researchers in the Research Institute of Contemporary International Relations, February 1995.
36 Xu Jian 1994, pp. 20–1.
37 ibid.
38 In a report to the Party's Central Advisory Commission of the CCP in late 1992, Jiang Zemin, on behalf of the Central Committee (CC) and CMC, talked in gloomy words about the 'new situation' in Taiwan (the deepening independence movement) and Hong Kong (Chris Patten's political reform plan) and outlined strong countermeasures. When he addressed a meeting on Taiwan affairs in December 1992, he issued a blunt warning, saying that 'China will take drastic countermeasures against Taiwan's attempt of independence' (*People's Daily*, 16 December 1992).
39 Sun Yanjun 1995, p. 20.
40 Zhang Xusan 1987, pp. 975 6, 984 (this author's comments in parentheses).
41 Wang Yunlan 1995, pp. 7–10.
42 Jiang Minfang & Duan Zhaoxian 1995, p. 9.
43 ibid.
44 Sutter 1997, pp. 57–80.
45 You Ji 1997b, pp. 300–3.
46 *Ta Kung Pao*, 24 March 1996.
47 Niu Li 1995, pp. 3–6.
48 *Ta Kung Pao*, 24 March 1996.
49 *Nikkei Weekly*, 25 March 1996.

50 *Ta Kung Pao*, 19 March 1996.
51 He Fudong 1994, p. 1.
52 Personal correspondence from Beijing in 1997.
53 Xiao Jun 1989, pp. 2–4.
54 Milivojevic 1989, p. 21.
55 *The Asian Defence Journal*, no. 3, 1993, p. 43.
56 Mack & Ball 1992, p. 2oo.
57 China started construction on the Yongshu Reef in February 1988 without a fight. But a naval reinforcement was standing by the reef at all times (*Jianchuan zhishi*, no. 8, 1992, p. 6).
58 The action broke out at Johnson Reef one month after the Chinese occupation when the Vietnamese saw the Chinese building the reef into an artificial islet and realised that the PLA would stay.
59 For a fairly detailed description of the 14 March incident, see Hiramatsu 1992, pp. 22–8.
60 For a good analysis of the rationale of the Chinese action, see Leifer 1991, pp. 130–2.
61 However, Article 60 of the Law of the Sea stipulates that an artificial islet, its facilities and constructions do not possess the legal status of an island and thus provide no legal grounds for the claim of territorial waters, exclusive economic zones and shelves. For the Chinese, the occupation of these islets was based on a historical claim, but more importantly it served a strategic purpose.
62 Blanche & Blanche 1995, p. 511.
63 Garver 1993, p. 1023.
64 The PRC's diplomatic history is full of such examples. The Sino–Indian conflict was a typical one. Immediately after the South China Sea clash in 1988, the spokesman of the Ministry of Foreign Affairs sought to scale down the significance of the incident.
65 Godwin 1991, p. 657.
66 Sha Li & Min Li 1992b, pp. 7–72.
67 For a good argument against such a concept, see Klintworth 1995.
68 For instance, there is a debate on what constitutes the motivation for the current arms build-up in Southeast Asia. In his seminar at the Australian National University in April 1993, Dr Amitav Acharya pointed out that contrary to the argument that the arms build-up in Southeast Asia was related to the South China Sea dispute, it was largely driven by internal factors.
69 Harding 1992, pp. 36–48.
70 There certainly are many China specialists who hold a pessimistic view on China's long-term development, given its weak legal system, lack of commitment to democracy on the part of a large number of people and the uncertainties concerning political succession.
71 Harris 1997, pp. 134–55.
72 Peng Guangqian et al. 1994, p. 102.

73 *Straits Times*, 2 July 1992.
74 As far as China is concerned, this flexibility is reflected in its proposal to shelve the issue of sovereignty for the time being.
75 *International Herald Tribune*, 7–8 October 1995.
76 Pan Shiying 1993, p. 265.
77 *Zhongguo Qingnianbao*, 8 August 1995.
78 Glaser 1993, p. 268.
79 Tai Ming Cheung 1991, p. 9.
80 You Ji & You Xu 1991, pp. 137–49.
81 This argument may be speculative, but it is plausible. Since the early 1990s, the PLA has been forced to cope with domestic problems following 4 June and then the effects of the Gulf War, as expressed in the shift to a high-tech strategy. The result is that, since 1990, there has been a visible decline in the navy's exercises in the South China Sea.

Yet, in personal contacts with these officers, some of them openly question the civilian leaders' intention to appease the ASEAN countries over the South China Sea dispute. Even immediately after the 14 March 1988 incident, a prominent American diplomat opined that the South China Sea threat was remote to ASEAN (Holdridge 1988, p. 25). This was also the prevailing view of the participants of the Canberra conference, Enhancing Security in Southeast Asia, in May 1993.
82 For instance, a Japanese government spokesman, Sadaaki Numata, expressed the view that 'China's military build-up has not come to the point of being a destabilising factor in this part of the world' (*Japan Economic Newswire*, 30 March 1993).
83 The US would undoubtedly oppose a drastic Chinese action in the Spratlys. As pointed out by Harry Harding, American sympathies will be with other claimants, including Vietnam, if China repeats its 1988 initiative. *(Worldnet* [USIS], 26 October 1993).
84 Information gathered from interviews with Chinese diplomats in Beijing in 1992. This was confirmed in a personal talk with a deputy foreign minister of Vietnam in November 1995 during a conference on the Spratlys in Manila.
85 According to a naval officer from the South Sea Fleet, the preparation for the South China Sea move in 1988 included a number of contingency plans for a possible Soviet intervention (interview with him in 1992). He refused to comment, however, on how the navy would handle American intervention should a conflict erupt between China and other claimants (excluding Vietnam).
86 Leifer 1996, p. 11.

CONCLUSION

1 Pillsbury 1997, Introduction.
2 Shambaugh 1996, p. 34.
3 Lin Chong-pin 1992, pp. 179–83.
4 Dr Pillsbury's speech at the US Consulate in Sydney on 5 November 1997.
5 Dibb 1993, pp. 5–6.
6 Over 3800 high-tech projects have been initiated under the 'Touch' program. Many of them are military-related (*Beijing Review,* 22 September–3 October 1993, p. 8).
7 Yu Zonglin 1996, p. 23.
8 Nation-wide, there are 52 centrally approved high-tech industrial development zones where 5569 high-tech enterprises are set up in the fields of electronics, information, biology, new materials and new energy resources (*Beijing Review,* 27 September–3 October 1993, p. 8).
9 *CCTV,* 12 October 1993.
10 The navy has received numerous donations from retired workers, primary school pupils and university teachers (*Zhongguo Gongshang Shibao* [The Chinese industrial and commercial times], 11 November 1992).
11 Joffe 1997, pp. 53–70.
12 With the collapse of the former triangular relationship, the dominant PLA view of the new world order is that China should no longer rely on playing big powers against big powers but develop its own power to make itself a key player (Huang Hanbiao 1993, p. 24).

Bibliography

English translations for titles of the Chinese journals most often used:
Jianchuan zhishi (Naval and merchant ships)
Liaowang (Outlook)
Guangjiaojing (Wide angle magazine)
Junshi jingji yanjiu (The research of military economics)
Haijun zazhi (The navy)
Zhongguo junshi kexue (Chinese military science)
Junshi xueshu (The study of military science)

Ahrat, Ehsan, 'Chinese prove to be attentive students of information warfare', *Jane's Intelligence Review*, October 1997

Allen, Kenneth, Krumel, Glenn and Pollack, Jonathan, *China's Air Force Enters the 21st Century*, Santa Monica: RAND, 1995

Ashton, William, 'Chinese bases in Burma—fact or fiction?', *Jane's Intelligence Review*, vol. 7, no. 2, 1997

Bai Keming, 'Zhongguo haijun de weilai fazhan' (The future development of the PLA Navy), *Jianchuan zhishi*, no. 12, 1988

Ball, Desmond, *Signals Intelligence in the Post-Cold War Era: Developments in the Asia–Pacific Region*, Singapore: Institute of Southeast Asian Studies, 1993

——'The post-Cold War maritime strategic environment in East Asia', in Dick (ed.), *Maritime Power in the China Seas: Capabilities and Rationale*, Canberra: Australian Defence Studies Centre, Australian Defence Force Academy, 1994

——'Signals intelligence in China', *Jane's Intelligence Review*, vol. 7, no. 8, 1997

Bao Zhongxing, 'Jianshe tianjun guoxiang' (The initial design for the creation of a space force), in PLA NDU (ed.), *Jundui xiandaihua jianshe de sikao*, Beijing: PLA NDU Press, 1988

Bernstein, Richard and Munro, Ross, *The Coming Conflict with China*, New York: Knopf, 1997

Blanche, Bruce and Blanche, Jean, 'Oil and regional stability in the South China Sea', *Jane's Intelligence Review*, November 1995

Cable, Vincent and Ferdinand, Peter, 'China as an economic giant: threat or opportunity', *International Affairs*, vol. 70, no. 2, 1994

Chanda, Nayan, 'George Bush, Japan, and the China card', *Christian Science Monitor*, 15 February 1990

Chen Baojiang and Huang Xing, 'Wojun junshi sixiang huigu' (Review of our military strategy concept), *Zhongguo junshi kexue*, no. 4, 1995

Chen Fangyou and Lu Jianxiu, *Haijun zhanyixue jiaocheng* (Textbook for naval campaign theory), Beijing: PLA National Defence University Press, 1991

Chen Hongyou, *Xiandai fangkonglun* (On modern air defence), Beijing: PLA Publishing House, 1991

——'Lielun xiandai guotu fangkong dediwei tedian he jianshe' (On the status, special characters and build-up of a modern air defence system), *Zhongguo junshi kexue*, no. 1, 1992

Chen Xiaoxing, 'The requirements placed by coastal economic development on naval building', *Junshi jingji yanjiu*, no. 7, 1989

Chen Youyuan, 'Junshi jishu gemin yu zhanyi lilun de fazhan' (RMA and the development of combat theories), *The Journal of the PLA National Defence University*, no. 10, 1997

Cheng Shenxia, 'Lianhe zhanyi kongjun yunyong ying zhaozhong bawo de jige wenti' (Several key questions for the use of the air force in united campaigns), *The Journal of the PLA National Defence University*, no. 1, 1997

Chou Shi, 'Bunen ba "sanzhi" shoucheng wojun jianshe de zongzhengce' (The policy of self-improvement cannot be regarded as the overall policy for the PLA's development), *Junshi jingji yanjiu*, no. 9, 1989

Chu Shulong, 'The second Sino/US hot war', in Greg Austin (ed.), *Missile diplomacy and Taiwan's future*, (*Canberra Paper* no. 122), Canberra: Australian National University, 1997

Cohen, Eliot, 'The mystique of US air power', *Foreign Affairs*, January 1994

Commanding Academy of the PLAAF, *Dierci shijia dazhanhou jici jiubu zhanzhenzhong kongzhong liliangde yunyong* (The employment of air force in several limited wars since the end of WWII), Beijing: PLA Publishing House, 1986

——'Guanyu zhanqu kongzhong jingong zhanyi de tantao' (On the campaign of air attack in regional warfare) in Editor Group (eds), *Tongxiang shengli de tansou* (Exploring the ways towards victory), Beijing: PLA Publishing House, 1987

Cui Longzhu, 'Jianli zhanque jidong fangkung budui' (Establishing war zone air defence troops), *Junshi xueshu*, no. 11, 1994

Dai Jingyu, *Kongjun zhanyixue jiaocheng* (Textbook for the course on the air force campaigns), Beijing: PLA NDU Press, 1991

——'Gaojishu jubu changgui zhanzheng de tiaozhan' (The challenge of high-tech conventional limited wars), *The Journal of the PLA National Defence University*, no. 1, 1993

Dantes, Edmond, 'Changing Air Power Doctrines of Regional Military Powers', *Asian Defence Journal*, no. 3, March 1993

Deng Xiaoping, 'Talks after inspecting Jiangsu and other places', *Selected Works of Deng Xiaoping*, vol. 3, Beijing: Renmin chubanshe, 1993a

——*Guanyu xinshiqi jundui jianshe lunshu xuanbian* (Deng Xiaoping on the building of the armed forces in the new era), Beijing: Bayi chubanshe, 1993b

Dibb, Paul, 'Key strategic issues for Asia and Australia', paper presented at conference Australia's Maritime Bridge into Asia, Sydney, 17–19 November 1993

Ding, Arthur, 'China's defence finance: content, process and administration', *The China Quarterly*, no. 146, June 1996

Dong Wenxian, 'Tan xingshiqi kongjun guimo he zuozhan liliang jieguo' (The size and structure of the PLAAF in the new era), in *Jundui xiandaihua jianshe de sikao*, Beijing: PLA NDU Press, 1988

——'Shouxian yaoyou qiangda de kongjun' (First of all, we must have a powerful air force), *Zhongguo junshi kexue*, no. 1, 1995

Dong Wenxian and Hu Siyuan, 'Woguo kongjunzhanlie yunyong yiao queli de xinguannian' (Our air force must establish new ideas for its strategic operations), *The Journal of the PLA National Defence University*, no. 5, 1994

Dong Xingtai, 'Weiyu paihui yu jingan de huajun' (Report on the navy that zigzags the inshore waters), *Junshi jingji yanjiu*, no. 3, 1989

Dong Xuebin, 'Dier paobin zaifandi lianhe zuozhan yunyong zhong ying bawo de wenti' (The issues that the SMF must resolve in frustrating the enemy's united offensive), *The Journal of the PLA National Defence University*, no. 5, 1997

Downing, John, 'China's Maritime Strategy', *Jane's Intelligence Review*, April 1996

Dreyer, June Teufel, *China's Political System: Modernization and Tradition*, New York: Paragon House, 1993

Duan Ruanlin, 'Zhongguo de yuanyang yuchuandui' (China's ocean fishing fleet), *Jianchuan zhishi*, no. 3, 1989

Editor group, 'Zhanlie daodan budui zhai chengzhang' (The development of the SMF), in CCTV Press (ed.), *Junwei jinxingqu* (The marching song for the PLA), Beijing, 1987

Editors, '1992 shijie zhanlie xingshi zongshu' (A general analysis of the world strategic constellation in 1992), *The Journal of the PLA National Defence University*, no. 2, 1993

Editors, 'Zouxiang 21 shiji de zhongguo zhoubian huanjing yantaohui' (Conference on China's peripheral environment toward the 21st century), *Contemporary International Relations*, no. 11, 1994

Espeland, D. and Curr, A.J., 'Air operations in the Gulf War', in

Andrew Ross (ed.), *The Military Significance of the Gulf War*, Canberra: Australian Defence Studies Centre, Australian Defence Force Academy, 1991

Fan Li, '*Taiwan zhikong binli jiegou zhi tantao*' (Some analysis on the structure of air control power in Taiwan), *National Policy Dynamic Analysis*, no. 104, 24 January 1995

Fang Lin, 'Tankongzhong jinggong zhanyi de zhisheng yingsu' (On the factors that are decisive to victories of air attack campaigns), *The Journal of the PLA National Defence University*, no. 10, 1995

Fang Shaolei, 'Zhanhao diyuan zhengzhi yu dangdai zhongguo de duiwai zhanlie' (The post–Cold War geopolitics and China's contemporary foreign policy strategy), *Zhanlie yu guangli* (Strategy and management), November 1993

Feng Changhong, 'Guoji anquan xingshi huigu yu qianzhan' (A review and forecast of the international security situation), *The Journal of the PLA National Defence University*, no. 2–3, 1997

Fulghum, David, 'New Chinese fighter near prototyping', *Aviation Week and Space Technology*, 13 March 1995

Galdorrisi, George, 'China's PLAN', US Naval Institute, *Proceedings*, March 1989

Gao Jinxi, *Guoji zhanliexue gailun* (An introduction to international strategic studies), Beijing: PLA NDU Press, 1995

——'Shijie junshi fazhan yu makesi zhuyi junshi lilun de lishi shimin' (The world military evolution and the historical task of Marxist military theory), *The Journal of the PLA National Defence University*, no. 1, 1998

Garver, John, 'China's push through the South China Sea: the interaction of bureaucratic and national interests', *China Quarterly*, no. 133, March 1993

Gerardi, Greg and Fisher, Richard, 'China's missile tests show more muscle', *Jane's Intelligence Review*, March 1997

Gill, Bates and Kim, Taeho, *China's Arms Acquisition from Abroad: A Quest for 'Superb and Secret Weapons'*, London: Oxford University Press, 1995

Glaser, Bonnie, 'China's security perceptions', *Asian Survey*, no. 3, 1993

Godement, Francois, 'Does China have an arms control policy', in David Goodman and Gerald Segal (eds) *China Rising: Interdependence and Nationalism*, London: Routledge, 1997

Godwin, Paul, 'Chinese defence policy and military strategy in the 1990s', in Joint Economic Committee, Congress of the United States, *China's Economic Dilemmas in the 1990s*, Boulder: Westview, 1991

Goodman, David and Segal, Gerald (eds), *China Rising: Interdependence and Nationalism*, London: Routledge, 1997

Gronlund, Lisbeth, Wright, David and Yong Liu, 'China and a fissile material production cut-off', *Survival*, vol. 37, no. 4, 1995–96

GSD and GPD, *Gaokeji zhai junshi lingyu de yingyong jidui zuozhan de yingxiang* (The military application of high-tech and its impact on warfare), Beijing: Bayi chubanshe, 1993

Guo Qiqiao and Yao Yanjing, *Jundui jianshexue* (The study of the PLA's development), Beijing: PLA NDU Press, 1991

Guo Xilin, 'Dui guojia yujing xitong jianshe wenti de tansuo' (On the construction of a national defence early warning system), *Junshi xueshu*, no. 3, 1995

Guo Yongjun, 'Fangkong zuozhan ying shuli quanquyu zhengti fangkong de sixian' (Air defence should be guided by the theory of area and integrated defence), *Junshi xueshu*, no. 11, 1995

Gupta, Vipin 'The status of Chinese nuclear weapons testing', *Jane's Intelligence Review*, January 1994

Hahn, Bradley, 'Hai Fang', *Proceedings* (US Naval Institute), March 1986
——'China: nuclear capability—small but growing', *Pacific Defence Reporter*, May 1989

Hang Suwei and Yang Zhonghua, 'Zouyou zhongguo tese de guofang keji fazhen daolu' (Follow the path of defence R&D with Chinese characteristics), *The Journal of the PLA National Defence University*, no. 10, 1995

Harding, Harry, 'China at the crossroads: conservatism, reform and decay', *Adelphi Paper*, no. 275, 1992

Harris, Stuart, 'China's role in WTO and APEC', in David Goodman and Gerald Segal (eds), *China Rising: Interdependence and Nationalism*, London: Routledge, 1997

He Fang, 'Xifan daguo zhijian de maodung yi chengwei guoji guanxi zhong de zhuyao maodung' (The contradiction among western powers has risen to become key contradictions in current international relations), *The Journal of the PLA National Defence University*, no. 1, 1993

He Fudong, 'Linghuo yingbian zhangwo junshi douzhan de zhudongqun' (Flexible response to control the military initiative), *The Journal of the PLA National Defence University*, no. 11, 1994

Hiramatsu, Shigeo, 'The Chinese navy's advance into the South China Sea', *The National Defence* (Japan), no. 1, 1992

Holdridge, John, 'Threat to ASEAN remote', *Pacific Defence Reporter*, March 1988

Hong Shisheng, 'Guofang jingfei touxiang fenxi' (An analysis of distribution of the defence budget), *Junshi jingji yanjiu*, no. 3, 1995

Hou Shanzhi, '*Jingque zhidao wuqi de fazhan dui jundui bianzhi zhuangbei he zuozhan xingdong de yingxiang*' (The effect of equipping precision weapons on the structure and operations of the armed forces), PLA Academy of Military Science (ed.), *Zhanyi zhanshu yu xiandai zuozhan* (Military campaigns and tactics and modern warfare), Beijing: PLA Academy of Military Science Press, 1987

Hu Changfa, 'Guanyu gaojishu tiaojian xia jubu zhanzhen zhanyi lilun yanjiu de jige wenti' (Several key questions on the theory of high-tech campaigns), *The Journal of the PLA National Defence University*, no. 1, 1997

Hu Guangzheng, '20 shiji jundui tizhi bianzhi de fazhan jiqi qishi' (The development and lessons of force structure and establishment in the 20th century), *Zhongguo junshi kexue*, no. 1, 1997

Hu Siyuan, 'Tan daying gaojishu jiubu zhanzheng de duice zhunbei' (On the countermeasures to win a high-tech regional war), *The Journal of the PLA National Defence University*, no. 5, 1993

Hu Wenlong, 'Tigao wojun zhiliang xu youhua ge junbinzhong jiegou' (To raise our army's quality necessitates rationalising the structure of the services and arms), PLA Academy of Military Science (ed.), *Xinshiqi changbeijun jianshe yanjiu*, Beijing: PLA Academy of Military Science Press, 1990

Hu Wenlong and Cha Jinlu, *Xiandai junbingzhong zhanshu* (The contemporary tactics of services and arms of services), Beijing: PLA Military Science Academy Press, 1991

Hua Renjie, *Kongjun xueshu sixianshi* (The history of ideas concerning air force development), Beijing: PLA Publishing House, 1992

Huang Bin, *Zhangqu you zhangqu zhanyi* (Theatre and theatre campaigns), Beijing: PLA National Defence University Press, 1990

——*Zhanqiu yu zhanqiuzhanyi* (War zones and war zone campaigns), Beijing: PLA NDU Press, 1992

——*Luhaikongjun guojishu tiaojianxia zuozhan zhihui* (The command of military operation of the army, air force and navy under high-tech conditions), Beijing: PLA NDU Press, 1993

Huang Caihong, 'Haijun hangkonbin fazhan de xinjieduan' (The new evolutionary stage of the naval air force), *Jianchuan zhishi*, no. 2, 1989a

——'Zhongguo haijun de fazhang zhanlie' (The PLA Navy's development strategy), *Jianchuan zhishi*, no. 4, 1989b

Huang Hanbiao, '*Miandui tiaozhan youxuan duice fazhan ziji*' (Facing challenge, make rational countermeasures and strengthen our own power), *The Journal of the PLA University of National Defence*, no. 2, 1993

Huang Xinsheng, 'Gaojishu tiaojianxia yuanjuli zhanyi jidong zuzhi zhihui wenti chutan' (The question of organising and commanding long-distance troop movement under high-tech conditions), *Jundui zhihui lilun jijing* (Collection of papers by senior PLA comanders on the theory of commanding), Beijing: PLA NDU Press, 1992

Huang Yuzhang (ed.), *Jiubu zhanzheng, zuotian, jintian he mingtian* (Limited war: yesterday, today and tomorrow), Beijing: PLA NDU Press, 1988

International Institute for Strategic Studies (IISS), *Strategic Survey 1996/1997*, London: Oxford University Press, 1997

——*The Military Balance 1997/1998*, London: Oxford University Press, 1998

Jacobs, G. 'Chinese navy destroyer *Dalian*', *Navy International*, no. 9–10, 1992

Jencks, Harlan, 'People's war under modern conditions: wishful thinking, national suicide, or effective deterrent?', *China Quarterly*, no. 78, June 1984

Ji Guoxing, *Maritime Security Mechanisms for the Asian Pacific Region*, Centre for International Security and Arms Control, Stanford: Stanford University Press, 1994

Ji Rongren, 'Zuzhi konhzhong jinggong zhanyi ying gaohao wuge jieheng' (In organising offensive air campaigns there should be five good coordinations), *The Journal of the PLA National Defence University*, no. 10, 1995

Jiang Lingfei, 'Lizu fazhan chuoniao heping' (Base the efforts of securing peace on development), *The Journal of the PLA National Defence University*, no. 2–3, 1997

Jiang Luming, 'Guofangfei de biandong qiushi jiqi zhanlie xuanze' (The changing trend of defence expenditure and the PLA's strategic choice), *Jingji junshi yanjiu*, no. 1, 1995

Jiang Minfang and Duan Zhaoxian, 'Taiwan zhanlie diwei danxi' (The analysis of Taiwan's strategic position), *Haijun zazhi*, no. 8, 1995

Jiang Tiejun, 'Shixing shehuihua baozhang shi jundui houqing gaige de biran quxian' (Socialised supply is the inevitable trend of the PLA's reform on the logistical supply system), *The Journal of the PLA National Defence University*, no. 10, 1997

Jing Weixin, 'Didi daodan zuozhan sitong shengcun nenli yanjiu' (Research on the survivability of surface–surface missile systems), *Junshi xitong gongcheng* (Military engineering), no. 3, 1995

Jing Xueqin, 'Shenru guanche xinshiqi junshi zhanlie fangzhen nuli tuijing kongjun xiandaihua jianshe' (Deepening the efforts of implementing the new military strategy, working hard to advance the air force's modernisation), *The Journal of the PLA National Defence University*, no. 8–9, 1997

Joffe, Ellis, *The Chinese Army after Mao*, Cambridge: Harvard University Press, 1987

——'How does the PLA make foreign policy?', in David Goodman and Gerald Segal (eds) *China Rising: Interdependence and Nationalism*, London: Routledge, 1997

Johnson, Alastair, 'China's new "old thinking": the concept of limited deterrence', *International Security*, vol. 20, no. 3, 1995/96

Junshi xueshu (ed.), *Quanjun bufen gaoji ganbu junshi xueshu lunwen xuan* (Selected papers on the study of military science by senior PLA generals), Beijing: PLA Academy of Military Science Press, 1984

Karp, Regina Cowell, (ed.) *Security Without Nuclear Weapons?*, Oxford: Oxford University Press, 1990

Klintworth, Gary, 'Greater China and global regional security', in Stuart Harris and Gary Klintworth (eds), *China as a Great Power in the Asia–Pacific: Myths, Realities and Challenges*, Melbourne: Longman-Cheshire, 1995

——'The Chinese navy to get some big guns, at last', *Asia–Pacific Defence Reporter*, April–May 1997

Kong Congzhou, *Kong Congzhou huiyilu* (Autobiography of Kong Congzhou), Beijing: PLA Publishing House, 1991

Kristof, Nicholas D., 'China's rise', *Foreign Affairs*, vol. 72, no. 5, 1993

Ku Guisheng, 'Shehui zuyi shichang jingji yu guofang jianshe' (The socialist market economy and military development), *The Journal of the PLA National Defence University*, no. 6, 1993

Lan Shuchen, 'Tuokuan wojun peiyang junguang de quado' (Widening the channel of training for the officers in our army), *Junshikexuexinxi* (Information about military studies), no. 10, 1986

Lasater, Martin, *U.S. Interests in the New Taiwan*, Boulder: Westview, 1993

Latham, Richard and Allen, Kenneth, 'Defence reform in China: the PLA Air Force', *Problems of Communism*, May–June 1991

Le Renshi, 'Lengzhanhou yiatai diqu de zhanlie dongxiang' (The strategic trend in the post–Cold War Asia–Pacific), *Guoji zhanlie yanjiu*, no. 3, 1994

Lee, Ngok, *China's Defence Modernisation and Military Leadership*, Canberra: Australian National University Press, 1989

Leifer, Michael, 'The maritime region and regional security in East Asia', *The Pacific Review*, vol. 4, no. 2, 1991

——'Chinese strategy in Southeast Asia', paper for the conference China and Southeast Asian Security, IISS/CCAPS, Canberra, 5–6 May, 1996

Lewis, John Wilson and Hua Di, 'China's ballistic missile programs: technologies, strategies, goals', *International Security*, vol. 17, no. 2, Fall 1992

Li Cheng and others, *Jianguo yilai junshi baizhuang dashi* (The 100 major events in the history of the PLA since 1949), Beijing: Zhishi chubanshe, 1992

Li Dexin et al., 'Haijun de junheng fazhen shi xinshiqi haijun jianshe de tuchu wenti' (A balanced development is the key task for the navy in the new era), in Academy of Military Science (ed.), *Xinshiqi changbeijun jianshe yanjiu* (The standing army in the new era), Beijing: PLA Academy of Military Science Press, 1990

Li Hong, 'Women de lishishiming' (Our historical missions), in *Houyujian* (The fire and sword), Langzhou: Gansukeji chubanshe, 1992

Li Jiang, 'Shilun 2000 nian wuqi zhuangbai fazhan zhanlie' (On weapons development strategy to the year 2000), in PLA NDU (ed.), *Jundui xiandaihua jianshe de sikao* (Study of the modernisation programs for the PLA), Beijing: PLA NDU Press, 1988

Li Jijun, 'Guanyu jianli zhanyi lilun tixi wenti de jidian renshi' (Some reflections on the development of campaign theory), Editor Group (eds), *Tongxiang shengli de tansou* (Exploring the ways towards victory), Beijing: PLA Publishing House, 1987

Li Jingchun, Li Zimin and Zhou Xie, 'On how to achieve maxium efficiency out of the limited military budget', *Junshi jingji yanjiu*, no. 1, 1993

Li Ke and Hao Shengzhang, *Wenhua dagemin zhong de renmin jiefangjun*, (The PLA in the Cultural Revolution), Beijing: Zhongguo dangshi ziliao chubanshe, 1989

Li Mingshen, *Tienhu yaoyao: Zhongguo huojian weixing fashe jishi* (The long way to space: the record of Chinese missile and satellite launches), Beijing: Zhongyang dangxiao chubanshe, 1995

Li Qingshan, *Xinjunshi gemin yu gaojishu zhanzhen* (New revolution in military affairs and high-tech warfare), Beijing: PLA Academy of Military Science Press, 1995

Li Yuliang, 'Shilun kongjiang zuozhan zhutihua qushi' (On the tendency of the airborne troops as strategic independent forces in future wars), in Editor Group (eds), *Tongxiang shenli de tansuo* (Exploring the ways towards victory), Beijing: PLA Publishing House, 1987

Liang Minglun, 'Gaojishu changgui jiubu zhangzheng tiaojian xia wo jun hetong zhanyi de jiben tidian' (The basic features of the PLA's combined campaigns under the conditions of high-tech conventional regional wars), *The Journal of the PLA National Defence University*, no. 1, 1993

Liao Rishen, 'Zhongguo hewu fazhen yu zhanbei' (China's nuclear development and strategy), *Cheng Ming*, no. 10, 1995

Liao Xinqun and Wu Xuansheng, 'On the priorities in the military budget allocation', *Junshi jingjixue*, no. 7, 1989

Lin Chong-pin, *China's Nuclear Weapons Strategy: Tradition within Evolution*, Massachusetts: Lexington Books, 1988

——'The Chinese military modernisation and its implications on Taiwan', in Taiwan Information Agency (ed.), *Defence and Foreign Policy White Paper*, Taipei: Yeqiang Publishing House, 1992

Lin Mu and Jin Yan, 'How big is China's territory?', *New Century*, no. 6, 1995

Ling Yu, 'Zhonggong heliliang de kouzhan (The expansion of the Chinese nuclear capabilities), *Guangjiaojing*, no. 11, 1989

——'Zhingguo daodan yanxi he dier paobin' (The Chinese missile exercises and the SMF), *Guangjiaojing*, no. 8, 1995

Liu Beiyi and Yun Qing, *Zhongguo junshi zhi zeidaguan* (The record of the Chinese military), Beijing: Zhishi chubanshe, 1994

Liu Cunzhi, 'Congduiyue zuozhan kan jiubu zhancheng' (Limited wars as seen from the Sino–Vietnam War), in Selected Papers of the PLA's First Conference on Campaign Theory, Editor Group (eds), *Tongxiang shengli de tansou* (Exploring the ways towards victory), Beijing: PLA Publishing House, 1987

Liu Huajin, 'Lunjunshi jingji guanli zhongde maodunqun' (On the multiple contradictions in managing the military economy), *Junshi jingji yanjiu*, no. 3, 1991

Liu Huaqing, 'To bring up new talents for the building of a powerful navy', *Hongqi*, no. 2, 1986

Liu Jingsong, 'Jiaqun gengban lilun zhidao zhuajin budui jianshe gaige' (To strengthen studies of guiding theoretical principles and quicken the PLA modernisation and reforms), *The Journal of the PLA National Defence University*, no. 5, 1993

Liu Jishan and Qian Zunde, *Dangdai waiguo junshi sixiang* (Contemporary military ideas in foreign countries), Beijing: PLA Academy of Military Science Press, 1988

Liu Jixian, *Junshi lilun yu weilai zuozhan* (Military theory and future warfare), Beijing: NDU Press, 1992

Liu Qingzhong, 'Xingshiqi wojun gaige he jianshe de zhinan' (The guiding principle for the PLA's reform and development), *Junshi xueshu*, no. 7, 1992

Liu Tongzu et al., 'Mianxian 2000 nian, jianli yige xiandaihua de zhanyi zhihui kongzhi tongxin qingbao xitong' (Facing the year 2000, establish a modernised C³I system), *Tongxian shengli de tansou*, Beijing: PLA Publishing House, 1987

Liu Yicang, *Gaojishu zhanzhenglun* (The study of high-tech warfare), Beijing: PLA Academy of Military Science Press, 1993

Liu Zhenhuan, 'Guanyu lianheguo haiyangfa gongyue yu zhongguo xinshiqi haifang jianshe de sikao' (Thinking on China's maritime defence after the signing of the UN Convention on the Law of the Sea), *Zhongguo junshi kexue*, no. 2, 1997

Liu Zhongyi, 'Taiyuan weixing fashe zhongxin ceji' (A brief look at the Taiyuan satellite launching centre), *Jingyang wenyi*, no. 2, 1992

Liu Zuoxin, 'Kongzhong jingong zhanyi liliang goucheng he zhanyi zhihui chutan' (Initial research on force structure and command for offensive air campaigns), *The Journal of the PLA National Defence University*, no. 10, 1995

Lu Ruchan, et al. (eds), *Dangdai zhongguo haijun* (The contemporary Chinese navy), Beijing: Zhongguo shehui kexue chubanshe, 1989

Ma Diansheng, 'Weilai zhanzhen dui zhihuiyuan de suzhi yaoqiu' (The quality demand on commanders by future war), *The Journal of the PLA National Defence University*, no. 7, 1997

Mack, Andrew and Ball, Desmond, 'The military build-up in Asia–Pacific', *The Pacific Review*, vol. 5, no. 3, 1992

Mao Huangli, Jia Xilin and Li Hiatao, 'Jiaqiang kongjun zhanyi xunlian de jige wenti' (Several questions concerning the tightening up of the PLAAF's campaign training), *Junshi xueshu*, no. 3, 1993

Menon, Rajan, 'The strategic convergence between Russia and China', *Survival*, vol. 39, no. 2, 1997

Mi Zhenyu, 'Guanyu jianli jubu zhanzheng zhanyi lilun tixi de chubu yuanjiu' (An initial study of the campaign theory of limited wars), *Junshi xueshu*, no. 12, 1986

——'Jiubu zhanzhengde tedian, fazhan qushi ji dui jundui jianshe de yingxiang' (The basic features and tendency of limited wars and its influence on the development of the PLA), *Hangkong zazhi* (The journal of aviation), no. 11, 1987

Milivojevic, Marko, 'The Spratly and Paracel Islands conflict', *Survival*, January–February 1989

Min Zengfu, 'Ganyu guojia fangkong zhihui tizhi jianshe de sikao' (On the restructuring of the commanding system of air defence), in PLA NDU (ed.), *Jundui zhihui lilun jijing* (Collections on the commanding theories of the PLA), Beijing: PLA NDU Press, 1992

——'21 shiji kongzhong zhanchang guankui' (A quick analysis of air warfare in the 21st century), *Zhongguo junshi kexue*, no. 1, 1995

Molander, Roger and Wilson, Peter, *The Nuclear Asymptote: On Containing Nuclear Proliferation*, Santa Monica: RAND, 1993

Morrison, Charles and Oksenberg, Michel, 'Japanese Emperor's visit to China sends important signals to the United States', *Asia–Pacific Issues*, October 1992

Mulvenon, James, *Professionalisation of the Senior Officer Corps: Trends and Implications*, Santa Monica: RAND, 1997

Munro, Ross, 'Eavesdropping on the Chinese military: where it expects war—where it doesn't', *Orbis*, vol. 38, no. 3, Summer 1994

Niu Li, 'Yao shizhong ba guojia de zhuquan he anquan fangzai diyiwei' (Always make the national sovereignty and security the number one task), *Junshi xueshu*, no. 10, 1995

Norris, Robert, Burrows, Andrew and Fieldhouse, Richard, *Nuclear Weapons Databook Volume V: British, French and Chinese Nuclear Weapons*, Boulder: Westview Press, 1994

Olsen, Edward, 'Target Japan as America's economic foe', *Orbis*, Fall 1992

Ou Jingu, 'Denglu zhanyizhong tu ji shanglu de zhanfa yunyong wen ti' (The tactics of seizing a landing platform in a landing campaign), *The Journal of the PLA National Defence University*, no. 4, 1997

Ouyang Wei, 'Guanyu jundui bushu wenti' (On the question of troop deployment), *The Journal of the PLA National Defence University*, no. 6, 1995a

——'Lung guojishu jiubu zhancheng de zhanyixing zuozhan xintai' (The forms of campaign operations under high-tech warfare conditions), *The Journal of the PLA National Defence University*, no. 4, 1995b

Pan Shiying, *Xiandai zhanlie sikao* (Thinking on contemporary strategy), Beijing: Shijiezhishi chubanshe, 1993

Peng Guangqian et al., *Deng Xiaoping zhanlie sixiang* (Deng Xiaoping's strategic thinking), Beijing: PLA Academy of Military Science Press, 1994

Pi Guoyong, 'Xinshiqi haijun zhanlie yunyong zhongde gongshi fangyu' (On the employment of an offensive-oriented defence as the naval strategy in the new era), *Haijun zazhi*, no. 8, 1995

Pillsbury, Michael (ed.), *Chinese Views of Future Warfare*, Washington: US National Defence University, 1997

Pin Fan and Li Qi, 'Ganyu junshi hangtian liliang fazhan jige wenti de lilun yanjiu' (On several theoretical questions of the development of military space capabilities), *Zhongguo junshi kexue*, no. 2, 1997

Pin Feng, 'Hangtian liliang zhai gaojishu jubu zhanzheng de yunyong ji duice' (The application of and countermeasures to the space force in high-tech limited wars), *The Journal of the PLA National Defence University*, no. 5, 1996

Pin Kefu, 'Zhongguo qianghua hewu liliang: eluosi de guandian' (The CCP is strengthening its nuclear force: views from Russia', *Dangdai Zhongguo* (Contemporary China), no. 31, October– November 1993

PLA Academy of Military Science, *Weilai de guofan jianshe* (The future development of Chinese national defence), Beijing: PLA Academy of Military Science Press, 1988

PLA NDU, *Dangde junshi zhanlie zuanbian yu renmin jundui jianshe* (The Party's alteration of military strategy and development of the people's armed forces), Beijing: NDU Press, 1991

——*Guojishu jiubu zhancheng yu zhanyi zhanfa* (High-tech limited wars and the campaign tactics), Beijing: PLA NDU Press, 1993

Qu Xing, 'Shilun dongou jiupian he suliang jieti hou de zhongguo duiwai zhengce' (China's foreign policy since the radical changes in Eastern Europe and the disintegration of the USSR), *Journal of Foreign Affairs College*, no. 4, 1994

Reng Xiufeng and Wang Guangxu, 'Youshenmo wuqi dashenmo zhang bingbu guoshi' ('Fighting whatever war in accordance with whatever weapons' is not an obsolete concept), *Junshi xueshu*, no. 5, 1986

Research Institute for Strategic Studies, PLA Academy of Military Science, *Zhongguo junshi dili gaikuang* (The outline of China's military geography), Beijing: PLA Academy of Military Science Press, 1988

Run Bei, 'Senshinian de weida hangcheng' (Thirty years of a great course), *Jianchuan zhishi*, no. 5, 1989

Segal, Gerald, 'Nuclear forces', in Gerald Segal and Bill Tow (eds) *Chinese Defence Policy*, London: Macmillan, 1984

——'China: the maverick nuclear power', in Regina Cowell Karp (ed.), *Security Without Nuclear Weapons?*, Oxford: Oxford University Press, 1990

——'Tying China into the international system', *Survival*, vol. 37, no. 2, Summer 1995

——'Constrainment' of China, *International Security*, vol. 20, no. 4, 1996

Sha Li and Min Li, *Zhongguo guonei shici junshi xingdong* (The PLA's ten major domestic military operations), Chengdu: Sichuang keji chubanshe, 1992a

——*Zhongguo jiuci dafabin* (The nine overseas missions of the PLA since 1949), Sichuan: Literary Publishing House, 1992b

——*Zhongguo kongjun shili* (The capabilities of the PLA air force), Beijing: Beijing Electronic Engineering University Press, 1993

Shambaugh, David, 'China's military: real or paper tiger?', *The Washington Quarterly*, vol. 19, no. 2, 1996

Shaoguang Wang, 'Estimating China's defence exenditure: some evidence from Chinese sources', *The China Quarterly*, no. 147, September 1996

Shen Lijiang, 'The mysterious course of the pilot warship captains', *Jianchuan zhishi*, no. 7, 1989a

——'A visit to the PLA Navy's nuclear submarine unit', *Jiangchuan zhishi*, no. 8, 1989b

Shi Fei, *Zhongguo junli da qiushi* (The general developmental trend of the Chinese military), Chengdu: Sichuan kexue chubanshe, 1993

Shichor, Yitzhak, 'Israel's military transfers to China and Taiwan', *Survival*, vol. 40, no. 1, 1998

Skebo, Robert, Man, Gregory and Stevens, George, 'Chinese military capabilities: problems and prospects', in the Joint Economic Committee, Congress of the US (ed.), *China's Economic Dilemmas in the 1990s*, Armonk: New York, 1992

Song Shilun, 'Guanyu jinhou fanqinlie zhanzheng jige wenti de tantao' (Several questions on our anti-aggression warfare), in the Academy of Military Science (ed.), *Junshi xueshu lunwenxuan* (Selected papers on military research), Beijing: the PLA Academy of Military Science Press, 1984

Stockholm International Peace Research Institute (ed.), *SIPRI Yearbook*, Frosunda: SIPRI, 1988

Su Yu, 'Several questions on strategy and tactics during the initial phase of a war against aggression', *Junshi xueshu* (The study of military science), no. 3, 1979

Sun Yanjun, 'Qiantan dongyong junshi shouduan zhizhi guojia fenlie' (On using military power to prevent a national split), *The Journal of the PLA National Defence University*, no. 6, 1995

Sutter, Robert, 'The Taiwan crisis of 1995–96 and US domestic politics', in Greg Austin (ed.), *Missile diplomacy and Taiwan's future* (*Canberra Paper* no. 122), Canberra: Australian National University, 1997

Swaine, Michael, *The Military and Political Succession in China*, Santa Monica: RAND, 1992

Tai Ming Cheung, 'Growth of Chinese naval power', *Strategic Papers*, Institute of of Southeast Asian Studies, 1991

Tang Daoshen, 'Dui xingshiqi zhanlie daodan budui zhiliang jianshe de sikao' (On the qualitative development of our strategic missile troops in the new era), in PLA Academy of Military Science (ed.), *Xin shiqi changbeijun jianshe yuanjiu* (The development of the standing army in the new era), 1990

Tang Fuquna, Du Zuoyi and Zhan Xiaoyou, 'Deng Xiaoping: xinshiqi haiyang zhanlie sixiang yanjiu' (A study of Deng Xiaoping's maritime strategy in the new era), *Zhongguo junshi kexue*, no. 2, 1997

Taylor, John, 'The Su–27 Flanker series', *Jane's Intelligence Review*, no. 5, vol. 7, 1995

Teng Lianfu and Jiang Fusheng, *Kungjun zuozhan yuanjiu* (The study of air force operations), Beijing: PLA NDU Press, 1990

US Defence Intelligence Agency, *Soviet and People's Republic of China: Nuclear Weapons Employment Policy and Strategy*, March 1972

——*China: National Command, Control and Communications—Beijing (U)*, December 1984

Wang Chuanyan, *Dangji shijie yu women de junshi xiandaihua* (The world today and our military modernisation', in Editors (ed.), *Lilun zongheng* (Theory forum), Hebei: Renmin chubanshe, 1989

Wang Dongpo, 'The strategic rivalry in the West Pacific and our country's security and development', *Xinyazhou* (New Asia), no. 1, 1990

Wang Gezhen and Li Mindtang, 'Junshi geming souyi' (Some discussion on the Revolution in Military Affairs), *The Journal of the PLA National Defence University*, no. 11, 1997

Wang Hai, 'Xiandai hetong zhanyi zhong de kngjun shiyang' (The role of the air force in contemporary warfare), in Editor Group (eds), *Tongxiang shengli de tansou* (Exploring the ways towards victory), Beijing: PLA Publishing House, 1987

——(chief editor), *Dangdai zhongguo kongjun* (The contemporary Chinese air force), Beijing: Zhongguo shehui kexue chubanshe, 1989

Wang Huangping and Xu Jian, 'Ai, zhuzao daodan bulou de junhun' (Love constitutes the soul of missile troops), *Liaowang*, no. 25, 1993

Wang Jianghuai and Zhu Guolin, *Gaojishu tiaojian xia hetong zhanyi honglan liangjun shouzhang jiguan duikang yanxi jiaocheng* (A teaching course on the combined campaigns under high-tech conditions conducted by the red army and blue army headquarters), Beijing: PLA NDU Press, 1994

Wang Jing, 'Chen Yi he zhongguo waijiao zhence' (Chen Yi and Chinese foreign policy), *Chunchiu*, no. 4, 1978

Wang Pufeng, 'Queli dajiubu zhanzheng de linghuo fanying zhanlie' (Establishing flexible and quick response strategy for limited wars), *Junshi xueshu*, no. 9, 1986

Wang Qunbo, 'Jidong zhanzhong de kungjun zuozhan zhidao' (The guideline for air force mobile campaigns), *Junshi xueshu*, no. 12, 1994

Wang Shaoguang, 'Estimating China's defence expenditure: some evidence from Chinese sources', *China Quarterly*, no. 147, September 1996

Wang Shichang, 'Zhengshi haiyang, tiaozhan julang' (Confronting the high seas and challenging the big waves), *Tiaozhan: yanhai fazhan yu guofangjianshe* (Coastal development and defence modernisation), Beijing: Guangming ribao chubanshe, 1989

Wang Weixing, 'Above is the sea territory of a foreign country', *Qingchuan*, no. 5, 1988

Wang Wenpo, 'Qiantan gaojishu zhanzheng danyao xiaohao qiushi' (A study of the consumption of ammunition in a high-tech war), *The Journal of the PLA National Defence University*, no. 5, 1993

Wang Yamin, 'Jiakui wojun bingqi zhuangbei fazhan bufa de jidian sikao' (Some thoughts on how to quicken the development of our weaponry and equipment), *The Journal of the PLA National Defence University*, no. 5, 1993

Wang Yongguo and Sun Meisheng, 'Bei hushilede haijun zhanlie mugang jianshe wenti' (The construction of a strategic naval base: a long-neglected question), *Junshi jingjixue*, no. 3, 1989

Wang Yongzhi, *Hangtian dashiji* (The major events of China's aerospace industries), Beijing: First Academy of the Aerospace Ministry, 1987

Wang Yunlan, 'Zhoubian guojia haijun lilang de fazhan ji duiwoguo de yingxiang' (The naval development of our periphery countries and its impact), *Junshi xueshu*, no. 10, 1995

Wang Zhenxi, 'Continued shock of the post–Cold War and uncertainties in the adjustment process', *Zhongguo junshi kexue*, no. 1, Spring 1994

Wang Zhiyi, *Wuzhuang liliang tizhi gailun* (An introduction to the structure of China's armed forces), Beijing: PLA Academy of Military Science Press, 1991

Willett, Susan, 'East Asia's changing defence industry', *Survival*, vol. 39, no. 3, 1997

Wilson, Ian and You Ji, 'Leadership by "lines": China's unresolved succession', *Problems of Communism* (Washington, DC), vol. 39, January 1990

Woolley, Peter, with C.D.R. Marks and S. Woolley, 'Japan's sea lane defence revisited', *Strategic Review*, Fall 1996

Writing Group of the PLA NDU, *Guofang fazhan zhanliexue jiaocheng* (Textbook for teaching the course of development strategy of national defence), Beijing: PLA NDU Press, 1990

Wu Guoqing, 'Duidangdai zuozhan lilun fazhan qiushi de tantao' (On the developmental trends of the theory of modern warfare), *Zhongguo junshi kexue*, no. 2, 1994

Wu Qinwen, 'Lunguofang jianshe yu jingji jianshe de youji jiehe' (On organically combining defence building and economic construction), *Junshi jingji yanjiu*, no. 4, 1987

Wu Xiangyun, 'Qianting gongfang xunlian jixu gaige' (Reform is urgently required for the training of submarine attack), *Haijun zazhi*, no. 1, 1994

Xiao Jingguang, *Xiao Jingguang zizuan* (Autobiography of Xiao Jingguang), Beijing: PLA Publishing House, 1988

Xiao Jun, 'Zhongdian yu pingheng' (Priority and balance), *Jianchuan zhishi*, no. 11, 1989

Xiao Ping, 'The Chinese navy and its nuclear forces', *Jianchuan zhishi*, no. 1, 1989

Xu Chuangjie, 'Military revolution gives impetus to evolution in command', in Michael Pillsbury (ed.), *Chinese Views of Future Warfare*, Washington: US National Defence University, 1997

Xu Fangce, 'Jiqu jubu zhanzheng de xinjingyan' (Learn from new experience in limited wars), in PLA Academy of Military Science, *Zhanyi zhanshu yu xiandai zuozhan* (Military campaigns and tactics and modern warfare), Beijing: PLA Academy of Military Science Press, 1987

Xu Fangting and Liu Hongji, 'Xinshiqi junshi douzhan zhunbei juyao' (Some major points on war preparation in the new era), *The Journal of the PLA National Defence University*, no. 10, 1995

Xu Guangyu, Yang Yufeng and Sang Zhonglin, 'Zhanqiu hezhanzheng de kenenxin jidui wojun zhanyi zuo de yingxiang' (The possibility of theatre nuclear warfare and its impact on our army's campaign operations), *Tongxiang shengli de tansuo* (Exploration of the path toward victory), Beijing: PLA Publishing House, 1987

Xu Jian, 'Yatai anqun jizhi de shuangchong jiagou wenti' (The convergent security strategy in Asia and the Pacific), *Research Report*, no. 146, International Studies Centre of the State Council, June 1994

——*Daguo changjian* (The large country and long sword: the evolution of the SMF), Beijing: Zuojia chubanshe, 1995

Xu Shiming, 'Jiubu zhanzheng zhong haijun de diwei yu zuoyong' (The navy's status and role in a limited war', in Huang Yuzhang (ed.), *Jiubu zhanzheng de zuotian, jintian yu mingtian* (Limited war: yesterday, today and tomorrow), Beijing: PLA NDU Press, 1988

——'The status and role of the navy in a limited war', in Li Dexin et al., 'Haijun de junheng farzhan shi xinshiqi haijun jianshe de tuchu keti' (A balanced development is the key task for the navy in the new era), in the Academy of Military Science (ed.), *Xinshiqi changbeijun jianshe yanjiu*, 1990

Xu Xiaojun, 'Helping shiqi zhanzheng zhuanbei de sikao' (On war preparation in the era of peace), *Junshijingjixue*, no. 6, 1991

Xu Zhongde and He Lizhu, 'Yuce weilai zhanzheng buke hushi hewuqi de weixie' (The nuclear threat should not be ruled out in study of future wars), in PLA Academy of Military Science (ed.), *Junshi lilun yu guofa jianshe* (Military theory and development of national defence), PLA Academy of Military Science Press, 1988

Yan Xuetong, '21 shiji zhongguo jieqide guoji anquan huangjing' (The security environment for China's rise in the 21st century), *The Journal of the PLA National Defence University*, no. 1, 1998

Yan Youqian and Chen Rongxing, 'Lun haiyang zhanlie yu haiyang huanjing' (On maritime strategy and the ocean environment), *Zhongguo junshi kexue*, no. 2, 1997

Yan Youqian, Zhang Dexin and Lei Huajian, 'Haishan zhanyi fazhan jiqi duiwojun zhanyi de yingxian' (The development trend in campaigns at sea and its impact on the PLAN campaign actions), Editor Group (eds), *Tongxiang shengli de tansou* (Exploring the ways towards victory), Beijing: PLA Publishing House, 1987

Yang Dezhi, 'Weilai fanqinlie zhanzheng chuqi zuozhan fangfa jige wenti de tantao' (Exploration of several questions concerning the strategy and tactics during the initial phase of the war against aggression), *Junshi xueshu*, no. 11, 1979

Yang Jinhua, 'Zhaitan gaojishu taojian xia wojun zuozhan zhihui wenti' (The C^{3}I problems in our army's combat preparedness under high-tech conditions), *The Journal of the PLA National Defence University*, no. 7–8, 1993

Yang Zhenggang, 'Kongzhong jingong zhanyi zhong kongjun liliang de yunyong' (The employment of air strike power in air strike campaigns), *Junshi xueshu*, no. 3, 1995

Yao Yanjin and Liu Jingxian, *Deng Xiaoping shiqi junshi lilun yanjiu*, Beijing: PLA Academy of Military Science Press, 1994

Yao Zhenyu, 'Wojun wuqi zhuangbei xiandaihua de kexue sixiang' (The scientific guidance for our army's weapons program), *The Journal of the PLA National Defence University*, no. 7–8, 1993

Ye Zhi, 'Laixi, hangkung mujian' (Come, the aircraft carriers), *Junshi jingjixue*, no. 1, 1989

Yin Changzhi, 'Xuexi Deng Xiaoping tici, nuli beiyang hege rencai', (Study Deng Xiaoping's inscription and do a good job in training qualified pilots), *Hiajun zhaizhi*, no. 1, 1994

You Ji, 'A test case for China's defence and foreign policy', *Contemporary Southeast Asia*, vol. 16, no. 4, March 1995a

——'In quest for a hi-tech military power: the PLA's modernization in the 1990s', in Stuart Harris and Gary Klintworth (eds), *China as a Great Power in the Asia–Pacific: Myths, Realities and Challenges*, New York: St Martin's Press, 1995b

——'Jiang Zemin: in quest for the post-Deng supremacy', in, Maurice Brossea, Suzanne Pepper and Tsang Shu-ki (eds), *China Review 1996*, Hong Kong: The Chinese University of Hong Kong Press, 1996a

——*In Quest of High Tech Power: The Modernisation of China's Military*, Sydney: ADSC, the University of New South Wales, 1996b

——'A blue water navy, does it matter', in David Goodman and Gerald Segal (eds), *China Rising: Interdependence and Nationalism*, London: Routledge, 1997a

——'Making sense of war game across the Taiwan Strait', *Journal of Contemporary China*, vol. 7, no. 2, 1997b

——'Economic interdependence and China's national security', in Stuart Harris and Andrew Mack (eds), *Asia–Pacific Security: The Economics–Politics Nexus*, Sydney: Allen & Unwin, 1997c

——'The Chinese navy and China's national interests', in Jack McCaffrie and Alan Hinge (eds), *Sea Power in the New Century*, Australian Defence Studies Centre, Canberra: Australian Defence Force Academy, 1998

You Ji and Jia Qingguo, 'China's re-emergence and its foreign policy strategy', in Joseph Cheng (ed.), *China Review 1998*, Hong Kong: The Chinese University of Hong Kong Press, 1998

You Ji and You Xu, 'In search of blue water power: the PLA Navy's maritime strategy in the 1990s', *The Pacific Review*, no. 2, 1991

Yu Hao et al., *Dangdai zhongguo: zhongguo renmin jiefajun* (Contemporary China: the PLA), two volumes, Beijing: Renmin chubanshe, 1994

Yu Hongmin and Wang Xingwang, 'Wuqi zhuangbei zhiliang jianshe de zhanlie sikao' (The strategic thinking on the PLA's development of its priority equipment), *The Journal of the PLA National Defence University*, no. 6, 1993

Yu Huating and Liu Guoyu, *Gaojishu zhancheng yu jundui zhiliang jianshe* (High-tech warfare and the PLA's quality improvement), Beijing: PLA NDU Press, 1993

Yu Juliang, 'Meiri anquan baozhang lianhe xuanyan fabiao yizhounian tuoxi' (A review of US–Japan joint security communique one year after it was announced), *The Journal of the PLA National Defence University*, no. 6, 1997

Yu Yongzhe, 'Jiaqan houqin jishu baozhang zhuangbei yanzhi yu fazhan de duice yu cuoshi' (On the policy and measures of strengthening logistical safeguards and technological research), *The Journal of the PLA National Defence University*, no. 1, 1997

Yu Zonglin, 'Zhengque chuli jingji jianshe yu guofang jianshe de guanxi' (Correctly handling the relationship between economic and defence construction), *The Journal of the PLA National Defence University*, no. 5, 1996

Zhai Zhihai, 'The future of nuclear weapons: a Chinese perspective', in Patrick Garrity and Steven A. Maaranen (eds), *Nuclear Weapons in the Changing World: Perspectives from Europe, Asia, and North America*, New York: Plenum Publishing Corporation, 1993

Zhang Aiping, 'Fazhan wojun wuqi yao jianchi shishi qiushi de yuanze' (The weapons program should be based on the principle of seeking truth from facts), in Editors' Board (ed.), *Junshi xueshu lunwenxuan* (Selected papers of military science), Beijing: PLA Academy of Military Science, 1984

Zhang Baotang, 'Dui xingshiqi zhanlie daodan budui zhanbei jianshe jige wenti de chutan' (On a few questions concerning the

development of the SMF in the new era), in PLA NDU (ed.),
  Jundui xiandaihua jianshe de sikao, Beijing: PLA NDU Press, 1988
Zhang Cangzhi, 'On the reorientation of the PLAAF from a defence
  force to one combining defence and offensive components', in
  Jundui xiandaihua jianshe de sikao, Beijing: PLA NDU Press, 1988
——'Weilai kongzhong jinggong zhanyi zhidao tanyao' (The outline of
  the guiding principle for future offensive air campaigns), *The
  Journal of the PLA National Defence University*, no. 10, 1995
Zhang Feng, 'On the overall policy of self-development and
  self-improvement', *Junshi jingjixue*, no. 2, 1989
Zhang Guangting, 'Qiantan woguo zhanqiu jianshe yu tizhi sheji de
  jige jiben zhiaoyandian' (A brief discussion on the construction
  and design of war zones in our country), in PLA NDU (ed.), *Jundui
  xiandaihua jianshe de sikao*, Beijing: PLA NDU Press, 1988
Zhang Jingxi and Zhang Mengliang, 'Shilun zhanliexing zhanyi
  heliliang de yunyong he zhujunbingzhong de xietog' (On the use of
  nuclear force in strategic campaigns and the coordination of the
  SMF with other services), Editor Group (eds), *Tongxiang shengli de
  tansou* (Exploring the ways towards victory), Beijing: PLA
  Publishing House, 1987
Zhang Liangyu, 'Weilai zhanchang sheizhu chenfu' (Who will decide
  the victory of the future wars—the role of the specialised services),
  The Journal of the PLA National Defence University, no. 6, 1993
Zhang Songshan, 'Zhongguo kongjiangbin de fazhan' (The evolution of
  the Chinese airborne force), *Kunlun*, no. 3, 1992
Zhang Xusan, 'Shilun weilai haishang zhanyi de zhidao sixiang' (On
  the guiding principle of our campaign tactics in future wars), in
  Editor Group (eds), Selected Papers of the PLA's First Conference
  on Campaign Theory: *Tongxiang shengli de tansou* (Exploring the
  ways towards victory), Beijing: PLA Publishing House, 1987
——(ed.), *Haijun dacidian* (The navy encyclopaedia), Shanghai:
  Shanghai cibu chubanshe, 1997
Zhang Yihong, 'China heads toward blue waters', *International
  Defence Review*, no. 11, 1993
Zhang Yuliang, 'Gaojishu tiaojianxia kangdenglu fangkong zuo tantao'
  (The study of anti-air attack in landing offensive campaigns), *The
  Journal of the PLA National Defence University*, no. 11, 1994
Zhang Zhen, 'Guanyu wojun zhanyi lilun fazhan de jige wenti'
  (Several questions concerning the development of our campaign
  theory), in Editor Group (eds), *Tongxiang shengli de tansuo*
  (Exploration of the path toward victory), Beijing: PLA Publishing
  House, 1987
Zhang Zhen and Su Qingyi, *Guojishu yu xiandai kongjun* (High-tech
  and the modern air force), Beijing: Junshikexue chubanshe, 1993
Zhao Hongmei, 'Riben haijun jiajin tuixin niangjin zhanlie' (The
  Japanese navy is speeding up its southward expansion strategy),
  Haijun zaizhi, no. 9, 1994

Zhao Ji, 'Tantan tankeshi fangyu zhuozhan zhong de fangkong wenti', *Junshi xueshu*, no. 6, 1992

Zhao Wei, 'Colonel General Liu Huaqing—the new vice-chairman of the CMC', *Mingpao Monthly*, no. 1, 1990

Zhao Yunshan, 'Zhonggong hezi wuli jiqi zhanlie' (The nuclear capability and strategy of the Chinese Communist Party), *Minzhu zhongguo*, no. 10, June 1992

——'Zhonggong hedaodan zhanlie sixiang de guoqu, xianzhai yu weilai' (The past, present and future of the CCP's nuclear strategy), *Zhonggong yanqiu*, vol. 31, no. 5, 1997

Zheng Wenhan, 'Guanyu changbeijun jianshe wenti' (On building a standing army), *Junshi xueshu*, no. 1, 1990a

——'Jundui jianshe xueshi taolunhui shang de jianghua' (Speech at the conference on army-building), PLA Academy of Military Science (ed.), *Xinshiqi changbeijun jianshe yanjiu*, Beijing: PLA Academy of Military Science Press, 1990b

Zheng Xianli, 'Dui jundui biancheng shijing zhanzheng bianhua de kanfa' (Opinions on how to restructure the army in order to make it more responsive to the changing forms of war), in PLA NDU (ed.), *Jundui xiandaihua jianshe de sikao*, PLA NDU Press, 1988

Zhong Su, 'Daqushi' (The Mag-trend), *Kunlun*, no. 5, 1989

Zhou Shijian, 'China's role important in APEC', *Intertrade* (Monthly), May 1995

Zhou Yingcai, 'Guanyu gaojishu jiubu zhanzheng bujiubu xianxiang de sikao' (Think of the phenomenon of limited war that cannot be limited), *The Journal of the PLA National Defence University*, no. 1, 1995

Zhu Kunling, 'Erpao zuozhan zhihui xu jiejue de jige wenti' (Several problems concerning combat command and control that the SMF has to resolve), *Junshi xueshu*, no. 8, 1995

Zhu Yingcai, 'Guanyu gaojishu yiubu zhanzhen bujiubu xianxiang de sikao' (The feature of unlimited war in a high-tech limited war), *The Journal of the PLA National Defence University*, no. 1, 1995

Index